Memorial Book of Goniadz Poland

Translation of
Sefer Yizkor Goniadz

Originally in Yiddish, Hebrew and English

Edited by Moshe Shlomo Ben-Meir (I. Treshansky)

Published in Tel-Aviv, 1960

Published by JewishGen

**An Affiliate of the Museum of Jewish Heritage - A Living Memorial to the Holocaust
New York**

Memorial Book of Goniadz
Translation of Sefer Yizkor Goniadz

Copyright © 2016 by JewishGen, Inc.
All rights reserved.
First Printing: September 2016, Elul 5776
Second Printing: March 2019, Adar II 5779
Third Printing: February 2022, Adar I 5782
Fourth Printing: March 2022, Adar II 5782

Translation Project Coordinator: Suzanne Scheraga
Layout: Joel Alpert and Suzanne Scheraga
Caption Translators: Ala and Larry Gamulka and Gloria Berkenstat Freund,
David Goldman, Shayna Kravetz, Selwyn Rose and Amy Samin
Cover Design: Nina Schwartz

Published by JewishGen, Inc.
An Affiliate of the Museum of Jewish Heritage
A Living Memorial to the Holocaust
36 Battery Place, New York, NY 10280

Printed in the United States of America by Lightning Source, Inc.

Library of Congress Control Number (LCCN): 2016934387
ISBN: 978-1-939561-40-4 (hard cover: 558 pages, alk. paper)

Cover illustration from the original Yiddish book
Front and Back Cover Photographs Courtesy of Michael Rothschild

JewishGen and the Yizkor-Books-in-Print Project

This book has been published by the **Yizkor-Books-in-Print Project,** as part of the **Yizkor Book Project** of **JewishGen, Inc.**

JewishGen, Inc. is a non-profit organization founded in 1987 as a resource for Jewish genealogy. Its website [www.jewishgen.org] serves as an international clearinghouse and resource center to assist individuals who are researching the history of their Jewish families and the places where they lived. JewishGen provides databases, facilitates discussion groups, and coordinates projects relating to Jewish genealogy and the history of the Jewish people. In 2003, JewishGen became an affiliate of the **Museum of Jewish Heritage - A Living Memorial to the Holocaust** in New York.

The **JewishGen Yizkor Book Project** was organized to make more widely known the existence of Yizkor (Memorial) Books written by survivors and former residents of various Jewish communities throughout the world. Later, volunteers connected to the different destroyed communities began cooperating to have these books translated from the original language— usually Hebrew or Yiddish—into English, thus enabling a wider audience to have access to the valuable information contained within them. As each chapter of these books was translated, it was posted on the JewishGen website and made available to the general public.

The **Yizkor-Books-in-Print Project** began in 2011 as an initiative to print and publish Yizkor Books that had been fully translated, so that hard copies would be available for purchase by the descendants of these communities and also by scholars, universities, synagogues, libraries, and museums.

These Yizkor books have been produced almost entirely through the volunteer effort of researchers from around the world, assisted by donations from private individuals. The books are printed and sold at near cost, so as to make them as affordable as possible. Our goal is to make this important genre of Jewish literature and history available in English in book form, so that people can have the personal histories of their ancestral towns on their bookshelves for themselves and for their children and grandchildren.

A list of all published translated Yizkor Books in the project with prices and ordering information can be found at:
           http://www.jewishgen.org/Yizkor/ybip.html

Lance Ackerfeld, Yizkor Book Project Manager
Joel Alpert, Yizkor-Book-in-Print Project Coordinator

This book is presented by the
Yizkor Books in Print Project
Project Coordinator: Joel Alpert

Part of the
Yizkor Books Project of JewishGen, Inc.
Project Manager: Lance Ackerfeld

These books have been produced solely through volunteer effort
of individuals from around the world. The books are printed and
sold at near cost, so as to make them as affordable as possible.

Our goal is to make this history and important genre of Jewish
literature available in English in book form so that people can have
the near-personal histories of their ancestral towns on their bookshelves for themselves and for their children and grandchildren.

Any donations to the Yizkor Books Project are appreciated.

Please send donations to:
Yizkor Book Project
JewishGen
36 Battery Place
New York, NY 10280

JewishGen, Inc. is an affiliate of the
Museum of Jewish Heritage
A Living Memorial to the Holocaust

Acknowledgements

The translation of the Memorial Book of Goniondz was the result of fifteen years of effort with a large number of Goniadz descendants contributing what they could. Thanks to:

Harold Black, and Bradley and Kathy Fisher for their donations of previously translated articles.

Our translators: Marvin Galper, David Goldman, Martin Jacobs, Yocheved Klausner, Shayna Kravetz, Selwyn Rose, Amy Samin and Sherry Warman.
And especially Gloria Berkenstat Freund, who has worked on this project from the beginning and is responsible for most of the Yiddish translations in the book. We consider Gloria to be an honorary Goniadzer.

Special thanks to The New York Public Library, Yad Vashem, Michael Rothschild and Carole Rosenfeld for supplying photos.

This has been a labor of love and we are thrilled to be able to offer the translation in print.

Geopolitical Information

Goniadz, Poland is located at 53°29' North Latitude, 22°45' East Longitude and is 17 miles SE of Grajewo, 29 miles NW of Bialystok, 46 miles WSW of Grodno.

Alternate names for the town are: Goniadz [Pol], Goniondzh [Yiddish], Gonyendz [Russian], Gonyadz, Gonyandz, Gonyondz, Gonyondzh, Goniondz

Period	Town	District	Province	Country
Before WWI (c. 1900):	Gonyendz	Bialystok	Grodno	Russian Empire
Between the wars (c. 1930):	Goniadz	Bialystok	Bialystok	Poland
After WWII (c. 1950):	Goniadz			Poland
Today (c. 2000):	Goniadz	Monki	Podlasie	Poland

Jewish Population in 1900: 2,056 (in 1897), 1,135 (in 1921)

Yiddish: גאָניאָנדז Russian: Гонёндз

Nearby Jewish Communities:

Trzcianne 11 miles SSW

Knyszyn 13 miles SSE

Jasionówka 14 miles ESE

Korycin 15 miles E

Radzilów 16 miles WSW

Suchowola 16 miles ENE

Grajewo 17 miles NW

Rajgród 17 miles N

Wasosz 18 miles W

Szczuczyn 19 miles WNW

Tykocin 20 miles S

Janów Sokolski 20 miles E

Sztabin 20 miles NE

Jedwabne 23 miles SW

Zawady 23 miles S

Wizna 25 miles SW

Choroszcz 25 miles SSE

Stawiski 26 miles WSW

Augustów 27 miles NNE

Wasilków 27 miles SE

Dabrowa Bialostocka 28 miles ENE

Elk 29 miles NW

Bialystok 29 miles SE

Sidra 29 miles ENE

Rutki 30 miles SSW

Current Map of Goniadz Poland

A Short History of Goniadz

According to old historical documents, Goniadz was in existence during the 13th century. Thanks to her geographic location as a connecting link by land and water between Poland, Lithuania and Prussia, Goniadz played an important role both strategically and economically. Under the feudal Polish Government, Goniadz enjoyed the dubious "privilege" of not tolerating the Jews. In the year 1597 the town was granted the so-called "Magdeburg Rights", which permitted the Jews to settle there. The town was at various times part of Russia, Prussia, Poland, and Lithuania, and now, after the fall of the Soviet Union, it is in Poland.

The town went through good and bad times: economic and commercial growth and also fires and epidemics. The proximity of the railroad and the fortress of Osowiec that were built in the second half of the 19th century, brought about the growth of the Jewish population and a marked improvement in their conditions of life. The market-days and the fairs attracted the peasants of the surrounding village. Goniadz became a lively trading center for lumber and grains, horses and cattle. The number of Jews in Goniadz varied at different times. In 1847 in a total population of 2,050, the Jews numbered 1,337, or 67% of the total population. The Jewish Goniadz was very lively and interesting. The small Jewish population was very active, established many parties and clubs and gave to the world outstanding intellectuals in many fields, both Jewish and general. This vibrant small Jewish community was best known for an intellectual and social culture which included creating the first Hebrew public school in Poland and an active Zionist community. In 1897 the number of Jews was 2,056 out of a total population of 3,436. In 1921, By the end of the First World War only 1,135 Jews or about 43% of the population still resided in Goniadz.

When the Second World War broke out and Poland was crushed by the Nazis in a matter of days, the Jews of Goniadz lived through days of panic and terror. The Nazis entered Goniadz on the 26th of June, but from the first days of the Nazi invasion of Poland, the local Polish population took over power and began a systematic reign of terror and barbarism against the frightened, helpless Jews. At first, almost all the murders were perpetrated by the Poles. All Jews were forced to shave off their beards. Those who survived were subjected to merciless tortures both physical and moral.

When the power in Goniadz was taken over by the Nazis, a more quiet occupation prevailed in town. For a time the Jews would gain some surcease by giving their tormentors the few belongings still left to them, such as: clothing and jewelry until they became completely ruined and impoverished. Thus, the painful tortured life of hunger, forced labor and degradation dragged on until the tragic end came.

On November 2, 1942 came an order from the Nazis to the effect that all the villages around Goniadz have to deliver 200 wagons for the town. In a few hours the wagons were packed with about 1,000 fainting and crying Goniadz Jews - young and old. This wretched transport was sent to the village of Bogushe, a few miles from Greive. There were assembled thousands of Jews from the all the neighboring towns and from Trestine. In the camp of Bogushe many old and sick died. Those who survived were transported to the death camps, some to Treblinka and some to Auschwitz.

Thus, after undergoing indescribable pain, degradation and barbarities perpetrated upon them, the beloved, tortured community of Jewish Goniadz was gone.

Goniadz Yizkor Book Summary

This Yizkor (Memorial) Book for the Jewish Community of Goniadz, in Poland is over 500 pages long. It contains information on the town's institutions, organizations, buildings, and families as recounted by survivors and prewar emigrants in addition to first-hand reports of survivors of the massacre and of Jews who joined the partisans, family histories of extended families of the town and all the photographs and illustrations from the original Yizkor Book.

Jews may have been living in Goniadz as early as 1597 when the town was granted the right to have Jews settle there. Goniadz became a lively trading center for lumber and grains, horses and cattle. At the beginning of the twentieth century there were about 2,600 Jews or about 67% of the population. The Jewish Goniadz was very lively and interesting. The small Jewish population was very active, established many parties and clubs and gave to the world outstanding intellectuals in many fields, both Jewish and general. This vibrant small Jewish community was best known for an intellectual and social culture which included creating the first Hebrew public school in Poland and an active Zionist community. By the end of the First World War only 1,135 Jews or about 43% of the population still resided in Goniadz.

This Memorial-Book portrays to a great extent the many-sided life of Goniadz before its destruction, as told by pre-war emigrants. Several people who survived the holocaust have given us a heartrending description of the horrors and destruction they witnessed. Their stories, and those of the efforts of those fortunate enough to escape, are presented in this volume. Today there are many descendants of Goniadz living around the world and several have contributed to create this translation.

"Let this Goniadz memorial book be a living memorial to the annihilated-lost splendor of the past – for us and for our children, for eternity."

Fishl Yitzhaki, page 806

List of contributors to Goniadz Yizkor Book Fund

*This list was printed as an insert in English to the Yizkor Book. It includes the
names of those who funded the initial publication of the book in 1960.*

**The following is a list of the Goniondzer in the United States and Canada who
have donated for the Yiskor Book of the town of Goniondz, Province Bialystok,
Poland:** *[surnames have been capitalized by the transcriber]*

NEW YORK, N.Y.	
Mrs. Sarah SEID, in memory of her beloved husband, Gus SEID, first chairman of the Goniondzer Relief Committee of N. Y.	$800.00
Mrs. Katy ATLAS & Children	100.00
Mr. Israel ATLAS	25.00
Mr. & Mrs. Joe ATLAS	5.00
Mr. & Mrs Pearl ALLAN	10.00
The children of Marcia & Benjamin Joseph BYER	50.00
Sol & Ruby BINDLER	25.00
Mr. & Mrs. Kalmon BACHRACH	10.00
Mr. & Mrs. Sol BYER	10.00
Mr. Simon BLOOM	5.00
Mr. & Mrs. Sam CHUDEN	5.00
Mr. Irving CANTER	5.00
Mr. David FORMAN	10.00
Mrs. Gussie FRIEDMAN	10.00
Mr. & Mrs. Louis GOLDBERG	50.00
Mr. & Mrs. Izy GREEN	5.00
Mr. & Mrs. Sam GROBARD	5.00
Mr. GUMBINER	10.00
Gondiondzer Ladies Auxiliary	100.00
Mrs. Bella KAYE	5.00
Mr. & Mrs. Max KAPLAN	10.00
Mr. & Mrs. David LIPSCHITZ	5.00
Mrs. Bessie LICHTENSTEIN	10.00
Mr. & Mrs. Morris MOLOZOFSKY	5.00
Anna & Molly NEWMAN	25.00
Mr. Phillip OTTENSTEIN	15.00
Mr. Sam PINSKY	15.00
Mr. & Mrs. Myrim RUBIN	30.00
Mr. Alter ROSEN	20.00

Mr. & Mrs. Sylvia SEID MORGAN	75.00
Irving & Jack SCHWARTZ, in memory of father, Max SCHWARTZ, secretary of the Detroit Relief Committee	100.00
Mrs. Sophia SEID	10.00
Mr. Abe TUDOR & sister, Chaya Leah	75.00
Mr. & Mrs. Gershon TUDOR	5.00
Paul YONOFSKY	10.00
TOTAL	$1,655.00

DETROIT, MICHIGAN

Mrs. Marcia APELL	$ 10.00
Mr. & Mrs. Human BALIS	10.00
Miss Mary BANKLER	10.00
Mr. & Mrs. H. CHERON	10.00
Mr. & Mrs. L. CHOLNICK	30.00
Mr. & Mrs. Abe GLUCK	5.00
Mr. & Mrs. Abe GRODMAN	20.00
Mr. & Mrs. Eli GRODMAN	10.00
Mr. & Mrs. Jack GRODMAN	10.00
Mrs. L. MARKOVITZ	10.00
Mrs. MARKELSON	10.00
Mrs. Tillie SCHOLNIK	50.00
Mr. & Mrs. H. SCHWARTZ	10.00
Mr. & Mrs. Abe SCHWARTZ	5.00
Miss Rose & Roe BOBER	10.00
Mr. & Mrs. M. WARSHAW	10.00
Mrs. B. WEIDER	10.00
Mr. & Mrs. Hyman WEINER	10.00
Mr. Abe WARSHAW	10.00
Detroit Committee	100.00
TOTAL	$350.00

LOS ANGELES, CALIFORNIA

Mr. & Mrs. Morris BACHRACH	$ 10.00
Mr. & Mrs. Max BLOOM	10.00
Mr. & Mrs. Morris FORMAN	10.00
Mr. & Mrs. Ben IZAKOVITZ	10.00
Mr. & Mrs. I. IZAKOVITZ	5.00
Mr. & Mrs. Jack KOBRIN	10.00
Mrs. H. KRAVETZ	25.00
Mr. & Mrs. Jack SEBULSKY	25.00
Mr. & Mrs. Raya SOLOMON	10.00

Fannie, Raya's sister	5.00
Mr. & Mrs. Rubin LEVINE	25.00
Mr. & Mrs. L. TICOTZKY	10.00
Mr. & Mrs. Milton WEINER	10.00
TOTAL	$165.00

GENERAL

Mr. [sic] Mrs. Chona BYER, Montreal Canada	$ 25.00
Mr & Mrs. Max BYER, Montreal, Canada	25.00
Mr. & Mrs. Max BYER WOLKOFF, Newburgh, N.Y.	25.00
Mrs. Esther BOBROWSKY, Norwalk, Conn.	40.00
Mr. & Mrs. Peretz FORMAN, Taunton, Mass.	10.00
Mr. Abraham GOLDBERG, New Orleans, La. (David FRANTZAILZUL's son)	55.00
Mr. & Mrs. Bernard HALPERN, Atlanta, Ga.	50.00
Mr. & Mrs. Samuel HALPERN, Salem, Mass.	5.00
Mr. Isador KOBRIN, Waren, Mass.	40.00
Mr. & Mrs. KULBASH, Roxbury, Mass.	5.00
Mr. & Mrs. Jack MOREN, South Bend, Ind. (Yeaske's son)	200.00
Mr. & Mrs. E. ROSENZWEIG, Troop, Pa.	15.00
Mr. & Mrs. Berul SLOMIANSKY, Atlanta, Ga. (Smuel BEAR's grandson)	15.00
Mr. & Mrs. Dora SCHOLNICK, Salem, Mass.	10.00
Mr. Aviezer ZARICHANSKY, Columbia, South America	20.00
TOTAL	$540.00
New York, N.Y.	$1,655.00
Detroit, Michigan	350.00
Chicago, Illinois	550.00
Los Angeles, California	165.00
General	540.00
TOTAL INCOME	**$3200.00**

Moshe Shlomo Ben-Meir, Editor
By his son, Nakhum Ben-Meir

Moshe Shlomo Ben-Meir, (Idel Treszczanski, changed to Idel Treshansky upon entering the United States), was born on October 26, 1895, in Goniondz (Bialystok District), Poland. At a very early age, he was recognized as a prodigy, who memorized the Old Testament and was able to quote passages in full from random prompts (a "parlor game" he used to play with his students). He was playing in major chess tournaments in Eastern Europe before the age of ten. At the time of his death, he was fluent in 13 languages.

He received his higher education in Warsaw, but it is likely that he never obtained the kinds of formal degrees that would be recognized outside of Eastern Europe, a condition which limited his ability to advance professionally within the education community in later years.

After World War I, he emigrated to Belgium (Antwerp), where he found work as a diamond cutter and teacher in the Jewish Community. He met his wife, Chana, in Belgium, and they married in 1929. Their first child, Frieda, was born in 1930. Very early during his time in Belgium, he became a member of the Zionist movement, and his writing and oratorical skills led to his becoming a leading figure in that organization. With the rise of Fascism, the Zionist Labor Organization in Antwerp felt the need to provide him with protection, as its intellectual leaders became targets of Nazi attacks. His wife remembers she always had bodyguards, along with two well-trained Belgian Shepherd police dogs. She lamented greatly having had to leave them behind when they left Belgium.

As Nazism grew during the 1930's, it was apparent that it was no longer safe for him and his family in Belgium. Thus, in 1939, barely ahead of the invaders, he fled South, through France and Spain, to Lisbon, where some of his wife's North American family were able to secure boat passage for the family out of Europe. They landed in Montreal, Canada in 1940, and, with the help of those same family members, entered the United States (New York) in September, 1943. Their second child, Nahum, was born later that year.

Moshe initially was unable to find work in the educational field in the U.S. because of his lack of credentials, so he again found employment as a diamond cutter and polisher, and taught private lessons in Hebrew. But his enormous writing talents and interests in Zionism soon found him writing essays and poetry regularly for Ha'Doar, a major publication of the time. He also commenced working on one of his favorite projects: the reintroduction of Hebrew as a modern language, and spent many years translating the works of the great Yiddish writers (Sholem Aleichem, Mendele Mocher Sforim, etc.) into Hebrew. He very soon was in the midst of the Hebrew and Yiddish intellectual circles of New York.

In the late 1940's, despite his lack of credentials, he was finally able to secure a teaching position at Yeshiva University in New York, where he taught Hebrew, Bible and Literature. He retained that position until his death, on January 18, 1959, of heart failure. His heart condition had, sadly, prevented him from taking an offered Full Professorship at the University in Jerusalem, because of concerns about the altitude. His most important work, a book of poems entitled "Tzlil Vatzel" (Sound and Shadow), was published shortly after his death, and earned much praise and prizes within Hebrew language circles.

Wife, Chana, preceded him in death, in August, 1957. Daughter Frieda died in 1996.

He passed away while indulging in his favorite hobby: kibitzing a chess match between masters at a Manhattan chess club.

Moshe Shlomo Ben-Meir

English Title Page of Original Yizkor Book

OUR
HOMETOWN
GONIONDZ

PUBLISHED BY THE COMMITTEE OF GONIONDZ
ASSOCIATION IN U. S. A. AND IN ISRAEL

Tel Aviv, January 1960

Hebrew and Yiddish Title Page of Original Yizkor Book

ספר
יזכור
גוניונדז
*
יזכּור
בוך
גאָניאָנדז

הוצא על־ידי ועדי יוצאי גוניונדז בארצות־הברית ובישראל
אַרויסגעגעבן דורך די קאָמיטעטן פון גאָניאָנדזער לאַנדסלייט אין אַמעריקע און אין ישראל

תל־אביב • טבת תש״ד • ינואר 1960

Translation of the Title Page of Original Yizkor Book

Memorial
Book
of Goniadz

PUBLISHED BY THE COMMITTEE OF GONIONDZ
ASSOCIATION IN U. S. A. AND IN ISRAEL

Tel Aviv, January 1960

Page of Editorial Board in Yiddish and Hebrew from the Original Yizkor Book

Page of Editorial Board in English from the Original Yizkor Book

Table of Contents

PART III – MEMOIRS AND PORTRAITS   245

The Shul

These Roman numeral pages are from the English section of the book

[Pages IX-XX]

Our Hometown Goniodz
Province of Bialystok, Poland

I.

We consider it important and necessary to represent a review of our Memorial-Book to the children and friends of the Goniondz Society who do not read Yiddish or Hebrew. Let all of them get an idea about the Hometown of their parents and relatives and together with them hold dear the memory of the small Jewish community, that went to martyrdom during the black period of the bestial Nazi rule.

6,000,000 Jews perished during the 2nd World War in Eastern and Central Europe. Many bigger and smaller towns were immortalized in memorial books. They stand out like living symbols, spiritual monuments for the coming generations.

Our beloved Goniondz has surely earned such a monument. The Jewish Goniondz was very lively and interesting. The small Jewish population was very active, established many parties and clubs and gave to the world outstanding intellectuals in many fields, both Jewish and general.

Citizens of Goniondz are spread out all over the world. The majority of them live in the United States and in Israel, where they have established many societies and cooperatives in the socio-philanthropic field, giving financial and moral support to needy townspeople.

The Memorial-Book portrays to a great extent the manysided life of Goniondz before its destruction.

The Chronicle is divided in 4 parts, each with a different content. The *first*-historico-social part contains articles and notes about the history of Goniondz in general and the development - economic and cultural - of the Jewish community through the generations, who left behind them documents and witnesses.

The *second* part is devoted to the catastrophy. It brings to the reader the heartrending account of how the town, after having undergone indescribable sufferings, was completely obliterated together with all the Jewish communities in Eastern Europe.

The *third* part immortalizes outstanding personalities no longer with us, such as: Rabbis, public figures, talented young people, gone before their time.

II.

According to old historical documents, Goniondz was in existence already in the 13th century.

Thanks to her geographic location as a connecting link by land and water between Poland, Lithuania and Prussia, Goniondz played an important role both strategically and economically.

For a long time the town was a battle-ground between the Crusaders and the Polish Gentry.

Under the feudal Polish Government, Goniondz enjoyed the dubious "privilege" of not tolerating the Jews. In 1425 the town was taken over by the Lithuanians. In the year 1597 the town was granted the so-called "Magdeburg Rights", which permitted the Jews to settle there. In the beginning of the 16th century, Goniondz was occupied by the Swedes on their march into Russia. In the surroundings of the town can still be found traces of the Swedish occupation. In the second half of the 18th century Goniondz belonged to Prussia. After the division of Poland, Goniondz became part of Russia.

For a period of 100 years, the town goes through good and bad times: economic and commercial growth and also fires and epidemics. The proximity of the railroad and the fortress of Osowiec that were built in the second half of the 19th century, brought about the growth of the Jewish population and a marked improvement in their conditions of life. The market-days and the fairs attracted the peasants of the surrounding village. Goniondz became a lively trading center for lumber and grains, horses and cattle. The number of Jews in Goniondz varied at different times. In 1847 in a total population of 2050, the Jews numbered 1337. In 1897 the number of Jews was 2056 out of a total population of 3436. In 1921, after the first World War, there lived in Goniondz 1135 Jews of a total of 2642.

The reason for the decline of the Jewish population was emigration and war. The 2 great fires in 1906 and 1912 intensified the emigration of the Jews to the USA.

In the first World War, that started in 1914, Goniondz suffered from the shelling of the fortress of Osowiec by the Germans. The Jews were forced to flee and the town was plundered by the Russian soldiers. During the German occupation many Jews returned, but the town was impoverished.

Under the rule of the new Poland, after the first World War, Goniondz went through hard times: mental anguish and torment, economic difficulties, all this due to the nascent antisemitism of the Poles. The emigration became intensified. The Jews who had the means emigrated to the United States, the Zion pioneers to Eretz-Israel.

III.

Among all the neighboring towns, such as: Trestine, Yashinovke, Kniesin, was Goniondz the most interesting and the liveliest town in the socio-cultural field.

At the very inception of political Zionism, there became active in Goniondz a Zionist group, that sent a delegate to the Zionist Congress - the businessman and erudite Yakov Rudski. A short time thereafter, there came into being different Socialist groupings, such as: the "Bund" the "S.S.", that were very active among the working class and the youth.

They participated in revolutionary activity and propaganda that even reached the soldiers in the fortress of Osowiec. As a result, many Jewish boys and girls were from time to time arrested by the secret police and a number of suspects were forced to flee to escape the danger of being exiled to Siberia. The Zionist and Socialist activities went on unabated even during the black period of severest Russian reaction in the years of 1906-1914. It became intensified and came out in the open during the time of the German occupation in the first World War.

When Poland achieved he independence, there arose different political parties and groups, such as: "Misrachi", "General Zionists", "Zeirei Zion", "Poalei Zion", "Hashomer Hatzair", "Hechalutz", "Bund". After the Bolshevic Revolution - there came into being also the Communist Party, led by the returnees from Russia. All these parties and groups were very active. Goniondz excelled particularly in the field of Jewish education. The very first Zionists with the intellectual Efraim Halpern at the head established a modern "Cheder", where besides prayers, there was instruction in "Tanach" (Bible) and "Gemara" (Talmud) as well as reading and writing in Russian and Hebrew in a modern way. The first teacher of this school was the Hebrew scholar Gedalie Koslowski.

During the time of the first German occupation there was established in Goniondz *the first Hebrew public school in* Poland under the direction of the beloved pedagogue Moishe Levin. The hebrew school, where all the subjects were taught by lectures and study-books, especially written for this purpose by Moishe Levin, became a model school for the entire province and even for Bialystok, where similar schools were opened after the creation of the Polish state. The school attracted a healthy Hebrew-speaking and chalutz-oriented youth, that for the most part saved themselves from the catastrophy by emigrating to Eretz Israel.

Goniondz possessed a rich library in different languages, but mainly in Yiddish and Hebrew. The radical groups have established a library of their own. They also prevailed upon to introduce in their school the study of Yiddish. The non-partisan "dramatic circle" produced a great number of Yiddish plays, both drama and comedy, with Jewish and general motif. The plays were shown in a hall specially fitted for this purpose in the brewery building of Yakov Rudski.

The clubs used to arrange entertainments, discussion-evenings and excursions. Goniondz had charitable institutions that dispensed medical and financial aid to the sick and needy. This relief work was made easier for these institutions to bear thanks to the steady flow of subsidies from the Goniondz societies in the United States.

VI.

The "Goniondz Relief Committee in America" stands out by itself as a lodestar, a shining example of fraternal help. The members have never forgotten their friends and kinsmen and have always cared for the sundry needs of their native town. Thousands of dollars and hundreds of food-and-clothing packages have reached the Goniondz brethren though different ways and means.

With the cooperation of the ladies auxiliary, the "Goniondz-Trestine Society" created the necessary funds for the erection of a school building atop the famous "School-Mountain". With the help of the Society was also established the "Goniondz-Loan-and Savings Fund."

When the second World War broke out and Poland was crushed by the Nazis in a matter of days, the Jews of Goniondz lived through days of panic and terror. There took place attacks on Jews, plunder was widespread. However, the Soviet Army soon occupied the eastern part of Poland and marched into Goniondz. The town enjoyed relative quiet and the population gradually adjusted itself to the new regime. These conditions obtained until June 22, 1941, when the Nazi armies started on their march into Russia. Several Goniondz people, who survived the holocaust, have given us a vivid account, a heartrending description of the horrible catastrophy and destruction that befell our town. In the second part of this Memorial-Book Tovia Yevreiski portrays in grisly detail how our town perished. Other Goniondz inhabitants, like Z. Altschild, described the tragic events, but it is imperative to bring to light a resume in English so, that everyone should know what unbelieveable cruelties were visited by the Nazi beast upon our beloved people. How this wildbeast decimated, destroyed helpless, innocent human beings - young and old, woman and child - our own flesh and blood. You shudder when you read all this!

The Nazis entered Goniondz on the 26th of June, but from the first days of the Nazi invasion, the local Polish population took over power and began a systematic reign of terror and barbarism against the frightened, helpless Jews.

The Jewish homes were closed, the doors and shutters locked. On Friday, June 26, they issued an order that the entire Jewish population - men, women and children - the old and the sick be assembled at a certain hour on the market- place.

The Poles, under the direction of a Gestapo officer, made a "Selection". Those whom they pointed out as "Communists" or those against whom they carried a grudge, were assembled separately. The order of the Gestapo officer read: "The unofficial Communists are to he sent to work, as to the 'official ones' you are free to do with them as you like".

The Poles began to carry out this horrible order with great glee. Beating them mercilessly, they drove them, the "Communists" - into the synagogue and planned to set it afire. However, the neighboring Poles did not permit that, for fear that the conflagration may engulf their own homes. Then they marched them through the market place to the cellar of Mordechai Klap. An attempt was made to rescue them by offers of money and clothing - to no avail. In a few days they were all brought to the cemetery and murdered in the most gruesome way.

Among those who perished were: Shimon Yevreiski with two daughters, Boruch Trochimovski, Yakov Theodorowicz, Zalmon Niewodowski, Leibl Kravetz, the brothers Green, Aaron Bialy, Moishe-Faivel Bialosukenski, Efraim Kravetz and others.

The second group that was locked in a barn, was for weeks dragged to heavy labor. The Polish hooligans, however, did not cease their bestialities against the Jews. They murdered another number of them, among whom were: Wolf Reigrodski with wife and children, Mary Bialy with her son Yosef, Yosel Kobrinski, Sonia Lurie, Niesel Friedman with his son-in-law Yudel Linchewski with wife and children. Yoshua Halpern with wife and 3 children were murdered in the Jewish cemetery.

A few weeks later came the Gestapo and took away 15 persons, among them:

Asher Kobrinski, A. Brzezinski, Noiach Barski, Shimon Felsinowicz, Yerachmiel Halpern. They were led out of town and shot there.

Almost all these murders were perpetrated at the beginning by the Poles with the local priest and "intelligentzia" at the head. All Jews were forced to shave off their beards. Those who survived were subjected to merciless tortures both physical and moral.

When the power in Goniondz was taken over by the Nazis, quiet prevailed in town.

The Jews were going to work under the direction of the newly-created so-called "Juden-Rat" (Jewish Council).

The Polish city council would invent daily new methods to oppress and plunder the frightened Jewish population.

For a time the Jews would gain some surcease by giving their tormentors the few belongings still left to them, such as: clothing and jewelry until they became completely ruined and impoverished.

Thus, the painful tortured life of hunger, forced labor and degradation dragged on until the tragic end came.

On November 2, 1942 came an order from the Nazis to the effect that all the villages around Goniondz have to deliver 200 wagons for the town.

No one knew the meaning of this order, but there was foreboding. The local commander, however, assured everyone that the order has nothing to do with the Jewish population. A few days later came a heavy truck with armed soldiers. They stopped all Jews going to work and warned them that anyone trying to escape will be shot. The peasant wagons began coming in. The Nazis with the help of the Polish police began to chase the Jews out of their homes. Many hid in cellars and attics, but all were fished out of their hiding places. The Nazis started to shoot in order to stop those trying to flee.

In a few hours the wagons were packed with fainting and crying Jews - young and old. This wretched transport was sent to the village of Bogushe, a few miles from Greive. There were assembled thousands of Jews from the all the neighboring towns and from Trestine.

The local Polish bandits immediately swarmed all over the town like a locust plague, plundering the empty houses of the martyred Jews and taking away the few pitiful belongings left there. Then they started an orgy-dancing, singing and drinking full of joy of making the town of Goniondz "Juden-rein" (free of Jews).

In the camp of Bogushe many old and sick died. Those who survived were transported to the death camps, some to Tremblinka, some to Auschwitz.

Thus, after undergoing indescribable pain, degradation and barbarities perpetrated upon them by the savage beasts, perished our beloved, tortured town of Goniondz. Only a pitiful few survived as if by a miracle!

Let the blood of the martyrs come forth from the earth and to the end of time follow those 2-legged swine and their evil spirits be forever damned in Hades!

The Higher Power will avenge the deaths of the loved ones! The memory of the martyrs will forever and ever live in our hearts in love and reverence!

Looking Out of My Window Toward Goniondz
Recollections From My Childhood
by Maurice Gelbort

The countryside where I was born and grew to manhood among surrounding hills, green pastures, wild flowers in the summer, and icebergs in the winter, was known as Dolko.

On a summer night, a stout and odd shaped moon slowly rose on the horizon and crept up from behind the trees, lighting up the countryside with her magic light. It was so serene and quiet that I could hear the moon whispering, 'I am coming to bring you rest and quiet from your days' worries and toil."

While the town and surrounding countryside lay down to rest, another world was awakening. Creatures of all kinds, from the tiniest insect to the croaking frog, and to the melodious trill of the nightingale, greeted the moon with prayer in their own mysterious language; for them a busy day starts.

Who has not experienced a frosty moonlit night with trillions of diamonds sparkling on a white blanket of snow? The moon rose above the roof-tops, as though watching over us so that we would not be disturbed from our slumber, assuring us, "all is well and no harm will come to you".

It is dead quiet and holy in the still of the night only an occasional disturbance by a barking dog who is displeased with something or has some grievance, or insomnia.

The moon completed her mission, hastily disappearing in the light of the dawn, making way for the rising sun.

Robed in flames and amber light, majestically, the sun rose from the eastern gate, awakening man and beast from their deep slumber, bidding them a cheerful good morning.

Then a new day of hustling and bustling and back to the daily routine.

I wonder whether the sun and moon darkened when they looked down upon Goniondz after the Destruction!

The Goniondzer's Hymn

A little town, so jar and far away,

Is well remembered even today.

A group of people who once did live there,

Many years later still really care.

So many others were left behind,

And suffered much in body and mind.

We in America heard the pleas,

Of our ow'n "Landsleit" across the seas..

We joined together to give some aid,

To those from Goniondz sick and afraid.

We try to help them find a new life,

Away from poverty, hate and strife.

In a land of sun where brothers dwell,

In our old, new land - in Israel.

Idel Arenson
Daughter of a friend Eva Arenson of Chicago

Map of the Surrounding Area

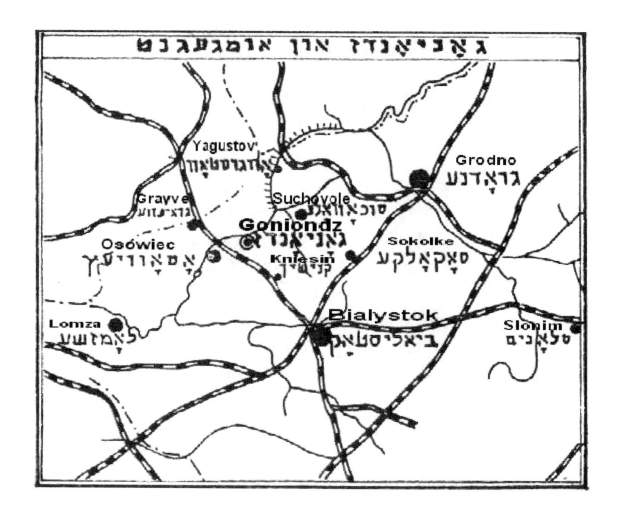

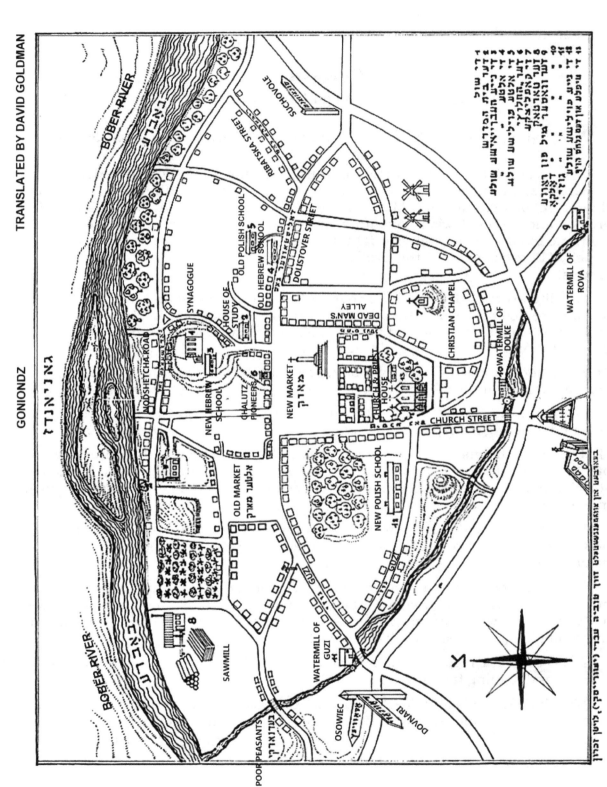

GONIONDZ   TRANSLATED BY DAVID GOLDMAN

DEVELOPED & DRAWN UP BY TUVIA IVRI (YEVREYSKY) FROM MEMORY

[Pages 21-22]

Foreword
Translated from Yiddish by Shayna Kravetz

"If only my words were written down, if only they were inscribed in a book!" Job 19:23

The dreadful Jewish destruction in Europe during World War II - a destruction unparalleled in history for its extent and cruelty - has led to the growth of a large "literature of destruction". Many monographs and memorial books about the greater and lesser Jewish communities destroyed in Europe have emerged and continue to emerge through special publications (such as "Cities and Ancestors of Israel", "Encyclopedia of the Exiled", etc.) and mainly through town dwellers' groups.

Our literature of destruction brings with it a terrible and anguished portrait of a giant cemetery filled with large and small tombstones, each with its own individual renowned name and personality, and with its local description of a rich Jewish life and its terrifying and tragic loss.

A memorial made of stone will be eroded and lost in the stream of time but a spiritual remembrance in the form of a book persists through the generations.

With our memorial book, we will perpetuate our beloved and dear town Goniondz, adding a chapter to the huge, bloody tale of the last Jewish destruction.

The four sections of the memorial book reflect the social and spiritual lives of our hometown in the last generations, although only in a limited way for, to our sorrow, we lack materials, documents, and comments from many interesting areas in old Goniondz life.

Like all Jewish cities and towns, Goniondz had its ups and downs, constructions and fires, good and beautiful achievements in unity and brotherhood as well as disputes and quarrels.

Goniondz contributed accomplished personalities in various areas with honoured names in the Jewish world, even including interesting folk-types. It was a lively town with virtues and flaws, greatness and smallness, storm and tranquillity, light and shadow like life itself.

From the dark region of its perishing there still beam out its beautiful, good, honest, and shining facets, pure and holy.

With bowed heads and deep sorrow, we establish through our memorial book a spiritual remembrance for our unforgettable destroyed hometown.

M.S. Ben-Meir (of blessed memory)

Pictures of Goniadz

Part I

Communal History

[Page 33]

Goniadz

By Moshe Bachrach, Los Angeles (California)
Translated by Gloria Berkenstat Freund

I suppose that each true Goniadzer feels as I do and it is "difficult" for him (or for her) to write about Goniadz, but a Yizkor Book is a document of generations and a spiritual *matzeyvah* [headstone] for a community - and the effort must be dear to us because the responsibility is great.

A *shtetl* [town], like a person, has its own physiognomy; it is different from its sister *shtetlekh* [towns] in some way. How is Goniadz different? How was our *shtetl* actually different - and was distinguished - from the surrounding *shtetlekh*?

Among the Gentile nations, a city usually excels with beautiful buildings, parks, gardens, monuments and art works that appeal to the esthetic senses. However, among we Jews, from primeval times on, everything points to spirituality and good qualities and in this sense, I think, Goniadz excels.

Surely, Goniadz, as regards "fashions," had its own portion of provincialism. Our *shtetl* at that time certainly had its so-called "curiosities." But this does not belong to the nucleus and the Goniadz that we from the last several generations knew possessed many strengths.

[Page 34]

Praise for the fathers and mothers must be included because they showed a great amount of tolerance for their sons and daughters by permitting and at times encouraging things and "changes" that would have been fought in other shtetlekh.

Goniadz was "equal with respectable people" in everything that has a connection to God. And yet individuals who were rooted in a traditional Jewish way of life and to whom everyone looked up with trust and respect, helped to raise the shtetl on the way to a modern, Hebraic education of Zionism, of education, of theater pieces and, finally - of the Halutz [pioneers who prepared for emigration to Eretz-Yisroel] movement, which transformed even the parents and set the tone of life in the shtetl - and of the environment.

Moshe Bachrach

It is a fundamental fact that the Goniadz Hebrew school was recognized as the *first* Tarbut [secular Hebrew school system] school in all of Poland. And it is symbolic that on the first day of the occupation and chaos in the fall of 1915, the Goniadz Jews requested from the Prussian commandant for the town only the chairs from the Russian school in the neighboring shot-up Russian fortress, Osowiec.

[Page 35]

It seems to me that only in Goniadz could it happen that a former Novoradoker [Novogrudok, Belarus] *yeshiva* [religious secondary school] young man who died as a modern Jew and, still a young man - Yehoshua Rozenblum (the son of Golda Elia Asher's daughter) - should be carried to the cemetery by first circling the *beis-hamedrash* [synagogue or house of prayer]... And it is hardly believable that it would have happened at that time in surrounding *shtetlekh*, that the diploma (graduating certificate) of the first *mahazor* (graduation) of the students who had finished the *modern* Hebrew school would be signed by the rabbi of the *shtetl* as had the Goniadz Rabbi, Reb Tzvi Hersh Wolf, of blessed memory.

[Page 36]

All Jewish cities and *shtetlekh* were ebullient with thoughtful life, but our *shtetl* had the luck that the generations tolerated one another and in many respects cooperated with one another.

Let all of us, who once took part in the life and creation of the shtetl think of it as justification that they can now take part in the *yizkor* [memorial] book and in making its publication possible.

[Pages 35-36]

Heads of the *Kehile* [organized Jewish community]

First row, standing (from the right): Elia-Hershl Nitvadovski, Yehoshaya Tsviklits, Moshe Furman, Zeidl Sidronski, Yehezkiel Perets Tshernia, Chana (?).

Second row, sitting: Shimshon Yevreiski, Josl Olshaniski, Chaim Treshtshanski, Leizer Trachimovski, Henokh Gelbard, Jakov Treshtshanski, Mishkovski (Chaim Kopelman's son-in-law), Leibl Mankovski, Dr. Blum, Wolf Piekorski, Zelig Nitvadovski, Sender Miltshan, Chaim Kopelman, Efroim Halpern, Beilach, Yakov Rubin, Leizer Tadaravitch, Ruwin Gelbard, Gedelia Treshtshanski.

[Pages 37-46]

Our Home Town
(Historical Notes)
By A. Miltshan
Translated by Marvin Galper

To the eternal member of my dear unforgettable sister and brother-in-law, Frida bas [daughter of] Reb Moshe and Zwi bar [son of] Meir Wilenski and their children Malka, Yosef and Yulek, of blessed memory, who perished at Treblinka in November 1942.

Our hometown Goniondz has a rich historical background. According to old documents, Goniondz has been in existence since the thirteenth century. Thanks to its geographical location as a connecting point through land and water between Poland, Lithuania and Prussia, our town played a very important strategic and economic role. For many generations Goniondz had been a battleground between Prussian crusaders and Lithuanian and Masovian (Polish) counts. This fact was confirmed by the accidental excavation of human bones and many skeletons, as well as old coins and weapon parts in various parts of town.

School children loved to tell stories about sunken houses and graves in the center of town. These childrens' stories were not entirely fantasy, but evolved from historical fact.

Under the combined rule of counts and clergymen in the fourteenth century, Goniondz was granted the so-called "privilege" to not permit Jewish residents. However, Jews moved into the city on an unofficial basis until Goniondz was transferred to the dominion of Lithuania in 1425. Goniondz received the Magdeburg Rights in 1547, which gave Jews permission to live in the city and become involved in commercial enterprise and the trades. The town grew, but this state of well-being didn't last long.

At the beginning of the seventeenth century, King Karl the Twelfth of Sweden undertook his march to Russia, and his path from Prussia lead through Goniondz. Brick ruins remain from construction of his army over the Bober River in the village of Shoshna. In memory of the period, the Russians named a section of the Osowiec fortress "The Swedish Fort".

The Swedish retreat and later return after their defeat in the famous battle at Poltava brought hunger and epidemics to Goniondz to which the greater part of the population succumbed. In the second half of the eighteenth century, after the annexation by Prussia, Goniondz experienced renewed vitality in all areas. A large town hall was built in the center of the new town square, and also a guild house for the education of manual laborers. The Prussians built a castle with the royal emblem as well as shops and houses for their employees. In order to shorten the water route to Prussia, they built a canal from the right side of the River Bober to the Prussian city of Lick. Grain from Goniondz silos was sent by special ships, "berlinkes", directly to Prussia. The Russian chronicles of that time described Goniondz as an important grain port on the Bober River.

After the wars and Partition of Poland (1795), Goniondz was given over to Russia. The town hall and the depots on the synagogue hill were destroyed at the end of the nineteenth century by the Russian government. The economic situation of the town fluctuated under Russian dominion. The town took on vitality from the construction of the Grayewo-Brisk railway line that connected it with the outer world-Russia on one side and Germany on the other

Later the fortress of Osowiec was built, which became a permanent source of Jewish livelihood. The fortress attracted Jewish military suppliers and experts from other places, for example, the military tailor Kantorowski and the photographer Karasik. The Jewish population adjusted itself quickly to the Russian regime and made business connections with the Osowiec military administration, providing various products and services. Prominent Goniondz suppliers were Bajkowski (Elioshers' son), Moishe Weintraub, Chayim Kobrinski (Chayim Poliaks), Moishe Katinko, Yakow Rudski, Moyshe Shilewski, and Moishe Kramkower.

Goniondz supplied the fortress with tradesmen-glaziers, metal workers, blacksmiths, coppersmiths, watchmakers, tailors, shoemakers, and so forth. Every Sunday groups of soldiers would come into town to buy their ordinary military goods--underwear, and all kinds of other supplies--and to buy clothing and other products of better quality than the standard military issue. Military personnel also came for the army camps at Monki and Downari. At noon time all the Jewish shops, teahouses and taverns were full, and it was a prosperous time. At times the order was disturbed by a drunkard or a group of drunkards, and the Jews would feel a little apprehensive. The military patrol would re-establish order in the town.

While Sunday was the time for commerce with military personnel, the Monday market was time for the farmers from the villages, who came to town to sell their produce and buy all kinds of merchandise for their needs. Both the new and the old town squares were filled with wagons of grain, chickens, potatoes, eggs, sheep, and so forth.

The old town square was the commercial center for horses and cows on market days, especially at the fairs which took place there three or four times a year. Merchants for grain, horses and cattle would assemble from near and far, even from the towns and villages on the other side of the river. Thanks to the connection of the River Bober with the Narew and Bug rivers, long barges laden with lumber would glide down towards Germany in the summertime.

Commerce in lumber developed in Goniondz. The most important lumber merchants were Chatzkel Bialototski (the wealthiest merchant in town), owner of the electric mill and the lumberyard, Alter Yisroel, Yisroel Yitzhak Farber, Yankel Shmerkes, and the Raigrodski brothers from Dolistower. The lumber merchants also arranged to have storage silos constructed for them on a custom basis because of the frequent fires in the surrounding villages. Many tradesmen derived their livelihood from the building construction industry--carpenters, painters, glaziers, shingle makers, and so on. Jewish millers who had a franchise from the princely owners of the wind and water mills in town were also successful.

Goniadz City Council

From right to left

First row : Hirsh Luria, Ah. Al. Lewin, Efraim Halpern, Tuvia Motl Kahn, Berl Rudski, Yakov Tikocki, Moshe Lewin

Second row: Klimaszewski, Khackl Bialostocki, Klicki (German official representative), Chaim Kopelman, Jan Potocki

The Monday market

The Jewish population in Goniondz fluctuated over the various periods, according to circumstances. According to available statistics, in 1847 there were 1337 Jews and 2050 in general population in the town. In 1897, there were 2056 Jews in the city, with a general population of 3436. In 1921 there were 1135 Jews in Goniondz with a general population of 2642. The decline in Jewish population can be ascribed to two causes--war and immigration. The two great fires, in 1906 and 1911, intensified the immigration to America. Some immigrants returned from America with the money they had earned, to build houses and open shops.

This situation continued until the First World War. The War, which broke out on Tish B'Av of 1914, caused much suffering in Goniondz due to its proximity to the front and the Osowiec fortress. After Rosh Hashono, the Jewish people were forced to flee. At that time the entire town was robbed by Russian soldiers at the front. That winter, after the German retreat, was a peaceful one. But at Purim time the Germans began a new offensive on all fronts. There was chaos in Goniondz.

On that day, the idealistic yeshiva student Yitzhok Laib Vitkowski (Laizer Isaac's younger son) met a tragic end. Yitzhok Laib had been arrested as the result of a false allegation and was taken to Osowiec, where he was killed by a German bomb. This tragic event threw the entire community into turmoil, which led to a massive flight from the town. Several weeks later the town was faced with the anti-Semitic edict of the Commander In Chief of the Russian Army, Nikolei Nikoleiwitch, that the entire Jewish population near the front be cast out of their homes.

Many people from Goniondz went to Bialystok and the surrounding towns-- Knyszyn, Yashinowka, and so on. Many traveled to central Russia, from which they returned after the revolution. During the period of the German occupation, many Jews were involved in reconstruction of the destroyed fortress and road repair. The Jewish population became very impoverished, but social life flourished. Under the dominion of the New Poland, Goniondz lived through difficult times with psychological and economic suffering. Immigration intensified and those who had the ability to do so moved on elsewhere. The dynamic Zionist youth migrated to Israel.

Stamp from the Post

Pajen Bank

From right to left:

First row: Bojarski, Wolf Rajgrodski, Simenow

Second row: Sh. Zachariasz, Zelig Poliak, Sh. Lipsztajn, Yehuda Mechaber, Hirsh Luria, Yehoshua Cwiklic

Third row: Zaliszanski, Chaim Kopelman, Hilel Biali, Wolf Piekarski, Zelig Niewodowski, Yehezkal Perec Czerniak, Mordekhai Kliap

A street in Goniadz

[Pages 47-48]

Historical Extract

A confirmation from the Goniadz *kehile* [organized Jewish community] in 1835 that four Goniadz residents presented themselves to it
Translated by Gloria Berkenstat Freund

Inscription on the stamp: *Kehile* **Committee of the Jewish people of the Holy Community of Goniadz**

Translation:
Mordekhai Aronowicz, Shmuel Ziskinowicz, Shlomo Zelmanowicz and Meir Ayzykowicz presented themselves to the Goniadz *kehile*, at which the same *kehile* signed and placed the *kehile* stamp. Given in Goniadz on the 3rd of July, in the year 1835.

Iczko Abramowicz

[Pages 49-50]

Goniadz in the Middle Ages
Translated by Gloria Berkenstat Freund

Many of the cities in Podlasze [Podlasie in Polish - the historic region of eastern Poland and west Belarus] were private during the first half of the 16th century. The most important of these belonged to the Queen Bori, for example, Bransk, Bielsk, Suraz.

During the reign of Count Radizwilow in Goniadz-Rajgrod. there were only a few very small *shtetlekh* [small towns], which began to develop relatively late. Rajgrod, which possessed bailiffs who received their office by inheritance, and Goniadz were already mentioned as *shtetlekh* in the acts of the year 1536.

In 1547 Goniadz received Magdeburg municipal rights [translators note: Magdeburg Rights were German laws granting towns a degree of internal autonomy. The laws were adopted by many Central and Eastern European monarchs.] and a city hall, which consisted of a mayor and three counselors. Rajgrod, then the property of Count Kizczyna, received the Magdeburg Rights 19 years later.

Lithuanian rule did not affect any Jewish interests, but from what we know Goniadz-Rajgrod was not in the area of the Lithuanian rule. In the known historical works by Professor [Sergei Aleksandrovich] Bershadski about Jews and even among his carefully collected materials, we have not found the least hint about Goniadz and nothing about Rajgrod Jews (page 16).

(Baranowski Tadeusz - about the occurrences of federalism on Podlasze, Radziwill Rajgrod-Goniadz rule in the first half of the 16th century. 11-187-476 B.N.

*

Goniadz in the 14th century was the object of quarrels between the Mazowiecka and Lithuanian dukes. Goniadz, was attacked from both sides, went from one side to the other many times and the city suffered greatly from this; the city lies opposite of the Bobra River - Biebrza.

Lithuania did not devote itself to capturing the entire actual area of Upper Podlasze.

The Mazowiecka dukes, who colonized the area from the west simultaneously with Russia, were not entirely expelled as a result of that defeat - and therefore they remained in Goniadz. And the Gemindoviches [Gediminidis], that is, the Lithuanian dukes, had to contend with them.

Thus, in 1358, an attempt was made to establish a mutual boundary.

(Excerpts from the book, Podlasze, in the Past and Today, November 1928, No. 1-2, Signature. F. 2442 B.N.)

[Pages 49-52]

Historical Information About Goniondz
Translated by Gloria Berkenstat Freund and Selwyn Rose

In his book of 1800, A[ugust] K[arl] Von Holsche, a German geographic researcher at the time of the reign of Brancki's widow in Bialystok, when the Prussians began during their annexation to rule in the Bialystok Department, lamented and said with bitterness about the Bialystok Department:

"This is an error: the majority of cities emphasized agricultural work and in general there was no industry in the agrarian cities; The consequences were that the Jews who were not engaged in agricultural work, firmly established themselves in all areas of providing food and many citizens had to move from the cities to the suburbs, to the villages and become farmers. The majority of cities had the privilege to have brewers and breweries, but it is rare to find a Christian citizen who is involved in this. [translator's note: in the 14th century through the 16th century, Polish kings granted the landowning nobility certain privileges including the right to exclude Jewish residence in cities and towns.]

This was the inheritance of the Jews along with taverns; Christians did not engage in trade and there were few professionals among them, but on the other hand Jews were engaged in various crafts because the crafts did not demand any physical exertion. An example of this is the city of Goniadz that according to available information was a flowering city of over 600 households 150 to 200 years ago and it had the privilege to not permit Jews to live in it. It became a complete ruin through fires and plagues.* But in the end the citizens began to move back..."

(A. Sh. Hershberg – Pinkas Bialystok 1949, vol. 1, pages 50-51)

* This is truly an admission that Jews then could not have any existence in any city in the district.

Goniadz Rabbis

The generations of the Holy Rabbi, Our Teacher and Rabbi Tuvia, (May G-d avenge his blood) son of Our Rabbi Yosef Shlomo (May his righteousness be remembered for a blessing) Bachrach...the seventh generation to Rabbi Mattityahu for sons and two daughters.

a) Rabbi, the Great Luminary, Pinchas Leib, Father of the Beit Din in the Holy Congregations of Goniadz and Orla, his wife was the daughter of Rabbi Moshe son of Rabbi Simcha, may he come to his place in the house of our fathers in pleasure and contentment... the eighth generation.

b). The Rabbi The Great Luminary, Our Teacher the rabbi Gedalia Ha-Cohen, Father of the Beit Din in the Holy Congregation of Goniadz .

"Da'at Kedoshim" Peterburg 1897: pp. 37, 39. ____

Goniadz

Goniadz is a town in the region of Grodno, County of Bialystok, on the left bank of the river Bober ----- 57 kilometers to the north-west of county capital Bialystok. The railroad station on the line Brest-Litovsk – Fryztak, and is from the old Russian south-west railroad near the Polish border.

According to an accounting there were 3300 residents in 1882. The town was especially known as a transport trade: boat passed by on the river. It was a very important factor. The river was navigable and many wooden lighters and barges plied up and down. Under Polish rule Goniadz received its City Charter in 1547.

In 1807 – the city was transferred to Russian rule.

(Sent from the Jewish Historical Institute in Warsaw)

Goniadz Statistics

The general number of residents 2,644; enterprises 127, of them 117 are active; number employed 204 people, of them owners 57.4%; assisting family members 22.1%; wage workers 20.5%, 88.1% of the wage workers are Jews.

(Jewish Industrial Enterprises in Poland, according to the questionnaire of 1921, Warsaw 1922, third volume; sent from the Jewish Historical Institute in Warsaw)

[Page 53]

[Political] parties in Goniondz
by Fishl Yitzhak Treshtshanski, Tel Aviv
Translated by Gloria Berkenstat Freund

Parties in Goniadz

Goniadz, our *shtetl* [town], as I remember it in the last era - in the years 1925-1935 - was active in many areas of communal life. In general I think that Goniadz boasted of itself in contrast to its "provinces." I do not know if it had a basis for this. In any case, Goniadz was the first in certain respects. Our Hebrew school was founded earlier than in the rest of Poland. The first who travelled to Eretz- Yisroel from our area, right after the First World War, were from Goniadz, such as: Efraim Halpern ("Efraim the writer"), Mordekhai the baker, Shakhna's son Leibl, Gedalia Grinszpan, Chashke Bachrach, Sholem Luria and many others.

In our *shtetl*, as in general then in Jewish community, they were parties and camps, of the right and left. Social workers and community activists stood at the head of the parties. I am not able to describe them properly; I will only mention them in a few words. I will begin with the smallest party.

The Bund

At the head stood Leibl Mankowski, who was the power of the Bund in the *shtetl*. I do not remember him well. In my memory remains only the impression of the large funeral that was arranged for him, with the many garlands of flowers - that was a rarity at Jewish funerals in the *shtetl* - and mainly that among the Jewish speakers, a Polish teacher also gave a short speech in the name of the Polish population.

[Page 54]

Henakh the tailor's son (Gelbard - Itshe the water carrier's son) or as he was called, "*der likhtiker tog*" [the bright day] was one of the most active Bundists; the nickname comes from 1920 when the Polish-Russian War took place and the Bolsheviks entered the *shtetl*. A large meeting under the open sky of the entire population, Jews and Christians, was called on one of the first days after the founding of the local *RevKom* (Revolutionary Committee). Henakh the tailor's son spoke as the representative of the Jews. He ended his speech with the words: "Today der likhtiker tog has come for us!" So he was given the name *der likhtiker tog...*

Henakh was solid and devoted to his party. He almost always appeared as an opponent in the name of the Bund at Zionist meetings. If Henakh was the opponent, Alter Machnowski was the "interrogator." His questions would flow at meetings. He was a baker by trade, the son-in-law of Ayzyk Abiezer and newly arrived in the *shtetl* [town]. He was a man of the people type, and he was often seen in the street with a creased *Folks Zeitung* [*People's Newspaper*] in his hand. His hat was always on the side and his long nose as well as part of his face was covered with flour. He would lead the first and best discussion as he went along, even when he hurried to work in the bakery.

[Page 55]

Another type from the Bund was Josl Alszanicki (Khinke's son Josl). He was the representative of the Bund in the city council for several years. He had a sensitive Jewish soul and wrote folk-poems (several of them were published in New York in the *Forvets*).

Josl Alszanicki

The Communists

Moshe Toykel was one of the most interesting figures among the "*royte* [reds]" - from outside [of Goniadz]. He arrived in Goniadz to work for Shimeon the cutter in his earliest youth and then he became his son-in-law. I remember his first appearance in the theater performance of Pinksi's play, *Di Familie Tzvi* [*The Tzvi Family*], in which he performed with great insight. He concentrated and led an entire group and was the guide of the Communist *Shulkhan Oruch* [Code of Jewish Law] in the *shtetl*.

[Page 56]

Zeydl Altszuld (Natke the farmer's son) belonged to this group. His party work was in another area. He was the "store" for the theater performances that were organized in the *shtetl* and whose income went for party purposes.

There were not only theater performances for the sake of art. The main factor was a party one. A demonstration of this fact was that performances were arranged separately by all parties, those on the "right' and on the "left."

The "stars" and "prima donnas" appeared at the performance. They prepared for these performances for weeks and on the designated day of the performance (it was usually at night after *Shabbos*) it felt as if the entire *shtetl* was preparing for it. On the *Shabbos* of the performance, young and old took longer naps after the *cholent* [*Shabbos* stew] because the performance would not begin earlier than 11 or 12 at night and it would end at four o'clock in the morning...

The interest was great notwithstanding that everyone knew before who would appear and how he (or she) acted and everyone was acquainted earlier with the details of the decorations and with the actors' clothing because everything was gathered from the entire *shtetl* - a long coat as a *tallis* [prayer shawl], an old chest of drawers as a broken table...

Each performance gave the *shtetl* something to speak about for weeks.

[Page 57]

Zelik Niewadowski

The Zionists

Goniadz was mainly a Zionist *shtetl*. Zelik Niewadowski (Leyshke's son, Zelik) stood at the head of the "general" Zionists. He was not only a Zionist activist, but also a general municipal activist. He was a representative everywhere: in the Hebrew school, in the city council, the *kehile*, the bank and so on. Zelik was an "intimate of the state," had the best relations with the police commissar and with the mayor of the *shtetl*, as well as with the *starosta* [head] of Bialystok. Zelik, it should be understood, was at the head of the Zionist meetings and he led the meetings so that it was certain that opponents would not disturb them and that they would not be disbanded by the police.

Zelik had an influence not only in Zionist matters or in general in city matters, but also in the houses of prayer and in the synagogue. I remember an episode from that time. This was in about 1927, after Rabbi Shomowicz, the new rabbi in the *shtetl*, was chosen. One *Shabbos* [Sabbath] a group of *halutzim* [pioneers preparing for emigration to *Eretz-Yisroel*] went on an outing to a nearby forest. The group left in orderly rows. The new rabbi noticed; he went into the street with a group of Jews - and when the *halutzim* approached, he stood across the width of the street and began to chastise them and did not let them pass. Understand that the *halutzim* did not want to be dictated to by the rabbi. There was turmoil - and Zelik Niewadowski appeared and he turned with anger to the rabbi and said as follows: "Rebbe, you will dictate to us only in the synagogue; you will not mix in outside of the synagogue. Excuse us and go inside the house." The noise immediately grew still greater, but Zelik's words resolved it and after an exchange of a few words on both sides, the rabbi and his people did go into the house - and the *halutzim* marched out of the city in victory (the episode was reported in the *Provinc Shpigl* [*Provincial Mirror*] of a Warsaw newspaper).

[Page 58-59]

Wolf Pekarski

Asher Szirotes

Wolf Pekarski (a son of Mushke's) also belonged to the (General) Zionists. He was a *lovnik* [alderman] on the city council and the only Jewish government official who received his salary from the city council. He was an intercessor for Jews in their small and large matters.

One of the Zionist "types" was Asher Szirotes (the black Yisroel's son), a teacher in the Hebrew school. He was one of the first makhzor (graduates) of the Hebrew school (in 1918), and thanks to his pedagogic capabilities he became a teacher in the school. He was the director of the Zionist theater performances and also of the children's performances at the Hebrew school. He was the recognized reviewer and expert on theater in the shtetl. Asher also gave lectures on this theme. He, himself, also took part, in the main roles in various plays: Got, Mentsh un Tayvl [God, Man and the Devil] Khashe der Yesoyma [Khashe the Orphan] Der Meturef [The Madman] and so on. He performed Der Meturef with so much heart that he was later called der meturef in the shtetl.

The basis of the Zionist education was the Hebrew school. The entire young generation studied, was raised and grew there. Only a few, who can be counted on the fingers, studied in the Polish school and the majority of them were those who after graduating from the Hebrew school, wanted to perfect their Polish speaking. And when in the later years the Yiddish school was founded, a small number of children studied there.

[Page 60]

The *Halutz* Movement

[Translators note: *Halutz* is the Hebrew word for pioneer. The *Halutz* movement prepared "pioneers" for emigration to *Eretz-Yisroel*. *HaHalutz*, the pioneer, was the name of the Jewish youth association preparing the emigrants]

The Zionist-*Halutz* Movement had a great influence in Goniadz thanks to the influence of the Hebrew school. The *haHalutz* organization was created earlier and then the *haHalutz haTzair* (the young pioneers). From the earliest age - from 10 to 11 - the children were organized and engrossed in their *Halutz* education. This was expressed in the systematic conversations, courses, evening classes and so on. Incidentally, at several evening courses in which our opponents took part, their participation in the discussions was permitted but only if they spoke Hebrew as we did.)

Summer colonies were arranged whose task was, firstly, to acquaint themselves with other living conditions than in the city and, secondly, to study problems of the pioneers and of *Eretz-Yisroel*. Outings to the closest *shtetlekh* also were arranged and a hectographic journal was also published that spread across the entire area.

Many conventions of the surrounding *shtetlekh* were arranged in Goniadz. The celebration that was organized for the tenth anniversary of *haHalutz-haTzair* in July 1934 particularly left a strong impression.

[Page 61]

All of the branches from the area took part in the celebration. The preparations were massive because preparing food for hundreds of people demanded their complete work. A guest was taken in at the house of each comrade. A kitchen immediately was created at which mothers also helped to prepare lunches that were served at large tables to the accompaniment of pioneer singing.

The entire *shtetl* looked *yom-tovdik* [like a holiday] as no time before. All of the guests were dressed in white blouses. Several balconies in the main market were specially trimmed and decorated with Zionist pictures, slogans and flags. The *shtetl* was brightly lit in the evening. At that time Goniadz possessed five or six large gas lamps that would only be lit in long, dark nights. But on the evening of the celebration all of the lamps in the shtetl were lit (at our cost).

The military trumpet that gave the signal that the celebration was beginning was heard at seven o'clock at night. We marched from every corner and courtyard, where each group had arranged itself, to the old market from where the solemn demonstration began. The orchestra walked at the head, especially invited from Bialystok; after it marched the long line with drums, through all the Goniadz streets and at the sides were organized the order keepers, riding on horses.

[Page 62]

Understand that the line was accompanied by the entire *shtetl*, young and old, until it dissolved on the synagogue hill. On the program of that night and into the morning was: a performance of the dramatic studio of the pioneer settlement in Bialystok, speeches and greetings, sport entertainments and other solemnities.

During the two days of celebrating the 10-year anniversary of *haHalutz- Hatzair*, everyone in Goniadz forgot their concerns about income and joined in the holiday that was unique - not like other holidays, such as Chanukah, but as something that does not repeat itself...

Therefore, it is no wonder that a significant number of Goniadz young, who were raised in the pioneer spirit, are found here in Eretz-Yisroel. If not for Hitler and the war, a larger part of our *shtetl* would be with us here where everyone had someone from their family - a brother or a sister - and to which we were drawn and strived for in the course of many years.

Tel Aviv, 1945

(From Goniadz-Trestiner Bulletin, published in America)

[Pages 63-68]

Zionism in Goniondz
by Yekhezquiel Peretz Tshcherniak
Translated by Marvin Galper

Once, when I was a youngster, Yossel Sheimus arrived at our home with a blue-white collection box with a Star Of David stamped on it, and also the printed phrase "Keren Kayemet L'Yisroel." He told us that on Friday he was going to be passing through the town collecting cash from the townspeople for the National Fund, for the purpose of redeeming land in Eretz Yisroel. At about the same time, I heard that Pinchas had gone through town with a little book, inscribing contributions to the Odessa Committee. One was required to pay three Russian rubles, in installments over the course of a year.

I remember being told that Chaim Dinkes, Efraim Eliyohu, Meilach Pekarski, and Nechemya Yankel (Zelig Isaac's) were enrolled as subscribers. The leader of the group was Alter Suprarski, who lived in Kursk, and visited Goniondz three times a year on religious festivals. Every Friday a young man would pass through the town collecting funds for Keren Kayemet. There were many who did not wish to contribute. They were generally either poor or tight fisted.

One of the wealthier men in town, Alter Yisroel, who was also a keen minded man, used to ridicule both the collection box and those who collected. They knew how to handle him. Alter Yisroel loved to stand at the lectern in the synagogue. He had the established prerogative to pray the beginning part of Slichos on the Saturday night of Rosh Hashana. The first group of young Zionist men consisted of Yankel (Dovid Rudskis'son), Hershel Finis, Hershel Leibel (Chayim Meyers'son), Yitzhok the son of the dayan's wife, Haikel (Schloime Yossels' son), Yossel Sheimus, Laizer Zelig, Mayer the watch repairman's son, Yisroel Yaysef Beryl, and a group of small kids.

Stamp of the Zionist Organization

They gathered behind the lectern and when Alter began to sing "Motzoi Menucha", everyone started to thump on the benches and seats, and he stopped. They said that they were not going to permit Alter to be the leader of the congregation from the lectern until he began to contribute regularly to the collection box. Almost all the worshippers were accustomed to donate to the collection box were in agreement with these young men. A tumult ensued, and Alter Yisroel swore that he would take care of those guys, "the unshaven ones." He gave the town constable, a heavy-set Russian with a thick mustache, the names of the young men.

It seemed like a good deal to the constable, He expected he'd end up with something in his pocket. He called the young men to him. Before going to see him they sent him in advance a fine pair of boots from Moishe Gershon the shoemaker. This dignitary scolded them a little for causing a disturbance in a public place, and then told them that he would let them go this time. The boots had cost the men three rubles. After that, Alter Yisroel regularly contributed a kopeck to the National Fund.

On another occasion, Alter Suprarski came to town from Kurtsk and established a local Zionist organization, mainly from among the laborers and tradesmen. The group included Schmuel Baer Malasofski, Berushki the tailor, Laizer the blacksmith, and others. They rented a place from Zeike the wagoneer, near to Benyomin the scribe. Every Sabbath they met there to study a little Chumash and Tanach. Gershon Boruch studied with them for a while. Yitzhok the dayan's son would read them a little history. Also, for a brief time, they were given lectures by Gedalke the teacher.

Goniondz also sent Yankel Rudski as delegate to the Fourth Zionist Congress. On that occasion, he served as representative for the town of Grajewo as well. When they arranged a Zionist congregation in the home of Schmuel Chodorowsky, Yankel Rudski told all those present what he had seen and heard at the Congress in Basel. Yankel Rudski was an intelligent man, but he had a problem with stage fright. He could tell a story clearly and cleverly, but he couldn't speak in public. He had been enormously impressed with Usishkin "The Iron General", and with

Dr. Max Nordau. But, Rudski said, they were like a drop in the ocean in comparison with Theodor Herzl--his striking handsomeness, his wisdom and his greatness. Rudski didn't succeed in being able to have a conversation with him, but could only manage a hello. To do that, he had to wait especially for Herzl in a corridor, and then give him his hello. When Rudski shared this episode, there was a tear in everyone's eye at the minyaan. At Simchas Torah time, the Zionists had their own minyan.

The Committee and Regiment for the Jewish National Fund – 1933

The Committee for Jewish National Fund Affairs– April 5, 1925

First row, standing from the right: Meir Treszczanski, Garber, Fishl Furman, Chaya Goldbard, Mordekhai Ribak, Shayna Markus, Sholem Niewodowski

Second row: Khona (Khone) Makai, Zandberg (Hebrew teacher), Baylke Kliap, Golda Rubin, Moshe Goelman

Third row in front: Rywka Kobrinski, Rywka Luria

[Page 69]

Agudas Tzeirei-Zion
[Association of Young Zionists]
by Prof. Dr. Engineer Mordekhai L. Abshalom
Translated by Gloria Berkenstat Freund

It would be unpardonable if when writing these memories of Goniadz were to forget the existence of the *Agudas Tzeirei-Zion*. The association was founded in an indirect manner thanks to General Zionists who formed under Comrade Jakob Rudski. When our unforgettable leader, Dr. T. Herzl, called together the Fourth Zionist Congress in Basel, the comrade, Reb Jakob Rudski, may he rest in peace, went as a delegate and when he returned he delivered his impression of the Congress and its various participants to a crowded circle of Jews. All who took part were convinced that Dr. Herzl was a true prophet sent from heaven to help in the final redemption of the Jewish people from their almost 2,000 year exile.

Present at the meeting were: Reb Jakob Rudski, Reb Pinkhas Kamenecki, Reb Chaim Kopelman, Reb Shimeon Chodorowski, Reb Moshe Halevy (today the latter is in Tel Aviv).

The Zionist World Organization created certain institutions for which we had to work and, chiefly, to develop the ideal of political Zionism. Thus were created: the institution of *Keren Kayemet leYisroel* [Jewish National Fund], to redeem the territory of *Eretz-Yisroel*, and the Colonial Bank to give financial support to the first colonists. In addition, the national spirit had to be developed among the young.

It also was necessary to draw a larger group as subscribers to the newspapers: *HaTsefirah* [*The Siren*], *Hazman* [*The Time*], to the journal: *HaShiloah* [*Of Shiloah*]; to bring new teaching methods into the old *kheder* [religious primary school] and to transform it into a modern *kheder*. It should be understood that the work fell on the General Zionists who, by the way, it must be remembered, were the most esteemed men, business owners in the city, who derived great pleasure from studying a page of the *Gemara* in the house of study every night; they never missed praying three times a day. However, these Jews had great difficulties then in Russia: they were busy with their livelihoods. Therefore, little by little the national work fell upon the young, who would listen with enthusiasm to the conversations of the old comrades on *Shabbos* between *Minkhah* and *Maariv* [the afternoon and evening prayers] and little by little prepared for the campaign for the redemption of the land and the people.

[Page 70]

Before beginning the work, the young created an association with the name *Tzeirei-Zion*. The following comrades took part in the organization: Josef Hercig, Yoal Meir Hacohan, Josef Bobrowski, Moshe Malozowski, Yehoshaya Rozenblum; Yehezkiel Perec Czerniak, Zundl Ben Akiva, Khunen Szilewski and Mordekhai L. Absholem (at that time he bore the family name Frydman-Furman), who was elected as the first president of the association. The main work of the association consisted of collecting money for *K.K.L.* Every Friday comrades with *puskhes* [cans] would go across the city and collect money for the National Fund. Others went on sales actions for the Colonial Bank (which was more difficult work); selling stamps for *Keren Kayemet* and the like. Every time a preacher would expound on Zionist thought in his sermon in the synagogue, the comrades would consider themselves lucky, particularly when he would attempt to draw the young to the ideal of Zionism.

[Page 71]

The dispute that the Zionists would carry out in the "occupied communities" cannot be described: they would consider themselves lucky when a Zionist candidate would win. The Zionist workers were, at that time, very fruitful and very successful. Because of the difficult circumstances that reigned at that time in Russia in regard to we Jews, the president of the association had to leave his dear city, Goniadz, and emigrate abroad. As recognition for his active work, he was recorded in the first Golden Book of *Keren Kayemet* by his comrades from his city.

Buenos Aires 31st July 1936

Precepts of the *Yehudiah* Zionist Union
Hebrew translated by Amy Samin
Yiddish translated by Gloria Berkenstat Freund

We publish an interesting document - the precepts of the Goniadz Zionist organization named Yehudiah. This document was sent to us by the first secretary of Yehudiah, Motya Leib Frydman, today known as Dr. L. Avshalom, professor of chemistry at the University of Buenos Aires.

On 23 Tishrei 5668 [1 October 1907] a Zionist association was founded in our town. Its regulations were as follows:

a. The name of the association is Ha Yehudiyah [The Jewess].
b. The location of the association is Goniadz, Grodno Region
c. The purpose of the association is to do Zionist work according to the first section of the Basel Program: "Zionism seeks to establish a home for the Jewish People in Eretz Yisrael secured under public law" which will be possible to obtain by means of practical work in the Land of Israel.

The methods for reaching this goal are:
d. To promote the Zionist idea among the people of our city at scheduled gatherings featuring lectures and discussions about Zionism.
e. To improve Hebrew education by means of the founding of a heder metukan [modern Talmud Torah school].
f. Anyone who desires the resurrection of our people and who pays the annual fee of one shekel in addition to the membership fee of ... per month for the expenses of the association may become a member of the association.
g. At the head of the association will be a committee of members: Mr. Yaacov Rudesky and Mr. Tuvia Mordechai, co-chairmen; Mr. Haim Kopilman, treasurer; Mr. Pinchas Kaminsky, secretary. Mr. Shimon Hodorovsky, Mr. Yosef Izzik Halperin, Mr. Efraim Halperin, Mr. Pinchas Kaminsky [sic], Mr. Yosef Tikutzky, Mr. Yehoshua Rozenbloom, Mr. Moshe Levin.
h. At the start of every year, the committee must call a general meeting in which at least two thirds of the association's members must participate, in order to make a report on the association's activities during the year and to elect a new committee.
i. The members of the committee must meet once a week, always in the same place, to discuss the work required of the committee and to determine whether each member has completed the assignments given to him by the committee during the previous week.
j. The association must maintain constant correspondence with the Galilean authority, to whom it also sends the reports of the association's activities.

[Page 73]

Photostat of a Letter
Hebrew translated by Amy Samin
Yiddish translated by Gloria Berkenstat Freund

Farewell letter that was written in the year 5679 (1919) from Agudat Tzeirei Zion [Union of Youth of Zion] in Goniadz to Moshe Malozowksi, before his departure from Goniadz.

Translation of letter:
Tzeiray Zion [Youth of Zion]
To our friend Moshe Molozovski,

We send you our warmest blessings of friendship. Peace, peace be unto you, our dear friend, in every place upon which you set foot, whether it be the mountains of Zion or Yehuda. May we be fortunate enough to see you and work with you on behalf of the Jewish people, as is your wish and the wish of all of your friends.

On behalf of the board of Tzeiray Zion, Goniadz, Signed,

Chairman, Executive Director, Board Member,
Head of the Yeshiva: Z. Niewadowski
Director of Studies in the Yeshiva: Moshe Furman
The Chief Rabbi of the Executive Committee: A. Milczan

[Pages 75-78]

A Homely Reflection on Various Movements
by Yosef Hertzig
Translated by Marvin Galper

Chassidism

In the beginning, only a small percentage of the people in Goniondz were Chassidim. These Chassidim were members of the merchant elite. The masses of the people were adherents of conventional Judaism. The Chassidim separated themselves from the mainstream. They established their own small prayer center where they would gather to worship. Tension between the townspeople and the Chassidim became so acute that, one Simchas Torah, the town unleashed their rage on the Chassidic worship center and tore it up. This resulted in the decline of Chassidism in the town.

Socialism

The Socialist movement had two currents in Goniondz which found expression in two separate organizations, the Social Revolutionaries and the Bund. The intelligentsia of the town youth became involved with the Russian Social Revolutionaries. Their mission was to distribute socialist propaganda among troops stationed at the nearby fortress of Osowiec. Their activities did not continue for a very long time. They were discovered as provocateurs by the military. They had to flee over the Prussian border. Among them was Dov Pekarski, may his memory be for a blessing. When he returned to Goniondz, he involved himself in Zionism and was very active in the movement.

The Bund consisted of a small group of workers and sympathizers. Goniondz was a poor town and did not have large factories as did the large cities. Attempts had been made to establish a textile factory, a pearl button factory, and also a bristle brush factory. None of these ventures, however, were successful. As a result there were no industrial workers available for recruitment. Consequently, the Bund involved themselves primarily in Yiddish cultural activities. They penetrated the town trilingual library (Hebrew, Yiddish and Russian) with the intent of shifting it's direction to learning Yiddish rather than Hebrew.

They were successful for a brief time period. However, they were ejected from the community and the folk library when the Tsire Tzion movement was established. Later the Bundists established a people's school with Yiddish as the language of instruction which operated at the same time as the Tsire Tzion Hebrew people's school.

Zionism

Zionism drew to itself nearly all the people of Goniondz. For legal reasons they attached themselves to the Lovers of Zion organization in Odessa. The youth organization entitled Tsire Tzion was established by the Vilna Zionist group. The Tsire Tzion fraternity was active in various areas. Their mission was to disseminate Zionist propaganda and instill a Zionist perspective in various organizations.

They also founded new institutions such as the people's school in which Hebrew was the language of instruction. They enriched the library with books written in Hebrew, with the intent of recruiting new membership by means of the shekel. They also collected funds for Zionist causes.

Two young friends visited all the Jewish homes every Friday afternoon seeking contributions. They attended every joyous family occasion, such as weddings or circumcisions, and solicited donations for the National Fund. Their wish was to have a Keren Kayemet donation box in every Jewish home. Those who made substantial contributions were inscribed for a perpetual memory in the Golden Book in the land of Israel.

Another activity was the establishment of the traditional Simchas Torah minyan organized by the Tsire Tzion. The Rudski home, the most attractive site on the town square, was made available to them on a gratis basis for this purpose. On Simchas Torah, all funds contributed for the honor of carrying the Torah were donated to the Keren Kayemet fund. These occasions were great Zionist demonstrations. The spacious area was filled to overflow with people. Masses of people also assembled outside due to the lack of sufficient space within. The tall and thin Yoel Mayer Cohen, with his serious face, would stand in the center surrounded by his chorus. They would sing "To The Bird Of Paradise" and "Hatikva." Yehatzkel Cherniak would sing "Shine Forth, O King From Your Abode" from the kedusha of the morning service in the musaf singing style of

Cantor Nochum, may his memory be for a blessing. One felt the powerful faith of the congregation as they responded in unison, "Soon, and in our days". Their passion is difficult to convey in a written document.

They also allowed themselves a little humor. At that time, the wealthiest man in Goniondz was given a Torah to carry around the room with the comment, "help the poor." All present would respond with hearty laughter. This was good- natured humor, and was experienced as friendly by all.

The powerful influence of Zionism on the town can be seen most clearly in the extraordinary number of persons who migrated to Israel. It is worthy of note that the Zionist influence was so extraordinary that, when the writer of these lines would pass through town selling shekalim, he didn't even neglect to stop at the home of Laib Maskovski, the leader of the Bund, may his memory be for a blessing. In response to my request that he buy a shekel, Laib answered, "As Bund leader I cannot buy a shekel. But I will accept one in the name of my wife."

[Pages 79-82]

The Bund
by Sarah Barqa'it
Translated by Amy Samin

In a chance meeting at a bar mitzvah celebration on a large kibbutz , one of the members - a son of the town of Radzilov, which was close to Goniadz said: "You don't know anything about how we, the youth of our town, felt about your Goniadz? We were very jealous of you, we were jealous of your school, of the way you spoke Hebrew so fluently, of your fervent enthusiasm for the Land of Israel, and the devoted work of the Jewish National Fund [*Keren Kayemet L'Yisrael*]. Indeed, you were an example and a paragon, and we tried to imitate your deeds to the best of our ability."

When I try to recall the source from which we, the youth of Goniadz, drew the strength and the courage to begin working on behalf of the Land of Israel, I recall the work we did for the JNF. The collection of donations for the JNF was wrapped up in every aspect of our lives. Virtually every celebration in Goniadz included the JNF. And when we would gather for meetings led by Bikla Claf of blessed memory, she would always open them thus: "In order to show both honor and affection for the work of the members and donors as one, we must find new ways to collect money." And indeed we knew how to find new ways. Who among us does not remember the bazaars of the JNF, for which we would prepare with days and

Bikla Cliaf [sic]

nights of painstaking work. The opening of the marketplace was quite an event in the life of our town, anticipated for weeks and months. How much thought and effort we invested in decorating the "Persian Room" and in the various raffles. How great was our happiness over every item that reached the bazaar, and how our hearts rejoiced over each additional bit of income!

[Page 80]

I recall that one Shavuot eve, we decided to hand out flowers among the houses and to allocate the money to the JNF. Since we did not have a place to grow an abundance of flowers like the Christian cemetery, at night we recruited all of the boys to pick lilacs in that place. Group by group the boys set off to "pick" while the girls stood watch... The flowers, whose pleasant scent carried quite a distance, were placed in pails of water, which filled the house and the yard. We sat on the floor and began weaving flower garlands. And here, in the midst of this feverish work of weaving flower garlands came the chief of the police who began to question us as to where we had obtained quite so many lilacs, and why we were suddenly so possessed by such a joyful spirit. We almost died of fright, until one of us recovered sufficiently to improvise a good excuse: next Shavuot she would celebrate her engagement, and she would be honored to take the opportunity to invite the honorable chief of police to join the festivities. Indeed, thanks to the cleverness and imagination of that young lady, we were spared from an investigation the results of which would most certainly have been very unpleasant for us.

Thus we tried to suit each project to a holiday. On Tu B'Shvat we handed out dried fruit from the Land of Israel. On Rosh Hashanah we distributed picture postcards with scenes from the Land of Israel, and during the Days of Awe the jangling coins would fill the bowls of the JNF at the synagogue and the House of Study. But the favorite was the blue box that adorned every Zionist house in our town. The JNF box was displayed in every home. The money from various arbitrations was dedicated to the blue box, and every family event: wedding, bris or the birth of a daughter, was commemorated the planting of trees in Herzl Forest.

[Page 81-82]

But the pinnacle of devotion to the JNF was felt in the donations of the school children. Fridays were dedicated to donations of the classes to the JNF. With anxious hearts, each child - poor and rich - would bring their donations to the box. Many times the mothers would come to complain to the teachers that their children were saving the money meant for bread and donating the meager pennies that they had received from their mothers to the JNF.

Especially great were the preparations surrounding donations to the JNF during Simchat Torah at the Zionist *minyan* [group of ten worshippers], where young people with nice singing voices would pass before the Holy Ark - it was an

The "Persian Room" at one of the JNF bazaars

From right to left: Chaya Palskovsky, Rubin, Dina Greenberg, Shifra Rivak, Rachel Palskovsky, Sarah Machbar

unforgettable experience for all Zionists in our town. Jews would come to that *minyan* whom you would usually never see in that synagogue. Many saw the aliyahs [being called up to recite the blessings over the Torah portions] in the minyan as a tradition and were not prepared to give up on the aliyah or the maftir [Haftorah portion] that they were once given, because they considered it to be a sort of possession. The stairs leading to the minyan and the yard of the minyan were crowded with lively children. The children greeted each donation announced from the bimah [raised platform in a synagogue] with cries of joy, and many of them also kept an exact accounting of each contribution that was made during the prayers for that holiday. And who among us does not recall the enormous impression made by the great amount of money donated, and how they could see in their mind's eye all that could be done in the Land of Israel with that money: endless forests and fertile plains as the country is redeemed.

[Pages 83-92]

The Bund

Edited by David Goldman, Avraham Yaffe, Tel Aviv, Israel
Translated from Hebrew to Yiddish by M. Goelman
Translated from Yiddish to English by Dr. Isaac Fine

Founders of the Jewish "People's Library" 17 February 1923

From right to left: Yankl Trachimowski, Zeidl Altszuler, Moshe Feiwl Bialosukenski, Henakh Gelbard, Leibl Mankowski, Goldberg, Toykel, Nakhum Yafa, Taybl Luria, Knone (Khone) Khazan

The Bund was a socialist labor movement that had a noticeable influence in the European Jewish world at the turn of the century. Its influence was felt in Goniondz. Goniondz, was not an industrial town, unlike some others in the environs of Bialystok. There was a folk saying, "When a rooster crows in Druskoenig, (a resort area near Grodno) it is heard in four provinces - Grodno, Vilna, Suvalk, and Kovno." So it was with Goniondz. Our shtetl was connected by the railroad with Bialystok on one side and with the town of Grayve, near the German border, on the other side. One could also reach the German border through passage on the Bober River, in several directions through the forests. The river Bober waterway led to the great lakes around Yagustove-Suvalk on one side and to the river Nemen near Grodno by the other side. In other words, Goniondz lay at a crossroads, and was open to winds from all sides.

The three major industries of the environs were (1) textiles - Bialystok and neighboring regions, (2) clothing - Smargon in Vilno province, and Krinke in Grodno province, and (3) pig-hair brushes in Trestine (near Grodno), Kniesin and other nearby towns, and also Vilkoviski in Suvalk province. This group of industries gave rise to a proletariat of hundreds and thousands of Jewish laborers, and provided the foundation for the Bund.

The Bund organization in Goniondz had its origins in the small pig-hair brush factory of Zeidke, the son-in-law of Chayim Trotz. Zeidke was a sharp-tongued temperamental young man. He loved to participate in the discussions of young men and women who were involved in the enlightenment. He wasn't interested in study at the House of Study, and relocated himself in the nearby town of Trestine. He became a brushmaker there, and at the same time was active in party propaganda for the local Bund group. When he returned to Goniondz he married and had children. He opened a little brush factory, in Feivel the baker's backyard, which looked out on the synagogue hill.

This happened at the end of the nineteenth century. At that time, I was still a child, a student of Yudl the melamed (teacher of elementary Hebrew). I had the opportunity to visit Zeidke's brush factory. Yudl's daughter had to bring dinner to her two brothers who worked for Zeidke. Once, at nine in the evening, when all the students had left school for home, she suggested that I accompany her to the brush factory. It was a cold winter night. Outside, a snow had fallen and a strong wind was blowing. Within the brush factory, however, it was light, warm and cheerful. Work tables were placed down the length of the room, with great iron combs placed upon them. The workers stood, each by his own comb, and combed the pig-hair. The hands of the workers moved quickly as they sang. Dust from the pig-hair filled the room. My rabbi's two sons stood in a corner of the room. They were making small packets of the cleaned pig-hair, then tying each pack with a string. We were fascinated by their work, and stayed there watching them. I found myself feeling drowsy about eleven at night. When we left at that time, the workers stayed on and continued at their tasks.

To me, as a child, the brush factory seemed full of light and song. When I became older, I saw it from a different perspective. The working conditions were oppressive, sixteen hours a day, from seven in the morning until eleven at night. Workers took their meals in the factory. During the summer, the windows were opened, and the breezes blew the dust away. In winter they were closed. The dust went into the eyes, the nose, the mouth, and from there to the lungs. Friday was a shorter day. Then on Saturday night, they had to work from sundown until eleven or twelve at night.

In that work-setting, the local Bund initiated a struggle for better working conditions. The organization demanded a maximum working day of twelve hours, which did not require working Saturday night. I remember the occasion when my rabbi, Rabbi Yudl returned from a talk with the shop owner. Zeidke responded, "What a nerve those workers have, demanding that I release them from work duties on Saturday night! After resting all day Saturday, they could do wonders on Saturday night!" Reb Yudl, whose sons worked there, felt that his reasoning was correct. The workers threw stones through the brush factory windows. At the end, the shop owner gave in to their demands, allowing a shorter workday and freedom from work responsibilities on Saturdays. This victory lent courage to those in smaller work settings where only one or two laborers were employed.

I recall that at that time there was a ladies' tailor in Goniondz. His name was Yankel, and he had come to town from Kobrin. Kobrin was my family's hometown, and we visited him often. Yankel was an observant Jew. He was a poor man, and was dedicated to his family. He had bought his sewing machine from a Singer sewing machine company agent in Bialystok by means of monthly installment payments. The contract was a strict and cruel one. The Singer Company would confiscate a machine after a default of one monthly payment, even after years of regular and reliable payments. When the agent came to town for his monthly visit, Yankel was terrified. The Singer man stayed at Rochul Maishe's , eating and drinking under the company expense account. More than once, Yankel came to us pouring out the bitterness of his heart. The agent was in town, and he didn't have the cash for his payment. The bandit will take away his machine, and his family will perish from hunger! My sister Esther, may her memory be for a blessing, who helped mother with domestic duties, was a friend of Rochul Maishe's' daughter. More than once she went to the agent to plead with him that he should not confiscate Yankel's sewing machine, and for him to extend the term of payment.

In the beginning of the Bund organization in the shtetl, Yankel the tailor suddenly became an "exploiter" because he had only one girl working for him. Yankel complained that his relationship with his worker had gone to wrack and ruin. As soon as it became eleven at night, his worker would start looking at the clock, God forbid she should work overtime. When I became an apprentice he told me we're going to work until midnight and before holy days until two or three in the morning, sleeping a few hours on the workbench or under the bench. The boss used to wake the employees up for work at five in the morning. But now better days came to our shtetl, brought about by the arrival of the Bund.

That was only one aspect of Bundist activity in our shtetl. The other more severe aspect was connected with the danger of arrest and exile in Siberia. I refer to the revolutionary agitation against the Tsar and his regime. The workers met in late night hours on the synagogue hill, or, during summer nights, in the Kolkovichisner Forest, which was about two kilometers from town. That was conspiratorial activity, and they were on the lookout for police and government agents.

I, a young boy who had just graduated the Russian school, was studying Gemara (part of the Talmud) in the House of Study. Once, between early afternoon and sundown prayers, Leibel-Akiva, the son of Bobers, took me to a corner and asked me to write letters for him in Russian which were invitations to a Bundist meeting in town. The invitation asked them to meet at a certain specified place in the forest, where he, Leibel, would make a speech. He hadn't wanted to write the invitations himself since his handwriting might be recognized. The end result was that he was shadowed by the police. They warned his sister that they would send him to Siberia if he didn't leave immediately for America. Leibel didn't wait to be asked. He went to the United States as soon as he heard the news. Later, he brought over his sisters.

On Sabbath and holy day evenings, the Bundists used to walk along the main road towards Osoviec singing songs of the revolution. I recall a part of one of these songs:

Our Messiah is coming!

The Jewish worker in Russia, Lithuania and Poland

He lifts up the flag of freedom!

The socialist cultural activities of the Bundists consisted of distributing leaflets in Yiddish among friends and sympathizers. They had a small illegal library in Yiddish. The more cultured members of the organization would visit the Hashachar Zionist library, and read periodical articles and books there.

From time to time, they would suddenly organize agitation assemblies, which frightened the Jews of town. Early one morning, they surrounded the House of Study during the prayer hour. They commanded that no one should leave and, by brandishing a revolver, threatened those who did to try to walk out. An agitator from Bialystok stood at the synagogue altar and made a speech. A fear fell upon all the worshippers within. They were afraid of being hit if they tried to leave the scene and also were fearful of the police, should they become aware of what was happening. I, a young boy active in all the Zionist work in the shtetl, was also among the Jews in the House of Study at that time. I tried to take a stand against those outside, "The Bund is not going to give me any orders!" I said to myself. I started to leave. Moishe Fievel the cobbler grabbed me and held me with his strong hand. He warned, "If you don't go along with us, we'll finish you off!" At that moment, he was approached by Mottel-Mendel's the grain merchant in the marketplace, my friend from Hebrew school. He said to Moishe-Fievel, "Don't forget that this is the son of Avrom the judge. Soon after that, Moishe-Fievel let me go. Later, on another occasion, I ran into Fievel in Grayve, when I was a Hebrew teacher there. My neighbor was a cobbler and Moishe-Fievel worked with him. He was arrested there for his Bund activities.

One of the Bund leaders in town was Slaveh, the son of Shusterke. He was a short fat fellow. He dressed very well, even on weekdays. Slaveh was a young tailor who had worked in Bialystok and came back to our shtetl a fervent Bundist. During the night meetings on the synagogue hill, when the walkers stood below and he stood at the lead, he would begin his speech, "Friends! Our task is to elevate the class consciousness for the benefit of the worker." While saying the word "elevate" he would always make a demonstrative gesture with his hand. He was also a frequent visitor to the Hashachar library, which was located in Shloime Yossel's' house. Chaikel was the most active organizer in this library. He would always come with a friend, read the periodicals and explain the implications to his friend.

Mottel-Mendel's was one of the best known and most loved of the Bundists. I remember his participation in the funeral of the youngest daughter of Avrom "Kurtzer" the teacher. He lived in a corner of the marketplace near the entrance to Dead Man's Alley (Meissim Gasse), through which all funeral processions passed, avoiding Church (Tifla) Street. Avrom the teacher had three daughters. They were all beautiful and were all seamstresses. Their mother would bake challah and kichel. The youngest daughter, who would sew until the late hours of the night, came down with tuberculosis and died very young, at 20 years old. At the funeral a group of Bundists participated with Mottel in the lead. He is the one who sang Peretz's song about the fate of a seamstress: "I sew and peddle, and peddle out gray braids." The song and the music cast a gloomy mood on all those present. After the father said Kaddish (the prayer often said by mourners), one of his friends cried out: "Down with the bourgeoisie! Down with the Tsar!" and shot a revolver. Immediately, everyone scattered in all directions. Neither the Burial Society, nor of course the father of the deceased girl, were pleased with this Bundist outburst, but everyone kept silent. The Bundist movement in Goniondz was a small sidestream in contrast to the great current of the Zionist movement, which captured all ranks of the townsfolk, especially the middle class, which constituted the majority of citizens in every city and town. Nonetheless, the Bundists did make significant contributions. They improved the working conditions of laborers in town, contributed to cultural development, and developed organizations which provided self defense against the wave of pogroms which fell upon the Jewish communities of Russia at that time.

Y.L. Peretz Library Managing Committee in Goniadz, 1926

From right to left: Nekhemia Altas, Ester Rubin, Zaydl Altszuld, Leibl Mankowski, Asher Szczuczinski, Sh. Grobard, Trachimowski

[Page 93]

He Chalutz – The Pioneer
by Aryeh Khativah, Kfar Witkin
Translated by Amy Samin

When the day came to create a memorial, in the form of a book, to the town of our birth, it was fitting that we also made note of the movement which came into being many years before the Holocaust. It is thanks to the mission and method of that movement that so many people remained alive to mourn the destruction.

The birth of the *He Chalutz* union in Goniadz came about when the second class of the Hebrew school completed its studies. On the evening of that last day, we – the students of the graduating class - were summoned by the distinguished educator Mordechai Nilovitzki, to a graduation party. It was not customary to invite any contributors or dignitaries to such a party, and the reason became clear that very night: that party turned into an emotional gathering marking the complete separation of the devoted educator from his students, who were like friends to him. His attention to and concern for the social solidarity of our group meant that we were fortunate enough to spend time with him earlier. It began with the conversations held prior to the publication of the class journal, Ha Nitzutz [The Spark] and our close mutual contact at the time it appeared. Now, with our parting, his heart grieved with the fear that this tight-knit group might turn into riff-raff with its first contact with life on the streets.

[Page 94]

On the street one could still hear at full strength all the enthusiasm over the great Russian Revolution. Its pretentious slogans for a comprehensive solution to all of the problems of human society, without distinctions between nationality and race, enchanted many and swept up countless Jews from every strata of society, including young men and women from our class at school, who looked on and were harmed a long time before we reached the end; and we were still just youth who had not yet reached the age of fourteen.

Indeed, the temptation was great, especially later on, when the Bolsheviks invaded Poland in 1920 following the withdrawal of the battered Polish Army. Certainly many still recall those fear-filled days for the acts of robbery and terror by the retreating army. Even on the last day of the withdrawal, three Polish cavalry officers committed a robbery in the city, and only a few hours later a single Russian cavalryman suddenly appeared on the entrance road (Tiplaa Gas). Dressed in a red shirt, with one bandaged hand holding a red flag, he slowly advanced, without fear, towards the town square with a friendly expression on his face. How spectacularly brave his youthful performance seemed to us! While our attention was still caught by this solitary cavalryman, we got another surprise: from a different direction, the Dolostova Street side, hordes of foot soldiers who began streaming into the square. Practically all of them, much to our amazement, were barefoot and in tattered uniforms, and all of them were carrying rifles. They all had one question: 'Is the road to Warsaw long?' One regiment had been delayed, and here they were in the town square. The children who walked among them were given pet names, and they called the adults "comrade". They spread out in the fruit and vegetable gardens like starving locusts, eating unripe fruit without noticing the difference.

[Page 96]

After they had left the city, the cavalrymen kept coming including Cossacks, notorious amongst the people of Israel, all of them polite and friendly. The heart pounded with the heroic songs and the hopefulness radiated by the flow of cavalrymen, and the splendor of their devotion to the idea.

He Chalutz Union, 1931

[Page 95]

He Chalutz Union, 1933

That same kind of fire was integrated in the soft hearts of schoolchildren with the coming of the news that there was hope for the founding of a Jewish state following the Balfour Declaration, and with the spread of the rumors of the existence of Jewish regiments in the Land of Israel, the flame ignited the New Spirit, which blew fiercely...Only the bloody clashes between Jews and Arabs that came later returned the balance in our uncertain hearts, but we did not give up.

Thus, at that same graduation party, the teacher spoke to the class demanding from us that we load upon our soft shoulders not only the burden of our newspaper, the character of which had yet to be formed, but also the burden of the revived nation, to join in the building of the homeland that was to be returned to us in the law of nations, to redeem the land that was empty and to fill it, not only with funds but, most particularly, with toil and also with weapons, if needed. His words fell like seeds on a plowed field.

[Page 97]

A few weeks later, with the end of the 'honeymoon' of our separation from school, there awakened a desire among the youth for initiative and action, and at the time, the goal seemed quite clear and tangible. The first group was made up of 11 youths. The process of unifying the group took a few months, and we refrained from admitting new members. Even after that, members were accepted one by one after meticulous investigation. All of this stemmed from the concern that broadening the organizational framework would create internal anarchy, and we didn't yet feel that we had the ability to control a group of youths who had no tradition of discipline, especially those youths who had not been students in the past. Attention was paid to integrity and fair behavior. The main period of growth was when we rented rooms for the club in the house of Eliezer Terschensky the carpenter, near the yard of the synagogue. We began cultivating connections with the *He Chalutz* Center, and we were fortunate to have visits from lecturers. We developed cultural activities and arranged question and answer receptions. Those activities brought many youth knocking on our doors. We absorbed many new members, including girls. Thus, the first group also constituted the subsequent dominant power which brought about the pioneering atmosphere. At that time, we felt powerful enough to create a new framework – *He Chalutz Hazair* [the Young Pioneer]. The role of leader was given to our friend Moshe Zakimovich, and activities were carried out separately. These were, generally speaking, the youths from the last class of the school. The activities branched out with the members' first trip to training sessions on the *He Chalutz* Center's training *kibbutzim* [cooperative farms]. Training was also given there on learning a trade, though principally we focused on agricultural training. This wasn't possible on the spot, and so we began to harass more than one farmer in the area surrounding the city to please allow us to do a little plowing on his land...At that time, plowing seemed to us to be the crowning glory of agricultural work. For a time we also performed exercises and drills, as a nod to the Torah verse to teach the sons of Judah archery, When we appeared on the streets and on trips on the roads outside of the city we would do so as a group, in friendship, in the way of youth – singing aloud. Thus, songs of all kinds filled a very honorable role, constituting a special gravitational force for our group, especially the choruses and romances of the Land of Israel, whose great magic lay in their pleasant contents. Many people asked to learn the songs, even the non-Jews, our neighbors. Among the many evenings, I recall one when I was on the bank of the river near the home of the fisherman Bochanki, leaping from boat to boat, which were tied together with chains to wooden pegs, when suddenly a familiar, pleasant song reached my ears. I was amazed to hear Hebrew words with a foreign pronunciation: "You promised me you would come. You promised – but did not come. I searched for you all night in the avenues." After a few minutes, I recognized the singer – the daughter of the Polish widow Veshinska, owner of the inn in the vicinity of our club, which was at that time in the Gerber house. I felt proud and content...

[Page 98]

The Goniadz *He Chalutz* Seal

Our connections with the outside increased thanks first of all to our members in the training programs, and to our friend Elimelech Sheinenzon, who had a job in Warsaw in Krobio's department store and who, in his free time, would visit the Grochov training farm and the *He Chalutz* Center. Those places were the first in which there were meetings with emissaries from the Holy Land.

With the passage of time our branch became known among the other branches in the area (apparently by the *He Chalutz* Center) as a unified branch, well-educated in Hebrew and Zionism, even though the number of its members – even during the peak days - never went above forty or fifty. The *He Chalutz* committee in Grodno, which was founded in the autumn of 1920, a short time after the withdrawal of the Bolsheviks from Poland, to which were sent two delegates from our branch, also helped to strengthen our connection to the area, and therefore to broaden our horizons and instill confidence in those who led our programs. I was one of the delegates, and even today the breathtaking impression made upon me by the committee in its discussions and even in the fact that it existed, still lives within me. The cars of the train on which we traveled were crammed full of soldiers, and anyone who remembers the atmosphere that prevailed within the Polish Army following the withdrawal of the Bolsheviks can certainly imagine our feelings – but our fear was ungrounded.

[Page 99]

Group of members parting from their friend who was immigrating to the Land of Israel

The Polish Army, under the leadership of Pilsudski, had made a hasty retreat to the gates of Kiev; the fortress in Grodno was one of the few places where the Poles were halted and fought a rearguard war. The signs of the battles were still quite evident in Grodno and the surrounding area.

The conference was held in an expansive, well-lit auditorium, and the gathering of a great many delegates swarmed the auditorium and the area around it. Loud and fluent speech in Hebrew was heard in the hallways, and even the group of delegates devoted to Yiddish could not dampen the sparkling, celebratory feeling. A surprise awaited us, the Goniadzniks, in the meeting between the guests in the auditorium and the daughter of our rabbi, Feige Wolf, who was a kindergarten teacher in that city. It is fair to say that our feeling, being among all of those delegates, was that although it was the first time we met and got to know them, it was as if we had known them for years. Thanks to the special and friendly atmosphere that prevailed there, we made the acquaintance of delegates from branches in Sovlak, Sochovolia, Grajewo and more.

[Page 100]

We made closer contact with the branches from towns located closer to our own: Knishin and Sochovolia. Of especial note was the visit of the delegation of pioneers from Raigrod, when they heard that our union was there and came to ask for our help in establishing a branch in their city. We spent the whole day together there, and in the evening went out together to accompany them to the Bosovich train station. Along the entire way to the station, located in the fortress, there was, so far as is known, no settlement. We made our way there and back in a spirit of sheer joy and wakefulness; it was an experience which was wrapped up in the essence of friendship.

[Page 101]

Such a feeling came about because of good relationships that bound the group together from the inside, especially among the members who had recently joined us, and who became a factor in the addition of even more members.

It is fitting to pause here to examine the relationship between ourselves and our parents, and the adult population in general. From the beginning there were signs of negativity and criticism. There were those who called us "*chalutzim parutzim* [broken pioneers]" because we had broken the yoke of *mitzvot* [commandments] and were not punctilious about keeping the Sabbath. In time, the attitudes towards us changed and we were given consideration and growing affection. Eventually, most of the public was imbued with Zionist awareness, which fed not only from the fields of religion, history, and romance, but also from the plight of the Jews in present times. The first Polish Legionaries harassed the Jews and insulted their dignity. Songs of hatred and incitement against Jews were heard, and the people of General Haller's army, among them Poles with American citizenship, cut off the beards of Jews on the trains.

The first time our members went out for training, and later also to the Land of Israel – the public became convinced that this wasn't, after all, a child's game. Now they were saying: although they don't keep the *mitzvot*, they are all in all good Jews – and maybe even better than many who are observant. Not like parties on the left, the Bund and the "Reds," our members would occasionally visit the house of study and the synagogue. We liked to hear cantorial music, especially on holidays when Rabbi Eliezer Zakimovich of blessed memory would pass before the Ark. We came to love his version of the prayers and melodies. Many days later, when we were far from the homes of our parents, we would pass the evenings with those melodies and thereby lessen our isolation (incidentally, Rabbi Eliezer lived out the remainder of his life in the Holy Land). We received a kind of approval and sometimes support from the *Zairei Zion* [Young Zionists] party, most of whose members were, at that time, scattered around the world and only a few individuals remained, including: Zelig Nivodovsky, Wolf Pikersky of blessed memory, and Yehezkel-Peretz Tesherniak, long may he live, who along with us lives today in the Land of Israel.

Committee of the League for *Eretz-Yisrael Haovedet* [the Working Land of Israel]

Standing (from the right): Yessia Burke, Malka Yanovsky, Yehudit Levine, Bilka Gornostaysky, Fishel Yitzhaki

Seated: Shoshana Pakrasky, Avraham Raigrodsky, Peltinovich, Belka Kleif

[Page 102]

He Chalutz brought life and activity to our city. Sometimes we put on theatrical performances, some of which were the fruit of our own creativity, on subjects involving the Land of Israel and the contents of which were mainly social or work-related matters. Also, sometimes celebrations and receptions were planned.

He Chalutz also worked for the benefit of the Hebrew school in town: advocating continuing Hebrew education – in gymnasia and seminaries – in the larger cities. We had a long and protracted struggle with the "Reds", who were not able to act constructively in any way, aside from their mouths being busy with

[Page 103]

Some of the first pioneers in the Land of Israel

First row (from right): Berel (Baris), Hannah Gelbord, Dov Tershchansky, Ziva Koberinsky

Second Row: Tova Friedman, Ariyeh Hatiba, Gittel Simcovitz, Moshe Zakimovich

abstract preaching. They harassed us in every possible way. The first stage was trying to pressure our active members, then they tried to bring us into their club to have political arguments, and when we avoided visiting their club, since we saw no value in fruitless arguments, they began coming to us and harassing us. After they were convinced that idle chatter would not sway us, they tried to bring "more compelling evidence" – fisticuffs, but we also stood firm before such tactics, even though they were older than our members. We felt that this gave us a foretaste of the struggle we could expect in the Land of Israel.

[Page 104]

Many of our members never arrived in our designated land, whose gates were securely locked in those days, and they scattered in countries across the seas. However, the many who arrived in the Land, by direct or indirect means, persisted in their faithfulness and devotion to her from the first day of their arrival.

[Page 105]

The Young Chalutz – The Young Pioneer
by Gershon Gelbort, Ramat Ha-Kovesh
Translated by Amy Samin

The year was 1922-23. The Hebrew school in Goniadz, which was founded around that time by *Zairei Zion* [Youth of Zion] and later joined the *Tarbut* chain, graduated its second class. The graduates of that class, boys and girls ages 16 – 17, some of whom went on to found *He Chalutz* [the Pioneer] and some of whom joined the Communist Youth; that group constituted the young men and women who returned from Russia, and who received their education and had spent all of the days of the war and revolution there. Those two youth movements waged a fierce battle for control of the youth. We, the students of the school, followed *He Chalutz* yet also listened to the stormy debates between that movement and the Communist Youth or, as they were called in our town, the "Reds."

He Chalutz appealed to us more, and even while in school we used to call every fearless or exceptionally strong young man by that name. The members of *He Chalutz* brought Hebrew speech and Hebrew song out of the walls of the school and into the streets, and they also worked at labor that had once been done by others, by *goyim* [non-Jews]. Cutting down trees, landscaping, and portage – all of those were matters of interest to the pioneers. And more than anything, the *He Chalutz* House, where people would gather to discuss and celebrate, to sing and to dance. And the house was also a center for youth who were not counted among the members of *He Chalutz*. We, young people aged 12 or 13, would gather outside, for we were not allowed to enter. We were accustomed to hosting the pioneers, and to accompanying them wherever they went. On evenings and Sabbaths we would assemble at the doors of the house. Their songs were not new to us, nor were their conversations about the Land of Israel foreign to us, for we were students of the Hebrew school. The only thing that was new to us was the activity surrounding immigration to the Land of Israel, the preparations. The arguments they had with the anti-Zionist youth regarding the Land of Israel and the Diaspora laid everything before us for re-evaluation and re-examination.

One Sabbath, we chanced upon a group of youth with one pioneer at the home of one of our friends. The pioneer told us of *HaShomer* [the Guardian] in the Land of Israel, and of the days of Tel Hai [a former Jewish settlement in the Land of Israel and the site of an early battle between Jews and Arabs]. We had a special connection with Tel Hai, because one of the fallen was Yaacov Tuker of Goniadz, whose family still lived in our town. We decided to form an organization. We heard of three people during that conversation whose names we wanted to tie to the name of our organization: Berele Shweiger of *HaShomer*, Tuker, and Joseph Trumpeldor. Tuker, as one of our own, was very close to our hearts, and Shweiger for some reason found special favor with us. But in the end we chose Trumpeldor; he was the symbol, the guide.

[Page 106]

We set these goals for our organization: a) Hebrew speech and b) physical education. They were intended as spiritual and physical preparation for the pioneer life.

When we rented a place and began operations, the wrath of our parents descended upon us: they saw it as a deviation from the regular way of life of a pupil in school. Some of us withdrew, and the first attempt at organization was undone.

Months went by. On one of our trips – we were a group of 8 members – we made an attempt to recreate the Trumpeldor organization, despite our parents' opposition. Our parents were not successful in destroying our organization, and the teachers – to whom they appealed for help – gave up. Our first months of activity were marked by growth and the organization of cultural programs. Our purpose was directed toward the youth from poor families. They tended to see Zionist organizations as the property of the bourgeoisie. We were able to bring a few of those youth into our organization, and we invested a great deal in them, starting with teaching them Hebrew and imbuing them with an elementary education and on to offering material assistance especially in the case of illness. The path we forged into the poor and artisan classes of our town broadened; in time, when in competition with the Tarbut school the Yesha school was founded (it only existed for a few years); we also infiltrated there and some of their students were active in *He Chalutz Hazair*.

We established our organized cultural activity through our own great efforts and with a little help from several older members. Only after a while did the members of *He Chalutz* become more interested in us, coming with a proposal to organize into a split-off group of *He Chalutz*, called *He Chalutz Hazair* [the Young Pioneer].

[Page 107]

In March of 1924, when rumors reached us of the founding of chapters of *He Chalutz Hazair* in other places, we asked to contact the *He Chalutz* Center. In June of 1924 we received the first letter from the main office of *He Chalutz Hazair* and attached to it was a circular and recommendation for how to found a chapter of *He Chalutz Hazair*.

The Goniadz Chapter of *He Chalutz Hazair*

The debates followed an accepted format in Question and Answer Evenings. Each person wrote down any question he wished to ask and put the paper into a box set aside for that purpose. Among those who attended these parties – which carried on late into the night due to the intense and vital atmosphere – were the Communist Youth, who tried to take advantage of the opportunity to spread their message to us. These evening conversations were conducted in Hebrew, and – with no other alternative - the Yiddish-speakers would speak Hebrew by way of pre-prepared texts.

[Page 108]

The second thing worth mentioning is the internal newspaper, <u>*Tel Hai*</u>, which was published from time to time for a number of years. The participation of the members was tremendous. Also here we were aided by the school. Every written assignment by one of our members that was praised by the teachers was published in our newspaper. Over time, the teachers also began participating in the paper. At the beginning, we would copy it by hand into a number of limited samples, later we would reproduce by means of a hectograph, which allowed us to introduce improvements. Every year we would publish an edition dedicated to Tel Hai. Sometimes we would work all night to ensure that the paper would be published on deadline. Its appearance was cause for celebration in our chapter.

[Page 109]

As one of the foundations of our education we decided upon getting close to nature, and began taking short trips outside of the city, to fields and nearby villages, and we eventually took more extended trips, to nearby cities. We dreamed of village life, of the farming life on the soil of our homeland. Therefore, we very much wanted to get an understanding of the life of the farmers and villagers nearby. We traveled in neat rows, and with both commands and songs in Hebrew our need to perform in public was also met. Our first big trip, to the nearby town of Trestina, was arranged especially and it led to the founding of a chapter of *He Chalutz Hazair* there. The trip had a major influence on the youth there. The chapter grew, and even young children began knocking on our door. We limited the acceptance of members to ages 14 and up.

The trips to nearby towns became a tradition. Through them we aided in the founding and strengthening of chapters in the surrounding area. Eventually we organized joint trips of several chapters together.

Those trips and meetings emphasized the need for frequent communication and mutual assistance every day of the year. For that purpose, in 1926 a regional council of six chapters was established. One of its roles was to found a joint library, a regional newspaper, and a subscription to *Davar* [a Hebrew language daily newspaper]. With the increase of chapters in the area and the founding of training *kibbutzim* [communal farms] the first area-wide bureau was founded.

Nevertheless, the trips could not satisfy the training needs of the pioneers: our hearts were drawn to agricultural work. How great was both the happiness and the jealousy when two of our members, happened upon a farmer plowing his land who allowed them to hold the plow and employ it for the length of an entire furrow. The plowmen were covered in pride and the others were terribly envious. Many went out into the fields in search of such a "good goy." The desire was awakened to request similar opportunities in the gardens of the Jews. And they found them. We began with the planting of a vegetable garden at the home of the parents of one of our members. On that first day of our work, when we appeared with hoes in that garden, it was like a holiday. Many people surrounded us and watched some with enjoyment and others with scorn. From that moment on we were the permanent vegetable garden workers. We put together plans for planting a large vegetable garden of our own. We had our eyes on a piece of land, and we had the required sum of money, but we were prevented from this plan by the question of how to guard the place. The whole plan failed because of this grave issue. In addition, we had begun cutting trees and we sometimes competed in that area with *He Chalutz*.

[Page 110]

Meanwhile, there was a training factory at the *He Chalutz* Educational Center. The important training points were located far away from us, so only a few left our chapter to go for training. There wasn't much information. And when two members of *He Chalutz* arrived on vacation, we immediately called together a large gathering of youth, dedicated to training. A great many youth from all levels of society attended the gathering, as did the Communists. The members revealed all in the matter of training, including in their remarks stories, songs and tunes from the training experience. For many hours we sat, crowded together, and never tired of listening. For us, those hours were an uplifting of our souls. But just when the gathering had reached its peak, the Polish police suddenly appeared and broke up the gathering, and forbade us to meet in the future.

The blow hit us right at the peak of our chapter's development, just when we had the feeling that we had sprouted wings and had developed the strength to stand up to opposition from outside. We held our activities in secret until we obtained a license. We began to organize into small groups of 5 – 10 members. We held conversations at some distance from the city, we arranged meetings in dwellings where the shutters were closed tight and someone stood watch outside. Announcements and information were delivered by word of mouth. This kind of activity had a bit of the romantic about it that united the minority, but took away the opportunity for growth, for establishing a large chapter that would captivate all the youth, as we wished we could have done.

(From the book *He Chalutz Hazair*, which was published in Israel)

[Page 111]

The Young Chalutz
by Fishl Yitzhaki, Tel Aviv
Translated by Amy Samin

Steering Committee of the Branch of Young Pioneer in Goniadz 15.?.1933

We were a group of young people, students at the *Tarbut* School, steeped in longing for the rebuilt Land of Israel. But we felt restricted at school, we were not content there, we were filled with a desire for a pioneering youth society.

In July of 1923, ten friends gathered together in the *Hehalutz* hall, for a frank discussion with one of the graduates. With the warmth and honesty of childhood, we revealed to him all that was in our hearts. It was decided to found an association called Herzliya, whose purpose would be scouting, the Hebrew language, and the Land of Israel. The method would be to speak Hebrew among ourselves, gather information about the Land of Israel through reading and lectures, and reading aloud from newspapers about the Land and such matters.

Within only a few days the association we founded was too narrow for us. Socialist overtones which had been hidden inside of us and played into our unconsciousness sought expression. The pioneer spirit, ideas and deeds of many Jewish youth, the enthusiasm for a life of work in the Land of Israel, all of these invigorated our lives. Without any specific decisions as a natural and understood thing, we added to the vague name Land of Israel in our program – the adjective "working."

[Page 112]

But that addition wasn't sufficient – something was still lacking. The rumors reached us of Trumpeldor, the hero of Tel Hai, the creator of Hehalutz. To us, the name Trumpeldor was the realization of the pioneering vision and the symbol of the movement. We decided to change our name – no longer Herzliya, but Trumpeldor. But the name alone determined nothing. We saw, but still we did not become integrated into the Jewish revolution which was: the pioneering movement. Those were the days of the Third Aliyah, an effervescent time of awakening, brothers and sisters going out to farms, living in the bosom of nature, gaining knowledge and experience of the agricultural work for which we longed: we saw the reality, the living existence of the pioneering movement, through which we discovered ourselves, and we began knocking on the doors of Hehalutz, full of expectations and faith.

Then the question arose: how will we move forward together with the graduates of *Hehalutz*, how will we work in cooperation with them, and how will we be elevated to positions, since we were still young, and members of *Hehalutz* must be at least 18 years old?

[Page 113]

We deliberated, and we looked for an opening. We negotiated with the local chapter of *Hehalutz*, and with the *Hehalutz* Center; we contacted them and eagerly awaited their reply. Eventually, we got some vague information that within the *Hehalutz* Center there was the opinion that a special department should be organized for matters regarding the Young *Chalutz*. So, after we received that information, we founded the Young *Chalutz* on 15 March 1924, and there was great rejoicing and a rising of spirits. No longer were we isolated youth in a remote town, but brothers to thousands of young people and multitudes who tied their fates to those of their pioneering older brothers to be reservists, young pioneers.

At first, we gathered fifty members, though they were not the only ones with us, mostly from our own town. Such was the feeling, and such was our work.

First of all we developed widespread publicity, about what had been done and was being done in the renewed Land of Israel: life in the new settlement, the first pioneers, and the Arabs in the Land of Israel. We had many arguments with the opposing youth, but even they would speak to us, unwillingly, in Hebrew. Those nights, and those stormy arguments, were deeply engraved upon our young brains.

When it came to cultural activities, we could never have enough. We immediately leased a garden. How the eyes of our friends lit up as they stood in the garden, caring for the furrows and the flowerbeds! Their eyes saw there a vision of the Land of Israel. Sometimes, two members would meet up by chance, and decide to set out of town together, heading to one of the farmers, who would allow them to plow a bit of his land. The happiness of these members after such an experience knew no bounds. A slight blush would rise up in the cheeks of a member upon receiving praise for his work from the farmer, so strong was the love for agricultural work and for every clod of earth, and so spectacular to the eyes was the appearance of every field and meadow.

[Page 114]

Our pioneering spirit required – and found - expression in our everyday lives and in the life of the entire town. Relationships changed, accepted concepts and values were turned on their heads, and dissention arose between the son of the shoemaker and the son of the wealthy. The horizon broadened, something new and sublime took root within us, and we had the feeling we were the talk of the town.

But the confines of our town were too narrow; we knew we needed to bring the Young Chalutz to the neighboring towns, and not just via lectures and discussions. Every time we visited a nearby town, we would take some of our members outside of their town, to spend a few days under the open sky, in field and forest. We brought a breath of fresh air to nearby towns, with song and dance, and a spirit of rebellion, and we returned home with an abundance of experiences and impressions. A spirit of educational pioneering excited the young people and united them around us. In this manner we founded a number of chapters in the neighboring towns.

We worked especially hard on the newspaper that was put out by our chapter. In it we put our passing thoughts, our impressions, waking dreams and noteworthy thoughts about life in our town, our school, and the chapter. There was tremendous interest in every edition that was published, and we worked on the newspaper with great love and devotion. The first time we printed it on the hectograph and removed the first printed page, our eyes lit up and were filled with joy, to the point of tears. That hectographed paper, Tel Hai was its name, was also distributed in the neighboring towns

Goniadz 1930

(From the anthology *Hehalutz Hazair* [The Young *Chalutz*] which appeared in Israel).

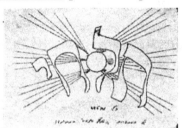

**Tel Hai Newspaper, which appeared at the
Goniadz chapter of the Young Chalutz.**

[Page 115]

The Library
Yekhezkeil-Perec Tsherniak
Translated by Gloria Berkenstat Freund

I remember when I was still a child, a covered wagon harnessed to an emaciated little horse, irritated at the neck from the rubbing of his horse collar, throwing his head back and forth, would come to the *beis-medrash* [synagogue or house of prayer]. A Jew, an itinerant book peddler, would crawl out of the covered wagon and would unpack his wares in the *beis-medrash*: *tefilin* [phylacteries], *tsitsis* [garments worn by observant Jewish males with fringes hanging from their four corners], *mezuzahs* [small boxes containing a piece of parchment with the central Jewish prayer, *Shema Yisroel* - Hear, O Israel], small prayer books, *Makhzors* [prayer books for Rosh Hashanah and Yom Kippur], *Mishnayos* [first section of the Talmud], *Yahrzeitn* [multiple year calendars to record the anniversary of a death], *Shire haMaalos* [Psalm 121 "...I raise my eyes upon the mountains; whence will come my help?" - recited to protect women in childbirth from evil spirits] for women in childbirth and other things. This was all openly done. In secret, he also traded in novels of Shomer [pseudonym of Yiddish writer Nakhum Meir Shaikewitz] and others. And if there were no people interested in buying, he would rent [the books] to them to read.

Although Goniadz stood higher culturally than the poor *shtetlekh* [towns], there was no city library in Goniadz. Several young men - Yankl Rudski's son Dovid, Yitzhak the son of the religious judge's wife, Hershl Vigodski (Bina's son), Chaim-Meir's son Hershl-Leib, Shlomo-Josl's son Kheikl, Sheime's son Josel, Moshe the Kievianker and others - came together and founded a library.

The first library was in a separate small room in Shlomo-Josl's house, for which we paid rent. At the beginning, the library consisted of gifts and some purchased Yiddish and Russian books and of a very small number of books in the holy tongue [Hebrew]. The library also subscribed to the first Yiddish newspaper that was published at that time in Petersburg, *Der Freind* [*The Friend*]. And the entire *shtetl* would make use of the newspaper, until after several weeks everyone had read it.

The official stamp of the library was *gezelshaftlekhe biblotek in Goniadz* [communal library in Goniadz] (*obszczezitelnyja biblioteka v Goniadza*). The above-mentioned young men also were the founders of the young Zionist movement. Thus all of the Zionist activity was concentrated around the library premises.

[Page 116]

The library moved from Shlomo-Josl's to a fine, new room at Matka Klap's. There the library received a new name, *Beit Eked haSefarim* [Book Collection] of Goniadz. The stamp was more distinguished - in the form of a book.

This was after [Theodor] Herzl's death. In 1904, we moved the library to Reb Benyamin the Scribe's house from Matka Klap's. The library then had over 4,000 books. Yiddish took the first spot, then Russian and Hebrew. At first, during the founding, a founder was "on duty" daily at the library; to provide care for the books, give suggestions as to what to read.

In about 1910-1911 the first confrontation occurred between the leaders of the library of the Zionist youth with the representatives of the Bund who demanded that, besides their participation in the management of the library Bundist literature be brought in. A general meeting of the subscribers of the library was called and the demand was rejected. However, Leibl Mankowski, the then representative of the Bund agreed to remain on the managing committee. Thus the conflict ended.

[Pages 117-118]

Managing Committee of the Tarbut-Library in 1925

[Ed: Tarbut was a Zionist network of Hebrew-language educational institutions founded in 1922]

First row (from the right): Fishl Yitzhaki, Sholem Neiwodowski, Fishl Furman, Chaya Gelbard, Meir Treszczanski Baylka Kliap

Second row: Gronya Kliap, Rywka Kobrinski, Chaya Bachrach.

Managing Committee of the Tarbut-Library in 1931

First row (from the right): Yehuda Bialostocki, Faygl Bajnstajn, Pesha Garber, Liba Frydman, Ruchl Rubin

Second row: Chaya Plaskowski, Ruchl Goniandzki, Fruma Halpern)

[Page 119]

The library developed very well until the war in 1914. When they began to bomb Goniadz, the library was moved to Moshe Bandke's shop cellar. An explosion near the cellar burned a portion of the books. We packed a number of the better books in crates and took them on our wandering way, first to Kniszyn, Yaszinowke and then to Bialystok. At the end of 1915, when the Goniadz residents returned home, they brought the books packed in the crates and founded the new library on the second floor of Baylka Pesha's house. The remaining books from Moshe Bandke's cellar served as the basis for the library in the surrounding *shtetlekh* [towns]. The library was the center of the Zionist organization until the destruction of Goniadz. The library was enriched with many new Yiddish and Hebrew books.

[Page 120]

Managing Committee of the Y. Kh. Berner Library in 1934

First row (from the right): Yeshaya Burak, Shayna Rajgrodski, Dovid Lichtensztajn

Second row: Ruchl Trachimowski, Ruwin Trescszanski. Ruchl Khazan

[Page 121]

The Dramatic Circle
Yekhezkiel Peretz Tsherniak
Translated by Gloria Berkenstat Freund

Goniadz intellectual youth had a lively interest in all kinds of cultural activities. A particular love for music and theater developed along with interest in literature, Hebrew, Yiddish and Russian. From time to time choirs would be founded that would appear on various occasions, as for example at the Zionist *Shimkhas-Torah minyonim** and Chanukah balls with a program of Hebrew and Yiddish songs.

Yiddish performances were carried out in Goniadz at various times at every opportunity during the time of the Czarist regime. Young men and girls from every party tendency took part. About 60 years ago, at the beginning of our century [20th], an amateur dramatic group was founded under the direction of Avraham'ke's son, Moshe Kopl, Khine's son, Hershl (Wigodki), Dinke's son, Lev Chaim (Koplman), Siomke Yidkowski (the midwife's son), Chaim Hersh Lewin, Pesakh, Zorakh and Yosl Szajmes and others. The performances took place in Itshe's Anshl's granary.

Several years later, the comedy, *Di Tsvei Kuni Lemelekh* [*The Two Kuni Lemels*] by A. Goldfaden was performed in the same granary under the direction of Reznik - an assistant of the photographer Karasik. Those taking part were: Yisroel-Yosef Rudski (in the role of Reb Pinkhasl), Yekheskiel Tsherniak (in the ... woman's role, "Karolina"), Ahron Rudski (in the role of the woman "Libela the seamstress"). There were no talented girls available to play the women's roles then.

[Page 122]

The dramatic circle became a stable institution in the years of the First World War under the German occupation, when the areas inhabited by the Jewish population were allowed to create Jewish culture and art unions.

Jewish dramatic circles were founded in Bialystok and in a number of other cities and *shtetlekh* that attracted professional actors and helped to develop many young artistic talents.

In addition to entertaining, the performances also were intended to create the financial means for certain cultural institutions, such as the school, library, as well as for Jewish communal and philanthropic purposes.

In 1915, *Di Shkhite* [*The Slaughter*] by Yakov Gordon under the direction of Goldberg (an employee of Avraham Rudski) was performed in Yankl Rudski's brewery. The performance was very successful and created a great interest in Yiddish theater art in the shtetl. A year later the play *Got, Mentsh un Tayvl* [*God, Man and Devil*] was performed with great success. Then came the plays: *Di*

Yesoyme [*The Orphan*], *Kreytzer Sonata* [*The Kreutzer Sonata*], *Di Teg fun Undzer Lebn* [*The Days of Our Life*] (by Leonid Andreyev). Later, *Yakov Boyle, Der Meturef* [*The Lunatic*] and also *Der Batlen* [*The Idler*] of Y.L. Peretz.

The members of the dramatic circle took part in the performances:

[Page 123]

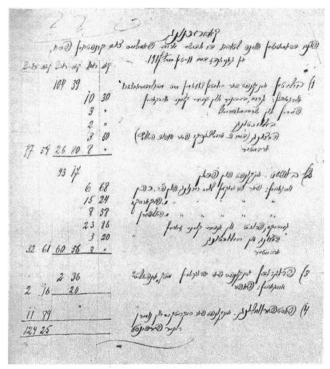

Handwritten treasurer's report

Itka Meres (Halpern), Zelig Polak, Avraham Rudski, Chaya Rubin, Shimeon Halpern, may he rest in peace, Chana Machey, the rabbi's daughter, Itka, and others. Itka Rudski, Yehezkiel Czarniak, Goldberg. Leibl Makowski had a great part in arranging the performances and the technical preparations were carried out by Moshe Furman.

[Page 124]

The last performances were arranged under the leadership of Zeydke Altshuld and others.

Thus, the dramatic circle always contributed to the communal, cultural life of our dear Goniadz.

*Translator's Note: *Shimkhas-Torah* is the autumn holiday celebrating the completion of the yearly Torah readings and the start of the new year of reading the Torah. A *minyon - minyonim* is the plural form - is the 10 men necessary for prayer. Here, *minyon* may have been used in an ironic sense.

[Page 125]

The First Sprouts of *Haskalah* in Goniadz
(From the memoirs of Reb Efraim Halpern, z"l)
Dovid Bachrach, Petah Tikva
Translated by Amy Samin

I was born in Goniadz to my parents, Elihu-Nechamia son of Shimon Halpern, and Chanah-Chaya, daughter of Reb Moshe Hillel. My father of blessed memory was one of a few well-educated men in our town, and was known as a man of books and languages. He was involved in the meetings of Russian intelligentsia in our town. He made a meager living through teaching, therefore my mother was inclined to offer her assistance and strength in earning an income, and together they were able to provide for the family.

When I was twelve I completed my studies in the *heder* [elementary school], and my father of blessed memory continued my education in Judaic studies and in secular subjects as well.

There was a Russian elementary school in our town that had only three classes, and only the children of Polish families studied there. I decided that I would be the first Jew to study in the state school in our town, and since my father of blessed memory was a crony of the principal of the school, he lobbied for my acceptance as a student, and his request was granted.

I was the first and only Jew among hundreds of Catholic students, boys and girls, but I tolerated my isolation in silence. The teacher received me warmly, since he was used to meeting my father of blessed memory on a daily basis at the postmaster's or in the rooms of the Catholic priest, Josef Malishowitz. He knew the Hebrew language fluently and was a righteous gentile. He was a lover of the Jewish people who suffered at the hands of his own kind for his tolerance of Jews.

[Page 126]

The other Jewish children my age became jealous of me, that I was a student at the school, and let me know that they also wanted to study there.

With the help of my father of blessed memory, I lobbied on behalf of my friends, that they also be accepted into the school. I was successful in my efforts. The following academic year the number of Jewish students reached eighteen, in spite of the opposition of the Catholics who objected.

Thus began the first breath of the spirit of Haskalah [Enlightenment] in our town.

[Page 127]

The *Kheder Metukan*
[Improved Religious School]
Dovid Bachrach, Petah Tikva
Translated by Gloria Berkenstat Freund

The Goniadz Hebrew School that was founded during the First World War (in 1915), and which existed until the Holocaust, excelled, as is known, with its very high level of achievement. All of the Goniadz young people who emigrated to *Eretz-Yisroel* during that period of time were actually former students of that school.

But historically this was not the <u>first</u> Hebrew school in our *shtetl* [town]. The very first Hebrew school in Goniadz was actually Gdalke Kozlowski's *Kheder Metukan* [improved religious school] where we learned *loshn kodesh* [the holy language – Hebrew]. A new approach to Jewish education in Goniadz began with Gdalke's school. The school existed from around 1901 until close to the First World War. I can write about the school from intimate acquaintance because I was one of its first students.

The founding of the *Kheder Metukan* truly signified a "revolution" in our *shtetl*. It is true that there was no active opposition to the divergence of the kheder [traditional religious school – *khederim* is the plural form] from the old style, but there were enough people in the *shtetl* who related to it with suspicion. Despite the fact that the founders and supporters of the *Kheder Metukan* were themselves pious Jews.

In 1957 it is difficult to show how much daring and effort was demanded more than half a century ago that only a few people could break down the "Chinese" wall represented by the traditional *kheder*, both as a fortress and a protection against foreign influences – from outside.

In *kheder* – in the best case – a child could learn *Khumish* with Rashi [the Torah with Rashi's commentary], a little of the *Prophets* and the *Writings* and sometimes a little of the *Gemara* [Talmudic commentaries]. The knowledge of *loshn kodesh* that a child could acquire there was very limited. (In a few *khederim* children were taught to write Yiddish, do calculations and sometimes also Russian. The supplementary "education" was supposed to teach a child to write a Yiddish letter and a Russian address. A teacher would come to certain *khederim* for an hour a day for this purpose).

Such an educational scope did not satisfy a number of people in Goniadz. Efroim Halpern, of blessed memory, with whom a son grew up, his first-born son, Josef, whom he wanted to give a more modern education in *loshn kodesh*, was particularly dissatisfied. This dissatisfaction led to the founding of the *Kheder Metukan*.

It is known that of all of the surrounding *shtetlekh* [towns], Goniadz excelled with its spirit of the *Haskalah* [Enlightenment], which reigned there. It is difficult to say with certainty how this "came" to Goniadz. A hypothesis that the nearness to *Krepost Osowiec* [Osowiec Fortress] with its large number of Russian military men, from whom the *shtetl* drew its income, brought "new winds" to Goniadz. But one thing is sure – that the Zionist spirit which ruled over the *shtetl* since the publication of Doctor Herzl was the decisive factor. For Zionism two things were necessary: the settlement of *Eretz-Yisroel* and the revival of Hebrew.

[Page 129]

Since that time it is an indisputable truth of more than half a century, but I remember how a number of young people would stroll around on the synagogue hill with Hebrew books in their hands... I remember several of them by name, such as: the four sons of Reb Gdelia the rabbi – Moshe-Meir, Pinkhas, Zalman and Welwl; the four sons of the wife of the religious judge; Dovid Rudski, and Moshe Lewin (Klewanker). (Abraham, the son of the wife of the religious judge, and Moshe Lewin now live in Israel.)

I also remember Yehoshua Sufraski as if in a dream. He left for "deep Russia" during my time – to Kursk. Later, he became a Zionist leader (a colony near Ramat Gan is named Neve Yehoshua for him).

The pious in the *shtetl* also looked at Zionism with suspicion because this meant the delay of the end of the Diaspora by sinful deeds. But the spirit of the time conquered: Goniadz became Zionist and the *Kheder Metukan* was founded and remained a permanent institution, parallel with the *khederim*.

Gdalke Kozlowski was one of the younger ones among the *maskilim* [followers of the Enlightenment] and the son of a teacher at a religious school (his father was Chaim Hersh the *Melamed*) and Efroim chose him as the appropriate teacher for the *Kheder Metukan.* The choice was a good one. Gdalke showed himself to be a capable pedagogue. The students loved and respected him and automatically "listened" to him.

It does not have to be said that the Kheder Metukan was religious in essence and that we studied in hats. We began the mornings with praying Shakharis [daily morning prayer] out loud – understand, with the correct "vocal music." After this we studied Torah (Khumish [The Five Books of Moses]) and Tanakh [Prophets, Writings]. We studied Khumish according to the textbooks of M. B. Sznajder, in which all the new words in each chapter were translated into Yiddish. There were also the "inclinations" of the old paper documents and the "edicts" of the verbs. We filled entire notebooks with the usual exercises and what we learned in childhood certainly had a great effect on our knowledge of Hebrew. There were also stories in Yiddish in the same schoolbooks, which the students had to translate into Hebrew. It should be understood that the spoken language in school was Yiddish.

[Page 130]

Gdalke would actually capture the hearts of the children by reading stories from the Hebrew children's newspapers, *Oyem Kotn* [Small World] and *HaKhaver* [*The Friend*]. Hebrew songs were an important "subject" in Gdalke's school. There we sang all of the Songs of Zion that were then popular.

We sat in a modern school on seats that we would call *skamyeikis* [benches] in Russian. These benches helped to create the character and the atmosphere of the school. There were regular breaks in the learning and the ring of a bell would call us back to studying. If a child received a punishment, it, too, was in a modern way – with a *lineyke* (ruler), or by being placed in a corner. When there was more than one boy in the school with the same name, an *alef*, a *beis*, a *gimel* [a, b, c] and so on were added to the name (for example: Moshe *alef*, Moshe *beis*).

We behaved according to the order of the Russian "school" in more than an external respect. For example, we also went home at three thirty in the afternoon and we would have a great deal of homework to do, such as: writing development, learning poems and pieces of *Tanakh* by heart and translating (Aramaic translations of the Bible) from Yiddish to Hebrew. Gdalke's students did not actually have more free time than the boys in the *khederim.*

[Page 131]

Strolling outside the city were wonderful experiences for us, which were a part of the teaching program. We would march in pairs according to military order and we would start singing as soon as we would be outside of the city. *Khushu Akhim Khushu* [*Feel Brothers, Feel* – known as the *Balfour Declaration March*] was the most popular marching song. On one of the strolls, I remember Zeydke Tikocki, the fervid Zionist, treated us with a full basket of cherries...

Josef Halpern, Jakov Murainski (Jankl Joyske's son], Yitzhak Bejkowski, Zuske Mechaber, Sender Miltszon, Moshe Kantorowski and Zeydke Tikocki's two sons, Tselke and Leizer, studied in my school group. Two others studied in a higher group: Zelik Newodowski and Mosh'ke Furman (Yitzhak Joske's son). The two "big young men," who were in a group of their own were: Motye Leib Frydman (Petye the Stoznower's son. He is now called Mordekhai L. Absholom, lives in Argentina) and Hilel Biali (Chaya Tsirl's son). They would help Gdalke with the schoolwork.

[Page 132]

Then, when Gdalke appeared for military service and he "surrendered" as a soldier, Efroim brought a teacher from Suchowolie [Suchowola]. He was named Leibl Wajnsztajn, but he was called "Leibl Suchowolier" in the *shtetl*.

When Gdalke returned from the Russian Army in 1906, he again took over the school and led it with great success until close to the First World War when he moved to deep Russia where he had the "right to live" as a result of his taking part in the Russo-Japanese War. With Gdalke's departure from Goniadz, the *Kheder Metukan* chapter ended. The road had then been paved for a modern school.

Grajewo *HaShomer HaTzair* [the youth guard – Socialist-Zionist youth movement] visits the *HeHalutz-HaTzair* - in Goniadz, 13.8.1928 [August 13, 1928]. Photographed on the river.

[Page 133]

Annals of the
Hebrew Elementary School in Goniadz
by Moshe Levin
Translated by Amy Samin

As the Zionist movement spread throughout the Diaspora there came the idea of reviving the Hebrew language. "It's obvious," said the proponents of the idea, "because it would be impossible to describe the renewal of nationalist Jewish life in the Land of Israel without the existence of the national language as the private property of the people." This lofty idea also stirred the hearts of some of the youth of our people in our small town of Goniadz in the Bialystok region, which at that time belonged to Russia.

At that time _ in the first years of the twentieth century _ there was in our town a group of about fifteen youths, some of whom were students at the Bialystok and Łomża yeshiva, - who began to diligently study, in addition to their studies in Gemara, "outside" subjects [secular subjects].

The place of study was the House of Study, where the youth would pass their time in the study of Gemara. Upon completing their studies in Talmud, they would remove their "outside" books from their hiding places and begin studying the Hebrew language, literature and grammar, Tanah [Bible], foreign languages, particularly Russian language and grammar, with great diligence and enthusiasm. Later, they also began studying mathematics, science and geography.

Among the members of that group, Yitzhak Yaffe was noted for his knowledge, and it was to him that the students would turn with their questions about things they didn't understand. Eventually, Yitzhak was accepted as a student into some pedagogical courses in Grodno. After completing his studies there he immigrated to the Land of Israel where he became the principal of the elementary school in Rehovot.

[Page 134]

The members of this group, as they gained more knowledge, began to influence others in the town, who became interested in Hebrew literature. The number of people who could read Hebrew increased. A small library was founded, where the youth would gather in the evenings and pass their time reading and discussing matters of interest in the Jewish world at that time.

During that time, there arose in the students the desire to speak the Hebrew language. Several of them set themselves the task of fulfilling this aspiration, despite the ridicule of several of their disbelieving friends, who said that it was impossible to make use of Hebrew as a spoken language. "How could one," they said, "use that language to speak of everyday matters if there is no word for such things as 'clock' or 'gazette' or 'railway'?" To this question our dear friend, Yoel Meir Cohen of blessed memory, who excelled at inspiring others as well as in the Hebrew language and its literature, responded, "Just because you do not know our language, since you are too lazy to learn it, we should abandon our lofty aspiration? Tell me, please, the origins of the word clock _ from the Polish word "zeiger", gazette [the words clock and gazette did not exist yet] _ from the Russian word "gazatta", or the word railway _ from the German word "eisen-ban" and the like. If you would make the effort, friends, to learn our national language, you will become convinced that your opinion of our language as lacking in everyday words is mistaken. In our modern Hebrew literature there already exist many of the words necessary for everyday conversations, and our authors are updating words to apply to daily usage, as an attribute of our language and its essence: the main thing is we must learn this literature."

[Page 135]

Conversations such as this, which took place frequently, greatly influenced the youth of our town, and encouraged them to study the Hebrew language and its literature diligently.

At the same time, a modern *heder* [Talmud Torah school] was founded in our town, where the study of the Hebrew language was introduced as a special subject.

Seated with the teachers are guest inspectors from Bialystok

One of the first students in the modern *heder* was our dear friend Yosef Halfran, whose father Efraim of blessed memory was one of its founders. Of course, study was done with the help of translation into Yiddish, but even so there was in the founding of the *heder* a sort of important renewal which introduced the study of the Hebrew language as a special subject. This was seen as an important advancement in the education of the children of our town.

[Page 136]

In those days (1906 _ 1910), after the failure of the Russian revolution, which ended in pogroms against the Jews, the Zionist movement gained strength. Many of the Jewish youth in our town joined the associations *Zairei Zion* [Youth of Zion] and *Poale Zion* [Workers of Zion], which were involved in a bitter struggle with the *Bund*, which was opposed to the nationalist idea. Thus the ambition to learn the Hebrew language spread amongst them. Once the desire to speak the Hebrew language amongst themselves took hold, the number of youths doing so grew by leaps and bounds. Knowledge of and conversations in the Hebrew language amongst the students became more wide-spread when I began teaching them using the new "Hebrew in Hebrew" method as it was called.

The first time this instruction took place with some difficulty. The children had a difficult time understanding the explanations, and their speech was hesitant and artificial. It was difficult for them to convey their thoughts on even clear and simple matters, because they lacked the words and the pronunciation required.

[Page 137]

Shimon Halfran

Yoel Meir Cohen

But after a short time it was as if there was a sudden revolution in the children's use of the Hebrew language. They began to understand the explanations and to answer questions without any particular difficulty. Their answers were brief, but they were clear and comprehensible. This progress encouraged the children, who began speaking Hebrew amongst themselves without too much effort.

This sudden, positive change which brought with it the development of Hebrew speech amongst my students raised my spirits as well as those of my young wife, who was also one of my students.

"From this day on…" _ my wife said _ "our home will be a true Jewish home where we will only speak Hebrew." That instruction was immediately put into effect. Our friends, who often gathered at our house, were also compelled to speak only Hebrew.

Later, when our eldest daughter Shulamit, may she rest in peace, was born, we decided that her mother tongue would be Hebrew. We kept to this decision completely. Thus ours was the first Hebrew household in the Diaspora and our daughter Shulamit was the first girl in the Diaspora who was raised and educated in our national language.

When the First World War broke out, our town of Goniadz was occupied by the Germans (1915). In those days the Germans still treated our people fairly and in a cultured manner. After the occupation, most of the Jewish residents returned to the town, after having been expelled by the Russians. With their return, the question of education for the children was raised, because there were only a few teachers, not enough to educate all of the children of the town. On the one hand, there were many parents who were not at all comfortable with the study arrangements of a traditional *heder*. Apart from that, the question came up of education for girls, who prior to that time had been educated in the Russian school. At first, I was hesitant to present my idea to them _ to open a school _ for fear that it could be that G-d was not on my side and I would be unable to put my idea into action. Nevertheless, a few parents approached me, among them Mr. Efraim Halfran of blessed memory, proposing that I take "this problem" (as they expressed it), in hand. After I clarified for them the difficulties involved in the matter, I told them "I will give you my answer in a day or two."

[Page 138]

That same night, I invited two of my best students over: Yoel Meir Cohen and Shimon Halfran of blessed memory, who excelled in their knowledge of both Hebrew and general studies. I put forward the proposal of the parents, and I inquired whether they would be willing to join me in founding a school and to work there as teachers. I also explained to them the great difficulties inherent in the task of realizing the idea of establishing a Hebrew elementary school especially given the fact that we had no textbooks for any of the general subjects _ not arithmetic, not science, and not geography. Could we create something from nothing? In spite of all of the difficulties, we felt obligated to make every effort to put this plan into action and to found a proper and well-organized Hebrew school, such as every other people in the world have. If we could actually make this thing work, wouldn't that be a revolution in the education of Jewish children in the Diaspora, because from this experiment Jews in other cities in the Diaspora will see and do the same. The two answered me that they would be delighted to join me in founding the first Hebrew school in the Diaspora, and that they were willing to dedicate all their energies and abilities to this important nationalist work. Later we discussed various practical matters relating to the founding of the school, and we made various decisions. Between them, they also decided that in this school, boys and girls would study together.

[Page 139]

The next day there was a gathering in one of the homes of the parents, and I informed them that I, together with Yoel Meir Cohen and Shimon Halfran, would take on the task of teaching in the school that was to be opened in our town. I also told them of the various decisions we had made in our meeting the day before. In addition, I informed them that I had the permission of Mr. Yaacov Rudesky (who had not yet returned to his home) to open the school in his house, where I was also living at that time.

[Page 140]

At that meeting, one of the parents announced that he already had ready the benches necessary for the school, and that he would bring them the next day and arrange them in the three rooms of the house of Mr. Yaacov Rudesky. Other parents took it upon themselves to supply the school with other necessary equipment, according to the list they would be given by the teachers.

The next morning, even before the benches had finished being arranged in the rooms, parents began to arrive to sign their children up for the school. Over the next two to three days, over eighty children were registered _ boys and girls.

After testing the children, we divided them into three grades. Only a few children were not accepted to the school, when it became clear they were not suited to any of the three classes. It was quite difficult for us to disappoint the parents and send their children home, but we weren't able to accept them. It was a very unpleasant situation. However, my wife rescued us from the unpleasantness by offering to care for those children, until a place could be found for them.

[Page 141]

After the testing, the teachers held a meeting wherein we discussed teaching methods. On the subject of the language of instruction there was no disagreement among us. It was obvious to all of us that we would soon begin teaching using the "Hebrew in Hebrew" method, that is to say, all instruction and explanation would be only in Hebrew, without using Yiddish at all. There were some disagreements as to how to actually put this method into operation. How would the teacher run the lessons, if the children didn't understand what he was saying? After much arguing, we reached certain decisions regarding the best and most suitable methods that the teacher must use to assure that the children understood him. Among other things, it was decided that in each class there would be some students who already knew some Hebrew who could answer the teacher's questions, and after them there would certainly be among the new children some who would be able to repeat the answers of the first to respond. In this manner the rest of the students would gradually begin participating in the lessons. We also decided that once a month a teacher would give a sample lesson, and afterwards the teachers would meet to discuss the quality of the lesson, its positive elements and its lacks, in order to fix mistakes and shortcomings.

These decisions brought great benefits: they greatly eased the work of instruction, and so the teachers made every effort to follow them precisely.

The greatest blessing was the sample lessons and the critiques that followed them. They greatly improved the work of the teachers, each of whom tried to find a number of innovations in teaching methods which did a great deal to facilitate the students' understanding of the subject being taught.

Every day after lessons were over, the teachers would gather to prepare the next day's lessons together. At the same time, I began writing textbooks for geography and science, which were published later by Tzantrel in Warsaw. I did this work after we had completed our daily preparation of lessons.

All in all we were very satisfied with our hard work, for we felt we were fulfilling a vital nationalist duty and were producing a new, valuable and lofty creation: we were building a national school, an original school, just like all of the other enlightened peoples of the world possessed.

Our students were also very pleased with their studies. They applied themselves diligently and with great enthusiasm to their studies, and made excellent progress in both their knowledge of Hebrew and of general subjects.

Many of the students learned their lessons by heart, for example chapters of the Tanah [Bible], various poems and articles, as well as certain things in geography, science and the like. Some of the children, a few months after the school opened, began speaking Hebrew amongst themselves even when not in school, even though it was not something required of them by their teachers.

There was never any problem with discipline. There was never an instance when a teacher complained about any shortcomings in the attentiveness of a student or a student's diligence in studying. The students' behavior was exceptional, and they always showed love and respect to their teachers. To this day, memories of those students come to my mind and heart, which is filled with love and longing for all of my dear students, both boys and girls, who are today scattered in various countries around the world. It is my hope that they have also not found it easy to forget me.

During that time, a young man named Yeroham Levin came to our town. He was one of the leaders of *Tzairei Zion* [Youth of Zion] in Bialystok (later _ a resident of the city of Afula in our Land). This young man, who was exceptional in his knowledge of the Hebrew language, came to my house and told me that a rumor had reached him of the founding of a Hebrew school in our town, and that he had come to see this great miracle with his own eyes, for he did not believe what he had heard. After visiting one of the lessons in the school, he said, "I am very excited and thrilled by all I have seen and heard here today. As I listened to the lesson, it seemed to me as if I was seeing and hearing everything in a dream, and I remembered something that my grandmother once told me: man sometimes sees things so clearly in a night vision [dream] that it seems to him he is seeing it while awake. Only when I began speaking with the children, and heard their clear and fluent speech in Hebrew, did I realize that it is not in a dream that I am seeing and hearing all of this, but in a real Hebrew elementary school. I am certain that this institution will bring about tremendous positive change in the method of educating our children in many countries of the Diaspora. Be strong, my dear friends, and you will be blessed."

[Page 143]

When I told Yeroham Levin in the course of our conversation of the difficulties we faced in the creation of the correct terms for general studies, he told me that two young men from Bialystok who had studied in the Herzliya Gymnasia in Jaffa had recently returned home. Those young men had brought back with them lists of their studies, upon which appeared at least some of the terms we needed. He said he would send those lists to us upon his return home. After a few days we received the lists from him, though we found on them only a little of what we needed, though that "little" was of great benefit to us.

In its second year of existence, our school grew and the number of students reached 120. We opened a new class and took on Yehonatan Neiman of blessed memory as a teacher. He was very young in years and even more so in his appearance, but he was so talented that he quickly adapted, with the help of his friends, to the work of teaching and after a short time became quite a good teacher.

[Page 144]

After the new class had opened and students added to the other classes, the rooms in which they studied were too small to hold all of the children. In addition, there were parents who complained that it was too difficult for their small children to walk all the way to the other side of the town, along the river, in the winter. We therefore moved the school to a different flat in the center of town. The new flat had larger and nicer rooms than the first location _ and very much resembled a proper school.

Our friend Yehezkel Peretz Cherniak helped us with the move to the new flat and began to take an interest in the school, engaging in many activities for its benefit.

One day, after the school had been founded, there came into my classroom during the Tanah [Bible] lesson a man with a kindly face, who said "good morning" in German and introduced himself as the school inspector for the occupied area. He said to me: "You must certainly be studying Bible, for the children are wearing hats." He put his own hat on his head and asked which chapter we were studying. After I answered him, he said I could resume my lesson. He listened for about half an hour, and told me he wanted to assess the children. I did not object, and he asked them various questions on the subject we had learned. The children answered him in Hebrew, and I translated their answers into German. In the next lesson, he quizzed the children in arithmetic, and later went on to visit the other classes.

[Page 145]

At the end of the lessons, after the children had gone home, the inspector gave us a summary of all he had found in the school, indicating the deficiencies he had found in the lessons and explaining how we had to repair the shortcomings. He gave us a valuable lesson in instruction. I thanked him for his remarks and explanations, and requested that he attend the sample lesson on the coming Friday.

Later he told us, "Explain to me, please, why you go to all the trouble of preparing lists for all of the general subjects that you teach? I can offer you all of the necessary textbooks, and you won't need to go to such lengths to prepare those lessons." I replied, "We greatly appreciate your good intentions in wanting to come to our aid, but we cannot take you up on your offer because we wish to educate the children in their national language, and not in the language of another people. And I think that a man such as you can understand that without any further explanation." "I understand your spirit" _ he answered _ "and I withdraw my suggestion." Later, he parted from us saying, "See you on Friday."

Later he told us, "Explain to me, please, why you go to all the trouble of preparing lists for all of the general subjects that you teach? I can offer you all of the necessary textbooks, and you won't need to go to such lengths to prepare those lessons." I replied, "We greatly appreciate your good intentions in wanting to come to our aid, but we cannot take you up on your offer because we wish to educate the children in their national language, and not in the language of another people. And I think that a man such as you can understand that without any further explanation." "I understand your spirit" _ he answered _ "and I withdraw my suggestion." Later, he parted from us saying, "See you on Friday."

On Friday the inspector arrived at the appointed hour. Yoel Meir Cohen gave the sample lesson in arithmetic, and at its conclusion the children went home and we sat around the table as was our custom. I told the inspector, "Long ago, when we dwelt in our land, there was a great court, on which there sat 71 judges. The trials were determined by majority opinion. Each and every one was asked to give his opinion on the matter at hand that was under discussion. In order that the younger judges not be swayed in their opinions by the older judges, they would start off asking the youngest for their opinions, working their way up to the eldest. However, this time I want to ask the eldest to express his thoughts first, so that the younger of us may listen and learn."

[Page 146]

The inspector said that first of all he wished to point out that the customs and practices in Germany were completely different. "There, strict discipline was enforced. Everything the students did was according to the orders of the teacher. Entering the classroom, sitting on the bench, taking out textbooks and opening them, and so on, are all done on commands: One. Two. Three. Although the behavior of your students here, so far as I could see, is very good, you should still be running your school with more precision and order. But we'll speak of that another time. In addition, our method of study is not like yours. So you can understand, I will give you an example of a language lesson. You will be the pupils, and I the teacher."

In that lesson, we learned that there stood before us an expert teacher with widespread and profound knowledge of teaching theory and that it would behoove us to take advantage of the opportunity to learn everything we could from him. At the end of the lesson, we conveyed to him our admiration for his impressive talent for instruction, and we requested that he continue to give us as much assistance as possible in our work through his vast knowledge, his tremendous experience, and his deep understanding. He was quite willing, and we parted fondly and with his promise to continue to visit us and to help us in any way he could. He kept his promise, and we made every effort to be good students and to use his methods in instructing our own pupils.

After some time, war refugees began coming to our town. Among them was a young man named Shmuel Skelot who had taken courses in Hebrew pedagogy in Grodno. I invited him to become a teacher in our school. This young man had a pedagogical education and was outstanding in his knowledge of Hebrew and general subjects, and he also possessed a fair knowledge of music and played the concertina. He could also draw a little. From the time he began to work at the school, he brought in a spirit of vitality. After a short time we began taking the students out on field trips in the area surrounding our town, and sometimes even to the forest.

On these trips the students learned to recognize many plants that grew in the area. There were some students who learned to classify the plants with the help of a field guide which we had translated from the Russian and German terms. In geography and herbology the students learned according to a list of text books - which were ready for print. We taught arithmetic and geometry according to a list of text books which we had translated from German and Russian.

[Page 147]

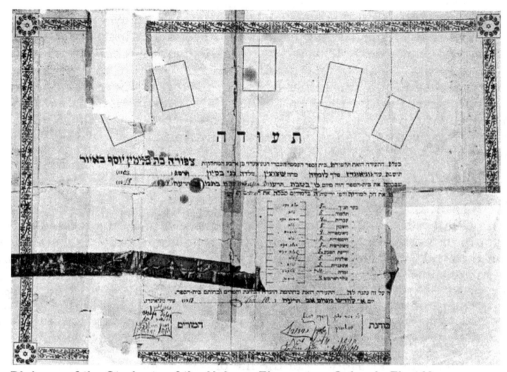

Diploma of the Students of the Hebrew Elementary School - First Year

The teachers acquired a great deal of experience in instruction of all subjects. Every teacher entered his classroom ready for anything _ not only in terms of knowledge of the subject but also all of the necessary teaching aids, such as: maps, pictures, plants, flowers and the like. The level of teaching in our school was much higher than in the Polish school, which opened quite a bit after our school was founded. Not a single Jewish child left our school to study in the Polish school.

[Page 148]

One day, when the inspector was visiting our school, a letter was delivered to me which invited me to the regional pedagogical office located in the city of Szczecin. When I got there, the manager gave me a certificate which appointed me the principal of the Hebrew school of Goniadz.

"We are giving you this certificate," said the manager of the office, "upon the recommendation of the inspector Radben, who has praised you highly and told us you are deserving of this position." This certificate was very important, and was most beneficial to the school, when the government was later turned over to the Poles.

In the third year of the school's existence, there were 21 students in my highest class _ boys and girls, almost all of whom had been my students even before the school opened. Most of them excelled in their studies in every subject, especially in their knowledge of the Hebrew language. All of them increased their reading in Hebrew, and spoke only Hebrew amongst themselves. There were some who also started speaking Hebrew to others. When they would go into a store to buy something, they would speak to the grocer in Hebrew. There was one case where a few children went to the store and asked the grocer in Hebrew for something. He told them he didn't understand, and suggested that they prepare a list for him of the items they were accustomed to purchasing from him. He would learn the list by heart and so be able to help them. They did as he suggested, and he kept his promise.

[Page 149]

The children's devotion to the Hebrew language had an enormous influence on the youth of our town. Many of them began reading Hebrew books, and thus were exposed to the Zionist idea and the rebirth of our national language. Three books in particular, which came to us by way of the library that was founded in our town, had a significant impact on our students and the youth of our town: *Ahavat Zion* [Love of Zion] by Avraham Mapo, *Shirat Hazamir* [The Song of the Nightingale] by Buki Ben Yagli, and Masa L'Eretz Yisrael B'shnat Taf Taf [Journey to the Land of Israel in the Year 2020] by A.L. Levinski.

The marvelous descriptions of the life of our people from days of yore, and the descriptions of the breathtaking scenery of our land, from the book *Ahavat Zion* deeply penetrated the hearts of our sons and daughters and awakened in them a boundless love for our dear land. Many of the students memorized a large portion of those descriptions.

In the book *Shirat Hazamir*, the story is told of a city boy who comes to the country and hears for the first time the marvelous song of the nightingale. In his fascination with that song, he loses touch with reality and begins hallucinating, imagining he sees various sights and scenes before him from the way of life and customs of our forefathers in days of yore in Eretz Yisrael, such as: pilgrimages, offerings, pouring out of water during the Sukkot holiday, and the like. Those visions awakened in the depths of the souls of those young readers an intense longing to renew the lives of our people in the land of our forefathers.

The third book, *Masa L'Eretz Yisrael B'shnat Taf Taf* was a utopia _ an imaginary description of the life of the Jewish people dwelling in the independent Land of Israel in the year 2020. The book tells the story of a Jewish teacher living in Russia who travels with his wife on a honeymoon to the Land of Israel, which is an independent Jewish state.

All of the residents of that country are Jews, and they are governed by a Jewish president. The Jews did not acquire the country by the sword or the spear, but rather they purchased it with their money.

[Page 150]

The main occupation of the Jews was to work the land. There is not a single resident of the country who does not work the land, which was owned by the state, and divided in equal portions amongst the residents _ a certain piece of land for each person. Every person made his living through the work of his hands. There were no exploiters and no exploited. There was no poor and no wealthy. There were no laborers and no lords. Each person worked for himself and was his own master. In other words, everyone was equal.

All of the residents set aside time to study Torah and science _ they were all honest and trustworthy people, living in brotherhood and affection with one another. In the country justice according to the law of the Torah of Moses, to which everyone was faithful, prevailed. In the country there was only one language _ Hebrew.

Descriptions of this ideal life in this Hebrew state that would be founded "soon and in our time" (according to rumors about the Balfour Declaration which filtered down to us from the front lines) kindled in the hearts of our young men and women a "strong love" for the idea of our resurrection. Frequently it was possible to see a young man or woman immersed in the reading of one of these books while tears rolled down their cheeks _ tears of longing, tears of dear and pleasant innocent children yearning for their homeland.

Typical of the feelings of our students in those days was the following fact: once one of the female students recited in front of her class the poem by Frug: "*Kos Hadmaot*" ["Goblet of Tears"], in which a child asks his mother: "The truth of the matter, told by my grandfather, that before G-d on the highest height there stands a wondrous and deep goblet" into which G-d cries a single tear for every time any sorrow befalls the people of Israel. "And when the wondrous goblet is filled with tears, the Messiah will come..." The mother answers: "Yes, that is right" and the child instantly asks: "And when, oh! Mother, will that goblet, the wondrous goblet, when will it be filled to the brim with tears? Or perhaps the tears, with the passage of the years, dry up and are lost? Or perhaps...or perhaps the bottom has a hole in it? And as every tear falls, it trickles out?" And when the student recited that final line, she was overcome with emotion and fainted.

This incident shows how deep and powerful was the yearning of our students to discover our people and our homeland, literally to the depths of their souls.

One morning when I arrived at the school, I discovered Mr. Redban sitting and waiting for me. When I asked him what brought him to the school so early, he replied that this was the day the Germans were going to hand the school, which was in the occupied area, over to the Poles, and he had come to say goodbye to us. Great indeed was my sorrow, and the sorrow of the other teachers as they arrived, over this sudden separation from this dear man who had played such an important role in the pedagogic improvement of our school. Later on, he entered the classroom of the highest grade and taught the students to recite a poem from

[Page 151]

The Hebrew School Building on the Synagogue Mount

the German textbook, and parted from them with great affection. Also from us, the teachers, he parted with warm-heartedness, saying as he departed, "Perhaps we will not meet again, but the affection that exists between us will not be obliterated so quickly from my heart." "And our affection for you will live on in our hearts," I replied.

[Page 152]

About two weeks after our parting from Mr. Redban, the teachers were gathered at the school one evening for a meeting to discuss various matters relating to the curriculum. Suddenly the door opened and a young Pole entered and, without a word of greeting, said, "I am the inspector of schools in this region and I have come to see your school. Are you the teachers? And who is the principal?" "Yes, Mr. Inspector," I answered. "These are the teachers, and I am the principal." "May I see your certificates?" I handed him my certificate. He glanced at it and said, "I would be more satisfied if you had a Polish certificate." "If you please, sir," I replied, "I would also be very satisfied if you would be so kind as to give me such a certificate in Polish."

Without replying to that, he pointed at Yehonatan and said, "Is he also a teacher? Listen _" he told him, as he wrote on the board "(a + b) _ explain how one would solve that exercise?"

[Page 153]

Yehonatan (who had paled a bit) got up from his place and began to approach the board. Nevertheless, I stopped him and told the inspector that while of course he had the right to test the teachers who work under his supervision, it was not right to single out only one teacher to test, even if he was the youngest one there. Would that not make the teacher feel terribly insulted? Perhaps he would like to sit with us for a while and discuss the matter...

"I don't have time to sit, I must go quickly to see the priest. If you would be so kind as to show me the way that leads to his house," he said. "Good bye." He left the room and I accompanied him so as to show him the way to the priest's house. When I returned, I found the teachers were very gloomy. We talked for a while about the unfortunate incident, then returned to our previous discussion of the curriculum.

Since the students in the highest class were making excellent progress and had already acquired the knowledge required for elementary school (according to the program of Department D of the Hebrew Gymnasia of Jaffa), we decided to graduate the first class of the Hebrew School of Goniadz.

After we had decided upon the date on which the examinations would take place, I notified our friend Yeroham Levin from Bialystok. After a few days I received a reply from him, that a few young people would come and take part in the examinations.

[Page 154]

On the day, three young people came to us, sent by the *Zairei Zion* Union of Bialystok. All of our students excelled in those examinations, which were oral as well as written, in Hebrew subjects as well as in general subjects. Great was the joy of those students, their parents, the teachers and the guests.

After the examinations, the guests from the *Zairei Zion* Union invited me to come to Bialystok and open a Hebrew school there. After consulting with my friends the teachers about the matter, they told me that I must not refuse that invitation, because the existence of the Hebrew school in Goniadz was already assured, and it would be a great national sin to leave a city such as Bialystok, which numbered more than sixty thousand Jews, without a Hebrew school, and therefore it was incumbent on me to make it happen. My wife agreed with the teachers.

When I parted from the teachers as I departed for Bialystok, they asked me to bring them to Bialystok and send other teachers to take their places in the school in Goniadz. I promised that I would try to fulfill their request, and after a short time I sent two good teachers to the school in Goniadz and brought two of my friends - Yoel Meir Cohen and Shmuel Skelot - to the First Hebrew Elementary School of Bialystok, which I founded with the help of *Zairei Zion* and *Hamizrahi*.

[Page 155]

Annals of the Hebrew National School in Goniadz
(Extract from Moshe Levin's article
"Annals of the Hebrew National School in Goniadz")
by Moshe Levin
Translated by Gloria Berkenstat Freund

The Hebrew movement in Goniadz emerged at the beginning of the [20th] century with the emergence of the Zionist movement. As a young movement, we its main workers, were young people, about 15 *yeshiva bokhirim* [young men attending religious secondary school] studying in the house of study who began to look at "booklets." The leading member of our group was Yitzhak Yaffe, who later went to study at the Grodno Hebrew teacher's course and became the director of *Yeshiva* studies in a school in Rehovot, *Eretz-Yisroel*.

We went from learning Hebrew and Hebrew grammar to speaking Hebrew. Then, the idea was born to create a modern school of Hebrew, a *kheder metaken* [reformed school]. One of the founders of the school was Efroim Halpern. I was designated to be the teacher. My wife, who also was one of my students, encouraged me greatly in the work. Thanks to her determination, our home became a center of Hebrew; we even spoke Hebrew with our children, a rarity at that time.

The war of 1914 interrupted our work for a while. About a year later, Goniadz was under German rule. As soon as life returned to normal, the question of the school surfaced again and with more enthusiasm than earlier because the Russian school had closed and many of the children did not have a place to learn.

[Page 156]

I was again appointed to open the Hebrew school. With the help of two of my best students, Yoel Meir Kohen and Shimeon Halpern and later also Yonatan Najman and Shmuel Skliut, I began the work of building a modern Hebrew school where the subjects, Jewish and secular, would be taught in Hebrew.

The work proceeded with enthusiasm and the number of children, boys and girls, grew from term to term. The main difficulty was that there were no nature and geography textbooks. Consequently, we had to put together written summaries for these subjects that the Warsaw publishing house, *Tsentral*, later published and spread across Poland.

[Page 157]

The responsibility also grew with the growth of the school. One of the main workers then was Yehezkiel-Perec Czerniak. He was very interested in the school and did a great deal to support it during the most difficult times.

Moshe Lewin and his wife, Khemda [Khinka]

A German school superintendent, who related to our school with great sympathy, came to help us with the question of pedagogy. Thanks to him, I was called to the county school managing committee in Szczyczyn and I was given an official certificate as director of the Goniadz School.

The transfer from German rule to the Poles was not a joyful one. The attitude of the new Polish superintendant was insulting and disparaging. Because of the change, we decided immediately to organize a graduation for the school (of which there is a picture in this book on pages 135-36). A short time after this, I was invited to come to Bialystok by the Bialystok *Tseire Tzion* [Youth of Zion] and to found a school there based on the pattern of our school in Goniadz. I accepted the proposal and this ended my connection to the school in our *shtetl* [town].

[Page 158]

The funeral of the teacher, Shimeon Halpern, of blessed memory

[Page 159]

The Wonderful Institution
by Yerukham Levine, z"l
Translated by Amy Samin

The name Goniadz is held in my memory since the day of the fire that broke out in that town (during the intermediate days of Passover, 1906): firefighters from Bialystok, the city in which I lived, were summoned there and there was great anxiety for the fate of that town. My parents owned a manufacturing shop and had commercial connections with the owners of manufacturing shops in Goniadz during the days before the First World War: Tybe Galchinski and Chaya– Rahel Luria (both of whom were the first to open shops in the Osowiec Fortress), Hershel Luria, Zerah Numoy, Alter Zimnoch, Yehuda Hertzig (milliner) and his sons, his daughter Shafrintza Goffstein, Pessah Friedman (Staznoaer). Her son, Mutiyeh–Leib, I knew to be an enthusiastic Zionist, and it was very hard to understand when, one night, he up and left Goniadz for...Argentina.

During the time of the German occupation, during the Second World War, I lived for a few years in Suchowola, close to Goniadz. My host would travel to Goniadz under a prohibition, for it was appended to Poland (General Government Pon Bazler), and the political rule there was more convenient. The trips to Goniadz were made in a sleigh belonging to a farmer from the border settlements. The purpose: Market Day. When I came to Goniadz in the winter of 1916 I found a pleasant surprise: an entire Hebrew School, including general studies; something which did not exist anywhere else in the Bialystok region at that time. The principal was Moshe Levin. The teachers were: Yoel–Meir Cohen, Shmuel Skaliut (studied pedagogical courses in Grodno), Shimon Halperin and Yonatan Naiman. I was friendly with two of those young teachers. Shimon had a grandfather in Suchowola, and we would meet there in the summertime, and Yonatan was in Bialystok the first year of the war. I learned from the teachers that the main difficulty they were pondering was the shortage of textbooks and the isolation from Hebrew cultural centers, since travel to Bialystok without a special license was forbidden and Warsaw was far away. Also in Warsaw there was still no school where the language of instruction in general subjects was Hebrew. I discovered that the principal had authored geography textbooks, but he had difficulty determining the professional terms. I took upon myself the negotiations between Bialystok and Goniadz, because I would frequently travel between Suchowola and Bialystok. I received notebooks from two former students who were graduates of the Herzliya Gymnasia in Tel Aviv and who had lived in Bialystok (Yaacov Ravich and Yeshbam Lipshitz) with their geography lists and transferred them to Moshe Levin, and therefore I made it easier for the one who was writing the textbook to put together a list of professional terms. In addition, I had a hand in founding an association for independent advanced study, *HaShachar* [the Dawn] among the students of the upper grades. I have a memento of that period: photographs of two students (Kalman Bacharach and Yezedka Gritz). The teachers Yonatan and Shimon helped the young association. Meanwhile, I publicized in the *Zairei Zion* [Youth of Zion] groups in Bialystok the existence of the Wonderful Institution – an entire school in Hebrew. Three teachers, from the elite of *Zairei Zion* (Shimon Rabidovich, Elimelech Magid, and Yaacov Ravich), were invited to be the examiners for the first class of students at the school. With the revolution in Germany, the gates to the Hebrew School were opened also in Bialystok, and it was decided to put Moshe Levin into that position.

[Page 160]

During the occupation, Zipora Wolf lived in Goniadz in the house of her father the rabbi, and she was unemployed. I offered her the position of assistant to the nursery school teacher in the Hebrew nursery school *Yaldut* [Childhood] in Bialystok, and she accepted the position. It served as her first seminar (under the expert guidance of the teacher, Rivka Rubin, the wife of Dr. Yisrael Rubin–Rivkai of blessed memory). In time she became one of the best nursery school teachers in Bialystok.

[Pages 161-162]

The Chalutz School
by Moshe Goelman, Tel Aviv
Translated by Amy Samin

The school in Goniadz was the first of the comprehensive Hebrew schools which later constituted the Tarbut chain of schools. I found that in a Yiddish encyclopedia which was published by YIVO [Yiddish Scientific Institute] in Vilna. Indeed, it was a pioneering school in every sense of the word. Today, it is difficult to speak of Zionism or a pioneer spirit, especially to the younger generation in Israel. But the spirit of Zionism was felt in Goniadz during the years I worked there between 1921 - 1925, both amongst the politicos and especially amongst the teachers. We held weekly pedagogical meetings in the teachers' lounge, during which reports were given on the situation in the classrooms, and we would argue and discuss the problems of methods and course of study of instruction and education relevant to the younger generation living in the Diaspora. At that time, many lived in the illusion of"autonomy"; in other words, that there existed the possibility of living a full spiritual and cultural Jewish life in Poland, despite the fact that the Land of Israel was the foundation of all of our educational work. It was not long after the Balfour Declaration and in the middle of the Third Aliyah [third wave of Jewish immigration to what was then Palestine], the founding of the *Chalutz* [Pioneer] Federation in the Diaspora, and the blossoming of various youth movements everywhere. Even in Goniadz the *Chalutz* organization existed, and several times I was invited to speak before those youths on Sabbath afternoons in private homes (the organization was illegal and was prohibited from holding public gatherings). As far as I can recall, my speeches were meant to expand upon the issue that I would teach the pupils in the school, but with a special emphasis on the Land of Israel, the pioneering spirit, and preparation for life in the Land of Israel. The Diaspora needed to be a sort of corridor leading towards the drawing room - that is, to immigration to the Land of Israel. We were not practical at all, and we did not take into consideration the likelihood that most of the youth would in fact remain in Poland and be forced to fight there for their very existence, and that it would have been more fitting for us to prepare them for that battle.

[Page 163]

The pioneering spirit also existed from another standpoint - the preparation of suitable textbooks; the teachers were compelled to translate books from other languages. I recall that in order to teach the history of the late Middle Ages to the fifth grade, I could not find suitable books and I would translate from Polish and hand out pages to the students. And in other courses - especially mathematics, we dedicated many of our evening hours to that difficult and exhausting work.

Third Graduating Class of the Hebrew Public School of Goniadz

As for the relationship between the teachers and the politicos and the parents, I must emphasize that in all my years of teaching in countries and places around the world, I have never experienced such complete understanding as I found in Goniadz. The treatment of the teachers was exceptional. Everyone treated the teachers with respect and admiration. More than once we were a bit prideful and looked down on the parents. We received full punishment for that sin when we arrived in Canada. There, teachers had to battle long and hard to raise the level of respect for teachers. And it still didn't reach the level of recognition and esteem awarded the teachers in Goniadz and in Poland in general. Until today the Hebrew school in Canada is called *Talmud Torah*, and teachers are called *melamed*. There is no doubt that one of the forces that kept teachers in small and remotes towns like Goniadz and others was the respect with which they were treated by the public.

I cannot forget the impressions of my first days in Goniadz. When I went to a house to rent a room, I found there a young woman sitting at a sewing machine. I asked her in Yiddish if there was a room for rent, and she answered me in Hebrew. I continued speaking in Yiddish to the older woman there, and her daughter answered me, explaining the conditions in perfect Hebrew. And then, when I entered a store to buy cigarettes, I spoke to the young woman standing there in Yiddish, and she answered me in Hebrew. It wasn't a kind of showing off for the teacher, but as I later became convinced, was born out of enthusiasm for the language that the teachers before me had instilled in their pupils. At the time, I felt as if I had already immigrated to the Land of Israel.

And if things were like that in homes and on the street, they were even more so in the school. More than once the Polish teacher left the classroom weeping. We had to lecture the students at length about how important it was to learn the Polish language - the language of the country in which we lived.

The students were different, of course, in their talents and knowledge, but they were equal in their love for and devotion to the school. The distress of a student sent home to bring tuition was quite terrible. We teachers suffered a great deal over that. More than one of us appealed to the politico Selig Nivodovsky, may his blood be avenged, to exempt us from the unpleasant debt that forced us to send home the students who did not pay the tuition? We demanded that one of the board members handle the awful task. In my opinion, we really robbed those pupils. I do not recall a single case where a student was pleased to get vacation from school. Absences from school were only brought about as a result of illness or other difficulties, and not by a love of idleness.

And in conclusion - a few words about the community of Goniadz. I must confess that I do not recall the city of my birth, Stawiski, the way I remember Goniadz. In my home town there were also genial and loving sorts, interesting and strange. But the Jewish spirit of Goniadz was different, more progressive. I cannot deny that a large portion of my feeling is due to my life companion, a native of Goniadz, and the members of her family, to whom I grew inextricably close over the years. Although when I remember Goniadz and think of her, I see the town first of all from the viewpoint of the school, its students, teachers and politicos.

[Page 165]

Tales of Goniadz
by Mordechai Nilovitzki, Haifa
Translated by Amy Samin

A. The Hebrew School

The school in Goniadz was an original creation - not an imitation of some foreign example, nor according to any other kind of model, but was rather created out of a very specific need and that was its magic for all of those who took part in the work. It was not a *Tarbut* School, it was established before the founding of *Tarbut* in Russia, and about four years prior to the founding of *Tarbut* in Poland. The unique character with which it was imbued at its founding was preserved for many years. Even though the teachers changed frequently, the school's advancement continued in the same direction and trend that it had had from the beginning. In its momentum and scope, the Hebrew School in Goniadz was different from all of the other Hebrew schools.

One institution, founded at about the same time as the school in Goniadz, was the Hebrew School of Lodz, which was started by the poet Yitzhak Katznelson of blessed memory. But what was the significance of one school among many in a large city and the one and only school for the children of a town? The school in Goniadz was, for much of its existence, the only source of education and knowledge for the Jewish children there. For only about the last ten years of its existence there was a Yiddish school, but the Hebrew School's standing as the first could never be undermined.

[Page 166]

And I can tell you something about its position among all of the other schools in the country. As is known, a network of schools sprang up along the geographic margins of Poland. In Congress Poland and Galicia there were almost no Hebrew schools for a very long time. And yet I had the opportunity to become well acquainted with a fair number of Hebrew educational institutions in Volhynia, on the outskirts of Vilna, in Bialystok and in Pinsk. The schools in Volhynia were reasonably modern, but they were established by *Tarbut* in Moscow, before the region became separated from Russia. In Vilna and its surroundings, there were local arts schools, but their tone was more local and relatively irregular. They had one significant good thing about them – they were the natural continuation of the *heder* [religious elementary school] and the modern *heder*. The most advanced and modern were the schools around Bialystok and Pinsk, and it is natural to think that the school in Bialystok itself would be at the top level. But it is known that in the establishment of the first Hebrew public school in Bialystok those who had the greatest part were the founders of the school in Goniadz.

Teacher M. Nilovitzki and his class

[Page 167]

The National Hebrew School in 5676 [1915-1916]

To date, there has been no written record made of the history of this special school, and certainly many have already forgotten the memories of the past due to the frequent change of teachers and management. And that is a shame!

Correcting the distortion of the neglected past is possible only through systematic study supplemented with the obtaining of evidence and written documents. Thank God more than a few of the teachers are still among the living (Mr. Moshe Levin and Shmuel Sakliot, Mrs. Shteigman-Sakliot, the columnist M.Z. Golman, Peretz Sandler, H.S. Raigrodski-Barkai, Aryeh Arad (Axelrod)), community leaders and students. I also have close to hand: copies of minutes, children's newspapers, letters and photographs; of course, others have such items as well.

Altogether, I worked in Goniadz for about five years, which was about one fifth of the school's years of existence. According to the distribution of my working years, indeed I was the last of the first (the years 1920 – 1921), after receiving my commission directly from Mr. Moshe Levin, and my three years of work later on (1930 – 1932). I was the last in and the first out. Also during the eight years' break (1922 – 1929) I was not completely out of touch with the school. I had contact both in person and through letters from pupils and teachers and public figures; those letters have remained in my possession ever since. Because of all that, I believe I have been given the opportunity to describe the history of the school from my own perspective.

[Page 168]

B. How was the Idea Realized?

A Hebrew school – the idea seemed clear to those in the know. No need to continue running after students from the *heder* system (even the modern *heder*). For those more advanced, the *heder* had basically ceased to exist. And what an insult it was, that an advanced, intelligent people with an ancient cultural heritage, would move to the institutions of foreigners – beneath them in terms of education – to teach their sons reading, writing and arithmetic, and even there not be able to find a spot! And even if you accept the decree that the beginning of wisdom and knowledge is in the study of the alphabet of a foreign language – in the words of Bialik – there still remains the question: which foreign language? Russian, German or Polish? And even so, we were then in the period of the First World War, when it was still impossible to know to which country the portions of the land currently occupied by the Germans would belong. Therefore, those people had no choice but to have a school of their own, and this of course must be based on the agreement of the cultural values of the entire people from time immemorial and on their national language, and not upon part of the culture of a small portion of the people during a brief historic time, and in Yiddish.

[Page 169]

A number of capable people were found, including the veteran, experienced teacher Mr. Moshe Levin, who took upon himself the role of establishing the Hebrew school. He hesitated over the monumental size of the task, and only after consulting with his young friends who promised to give him all the help they could, did he agree to accept the offer of the position. Then the group came together, Moshe Levin together with Y. M. Cohen, Shimon Halfran and Yonatan Neiman who brought along Shmuel Skaliot, a student of the pedagogical courses in Grodno who had tarried in Goniadz as a war refugee. The principal's wife, Hinka, (she and her husband established the first Hebrew home in Goniadz and then later in Bialystok), did her part in the work of helping the students who were struggling, so that they could remain in the school. And still there were not enough resources.

C. The School and Its Area of Influence

Teacher A. Gevirtzman and his Class

[Page 170]

The Goniadz Hebrew Primary School – that was the name given when it was founded, and that is what it was called for as long as it was in existence. The school maintained a level and method of instruction that was in no way inferior to that of any other culture. The founders had in mind the curriculum of educational institutions in the Holy Land, which was secular in nature and there was no need to publicly emphasize such agnosticism. In Goniadz, for example, they did not study sacred subjects bareheaded [i.e. without wearing a yarmulke] and, as a matter of fact, they always showed respect for the holy aspects of the people. That being the case, there was no longer a need for the *heders*, and even the sons of rabbis attended the school. And it truly was popular; no one remained outside its walls from any strata, not for spiritual reasons or for financial reasons. Hebrew was the language, a simple and clear Hebrew without hesitation or unnecessary phrases. The writing of the pupils which has been preserved – for over fifty years!

– is in no way deficient in comparison with the Hebrew used today in Israel. A significant emphasis was placed on language, on literature, on biblical verse, and on history. At various times they also taught *Mishnah* and *Talmud*. The school caused the permeation of Hebrew – to the home, the shops, the street, the society of young men and women, and even more so to the public institutions. It was possible to live in Goniadz and not know any other language. The graduates of the school promoted the Hebrew language in the training farms throughout Poland, from whence came teachers. An excellent library was founded in Goniadz, as were theatrical groups which put on performances in Hebrew, also in the surrounding areas. There were parties to welcome the Sabbath, as well as literary and practical speeches, literary discussions, newspapers, and journals for children. Someone might say, "provincial art", and it's possible that we ourselves belittled those things at the time, and concerned ourselves instead with other matters that seemed important at the time, and with financial enterprises and the like. In any event, this created a good social atmosphere – we didn't settle down with cards and as a result of that, "modern" matters. Hehalutz, Hehalutz Hazair, pioneering *moshavim* [settlements], "Youth Days" – all of these were a part of the school, and in all of them the teachers and employees played an active role. During Sukkot 1931 there was a *Tarbut* conference in Warsaw where for the first time a pioneering group was established, initiated and run by a core group from Goniadz. Thus, an island of modern Hebrew grew up in and around the school, whose influence spread out far and wide from there.

The *Tarbut* School of Goniadz 1928

However, that school, whose destiny it was to raise a generation of pioneers who built our country, did not exist in a vacuum: it was the fruit of the labor of common sense combined local social forces and was used as a fulcrum and a anvil for the local public in its struggle for real national autonomy. It must be remembered that during the days of the German government (1915), many special schools for Jewish children were opened in the neighboring cities with instruction in German, and a few in Yiddish which was like a form of German, from which were created typical Yiddish schools as they were known later. All of those schools were, of course, closed when the Polish government took over. The new government thought they would just as easily destroy the Hebrew school in Goniadz, and to further that goal they opened a Polish school for Jewish children. But they came up against the vigorous opposition of the entire public – the community leaders, the parents, and the children themselves. The matter reached the representative of the Jews in the capital and in the Sejm, and after a prolonged struggle the school was reopened. The Polish school closed for lack of pupils, and "Israel gained its inheritance"...It is no coincidence that among the leaders of the organizers of the autonomous community in the Bialystok region, the leaders of the Goniadz community held prestigious positions (an important note from Yeroham Levin of blessed memory: "At the time of the German occupation, all of the places in the area were under the *uberhost verwaltung* [over-host administration]. There, the Germans opposed the Hebrew school, although Goniadz, which was included in the area of Poland, was able to open a Hebrew school. That possibility was given to every place in the same range, but the others did not have enough desire for such.")

[Page 173]

D. The Goniadz Community

Goniadz was different from the neighboring towns and cities, with which it was very familiar. On my arrival there one fine spring day, I was impressed with the scenery, the Bobra [Biebrza] River curved to the foothills in the East, with the lively and vivacious youth and – most of all – with the school!

Goniadz was a typical border city. The elders of the city maintained the custom from the start of the previous century, when after Poland was divided the city changed from Prussian hands to Russian, and so forth, and on the walls of the synagogue could be found signs leftover from the wars. In the World War of 1914, Goniadz and the Osowiec Fortress were in close proximity to the line of fire, and many of its citizens fled to nearby towns. When the Russians left the line of the Bobra, the Germans took control of the area. Three years later, a third side – the Poles – came and occupied the place without lifting a hand. Soon the Russian wave returned for a time – in new packaging - claiming ownership of their little brother, the Belorussian. The Lithuanians also tried to make a claim, and so a place that was claimed by three kingdoms, was actually ours, and none of the other peoples in the area were able to impress their cultural stamp upon us, the Jewish population there. We left our mark there, and created a Hebrew school, in which we had complete spiritual control. Its spiritual fortress – insofar as we could have one in the Diaspora – was destroyed at the hands of those who were not spiritual at all. But the work we invested in the quarter-century (1915 – 1939) of its existence was not in vain. And the part of the Hebrew School in Goniadz in the process of our cultural rejuvenation is not negligible at all.

The Jewish community of Goniadz, which arose in the environment of society, and state, with the influences of various nationalist policies, was the most independent in terms of modern national integrity. It was never felt that we lived within the range of Polish culture. It's possible that the Jews of Goniadz did not see themselves as Polish Jews. Moreover, at one time they certainly felt themselves to be Jews of Russia, so in the days of the extensive Russian Empire, when an abundance of income and affluence flowed from the Osowiec Fortress and their trade relations with the large cities of Russia were strong. But even then there was no adherence to Russian culture or any blurring of the Jewish consciousness; they were far from devoted to the lords of the land.

[Page 174]

Goniadz was a modern, educated community – education acquired, of course, through independent study. There were wonderful types of autodidacts, people knowledgeable in the law, etc. there, including teachers, and there were attempts to establish modern educational institutions, partially in the format of a modern *heder*. Not surprisingly, it was here the need for a Hebrew school was felt most acutely. The presentation of Reb Yaacov Rudesky – a Torah scholar and knowledgeable man, a completely educated personality – who was a candidate for the rabbinate, can only be imaginable in Goniadz. Although he was not chosen - and it is only natural that as a local figure he would have opponents including the man who held the position before as head of the rabbinate, a great Torah scholar, a wise man, respected and enlightened, Rav Wolff of blessed memory – he could have graced a large and important community.

The population of Goniadz was an active one, lively and connected to the broader world. Once, there had been trade relations branched out throughout Russia, which furthered the establishment of spiritual connections with people of action in the yet-to-be-built Land of Israel. Goniadz was also represented in the pioneering section by one of its brightest sons, Yaacov Toker, one of the heroes of Tel Hai, the son of a widow of Goniadz. It was common to find there people who took bold action, imaginative people. In other words: people of action who also had vision, vision that could be made reality. They, of course, belonged to the upper strata, the commercial and the affluent. They were also homeowners, whose income to some extent was based on nature: owners of water stations, orchards, milk cows, and so on. Also common was income from the marketplace, and they were peddlers in the nearby villages and also craftsmen: carpenters, blacksmiths, bakers and tailors, including village tailors. Types of Mendele: the village tailor Isaac Nefha, and Hertzl the Carpenter, and their ilk, as well as characters from nature like Moshe Stabasky, "Laban the Aramean" – which stirred the hearts of the children and their creative imagination.

[Page 175]

Earlier, pioneers – good ones – from Goniadz had immigrated to the Land of Israel. Since then, the flow has not ceased. Among them were merchants and artists, and those holy instruments, the people who left, were people of action, founders of enterprises, foremen of major factories, people who did great things in the *Haganah*, members of the *kibbutzim* and founders of *moshavim*, exemplary artists, young women who acclimated well to farming, teachers, kindergarten teachers, school principals – men and women with drive. In short, typical of the youth of Goniadz.

[Page 175]

A Cherished Town
by Arieh Arad (Axelrod)
Translated by Selwyn Rose

I knew Goniadz intimately. For two whole years I lived there. I was engaged as the manager of the "Tarbut" school until the day World War II broke out. On September 1st 1939 I left town.

For two whole years I shared their joys and their sadness together with them; they were very close to my heart. I discovered in that town a national–cultural life, lively and effervescent. Among themselves her youngsters spoke rich, correct Hebrew. Songs of Eretz–Yisrael were heard in the streets and squares in the evenings. The "Hechalutz" ["Pioneer"] organization ...from among whose ranks, magnificent cultural work was done, with the best of their youth being sent to Palestine.

[Page 176]

Her Jews donated generously to national foundations. And above all – the local "Tarbut" school, in which the town's children acquired knowledge and wisdom in their people's tongue, was a national cultural center for the town. The children created a Hebrew–speaking group – "B'nei Yehuda" that took upon itself to speak Hebrew not only in school but also with their parents and acquaintances and thus, the sounds of the Hebrew language was heard throughout the town's streets. The teachers were not satisfied with the regular curriculum alone but introduced several different extra–curricular activities for the pupils in the evenings. Graduates of the school would come on Shabbat and festivals to hear Torah readings from the counselors and the teachers. Next door to the school a course was instituted for the town's family heads of families to study Torah. Among the participants were community leaders under the tutelage of Zelig Niewodovski. On one side stood the community Rabbi, Shlomowitz and on the other, the writer of these lines. Together they discoursed on the Torah...

Grief over the cherished town that is no more...

[Page 177]

The Yiddish School and People's Library
by Leibl Mankowski
Translated by Gloria Berkenstat Freund

The beautiful, colorful Jewish communal life in Goniadz drew its spiritual nourishment from the daily problems as well as from the various generational wells of knowledge that help to develop and validate the social and spiritual life of the *shtetl* [town].

The ideals and ideas of the various strata of the population came to expression in their activities. I will illustrate several of them here.

The erection and support of a Hebrew school and library and, later at the beginning of the 20th century, the Jewish children's school helped enrich and elevate the general spiritual life in the *shtetl* to a higher level of achievement.

Leadership strength moved into the foreground during the process of this and other accomplishments; that with their capabilities and with their sincere sensible relationship to the needs and problems of the time, many contributed to the improvement and beautification of city life, often with self-sacrificing efforts.

[Page 178]

One of those beautiful leading personalities, who won the love and respect of the entire city population, was Leibl Mankowski. Although he belonged to the Bund whose ideology stood in contradiction to the ideas of other groups, both on the right and on the left, particularly of the Zionists, this did not disturb the friendly and most respected relationship of everyone to him.

Founders of the Jewish School Organization (*YSHO - Yidishe Shul Organizatsye*) in Goniadz, 1921

From the right: Borukh Trachimowski, Yankl Trachimowski, Alter Michnowski, Shimeon Jewrejski, Nekhemia Atlas, Henokh Gelbard, Leibl Mankowski, Moshe Feywl Bialosukenski, Josl Alszanicki, Leyzer Trachimowski, Sholem Grobard, Yankl Ruwin)

[Page 179]

Leibl Mankowski always stood in the front rows of the workers, artisans and, in general, with the ordinary people and worked with them with all his strength to reach the achievements which they recorded in the economic and in the cultural realms. He particularly, contributed much to the founding of the Yiddish People's Library and Jewish Children's School.

These two institutions enriched the cultural life in Goniadz, fulfilling their assignments with success: systematically presenting the reader with the latest Yiddish books from the best Yiddish writers, as well as from world literature, which had been translated into Yiddish. And providing good teaching personnel and appropriate Yiddish and general scholars for the children's school.

In an indirect way, the two institutions helped expand the cultural life in Goniadz but the support and the constant expansion of these institutions brought great expenses that the low tuition or, in relation to the library, members' dues, could not cover. Even the support of the American *landsleit* [people from the same town], which was received from time to time, could not cover the deficits. A dramatic circle was founded for this purpose which, in a short time, presented capable young men and girls who produced performances from time to time for fully packed rooms; sometimes in the Polish school and sometimes in Yankl Rudski's *piwowarnje* (beer brewery). They would also sometime travel to give a performance in the nearby *shtetl* of Trestiny [Trzcianne].

Leibl Mankowski

[Page 180]

The school children would also present Chanukah and Purim performances with the help of their teachers.

Leibl Mankowski played a very great role in all of the undertakings. The events not only covered the deficits of the above-mentioned institutions, they also brought a great deal of joy and encouragement to the *shtetl*.

Leibl Mankowski was also a correspondent of the Warsaw *Folks Zeitung* [*People's Newspaper*], as well as the *Bialystoker Shtime* [*Bialystok Voice*].

For a time he was also a councilman in Goniadz city hall.

He died young, after a long illness, in his late 20s. But most of those who worked with him perished at the hands of the Nazi murderers along with all of Jewish Goniadz. They were all loved and dear to us without difference and they will eternally remain etched in our memory.

Sons and Daughters of Goniondz in the World

Goniondzers in America

Moshe Malozovsky, New York
Translated by Martin Jacobs

It is hard for someone as much "in love" with Goniondz and Goniondzers as I am to write objectively about them – but I will of course attempt to stay within the framework of the facts as they are, and principally I will focus my attention on Goniondzers in America.

About four thousand *landsmanshaftn* [people from the same town] are registered in New York (others consider the number to be much higher), some very big, such as Bialystock with about 20 organizations, Warsaw, Lodz, Minsk, etc. I don't want to denigrate the activities of these thousands of organizations, but the Goniondzers, although not as eminent in public life in such a big city as New York, are truly different. I believe that the cultural level of our *landsmanshaft* is higher than the average *landsmanshaft*, our scope has always been broad, we have always approached various problems with liberality, whether it is a question of local assistance or of allocating funds for our home town, and in recent years, our brotherly cooperation with our Goniondzers in Israel. We never use the words "charity", "donations", or "support", as is the fashion here. Our attitude is that we are in America, and are therefore better off, not because we are so wise; it might have been just the opposite, and we would be on the "other side of the fence", and the Gondiondzers would have acted against us as we against them*.

We are especially proud of our human resource, our dear, wonderful membership, which unfortunately has decreased considerably in recent years. I will mention some of them in what follows.

* * *

The present-day Goniondzer society was officially organized in September 1905, but there were already Gonionders in America at the end of the 19th century. They had organized themselves as a religious organization (unfortunately no documents remain, and I can only record what I have heard from elderly countrymen). They had their own synagogue, and since they lived close to each other in the early years, they prayed there every day. There was no problem in getting together a *minyan* [quorum of ten men necessary for prayer] . For reasons we do not know, they later joined the countrymen of a Ukrainian town, Khomsk, so that I still remember the "Goniondzer-Khomsker synagogue" from the beginning of the 20's of this century. It was at 25 Ridge Street in New York. Perhaps it is not important, but I will note here that as far as I know I am the only Goniondzer of the last immigration at the beginning of the twenties to get married in the Goniondzer synagogue. My bride was Soroke Kantshuk (Sore with the black hair from Trestine). Performing the ceremony was R. Benjamin Bayer z"l, beloved by all.

I have heard that only one member remained in the organization, and it is said that a large sum of money was left over, some tens of thousands of dollars, and that according to the laws of New York State (not the City) the entire sum belongs to this man or his heirs. (Unfortunately I have no documents confirming this.).

In September 1905 the Goniondzer organization was formed. It is now known by the name "Goniondzer-Trestiner Young Friends Benevolent Association". The founders of the *landsmanshaft* came from a completely different element. They were workers who had arrived from Goniondz at the beginning of the century, some fleeing conscription in the Czarist army, some because of revolutionary activity, etc. The founding took place in a bedroom in Willy Levine's home. In a few weeks 20 Gonziondzers were registered, and Simon Blum was elected the first president and Morris Levine was elected secretary.

Although the members paid a total of 10 cents each a week in dues, they immediately decided to pay a sum of four dollars a week to a member who became ill, without knowing where the money would come from. They also decided to buy land for a cemetery as soon as possible (land for a cemetery was an important matter for a *landsmanshaft* in a city like New York, although it seems to be no less important for Americans).

Despite the difficult conditions in those years, especially in the terrible crisis in America in 1907, and generally despite the long working hours and the low pay, they were able to sign up more members and to arrange some small activities and more or less fulfill their obligations to the members. When the first World War broke out in 1914 a new era began in the Goniondzer *landsmanshaft*.

* * *

At the beginning of the twenties of the present century, after the First World War, when the first immigrants were arriving in New York, we already find the organized Goniondz *landsmanshaft,* together with the Trestiners, in its own club rooms at 31 2nd Avenue, in the heart of Jewish New York, with a membership of over 200. The club rooms were tastefully furnished with a library having English and Yiddish books, and there was even a chess teacher and a dance teacher.

At this time we already find a well organized relief committee which sent the first sums of money to Goniondz and Trestine. As was then the custom, they also sent a delegate to Goniondz, our Dr. Blum, and later Aaron Rudsky.

A short time later we organized a mandolin quartet. Its members were Zalmen and Moshe Bachrach, Itshke Burak, and the present writer. We gave several concerts in the club rooms. From time to time there were also lectures. It goes without saying that almost all new arrivals joined, paying about $25 a year. Commonly a weekly meeting (every Tuesday) would draw 150 to 200 members.

We began publishing our bulletin in August 1929. It came out regularly for about four years. I had the honor, with some small interruptions, of editing the bulletin and the five special enlarged journals.

In November 1930 we published a special enlarged bulletin of about 60 pages, to celebrate the 25th anniversary of the organization of the *landsmanshaft* in America. About 500 people came to the great banquet, which was carried out with pomp and splendor. At that time also the Goniondz Ladies Auxiliary was organized, under the leadership of Mrs. Kamenetz, who has since then taken over the entire relief effort. It even published four issues of its own bulletin, called the "Shul-barg". Our *landsmanshaft's* activities went along in this manner (sometimes more strongly, sometimes less) until the beginning of the 40's, when everyone's great misfortune began.

In 1945, in connection with the fortieth anniversary of the organization, we published our first memorial journal, with about 100 pages, most of which were filled with accounts of the terrible tragedy which befell our town and the entire Jewish people. Our relief work took on a completely different character (Mayrim Rubin especially writes about this).

In 1955 we celebrated our 50th year. We had reached our peak (actually a bit earlier), and now things started going down hill. A great number of our townspeople are no longer with us, having gone to the next world. Our children do not have and cannot have the interest in our *landsmanshaft* which we had. The small number of active members still hold on firmly to our beautiful traditions, but the labor gets weaker and weaker. This is a normal process in American Jewry, of which more than 70 % are now born in America.

I consider it my duty, before concluding, to mention the names of at least some of the members who were always interested in our townspeople and always gave of their time for them. We will never forget them.

Zerah Tikotsky; Morris Levine (Moshe Sender the shoemaker's son), died September 22, 1947, in whose memory we published a special issue of the Bulletin; such beloved people as Gedalia Seid, Joseph Babrovsky, Dr. Kamenetz, Mendel Schwartz, and several others I cannot not now remember.

Among the living I must mention such devoted active members as Moshe Bachrach, Mayrim Rubin, the.Gradzinskys, Mrs. Kamenetz, Kaydi Atlas, Israel Atlas, Sholem Grobard, who is the present president of our organization; David Forman (son of Nisn the tailor); and devoted active members like Meyshke Gelbard in Chicago, and Warsho in Detroit, and several others in various cities in America, which Mayrim Rubin most likely mentions in his article.

Dr. Simon Blum during his visit to Goniondz

The four founders of our society
Morris Levine, Simon Blum, Leybele Greenberg, Jacob Greenstein

I will conclude these lines with an excerpt from the poem by Z. Weinper, a poet who died young. This poem is so much in accord with the mood of all of us.

- - - *Where has Mother's dear body gone roaming?*
I call and I call and I call
and no one answers.
desolate,
wiped out,
covered over,
and silenced,
and yet, how my heart now roars
next to the silent canyon!

* * *

Oh! Wickedness made a bacchanalian orgy from our blood!
I would now needs turn my song into a whipping rod,
except that I am tired, so tired
as every shattered Jew

everywhere, everywhere, everywhere,
a world of stone now looks at me
so hard, cold, and silent.
how can weeping from human emotion matter to it?
the world is granite.
so excuse me, Mother,
if there is no tin-roofed house over you.
You are in the temple of my word.
If I would wish to know where your grave is
I would come from afar with dust on my feet,
the dust which lies over you.
See, see - some strange color
has spread from somewhere.
Oh Mother, is it you?
Who else would walk so blindly and so glowingly over the granite?
I would have sworn – step!
I would have sworn – a voice
rises from the valley
and speaks
so softly, like a caress
and what it says is:
- one must bear it –because God, blessed be He, knows what he is doing...

* * *

- I am no longer able!
a god with a gun!
a god with a whip!
a god with a German!
Mother, forgive!
I do not accept
not even for God's sake
not even for your sake
a curse on life which would condone this!

*Translator's Note: The author presumably means that the non-Jewish Goniondzers would be fighting the Jewish Goniondzers, and the latter would be fighting back, at the time of the Holocaust.

[Pages 191-192]

Goniondzer Immigrants in Palestine
Prior to the First World War
Translated by Martin Jacobs

Zalmen Yirmes (son of Yirmiya) z"l

His name in Goniondz was Kravietz. He came to Petach-Tikva in the 80's of the last century, at the age of 15, with his uncle Leyzer-Shimon Yirmes from Tiktin, when Petach-Tikva was not yet ten years old. Died in Petach-Tikva in 1948.

David Seid z"l

Father of Gedalia Seid z"l of New York, who visited Palestine in 1951. In the old country his name was David Raver (of the Raver water mill). Not having money for transportation, he walked for two years to get to Odessa. There a relative of his gave him five rubles and he arrived safely in Palestine. Lived there about two years. Died in Jerusalem in 1895.

Hayim Eliezer son of Dov Miltshan

Was known in Goniondz as Hayim Leyzer Shikorer. A brother of Zerah Shikorer. Came to Palestine, to his uncle Yaroshevski, in 1884 as a boy of 14. Went through all the difficulties of getting settled faced by a new immigrant. Married and established a numerous family. Co-founder of Rehovot, was active in purchasing land and expanding the settlement. A permanent member of the Rehovot administration. He is considered one of the most respected persons of the old community.

We wish him the best of luck and long life.

Israel Krepchn z"l

In Goniondz he was called Israel son of Reuben ("the Pure Soul") of the old market. Had a large orchard behind the forge of Leyzer the blacksmith. Had two houses. Was an expert in horticulture. A victim of the fire of Passover 1906, he sold his property and left for Palestine, with his wife Feyge and his eldest son Zeydke, settling in Petach-Tikva. Baron Rothschild's officers recognized his ability and employed him professionally. He tried planting apples here and was successful, but when oranges became popular this was abandoned. He died in Tel-Aviv in 1926. His wife Feyge was buried in Afulah. His son is living in Paris.

Two girls traveled with Israel:

1. Khaye-Sore, daughter of Khatskel the water carrier. Married in Petach-Tikva. After the First World War she and her husband left for Chicago, where they still live.
2. Rokhl, daughter of Eti-Leye, of the Bandke family. Married in Petach-Tikva and lives there now with her family.

Joseph Halpern

Eldest son of Ephraim Halpern z"l. Came to Palestine in 1912 to study in the Herzeliya Academy. Finished in the second graduating class. Lives in Tel-Aviv.

Israel David Yardeni

In Goniondz – Yaroshevski. A son of Moses Michael the dyer of Dolistover Street. Came before the First World War. Completed the Mizrahi Teachers Seminar in Jerusalem. Lives in Rehovot.

Pua (Paye) Bloshteyn (Soloveitchik-Shalvi)

A daughter of Mordechai Bloshteyn, immigrated to Palestine as a young girl, before the First World War. Lives with her family in Ramat-Gan.

[Pages 193-230]

Goniadzers in Israel
by Fishl Yitzhaki–Treszczanski
Translated from Yiddish to English by Gloria Berkenstat Freund

(Seen through their families and places of residence in the old home)
Dedicated to the memory of my father, Yitzhak, may he rest in peace, who died on the eve of the Second World War and of my mother Rywka, sister Gitl and my brothers, Yudl, Ayzyk and Ruwin, who perished at the hands of the Hitlerist beasts.

After the First World War, after the historical act of the Balfour Declaration, there awoke in our *shtetl* [town] as in the entire Jewish world, a hope of the more rapid achievement of Zionism. The *haHalutz* [a Zionist pioneer group] was founded and it strengthened Zionist propaganda and activity. The first three families then traveled to *Eretz–Yisroel*. These were the families of Efraim Halperin, Mordekhai Rubak (the baker) and Leibl, Shakna's son.

Thus was drawn the cord of the pilgrim. Their number mainly grew in the years 1924–1925, until the last years before the outbreak of the Second World War. This era brought the most significant number of Goniadzers who today are found in Israel. The last dozen Goniadzers arrived after the Holocaust.

Today more than 150 Goniadzers are in Israel. Mainly, one or two from a family. It can be said that someone from every second or third house in the *shtetl* is in Israel.

We will try to recall from our memory our shtetl during the last years before the Jew. His two nieces are in the country [Israel].

[Page 194]

Further toward city is the house of Elia Dlugalenski. Elia, who was intelligent and educated, was a councilman and alderman at city hall. He defended the interests of the Jewish population in a clever manner. He had to remain in the *shtetl* because of his weak health and could not think of a life in *Eretz–Yisroel.*

His neighbor – the house of Borishke's son, Zeydke (Chanowski). He was one of the "regular Jewish" types who made himself heard. He fought in his way to aid and to lighten the situation of the artisans. He was among the founders of the cooperative bank that was organized before the Payen Bank. He also was in the opposition to the elected Rabbi Szlomowicz and one of the fervid followers of Yakov Rudski at the rabbinical election. His daughter, who was in Israel, had to return to Goniadz before the outbreak of the Second World War because of the condition of her health, and could no longer return [to Israel].

[Page 196]

Ribacke Street

Dowid Goldiner, one of the calm, good–natured and modest Jewish middleclass men, lived opposite. He lived a quiet life with his wife and children. His daughter, Yafa, is in Tel Aviv.

A few steps further – Mushke Pekarski and family. Mushke's children gathered friends from school and organizations around them in the house. Their house served as the meeting point for a significant number of young people. The first *Hahalutz–Hatzair* [Young Pioneers] room was in their house.

The first of this family who traveled to Eretz–Yizroel was Khatskl, then Dobka and Leyzer, who was one of the first educators with *Hahalutz Hatzair*. In the end, Mushke himself came with his daughter Hinda who in time emigrated to America.

[Page 197]

One of Mushke's children was Chaim–Arya. [He was] one of the most capable and most talented among the young, himself a student in the Hebrew school, and right after graduating in the first graduating class he became a teacher in the same school.

He was full of strength and energy. Right at his start as a teacher, he would enter the class where just yesterday he had sat as a student, with sure steps. With his blond head of disheveled hair, smile and with his fluid, pearly speech, his students focused all their interest on his lecture.

His home in the *shtetl* was restricting for Arya. He left for the wide world and in later years became an esteemed lawyer and an admirable Jewish and Zionist personality in Canada.

Yehoshoya Supraski, a Goniadzer who settled in the Russian city of Kursk and who would come to Goniadz from time to time, is a relative of the Pekarski family. After the outbreak of the revolution, he emigrated to *Eretz–Yisroel*, where he was very active as a Zionist and communal worker. [He is one of] the most eminent Jewish personalities in the Jewish community and one of the leaders of the general Zionists in the country.

Opposite, the Garber family from Jasionówka had moved into the Wajntrojb's house during the last years. The Hebrew school was located in the house for many years. Peshke, Garber's daughter, lives in Petar Tikva.

As a neighbor – Shmuel Ber Malozowski, a dear and good–natured Jew. He and Leyzer the blacksmith (Todorowicz), Borukh the tailor, Nisan the tailor and others, were the first worker–Zionists in the city at the beginning of the century [20th century] thanks to the influence of Supraski. They rented a room from Saika, across from Benyamin the scribe, and taught the geography of *Eretz–Yisroel*, history and the history of *Khibes–Zion* [first Jewish movement favoring the return to Palestine]. Shmuel Ber's younger son, Dowid, lives in the Gvat kibbutz.

[Page 198]

Asher's son Itshe, whose house served as an inn in the last years, lived in the same row of houses. His oldest son, Zeydl, was one of the first *Poalei–Zion* workers. He was the first secretary of the Hebrew school for many years. He emigrated to Argentina where he died.

His younger son, Asher, is in Cuba, and is one of the eminent people in Jewish society there. He visited Israel several years ago with his wife, Freydl (Szajnenzon).

ShmuelBer Malozowski

Avraham'l Rajgardski

For many years, [in the house] after Asher's [son] Itshe, lived Khatskl Bialastocki, who was the owner of the sawmill that he had erected right next to the river. Wood would be brought to the sawmill on the water from the entire area. Only Christians were employed in the sawmill. Therefore, the sawmill had no importance in the economic life of the *shtetl*. Khatskl himself was a charitable person and generous donor. He erected the fence around the synagogue hill.

Further, Avraham and Ida Rudski lived in the house of Chaim Polak (Kobrinski). Avraham was a merchant on a large scale. During the last years, he was a volunteer doing communal work and also was active in the Zionist area. The only son of simple parents, he attended the Bialystok *Tarbut–gymnazie* [secular Hebrew language secondary school] and several years later, the Strasbourg University. Avraham came to *Eretz–Yisroel* in 1935 and accepted with joy and enthusiasm everything he saw in the development of the country. However, because of his illness, he returned [to Goniadz] with great sorrow and pain. His son Tzwi lives in Ramat HaKovesh.

[Page 199]

His daughter–in–law and a grandchild live in Israel.

Next, Leyzer the blacksmith, and opposite – Avraham'l the shoemaker (Tshudak) and at the corner – the house of Moshe–Mendl's daughter, who lives in Jerusalem with her husband and family.

The old market starts from her house. At the start – Itshe Lichtensztajn's family. His son Chaim was one of the first *Halutzim* in Israel. The entire family emigrated to Israel in the 1930s with the youngest son, Dovid, who was one of the young social workers of *Hahalutz–Hatzair* in the *shtetl*.

The father and his two sons Chaim and Dovid died. Leah, the mother, and her daughter, Ruchl, are in Israel.

We pass several houses where Moshe–Mendl the tailor [and] Yehosha Cwiklic lived and we come to the last houses, before the expanse that led to the river.

The Mali family lived in one of the houses. Moshe, who was a Zionist all those years, today is in Israel with his wife and his daughter. Their son, Leyzer, also was in the country, but because of his communist activity, the mandate regime drove him out of the country and he perished in Goniadz.

Shmuel–Yoska Rubin's son–in–law, Y. L. Gradzinski, who was a Hebrew teacher in the Jewish school and carried out Zionist propaganda at various meetings in the city, also lived there. They gave their first daughter the name Bat–Ami [girl of my nation]. Even then, they lived in the *shtetl* in the spirit of the new *Eretz–Yisroel* settlement. He and his wife, Zahava (Golda), and their family live in Tel Aviv.

[Page 200]

On the other side of the old market – Sara'ke, Chaya–Cyrl's daughter, and her husband Wolf Rajgardski who had a bakery. Their children were in HaHalutz. The son, Avraham'l, was one of the active members of Hahalutz and Keren Kayemet [Jewish National Fund] and he perished with his parents. His two daughters are in the country, Yafa in Haifa and Yona in Tel Aviv.

[Page 201]

Next door to him lived Chaim Kobrinski who was the supplier to the government (*liferant*) for the soldiers in Osowiec. Rywka, one of his daughters, came here [*Eretz–Yisroel*] in 1924. His second daughter, Sara, came later. Then also Chaim and his family. Today Rywka, Arya, Sara and Leyzer are in the country.

A little further – the house of Chaya–Tsirl. Her son Hilke (Hilel) Bialy also carried on a large trade with wagons of flour and sugar, in addition to his large iron business. He was active as a Zionist, managing committee member of the Hebrew school. His son Moshe graduated from the *Tarbut–gymnazie* in Bialystok. He studied in England and arrived in *Eretz–Yisroel* as a volunteer to take part in the war of our country's liberation. He was a member of the *Kfar Blum kibbutz* [communal settlement] in the Galilee. He met his death in a tragic manner a few years ago, leaving a wife and two young children.

In the alley of the old market, we see a row of houses after the post office, the house where Yankl the refuah [traditional healer] lived, Atlas the photographer and we come to Yosl Tikoncki (Sheymele's [son]). He was one of the first who collected [money] for the [Jewish] National Fund. He was active as a Zionist volunteer, a teacher and one who loved Yiddish melodies.

Shlomo–Yosl's house is after his. [He was] a Jew, a scholar and a meticulous man. His older son, Yisroel–Shimeon, emigrated from America when he was old and has lived here for nearly 20 years. His younger son, Kheikl, visited the country several times.

Josl Tikocki [Sheymele's]

My father, of blessed memory

[Page 202]

From there we enter the alley that leads from the old market to the new market.

The Guzowski family lived on the left in the alley. Their daughter, Dwoyra, lives in Israel.

As a neighbor – Gela's son Yoal (my grandfather, may he rest in peace) and his children and their families. Itshe (my father, may he rest in peace), his sister Khinka and brother Yankl. The writer of these lines and his brother Meir are here in the country [Israel].

[Page 203]

As a neighbor – the Miltszan family. Their son Sender, who was a Zionist communal worker and one of the most active in the Zionist library, is in the country [Israel].

Opposite, in the courtyard of Chaya–Ruchl Luria, lived the Grynszpan family. Industrious people and one of the few whose entire family emigrated to *Eretz– Yisroel*. The mother and son, Gdalia, live in Kfar Malal near Tel Aviv.

Chaya–Ruchl Luria herself was a woman who ran large businesses. She was good–hearted and always ready to help everyone. Chaya–Ruchl "*Keynenhorenit*" was her nickname because she added the words "*keyn ayen hore*" [may there be no evil eye] to everything she said. So much so that when she said, he is dying, [she added] may there be no evil eye...

GONIADZ – Ulica Krotka [Krotka Street]

The "short street" (Przejazd)

Her children and their families played an important role in the life of the *shtetl*. However, not one of them had the merit to see *Eretz–Yisroel*, despite the fact that both of their sons–in–law, Zelik Poliak and Isak Zaliszanski, did everything that was possible to be able to come to *Eretz–Yisroel*.

[Page 204]

Henekh Frydman and his family lived in Chaya–Ruchl's building. He was one of the few Hasidim in the *shtetl*. He was one of the individuals in the city who during the great typhus epidemic was dedicated with his life and body, day and night, to bringing aid to all of the sick. Business mainly was carried out by his wife Feygl Fruma. His daughter Toba and his son Zeydl are in Israel. The youngest daughter Liba died here.

Yehuda the furrier (Hercig) [also called Yehuda the capmaker] lived opposite Chaya–Ruchl's building. He was a Jew, a man of the people, a wise man, a hospitable man, full of humor, always with a smile on his lips and a good word for everyone. It is said of Yehuda: After the First World War, when the various refugees without citizenship documents came to Goniadz, Reb Yehuda was the constant witness for them and confirmed that they were born in Goniadz. His testimony was reliable to the municipal authorities (city council), after which he was treated to a good whiskey and a snack...

[Page 205]

Yehuda Hercig [the furrier]

Reb Yehuda gave testimony for too many people... And a commission from Bialystok came specially to investigate him. Reb Yehuda "clarified" for them that there was a society in the city that went to every celebration and bris [circumcision] and because he was the *gabbai* [sexton] of this society he knew of all of the births in the *shtetl*...

And another episode:

After the great fire, the Goniadz *pristov* (police commissar) did not permit the building of houses without official construction plans. On a given day, Reb Yehuda left for Grodno and he succeeded in being received by the governor himself. In his usual manner, during a short conversation he persuaded the governor to fulfill his request and before Reb Yehuda returned to Goniadz the *pristov* had received a telegram: Permit everyone to build...

[Page 206]

His son Tovya was one of the first of the family to go to *Eretz–Yisroel*. Then Tsipora and Yosl. After Reb Yehuda's death, his wife Ruchl–Leah also came with their daughter Liba. After the [Second] World War, Yehuda's grandson, Leibl Gopsztajn, the son of his oldest daughter Tsipora, came here with the remaining refugees. Liba, Shprinca's daughter, is also here from before.

Further – Etl Mushke's house. Left with two children after the premature death of her husband, she took the yoke of earning a living on her shoulders and ran the businesses. She was devoted to her two daughters with her body and life. Her house was open to all. Every emissary from *Eretz–Yisroel* was a guest in her house. She was generous in her donations to Zionist funds. Her daughter Malka lives here in the country [Israel].

As a neighbor – the Luria family. A house with many visitors to the family and children. Hershl Luria was a *gabbai* at the synagogue and chairman of the *Linas haTsedek* [society for visiting the sick]. His son Sholem, one of the first *halutzim* who emigrated, today lives in *Kibbutz Ein–Harod*, the first kibbutz that arose in the country [The first kibbutz actually was Degania]. Yankl, Teybl and Rivl emigrated after Sholem. Finally, Hershl and his wife Ruchl, the grandmother Khina also came and died here several years ago.

***

The valley that led hill down to the river extended from the Lurias' house. A number of families lived in the valley who were far from the idea of Zionism, like the families of Shimeon Jewrejski, Brumer, Tyukl, Todorowicz, and others. Shimeon Jewrejski was active in the Bund during elections and with the Jewish school. Tyukl was a leading person in the leftist youth group.

[Page 207]

Shepsl the shoemaker also lived in the valley. His strongest desire was to go to *Eretz–Yisroel*. He even wanted to become a member of *haHalutz*. His love of the land probably came from his earliest youth. Perhaps he saw *Eretz–Yisroel* in the light of the *Khumish* [Torah] that he once studied in *kheder* [religious primary school]. However, his desire was not fulfilled. Due to his age, *haHalutz* could not accept him as a member and, naturally, at that time he could not obtain a certificate [from the British permitting him to emigrate].

Yankl Rudski's *pivovarnia* (beer brewery) stood deeper into the valley, near the river. Only the giant house remained of Yankl Rudski's attempt to build a large brewery in the *shtetl*. Much energetic zest as well as money was put into this unsuccessful try. This was characteristic of Rudski who had a broad, worldly approach to life. He was one of the nicest and most interesting Jewish men with his comprehensive point of view. [He was a] man full of charm, a synthesis of Torah and education, modern and simultaneously an ordained rabbi. One of the first Zionists in the city, he took part as a delegate at the fourth Zionist Congress in Basel. In addition to his grandson Tzwi, his daughter Chana Rudski and her husband and son, who recently arrived here after various wandering in Poland, are [in Israel].

***

Leaving the valley, we meet the house of Katinke. Once Feygl Szilewski lived there.

[Page 208]

Her daughter Chana and granddaughter Avigil live in Israel.

Further – Baylka Pesha's *piekarnia* (bakery). The premises of the Zionist organization *Hahalutz, Hahalutz Hatzair* and the *Tarbut* [secular Hebrew language organization] library were on the second floor of the house for many years. Zionist lectures with the participation of emissaries from Warsaw and from *Eretz-Yisroel* took place there as well as discussions among the parties. There on *Shimkhas- Torah* [the autumn holiday celebrating the conclusion of the yearly Torah readings and the start of the readings for the new year], the Zionist *minyon* [10 men needed for prayer], the collection for the *Keren Kayemeth L'Yisroel* [Jewish National Fund] and for the league for those working in *Eretz-Yisroel* took place. The sound of the songs from *Eretz-Yisroel* echoed across the entire *shtetl*.

On the bottom floor of the house, near Baylka Pesha's lived her sister Henya and her children. They came from Russia after the First World War and were permeated with the revolutionary winds there. They provided the main push for the development of the leftist camp in the *shtetl*. Two contradictory orientations, two camps – by chance, under one roof...

From Baylka Pesha's family, her son Avraham'l is here [in Israel].

As a neighbor – the house of Alter Trezczanski. Wolf Pekarski lived with him. [He was] a councilman and alderman at the city hall (city council) and the only Jewish official from the surrounding province who received a salary from the government.

Wolf was one of the leading Jews in the *shtetl*. We would come to him with the most difficult [problems for] arbitration thanks to his shrewdness. He was one of the active Zionist workers in the Hebrew school, in the bank, for *Keren Hayesod* [the Foundation Fund, now the United Israel Appeal] and others. He, nor his wife, nor his children lived to emigrate to Israel.

[Page 209]

Wall to wall – Mushka Rozencwajg and her two daughters. The younger daughter Dora was active at the Zionist library and went to *Eretz-Yisroel* in 1925. She lives in *Kfar Vitkin*. The mother and Hinda emigrated in 1935. The mother died here and the daughter Hinda lives in Jerusalem.

The further house was Tovya–Motl's and from there began the alley of the house of prayer. Of the families in the alley, there were no families from which someone emigrated to Israel, except for Moshe Dinka's daughter, Grunia, who lives in *Kibbutz Glil Yam*, Bajdan Gitl and Piekhote's daughter who live in Ramat Gan.

Wolf the rabbi and his family lived in the house of prayer alley. He was a modern Jewish rabbi, smart and ingenious. He belonged to *Mizrakhi* [a religious Zionist organization] and he himself distributed the Zionist Congress membership cards. He had a good reputation as a great arbitrator and was interested in life in the *shtetl* and was particularly concerned with those who needed communal charity, contributions for Passover necessities (Passover flour), and, in general, was a great help. His daughter Ida, the wife of Yosl Hercig, who provides a treatise about Friend Wolf in this book, is here in the country [Israel].

***

Exiting from the alley of the house of prayer, a row of houses begins on the left, one after the other. Someone from each of them lives in Israel.

Riwa–Tsirl Yafa lived in the first house. Her oldest son Nakhum escaped from Goniadz with the largest number of the young in 1920 when the Bolsheviks withdrew from the city and before the Polish military marched in, inspiring a strong fear among the young Jews. When Nakhum returned to the city, he brought with him customs from the great, modern world, as for example: walking in the street without a hat... He was one of those who appeared in the theater performances, whose income was designated for cultural or Zionist purposes.

[Page 210]

Yankl–Moshe, his second brother, was in *haHalutz*. He was always full of humor and witticisms. Both brothers are in Israel.

Their house abutted Manya Cuker's house. Her oldest son Yisroel studied in Italy and perished there. His youngest brother, Heczak (Tzwi), was a founder and active worker with the Revisionist youth organization *Betar*. He and his mother live in Israel.

In the house further along – Chaim Koplman. One of the nicest, most respected merchants in the city. A great philanthropist. One of the first members of the Odessa committee in the city. From his large family, only his daughter Sonya is here [in Israe].

Moshe Zylbersztajn

Moshe Zylbersztajn, one of the directors of studies at the Hebrew school in Goniadz, lived in the same house. In the course of long years of work at the school, he became a resident of Goniadz. In addition to the school, Zylbersztajn was very active in the city in all areas of Zionist work. His public appearances and basic clarifications about all Zionist and *Eretz–Yisroel* problems remain in our memories. I particularly remember his interesting lectures about Yiddish and Hebrew literature that were rich in content, given in a beautiful form and language and drew listeners from the right and the left. During the last years he dedicated himself with his entire soul to the new building for the Hebrew school.

The difficulties of going to Israel prevented him and his family from emigrating despite his great efforts in that direction.

[Page 211]

As neighbors – the house of Avraham and Gnendl Gelbard, one of the respected merchants in the city. Several members of the family live in the country [Israel]. Chaya and Yehudis in Kinneret, Gershon in Ramat HaKovesh. Gershon was one of the founders of *HaHalutz–Hatzair*, active in the pioneer movement and a member of the central committee of *HaHalutz–Hatzair* in Warsaw.

After their house, Sholem Hirszfeld's family lived in the courtyard. Leyzer, one of his youngest children, lives here in the country [Israel].

Further – the house of Dwoyra Rajgrodski. Dwoyra carried the burden of the businesses for all of her years. Her house was "open" with a generous hand for everyone, always ready to do a favor. She sent her children to study at the Hebrew *gymnazie* [secondary school] in Bialystok. Her daughter Yona traveled to *Eretz–Yisroel* in 1924 and, later, Dwoyra and Sura and Malka also came.

[Page 212]

Sura Bejnsztaun, the baker was a neighbor. She, too, ran the entire bakery with her own strength. Her oldest two sons are in America and her daughter, Tsipora, who was active in *haHalutz* and *Keren Kayemet*, is here in Israel.

The small alley, after Sura the baker, led to several houses in one of which Arka the tinsmith lived. His daughter, Shifra, lives in Israel.

Mordekhai Nielowicki, one of the most admirable teachers at the Hebrew school, and his wife Baylka from Trestina [Trzcianne], lived in the same alley, nearer to Dalistower Street, for many years.

Nielowicki, who came from Wizna, arrived in Goniadz at the beginning of the 1920s and became an educator of the second graduating class (graduates) of the school.

He was unusual in his special approach toward students. He attempted to avoid keeping a distance from them, but the opposite, searched for ways to come near to them and be their comrade and friend.

He brought the spirit of *Halutz* with him that influenced a large part of the Jewish youths in Poland and he set for himself the task of educating his students in the spirit of the *Halutz* ideas.

Thanks to him, the school class was the basis for the newly created *haHalutz* organization. A majority of his students were the first of the *Halutz* emigrants in the city, such as Sholem Luria, Moshe and Shaul Zakimowicz, Arya Khtiba, Berl Beris, Yankl–Moshe Yafa, Gitl Frydman, Chaya Gelbard, Ziva Kabrinski and others, who went immediately after graduation to *hakhshore* [preparatory training for prospective agricultural emigrants to Israel] and emigrated to *Eretz–Yisroel*.

In the course of time, Nielowicki almost became a citizen of the city, the main social worker and communal worker. He took part in the business flow of the *Halutz* and Zionist work and from time to time appeared with programs with *Eretz–Yisroel* and literary themes.

[Page 213]

Even during the time when he had ceased his work in the school and worked for the main central [office] of *Keren Kayemet L'Yisroel* in Warsaw, he visited Goniadz often because for him it was as near and his own as a birthplace...

Nielowicki and his wife Baylka live in Israel. Their families in Wizne and in Trestine perished there.

***

The Dalistower Street begins there. Efroim Halperin and his family once lived after Tserel's house.

Reb Efroim was one of the first followers of the Enlightenment in the city and one of the first in the Odessa *vaad* [council]. One of the nicest and most respected Jews. He was mayor during the German occupation [First World War]. In 1915 he was among the founders of the Hebrew school. He was also one of the first to emigrate to *Eretz–Yisroel* with his family.

His older son Josef came to Israel before his family. He was arrested in 1912 when he was at a wedding in Bialystok with the National Fund *pushke* [tin can used to collect contributions]. Thanks to the intervention of the then Bialystok Rabbi, Dr. Josef Mohilewer, may his memory be blessed (a grandson of the Rabbi Shmuel Mohilewer, may his memory be blessed, director of the Rehavia *gymnazie*, Jerusalem), he was freed and he emigrated to *Eretz–Yisroel* a short time after this.

His second son, Shimeon, one of the first Hebrew teachers, was gifted with great abilities. He died very young.

[Page 214]

The remaining children, Golda, Nekhama, Meir and Elkhanon, are in Israel.

Further – the Tawolinski family's house. The daughter Malka was one of the first Hebrew teachers abroad and is a pre–school teacher here [Israel] to this day. The second daughter Chana'ke, who graduated from the first course at the Hebrew school in Goniadz, also is a pre–school teacher. The third daughter, Chaya–Ruchl, is also here.

A few houses further – Ruwin the shoemaker. His daughter Chana was one of the first *halutzim* who emigrated to *Eretz–Yisroel*. She and her family brought her father here. He died several years ago.

Further – the Izraelski family. The Hebrew school was located [in their house] for a long time. The younger son, Ayzyk, is here in Israel. After them lived Gedelia the cabinetmaker. His older son Berl was one of the first halutzim. He brought his parents [here]. The youngest son, Dovid, also came here before the outbreak of the Second World War.

From this house on we pass several houses and come to the house of Bertshuk Polak (Kobrinski). His daughter Ziwa (Zelda) was one of the first halutzim. She lives in Tel Aviv.

Again several houses and we come to the last house on Dalistower Street. This is the house of Rwyka Ruchl, Moshe's daughter (Zakimowicz).

The oldest son Moshe was one of the Halutz founders in the city. He tried to enter Eretz–Yisroel illegally and was deported from the Romania border. He tried again and this time with success. Shaul came after him, then Nakhum and finally the parents with Masha– Gitl. The parents were with Nakhum in Kibbutz Ayelet HaShahar. Reb Eliezer and Rywka lived with respect in the kibbutz, esteemed by the entire kibbutz, young and old. Eliezer's ceremonial melodies and compositions for the Days of Awe prayers from the synagogue lectern were a big hit with everyone here.

[Page 215]

A few years after the death of Reb Eliezer, his youngest and most beloved son, Nakhum, tragically perished. The mother Rywka died a year ago at a very old age. Today, Moshe and Shaul live in Haifa; Masha–Gitl in *Ayelet HaShahar* and Nakhum's family in *Kibbutz haGoshrim*.

After their departure, the family of Nusan Lewin moved into Zakimowicz's house. Their son Melekh (Meilakh, or as we called him, Meilakh Shatan) was very popular in the *shtetl* in his own way. He was somewhat unpredictable. He liked a dance, a song and a leap, easy and carefree and was informally friends with all strata of the Jewish population in the *shtetl*.

He was educated in the Hebrew school, was in *haHalutz*, went for agricultural training, dabbled in communal affairs and was very active in Zionist matters. He also appeared in the theater performances for Zionist purposes when emigration to *Eretz–Yisroel* was closed. He tried his luck and left for Uruguay. He was unsuccessful in settling there and returned.

During the last years he was a Hebrew teacher in the surrounding *shtetl*ekh and perished there with his family.

Jewish Goniadz ended with the house of Moshe's daughter, Rwyka Ruchl. From there on was the Christian population and among them lived several Jews: Diodka the *melamed* [religious teacher] (Furman). His older daughter, Chaya was a chief nurse and died some time ago. Two more daughters, Peshka and Sura, are in Israel. Shmuel the blacksmith also lived there [among the Christian population]. A Zionist and philanthropist. His daughter Chaya–Itka and her family came [to Israel] with the last refugees.

[Page 216]

The road from there led to Klewianka where Moshe Lewin was born, one of the most meritorious people in the Hebrew school system, not only in Goniadz, but also in Bialystok where he founded the first Hebrew school and in the entire Hebrew education movement in Poland and then in Canada. There is a special appreciation of Moshe Lewin here in this book. Moshe Lewin, his wife and children live in Israel.

***

Returning from Dalistower Street, on the other side, one reaches still more houses until halfway down the street, where Sender Yaszwiler lives. His daughter Zelda lives in Israel.

Several houses further – the Tokar Family. Yakov Tokar, the son, was one of those who fell with Trumpeldor defending Tel Hel.

Libka the widow (Rubin) lived as a neighbor. Her son Avraham Rubin lived in Petar–Tikvah. Moshe Mikhl the dyer (Yaroszewski) also lives there. Their son, Yisroel–Dovid Yardeni, emigrated to *Eretz–Yisroel* before the First World War and became a well–known teacher here [in Israel].

Further – Leibl Ribak's house. An extensive family. After the father's death, Chaim, the oldest son, became the leader of the business and took care of all of the children as a father. A daughter, Chaya–Liba, who married Khona Makay, lives here [in Israel] and also Josefa, the youngest daughter.

[Page 217]

Chaim's brother, Yankl Rubak, lived in the next house. His daughter Kayla lives here in Israel. Moshe Szewc's daughter also lives here.

From there we come to the corner of the market where Barski's building stood. Years ago, the Goniadz religious judge lived on the spot. His son, Avraham Yafa, was one of the most successful people in Hebrew education. He graduated from the first Hebrew teacher's course in Grodno. He was proficient in Russian and Hebrew literature and took part in journals about education problems. He and his family live in the country [Israel].

After Barski – Yudl Bojarski, one of the Zionist workers, Meri Halpern, Krepcin – to the house of Penski. Berl Penski died tragically during the normal years, going to Bialystok. His daughter Chana lives here [in Israel].

From there we come to the Szajenzon family. The oldest son, Elimelekh, was one of the first halutzim who emigrated [to Israel] in 1924. His mother and the second brother, Leibl, came later.

From this house began the so–called *Maysim* [Dead Man's] Alley, which counted a few houses. And in one of them lived Yankl Janowski, a modest and honest Jew. His daughter Rywka lives here in Ramat HaKovesh. There, on the street, also lived Bobka the widow (Bialystocki). Her oldest son Motie emigrated to Uruguay. Ahron and Yankl, the remaining brothers, also emigrated here [to Israel]. Then the children brought their mother and their sister Yehudis.

The only one from the family who became stubborn and did not want to go was Meir, the youngest son, who is here in the country [Israel]. He married Mushke's daughter Malka Etl. The last to come from Uruguay was Yehudis, Meir's sister, and she settled in Israel with her husband and family.

***

[Page 218]

On the corner of the market, the Jewish library was in Arka Bailach's house. This was the gathering spot of the leftist faction of the young in the city. Extreme left parties were forbidden under the Polish regime. Therefore, the work was done in the name of the library where gatherings would take place from time to time that were ostensibly on literary themes. The library was rich in books; newly published books were bought immediately. The possibility of acquiring the books was thanks to the income from the theater presentations that were on an appropriate artistic level and had a cultural value.

Dovid Treszczanski, who lived here in the country [Israel], was one those of who was active in cultural work and took part in theatrical presentations.

Avraham Orki's daughter Hoga (Halpern) lived as a neighbor in the courtyard. The first Hebrew school was in her house. Her two daughters, Fruma and Ruchl, who were active in *haHalutz–haTsair*, live in Israel.

Nusan Trac lived there, too. Ahron Frydman, the brother, left for *Eretz–Yisroel* before the First World War. He lives in *Kibbutz Ein Harod*. He is an influential and leading comrade of the kibbutz movement. Yankl Trac's daughter also lives here in Rishon LeZion.

A little further – Kheikl Yerajski. The only family that hid in Goniadz during the time of the Nazi occupation and that went through all seven levels of hell of those difficult and cruel Hitler years. Two brothers came here to [Israel]: Tovya and Zalman as well as the youngest sister, Kayla. Tovya, the oldest son, provided a great description in this book of their survival during those years under the name "Goniadz Destruction."

[Page 219]

Diodia the baker also lived there. His son Yosl, who lived in the country [Israel] for many years, died several years ago. Zerah Miltshan and his family lived in the same house. [He was] a Zionist and the constant *bal–tefilah* [person reciting prayers] for the Zionist *minyon* [10 men required for prayer]. One of his brothers came to *Eretz–Yisroel* in the 1890s and created a large family with many branches. He lives in Rehovot. Zerah's oldest son Leyzer lives there. Zeydl, the youngest son, was among the last refugees who came to Israel.

In a further house lived Shimkha the leaseholder (Hativa). An honest man of the people, lessee of orchards and land from Polish noblemen. He loved agricultural work and raised his children in the spirit of love of agriculture. His son Arya was one of the founders and active members in *haHalutz*. He traveled illegally several times until he was successful in entering the country [Israel]. He lives in Kfar Vitkin and is actually one of the new Jewish farmers in the country. His sister Chaya lives here, too.

Moshe Furman also lives here, a son of Yoske's son Yitzhak, the *gabbai* [sexton] in the house of prayer. Moshe himself was a Zionist and technical leader in all undertakings with Zionist aims.

Itshe Biali lived in the narrow alley, near Yoske's son Yitzhak. [He was] one of the worshippers at the reader's desk in the house of prayer. His two daughters and son live in Israel.

[Page 220]

As neighbors – the house of Moshe–Leyzer Grodzenski. His son Mordekhai–Itshe was one of the mobilized soldiers that left for Russia. He came to Israel after the Holocaust and died several years ago, leaving a wife.

Notka the lessee (Altszuler) and his family lived in the next house. Notka the lessee was the holder of the *korobka* [community tax on the kosher slaughtering of meat] in the *shtetl* [The Russian government that controlled Goniadz at this time leased the right to collect the korobka to individuals]. He was one of the respected [members of the middle class]. He would be seen strolling at ease through the streets of Goniadz with his arms crossed behind his back, taking pleasure from God's world.

His son Zeydl, full of energy, devoted himself to communal and party work. He was involved with sports and organized theater presentations mainly within the framework of his communal work and he himself appeared in the main roles. The standards of these presentations were much higher than the usual amateur acting.

Zeydl was one of the few survivors from our *shtetl*. A few years ago he visited Israel.

***

From there we go to the corner where Yankl Tikacki's house stands, going past the house of Zalman Bialistocki and come to Mordekhai the baker. His two daughters are here [in Israel]. One in Hadera and the other in Kfar Haroeh. Further, after the house of Alter the iron shopkeeper, Fayga–Ruchl and Gornastajski, we came to the house of the Czerniak family.

Khatskl Perec Czerniak was one of the respected and most popular people in the city. [He] was active in Zionist matters and in the Hebrew school. He was one of the founders and leaders of the bank that financially helped all of the merchants and retailers. He had a special proclivity for theater. Thanks to his beautiful voice and theatrical abilities, all of the productions were directed by him in which he himself played the main role – [they were] on an appropriate artistic level.

[Page 221]

He, his wife and children are in Israel. His parents came in the later years and died here in deep old age.

After this house began the official residence of Koszcial the priest and his private house with a large garden that occupied half of Tiple Street.

***

After Koszcial, opposite, among the gentile houses, lived the family of Avraham'l Farber. His son Ruwin, who was active in *haHalutz*, lives in Tel Aviv.

From Farber's house – one returns to the city, passing the house of Rayna's son Leibl the blacksmith. Yankl the blacksmith (Ruwin) was a neighbor, one of the respected Jews, a *gabbai* in the house of prayer and *bal–tefilah*, one of the heads of the kehile and one of the strongest followers of Yakov Rudski. His son Leyzer was one of the fighters in the Bialystok ghetto and fell as a partisan two weeks before the end of the war. His two daughters, Chana and Leah, live here in the country [Israel].

[Page 222]

There is the house of Moshe's son Ayzyk Yankl the glazier (Rawer). His son Skharye was in *haHalutz* and lives in Israel. As neighbors – Avraham Rower's house in which the Jewish school was located for many years.

From there one goes to Ruwin the shoemaker, Sidranski and Moshe–Feywl Bialasurkenski.

Moshe–Feywl was one of the active Bund workers. When the Bolsheviks were in Poland for a short time in the 1920s, Moshe–Feywl was among the Bolshevik regime's most trusted people. In order to maintain order he received weapons. With pride he would go through the streets with a rifle and many of the young envied him, particularly his son.

Yankl Ruwin [the blacksmith]   **Motka Kliap**

Moshe–Feywl's brother, Avraham–Meir, was one of the founders of *haHalutz*. He was a teacher at the Hebrew school for a few years and later in other Hebrew schools in Poland. He spread and rejoiced in the idea of *Eretz–Yisroel* everywhere. However, he did not live to go to the country [Israel].

As neighbors – Tsalel's son Leibl – Tikacki. His youngest son Pesakh was one of the last refugees to come to Israel.

After Anshel's son Itshe, [lived] the shoemaker Moshe–Gershon and Alter Zimnach. The latter's son Chaim was mobilized in the Polish Army during the Second World War; he was in Russia and came to the country [Israel] with General Anders' Polish Army. His brother Motl, who was a Hebrew teacher, perished with the family.

[Page 223]

His house bordered with Motka Kliap's house. One of the respected families. All of his children were active in communal areas. Baylka, the oldest daughter, devoted her entire energy to the work for Keren–Kayemet, which she headed for the entire time. His second daughter, Grunya, and her brother Gershon were among the active workers for haHalutz haTsair. Both live in Israel. The two younger brothers and their parents perished.

As neighbors – the Bachrach family, one of the most esteemed Zionist families in the city. Every one of the children was active in his own way: in the Hebrew school, in the library or in the Zionist funds. Dovid, Moshe and Kalman went to America. Their sister Kayla, who married the Hebrew teacher, M. Gaelman, moved to Canada with her husband. Khasya, and then their mother Chaya, went to *Eretz–Yisroel*. Dovid came here from America in 1934 and Kayla and her family came to Israel from Canada and settled in Israel during recent years.

[Page 224]

After the departure of the Bachrach family, Rabbi Szlamawicz moved into the house. There was a quarrel in the *shtetl* for a long time after the death of Rabbi Wolf until the arrival of Rabbi Szlamawicz that divided the *kehile* [organized Jewish community] into two sides: Rabbi Szlamawicz's side and the side of Yakov Rudski. There is a special discussion about both of them in this book.

Dovid Leyzer Simchowicz lived on the second story of the house. His two daughters live in the country [Israel].

Further, the building of Zerah Niemai. The Hebrew school and the Zionist library were on the second story for a long time and sometimes the theater presentations. No one from Niemai's family is in Israel.

After Niemai, one went past the house of Chana Surozki, the Polish apothecary, Gerzon, and one arrived at Chaim Lejczke's (Niewodowski). His son, Eliahu–Hershl, also was among the mobilized soldiers and survived thanks to this and came to Israel.

Next door lived his brother Zelig Niewodowski who was one of the leading and most popular people in the city. He was active in all Zionist and general municipal matters. Zelig was beloved and respected by the Goniadz population. He always stood as the first representative in the city hall, *kehile*, and bank and in the Zionist institutions. Zelig fought for the Zionist idea for his entire life and tirelessly devoted himself to Zionist work. He led election campaigns to the Polish *Sejm* [lower house of parliament], the city council and kehile. He appeared at every Zionist gathering and election meeting and clarified Zionist ideas and interests in a logical manner, with much persuasive power in juicy Yiddish.

The Zionist ideas were interesting.

[Page 225]

Zelig always was engulfed in daily communal work: providing the Hebrew school with teachers, with monetary means, with its own building. He stood at the head of all money collections for *Keren Hayesod* and *Keren Kayemet*, welcomed all of the Zionist emissaries and also had time to intercede for Jews with the police commissar or village elder. In a word: everything connected to Zionist work in the *shtetl*, as well as what was important or simply, day–to–day, went through Zelig's hands.

However, fate willed that he, who personified everything connected with the idea of *Eretz–Yisroel*, would perish there [in Goniadz] tragically with his family and not live to come to the country [Israel], for which he sacrificed so much

After him lived Asher Szirates. He was educated in the Hebrew school and graduated from the first course. Then he was one of the most capable teachers

Market Street

[Page 226]

in the same school. He was drawn to the theater. He directed all of the children's performances in the school and also took part himself, showing much talent. He, who lived with the thought of *Eretz–Yisroel*, did not succeed in emigrating to *Eretz– Yisroel* for various reasons. During the last years, he married Shifra Ribak and had a child. He perished there [in Goniadz] with his family.

As a neighbor – the family of Ahron Grinberg, who sold his business and came here [to Israel]. His two daughters are here, Dina in Jerusalem and Ester in Haifa.

Near them – Ruwin the furrier. His daughter Yehudis and her family live in Israel.

In the same row of houses – Leibl Mankowski and his family. He was the most dedicated leader of the Bund.

[Page 227]

The Bund played a respected role in the Jewish life of the *shtetl* at that time. A large proportion of the working population belonged to the Bund.

After long–lasting difficulties, Leibl succeeded in opening the Jewish school and he supported it with great effort.

Leibl was an honest party man for whom the truth stood higher than the party. Who could have predicted at that time that Leibl, the dedicated member of the Bund, who as such, fought Zionism and everything connected with *Eretz–Yisroel*, would have sons who were such fervid Zionists... His youngest son Yankl was an active Zionist worker and his older son Ruwin was a police officer in the Jewish Zionist land [Israel] that was so strongly opposed by his father...

Yes, fate possesses a great deal of humor at times!...

***

The above–mentioned survey returned us to our former, old home for a while. A number of families close to us and far, whose children and family are now in Israel, passed before our eyes.

Understand that this survey does not pretend to gave an exact description of all of those mentioned, almost all of whom [deserve] a chapter for themselves.

[Page 228]

All who find themselves here in [Israel] come from families that perished; they are among those who found their way to Israel and in the course of time became rooted in the local way of life, for and in the new Jewish nation.

The Goniadz *landsleit* here [in Israel] are united by a common past in the old hometown. They are bound to the source of the former dear *shtetl*, from which we inherited our good Jewish traits from our parents who were personified by the best characteristics of good folksiness, reciprocal aid, enthusiasm, goodness, honesty and simplicity.

***

The last greeting from the two Goniadzers, Chana, Yankl Rudski's daughter and Elya Gamzon, who visited the ruined *shtetl* in 1955 is a very sad one.

They say that only some individual houses remain whole and gentiles who were partners in the annihilation live in them.

The streets were empty, not one living Jewish soul, the synagogue was a ruin, no trace of the house of prayer or of the school. Everything disappeared in smoke, erased and wiped away. Even the cemetery was plowed up and without a fence. Only seven headstones were located there, broken and erased. They could only read with difficulty the inscription on one headstone: here lies Yakov Rudski, Zionist heart and soul.

Seven broken headstones remain of an entire Jewish congregation that lived in the *shtetl* for hundreds of years, that boiled over with life and creativity, full of belief and hopes for a better tomorrow.

[Page 229]

The only inscription on one of the remaining headstones is a silent witness of the truth of the correctness of the road that always led a significant number from the city to *Eretz–Yisroel*. The only road that also remained for the last two refugees who stood on the ruins of our hometown that once existed, lived, fermented – and disappeared forever...

[Page 230]

Memorial Service Evening that took place in Tel Aviv

[Page 231]

Goniadzer Aid Activity in America
Meirim Rubin, New York
Translated by Gloria Berkenstat Freund

The charitable activities of the Goniadzer in America began approximately 50 years ago. As Avraham Warshah of Detroit reports, in 1908 the Goniadzer in America collected the sum of 600 dollars and sent this to Goniadz in order to found a loan and savings fund. They sent the money to the rabbi and according to the Russian rate of exchange it amounted to 1,200 rubles. The rabbi and the business owners chose Pinkhas, the rabbi's son, as treasurer and director.

Many remember how Goniadzer Jews would go to borrow money without interest. The bankl [small bank], that is what we called it, existed until the First World War.

The old Goniadzer in America also cared for their landsleit [people from the same town] in Goniadz. Immediately after the First World War, when no bank or post office accepted any money for Poland, the Goniadzer and Trestiner Young Men's Society sent out a special delegate, Doctor Blum, to personally bring the money for the poor and for relatives. When normal times returned and the Polish currency stabilized, the first Goniadzer emigrants, Benyamin the soyfer [scribe] and his children, came here.

[Page 232]

Benyamin went to the old Goniadzer who were members of the Goniadzer synagogue on Ridge Street in New York to ask that they tax themselves for the poor people in Goniadz for matzo for Passover. Meanwhile, they asked him to lay out his own hundred dollars. The hundred was not returned... But the young Goniadzer who joined the Goniadzer and Trestiner Young Men's Society gave their 200 dollars so that it became a tradition with the young Goniadzer of the Young Men's Society on every eve of Passover to send three hundred dollars for Goniadz and three hundred dollars for Trestina [Trzcianne]. The tradition continues today; they give this sum to the Goniadzer Aid Committee and also to the Trestiner Aid Committee every year.

[Pages 233-234]

Dr. Simon Blum in Goniadz

First row from the right: Zeidl Fidronski, Mishkovski, (son-in-law of Chaim Kopelman), Yehezkiel Perets Tshedniak, Miltshon, Leizer Sodorovitsh.

Second row: Moshe Furman, Zelig Nievadovski, Volf Piekodski, Dr. Blum, Chaim Kopelman, Efriam Halperin, Jakov Rubin, Beilach, Avraham Gelbard, Ezrial Hauptman.

Third row: Treshtshanski, Josl Oltanicki, Leyzer Trachimovski, Jakov Yevreyski, Chana (?).

Fourth row: Yehoshaya Tsviklic, Eli-Hirsh Niyevodovski

[Page 233]

In 1927 the Goniadzer Ladies Auxiliary in New York, with the help of the Goniadzer and Trestiner Society, decided to build a school with instruction in Hebrew and Yiddish on the synagogue hill and the building was completed over several years. They also supported the school, paying tuition monies to the teachers, clothing and lunches without cost for the poor children.

The school existed until the Nazi destruction.

[Page 234]

A group of 15 young people was arrested in Goniadz in 1938 because they had the courage to strke back the Gentiles who incited and beat the Goniadzer Jews.

The Polish police did not arrest the Gentiles and arrested the Jews and sent them to the Bialystok jail. The arrestees' parents turned to us in New York; we should collect money for a good lawyer (advocate), in order to free their children.

The Goniadzer and Trestiner Society contributed 25 dollars and a sum of 150 dollars was assembled and sent by telegraph.

[Page 235]

Benyamin the scribe, may he rest in peace, excelled in the aid work, which was his own initiative. In addition to money he also collected used clothing and shoes, made packages and sent them to poor people and poor brides.

From 1920 to 1939 he alone sent 1,400 dollars and 150 packages of clothing.

On *erev* [eve of] Rosh Hashanah, Benyamin would go to the Goniadzer *beis-olem* (cemetery) to recite the *El Male Rakhamim* [God full of compassion – prayer for the deceased]. He also would go to weddings to collect money and he would send this money to the Goniadzer poor.

Once, when we, all of his daughters and sons-in-law, were at a wedding and sat at one table, he stood up and went to collect donations from the Goniadzer *landsleit*.

His devoted wife also worked with him fully in making the packages.

I commented to him that it wasn't nice to ask for donations at a wedding. He answered: "You need to understand, I collected 35 dollars. Seven poor families will have income for a week from the 35 dollars. Are they worth less than my honor?"

In 1946 when the Goniadzers in New York learned about the Jewish destruction, the idea arose to create an aid committee on a great scale that would not only consist of the Goniadzers who belonged to the Young Men's Society, but also the Goniadzer Ladies Auxilary in New York and also all Goniadzers who did not belong to the Society, as well as those from all cities in America, New York, Chicago, Detroit, Los Angeles, Montreal and so on.

אַ נאָטיץ דערשינען אין ניו־יאָרקער
„פֿאָרווערטס" אין סעפּטעמבּער
1938, צוגעשיקט פֿון דוד פֿאָרמאַן.

אין גאָניאָנדז מאַכן אַנטיסעמיטן אַ בלבּול
אויף אַ איד, אַז ער האָט באַלײדיקט פּילסודס־
קי'ס נאָמען, און עס קומט צו אָנפֿאַלן אויף
אידן.

צו דער „היינטיקער נייעס" שרייבּט מען פֿון
גאָניאָנדז:

בּיי אונדז אין שטאָט האָבּן אַנטיסעמיטן גע־
מאַכט אַ בּלבּול אויף דעם אידיש איינוווינער
קאָסליאַר, אַז ער האָט באַלײדיקט דעם נאָמען
פֿון פּילסודסקי'ן. די אַנטיסעמיטן האָבּן קאָסליאַרן
פֿאַרוווּנדעט דעם קאָפּ. דער לערער פֿון דער
העברעאישער שול, אַשר סיראַטעס, צוזאַמען מיט
אַנדערע אידן האָבּן זיך אָנגענומען פֿאַרן באַפֿאַ־
לענעם אידן. עס איז געקומען צו אַ געשלעג, אין
וועלכן עס זיינען פֿאַרוווּנדעט געוואָרן בּיידע
צדדים. די פּאָליציי האָט אַרעסטירט פֿאָלגנדע אידן:
אַשר סיראַטעס, מאַקס יאַנאָצקי, לײבּ ריבּאַק,
נחום שעווויץ, גדליה גראָדזיענסקי, משה גראָד־
זיענסקי, פּסח פֿישער, יאַנקל ריבּאַק, מאיר
טרעששטשאָסקי און בּעריש ראָזענטאַל.
די אַרעסטירטע זיינען געבּראַכט געוואָרן קיין
ביאַליסטאָק צום אויספֿאָרשונגס ריכטער.

**A notice published in New York *Forvets* [Yiddish language newspaper]
in September 1938, sent by Dovid Forman**

The anti-Semites in Goniadz are accusing a Jew of a blood libel, that he insulted Pilsudski's name and attacks are being made on Jews.

To the *Today's News*, is written from Goniadz:

Anti-Semites in our city issued a blood libel on the Jewish resident Kosliar, that he insulted the name of Pilsudski. The anti-Semites wounded Kosliar in the head. Asher Sirames, the Hebrew school teacher, along with other Jews, defended the attacked Jew. A fight ensued in which there were wounded on both sides. The police arrested the following Jews: Asher Sirames, Gedelia Grodzienski, Pesakh Fiszer, Yankl Ribak, Meir Treszczoski and Berish Rozental.

The arrestees were brought to Bialystok to the Investigating Court.

Benyamin the scribe gave us the addresses of many Goniadzers in America, Canada and South Africa.

At that time we did not know anything about who among the Goniadzers had survived.

Moshe Malazowski received the only message from his neighbor's son who was in the American army in Germany. He met a sick man in a camp who asked about Mosheke Malazowski from Goniadz. This was Zeydka (the son of Notka the farmer) Altshuler. Moshe immediately wrote a letter to him and immediately received an answer. He asked us to find his relatives who were here in New York.

[Pages 237-238]

We learned from Benyamin the scribe that Notka the farmer came from Lomza. We found the address of Zeydka's relatives from the Lomza Society. We went to them immediately and told them the news that their relative had survived. But they received us very coldly; we realized that we could not rely on them and we immediately sent a food package to Germany.

Meanwhile, Zeydka found other Goniadzer who had survived and we immediately sent food packages to them.

The committee decided to hold a memorial evening in the Bialystoker Center in November 1946 that was announced in the newspapers. Two Goniadzer refugees (Hershl Beker – married in Goniadz and the second one, a Sztucziner, a relative of the Szilewskis) unexpectedly came to the memorial evening.

When they described to us what had happened to our dear parents, relatives and friends, there was not one person who did not shed tears.

One thousand eight hundred dollars was donated at the memorial evening.

At that time we learned of another 10 Goniadzer refugees who were in German camps.

[Page 240]

After the evening our committee was enlarged. Josef (Mendele's son) Bobrowski, may he rest in peace, our dear, beloved Goniadzer, of Norfolk, Connecticut, joined and became vice chairman. In a short time we had the addresses of 20 refugees.

We appreciate all of the devoted, noble work of Moshe Bachrach for writing letters of comfort to all of the Goniadzer refugees and his sincere wife, Chaya, for preparing clothing and food packages. The writer of these lines helped them greatly in buying, packing and sending the packages from the first day after the founding of the committee. We would go through the stores with a child's wagon, buying food and clothing, make packages and send them by mail to Germany.

Hilke Grodzenski,
Vice Chairman

Sura Seid,
Chairwoman

Meirim Rubin,
Executive Secretary

David Forman,
Member

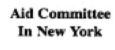

**Aid Committee
In New York**

Moshe Malazewski,
Vice Chairman

Louis Goldberg,
Accountant

Helen Atlas,
Bookkeeper

In 1947 Goniadzer refugees from Soviet Russia arrived. We also adopted Goniadzer "grandchildren."

We once called a meeting at Louis Goldberg's office. Gedelia Seid, Josef Mendels [This probably is referring to Josef, the son of Mendel, as in "Josef (Mendele's son")] , Moshe Bachrach and the writer of these lines came to the meeting.

Moshe declared that we had no money in the fund for packages, which we would send every three weeks for 300 dollars. Josef said to Gedelia: "You write a check for 150 dollars and I will do the same thing." It should be mentioned that Josef and Gedelia had earlier donated 200 dollars at the memorial evening.

At that time we would assemble about 4,000 dollars a year from the Goniadzer *landsleit*. We would immediately distribute it among the refugees.

In time the Goniadzer Aid Committees were created in Detroit – Avraham Warshah, chairman, Max Szwarc, may he rest in peace, secretary, Elihu Gradman, treasurer; Chicago – Moshe Gelbord (Dokler), chairman, Golda Hoyrst-Rubin, secretary, Moshe Tikocki (son of Josl Szmeker), treaurer; Los Angeles – Meir Farber, (Shlomo Moshe Shmeun's son), chairman, Mrs. Raye Salomon (Yenta Ruchl's daughter), secretary, Morris Forman (Moshe'ke Nekhema's son), treasurer; Montreal – Max Bayer, chairman and treasurer, Mrs. Ruchl Bayer (Leyzer's wife) and Mrs. Finczun, treasurers.

When Moshe arrived in Los Angeles, the committee unanimously elected the writer of these lines as secretary.

During Moshe's departure in February 1949, the sum of 10,000 dollars was collected. Up to now we have collected the sum of 30,000 dollars.

In time all of our refugees left Germany. Several of them came to America, others to Australia. The majority of them settled in the Land of Israel.

The refugees who made *aliyah* [immigrated] to Israel still needed our support.

In the course of 10 years of the existence of our aid committee, we gave support at the time and in the place, first in Germany, Austria and now in Israel.

The aid committee in the Land of Israel is led by our friends Dovid Bachman, Fishel Yitzhaki, Chatskl Perets Czerniak and Sura Rajgradski-Brkai. Our support for the *landsleit* in Israel is always sent according to their recommendations.

When Mr. and Mrs. Gedelia Seid visited Israel in 1950, the Goniadzer in Israel arranged a meeting for them. A loan fund was founded then with the purpose of helping our Goniadzer in Israel.

[Pages 241-242]

Goniadzer Aid Committee in Detroit

Sitting, from the right: 1. Avraham Warshah (son of Yona'khe), chairman; 2. Mrs. Sadie Winer, chairwoman; 3. Hyman Winer (son of Chona Benyamin), member.

Standing: 1. Abe Szwarc (son of Avraham'l Alter), member; 2. Eli Grodman (son of Elya Khaske), treasurer

Goniadzer Aid Committee in Chicago

Standing (from right to left): 1. Leo Majnkes, vice chairman; 2. Morris Gelbord (Moshe'ke Dokler), chairman; 3. Morris Tokor, treasurer.
Sitting: 1. Nemy Monarkh, (daughter of Chaim Welwl, the dyer), member; 2. Perl Rapoport,

recording secretary; 3. Golda Rubin-Hoyrst , secretary

[Pagse 243-244]

The fund exists with success until today.

At the same time each year we send certain sums of money from America especially for the loan fund. At the same time the Goniadzer in Israel asked that we in America create a yizkor [memorial] book in memory of our *shtetl*. Their plan for this book pleased us. Mr. and Mrs. Gedelia Seid and Josef Bobrowski promised their help and cooperation.

To our great sadness, Josef Bobrowski and Gedelia Seid were prematurely torn from us. I did not give up our plan to create the book and with the help of our chairwoman, Mrs. Sarah Seid, who provided me great effort as well as contributions over the course of four years, we succeeded in collecting the necessary sums for the yizkor book.

Our committee still has a great responsibility after the publication of our book. We will try every means to distribute it among all Goniadzer on the American continent, as well as among Jewish libraries, so that our dear home city will be immortalized in Jewish history.

Goniadzer Aid Committee in Los Angeles

[Page 245]

Goniadzer Ladies Auxiliary
by Mrs. Kamenietz, New York
Translated by Gloria Berkenstat Freund

The Goniadzer Ladies Auxiliary in New York was founded 35 years ago. I had the honor to be the founder. Myself, not from Goniadz, but as the wife of Moshe Meir *ben* [son of] the Rabbi, Gedalia Kamenietz, may he rest in peace, I immediately felt like a member of the large Goniadz family in America.

My husband, Moshe Meir, may he rest in peace, who came to America in 1901 was one of the first presidents of the Goniadzer Society and was very active as a speaker and writer and I decided to help him in his communal activities.

Only 13 women came to the first meeting, in the Goniadzer premises on Second Avenue, of whom I remember Mrs. Atlas, Szwarc, Lewin, Szapiro, Gradzenski and Ruder.

Goniadzer Ladies Auxiliary of New York

Standing from right to left: Mrs. Ni[illegible letter]an, Mrs. F. Rubin, Mrs F. Frydman, Mrs. Ruder, Mrs. B. Lichtensztajn, Mrs. M. Samuels, Mrs. R. Paperow.

Sitting: Mrs. B. Goldberg, Mrs. Sztroser, Mrs. Lewin (treasurer), Mrs, Kamenietz (executive president), Mrs. L. Kaplan, secretary, Mrs. B. Szwarc, Mrs. Atlas.

[Page 246]

The members paid one dollar a quarter. Our first activities had the character of communal recreation. We would often come together in order to quietly spend time together and create friendly connections. In time we began to think about how to help the Goniadzer needy who lived in America. Then we founded a loan fund that would lend smaller and larger sums without interest. Times got better and our members did not need our help anymore, so we decided to provide help to the needy in Goniadz. We established relations with one of our *landsman* [person from the same town], who traveled on a visit to Goniadz, asking that he find out the best ways in which we could help our dear *shtetl* [town]. Our *landsman* returned with a detailed report and clarified for us that the most important thing needed in Goniadz was its own building for the Hebrew and Yiddish school where the children would have a play area and opportunities for sports as well as the various classes. We went to work with great enthusiasm.

[Page 247]

We then received many new members, among them the energetic and good-hearted Mrs. Seid, the wife of Mr. Gedalia Seid, of blessed memory. Mrs. Seid has remained to this day the honorary chairwoman of the Ladies Auxiliary and she shows the greatest interest in our work from her new home in Florida.

The Ladies Auxiliary produced a journal with the name *Goniadzer Shul-Barg* [*Goniadz Synagogue Hill*] for a time, in which were published articles, letters, notes and announcements in connection with all the activities of our society. The journal was edited by Dr. M. M. Kameniecki and M. Malozowski.

We collected the sum of 2,000 dollars for the school. And our joy was great when we received a detailed description in September 1933 of the laying of the foundation for the new school on the synagogue hill.

I find it necessary to provide an excerpt from that description, which we published in the *Goniadzer Shul-Barg*.

"This day, Goniadzer Jews experienced the most beautiful and most glorious moments of their lives! An evening earlier, on *Shabbos* in the evening, all of the young people from the *shtetl* along with all of the school children marched out to the sounds of music with a torch procession through all of the streets, and all of Goniadz, big and small, took part in the march - many cried with joy that they were worthy to live to see this great holiday. 'This is how Jews build their own school for their children!'"

[Page 248]

"Early in the morning, representatives of the Bialystok and Warsaw Jewish cultural institutions arrived with the orchestra from the Bialystok Hebrew *Gymnazie* [secondary school]. - - - The procession with the orchestra in the lead arrived on the synagogue hill where the massively constructed foundation quietly and modestly welcomed us all. At the side a platform had been erected, decorated with plants, on which all of the members of the building committee sat with the guests. Mr. Zelig Niewodowski, the chairman, opened the holiday with sincere words, sending heartfelt blessings to the dear brothers and sisters in New York. The crowd gave a stormy ovation in honor of the Goniadzer Women's Committee in New York."

"On the spot, a pledging of money was proclaimed. Whoever did not see the way in which the poor, sick Jews were led by their arms to take part in the holiday and to sacrifice with their pledge has never seen true self sacrifice!... The noble Jewish spirit then floated over everything and everyone and this was our truly greatest people's holiday in Goniadz."

This is only a small excerpt from the long letter that was written in Hebrew and translated into Yiddish for the *Goniadzer Shul-Barg*. For a long time, this letter served as a source of inspiration for our further activities, such as money collections for our refugees who had been saved from the Nazi hell, for packages and finally, also for the Goniadzer Yizkor book [memorial book].

[Pages 249-250]

Mrs. M. Grodzenski,
vice president

Mrs. Kh. Bachrach,
member

Mrs. G. Frydman,
treasurer

Mrs. M. Walkow,
member

Mrs. Lewin,
member

Mrs. K. Atlas,
member

[Pages 251-256]

Aid Work in Israel
by Dovid Bachrach - Petah Tikva - Tel Aviv
Translated by Gloria Berkenstat Freund

It began in March 1947 when my brother, Moshe Bachrach, sent me a small sum of money to be divided among the old people and needy in our town and he even noted to whom it should be given. There were then three successful Goniadzer young men in the country who had come here [Palestine at the time] with the Polish Army from Russia, through Persia and had gone no further. However, they had not yet settled and needed more than a little aid. Our refugees also appeared with the flood of refugees and, then, the rise of our state. The first ones came in the middle of the night, right from the ship, with ocean water in their shoes. Their arrival in the country was illegal and it was necessary to do it quickly and under all kinds of circumstances. In May 1948 when the gates to the country were opened, the refugees first went to a *ma'abara* (transit camps) [refugee absorption camps] and in a short time they were spread across the entire land: Hadera, Ra'anana, Ness Ziona and Rehovot. I could not carry on the work alone; it was proposed to me from New York that we should create a *vaad* [council] (committee) of the following people: Khatskl-Perec Czerniak and I - from the old generation; Fishl Yitzhaki (son of the blond Itshe) and Chaya-Sura Rajgrodski - from the younger generation. Thus was created the *vaad* that exists to this day.

The work divides into two periods: before the Seids' visit to the country and after. Until the Seids' visit, the money was used for direct support; first for the most necessary things and then for [obtaining] a room, which was a very difficult matter at that time of great immigration. We visited our refugees in the transit camps many times in order to persuade them of what they needed to do and how to get out of there more quickly. This usually was done after a day of work and in the hot summer days in Israel that was not an easy thing. However, we did it willingly. We met the great expenses and the smaller ones together. When we dealt with a large sum we would first contact New York and receive a confirmation. We did not neglect any refugees. We also did not lose sight of the two little sisters, daughters of Kalman Treszczanski, Idl's brother, who lived in Belgium. The twins were born shortly before the war, but the mother died in childbirth. Kalman gave them to a Christian woman to be raised. When the war broke out, he gave the Christian woman a large sum of money. But when the money ran out they gave the children to a monastery. Kalman perished, but his two sons who had survived the war visited their sisters. They often took them out of the monastery for a stroll and once they did not bring them back and, with the help of the Jewish Brigade, they brought them to Holland and from there they came to Israel. Here, we clothed them from head to foot. They are in Israel.

[Pages 253 - 254]

The Committee in Tel Aviv

Dovid Bachrach

F. Tzerniak

Sura Rajgrodzki-Berkai

Fishl Yitzhaki

Until 1951 all had been settled and we thought that our mission had ended. However, then our unforgettable, dear *landsleit* [people from the same town], the Seids appeared with a new task, that we should create a *gmiles-khesed* [interest- free loan] fund and they brought cash for this purpose. According to their message, the idea came from our [*landsleit*] in Detroit.

Then a family of three souls came from China: a father, mother and daughter. We did everything that was possible to make it easier for them and to remove them from the transit camp. We even succeeded in getting housing for them (their own apartment) in Kiryat Bialystok and it was not an easy thing to do. We simply appealed to Mr. Ralph Wein of New York. We received money for the first payment from relatives of this family in Atlanta and in Israel. The committee also was ready to tax itself. However, this caused us effort and heartache.

[Page 255]

Alas, this was not crowned with success because they decided to immigrate to Brazil at the last moment. They did not go but we had given the house to another family. The money that we had received from their family they used for themselves. In April 1958 we lent them a larger sum of money for housing.

We received housing (our own apartment) in Kiryat Bialystok for a Goniadz grandchild, a daughter of Chaya-Witse's son Hershl, brother of Moshe-Feywl the shoemaker. The house simply saved her family. We loaned the first payment to them. They repaid us.

Several words about Sonia Gelbart, our "guerrilla fighter. " Her father was named Leibl and he was brought up by his aunt, Chaya-Ruchl Luria. His mother, Chanatsha, and Chaya-Ruchl were sisters; [they were] born in Goniadz, [and their maiden] name was Maranc. In the beginning of the century (20th), his mother emigrated to America with two sons, and she left two more sons, Leibl and Meir, with her sister. Leibl married in the Vilna area. During the war, he and his nine- year old daughter, Sonia, left for the woods and survived the war. His wife and a small son perished. When she [Sonia] arrived in the country we interceded and placed her in the Shfeya children's colony paid for by the [Jewish] Agency. When she graduated from the *Folks-Shul* [public school], we requested that she go to her father. However, she asked for help to continue her studies at a seminar. Just then, the Seids arrived. Mrs. Sura [Seid] took upon herself the obligation and the American *landsleit* carried this out in the best manner. We have no words to express our gratitude. She graduated from the teacher seminar and is now independent. Immediately after finishing the degree program she married a young man from one of the nicest families in Israel. He husband graduated as an engineer and she works as a teacher.

[Page 256]

In short, this is the sum of our work here. I will also mention that we had our own money collections when it was necessary.

We received the following sums:

From March 1947 to August 1951 - 1,159 *Eretz-Yisroel* pounds. From August 1951, Mr. and Mrs. Seid's visit, until 31 December 1957 - 5,640 pounds. Three year seminar, tuition and dormitory [costs] for Sonia Gelbart and a one-time support for an apartment, sent from New York for a family that came from Russian-Poland, with an expense of 2,085 pounds. 3,555 pounds remained for the *gmiles-khesed*. Nearly 25 people borrowed, some twice and several three times. We can count up to 50 loans. At the beginning the loans were up to 150 pounds; now the loans have to be larger if they are to have importance. Most times loans are for housing or a constructive purpose: such as a sewing machine, but also for necessary furniture. In general, there was not one case that we refused. The main condition is: [that there is] money in the fund.

In addition to this many food packages were sent from the New York committee directly to those in need in Israel.

I cannot end my short report without remembering our tireless friend, Meirim Rubin. Himself a heavy worker; he has been doing this work since 1948, cares for everything and everyone, with great dedication. We wish him and his wife, Benyamin's daughter Faygl, and all the dear *landsleit* in New York, Detroit, Chicago, South Bend, Los Angeles and wherever they are - a sincere thank you!

Part II

Images

[Pages 261-262]

Forward
by Moshe Bachrach
Translated by Gloria Berkenstat Freund

In his poem, *If Your Soul Knows*, Chaim Nachman Bialik called the *beis hamedrash* [synagogue or house of prayer] the creator of the nation's soul – the forge on which was formed the soul of the people. However a smithy is necessary to forge; nothing is forged by itself. So who in our *shtetlekh* [towns] were the "blacksmiths" who formed the soul of the people?

These were the individual Jews, men as well as women, who in the political, ethical and poetic sense had a daily effect on the life of the community and a direct influence on the path of life in the *shtetl* in general and on the sensitive individual in particular. Together, they all continually enriched, fertilized and made it easier. Those among us who were particularly perceptive and, especially those who had the luck to be under their influence, bless their memory.

The influence of these chosen few was quiet, but in sum total, very reciprocated in Goniadz.

[Pages 265-268]

My Father Rabbi Gedaliah Ha-Cohen Kamenietzki z"l
By Ze'ev Wolf Kamenietzki Haifa, Israel
Translated from Yiddish to English by Dr. Isaac Fine

My father, may his memory be for a blessing, was born in Semyatich, a city in the environs of Brisk. His grandfather had been in a very successful business in association with his brother, who later became the rabbi of Bielsk. They transported salt in ships from the Carpathian Mountains through Galicia to the port of Danzig. When my father was three years of age, his grandfather traveled with a transport ship in the direction of Danzig. There was a great flood while traveling on the Vistula River, and all the ships with their salt cargoes went under. On that occasion they lost all of their wealth. My father's mother died from the severe stress which followed, and my father became a young orphan.

My father didn't study in yeshivas. His goal was to study with great and distinguished scholars. He traveled to Vilno, which was called the Jerusalem of Lithuania. Vilno had great rabbis and also renowned figures of the secular enlightenment. He spent a number of years there. When he returned home they began to refer to him as a "Berliner" and a "free one". Soon afterwards he married my mother and subsequently accepted a position as dayan in Sokolke. He stayed there several years, and then became rabbi in Vishnieve, a shtetl not far from Voloshin.

Vishnieve was encircled by forests. My mother was frightened, seeing the wild animals in the nearby woods from a distance. She became so anxious that she was unable to leave the house. She traveled to Vilno for medical consultations, and the physicians advised her to spend some time in Frantzenbad, as a curative experience. Returning back home she stayed with her parents in Suchovole, and from there wrote my father, informing him that the physicians ordered her not to live any longer in Vishnieve. Soon afterwards, Father left that town to join my mother in Suchovole. After arriving in Suchovole, he discovered that the Goniondz rabbi had recently left Goniondz after a great dispute with the Chassidim. Father traveled to Goniondz at that point, and then was accepted there as the new rabbi.

He spent the rest of his life in Goniondz. For five years, he suffered through another great dispute in town. After the dispute ended, however, everyone considered him a good friend. In character, he was a rare, good man. My mother didn't let him handle money because he would give it away to the first guest who came to him. He would send every guest who came to him in the House of Study to the shtetl restaurant, and he would arrange to pay for that person's bill quietly with the restaurant owner so the person would have a good meal. He never argued with a person who disagreed with him. He would simply convey to him, quietly and peacefully, his intention. He would sit in the House of Study until one in the afternoon. When he saw a worker arriving in the House of Study, he would approach the man and inquire regarding his domestic affairs and also his work. Grandfather would walk with him around the House of Study, chatting with that person as one might with an important businessman. My grandfather was criticized for "lowering himself" too much by such behavior. His memory was quite extraordinary, and his mind was sharp and clear. I believe I do not exaggerate in stating that he knew the Babylonian Talmud by memory. He also was familiar with the old philosophical books. There were no cases in which protests were registered against his rabbinical judgments.

He was loved by all the inhabitants of the shtetl, including the Christians. When he was occasionally traveling outside of town, Christian passersby would fall on their knees before him. When a Christian had a dispute with a Jew, he preferred to go to the rabbi for settlement of the case rather than to the secular court. When a wealthy Christian saw that my father was going to the river to bathe, he would accompany him, and wait for him at the river edge until he was finished.

I recall an anecdote concerning a Christian who came to the rabbi complaining that a baker had been required to pay him five rubles and sixty kopecks in exchange for grain. The baker had paid him the sixty kopecks, but didn't give him the five rubles. At the time of the transaction, the baker had told him that he had forgotten to bring the rubles. Later on, when he came to the baker to collect, the baker did not want to pay. My father immediately called in the baker and asked him, "What is the situation with the five rubles that this man says you didn't pay him?" The baker didn't answer. My father told him that he should pay the Christian the five rubles. The baker immediately took out five rubles and paid the Christian. After he had paid, the baker said, "God has sent me a reward, the rabbi has become my partner." My father smiled broadly and remained silent.

My father was seventy-three years of age when he died, on the fourteenth day of the month of Sivan, 1907, on a Friday at sundown.

[Pages 269-270]

The Rabbi Mordekhai Yaffa z"l
(*Dayan* [religious judge])
by Avraham Yaffa, Tel Aviv
Translated by Gloria Berkenstat Freund

My father, may his memory be blessed, came from many generations of rabbis, from which the first was the famous *gaon* [sage], Reb Mordekhai Yaffa, known by the name "the *Levush*"(a shortening of the title of the book *Levush Malkhut* [*Robes of Royalty*] which he authored). He [my father] was born in Kobrin, Grodner *gubernia* [province] to my grandfather, the Kobriner Rabbi, Reb Yakov Yaffa. At the age of 15 my father married my mother, the God-fearing esteemed Bluma, may she rest in peace. As was the custom at the time, my father was *oyf kest* [support from in-laws while studying] for several years, studying in the *Beis-Medrash* [house of study or prayer] for several years. My mother of blessed memory was a woman of valor and helped carry the burden of earning a living. She had thirteen children, of which only six survived. I remember how my mother, my she rest in peace, in addition to the *Shabbos* candles on the table, would light seven more small candles that she would place in potato "candlesticks" at the edge of the chimney. At the blessing of the candles, her tears would flow for the life and health of the living children and also for the souls of those whose lives were cut off before their time.

After *kest*, my father moved to Kovno for several years to study and receive ordination from the Kovner Rabbi, the Rabbi, the *gaon* [genius] Rebbe Yitzhak Elchanan, of blessed memory. An interesting episode is told about my father's life in Kovno: once, on a hot summer day, sitting with a *gemara* [Talmud] for many hours in the *Beis-Medrash*, Reb Elchanan suggested that the young zealots go outside and get a little fresh air. They sat under a tree resting and the tired *yeshiva* man fell asleep. When he opened his eyes he saw how Reb Yitzhak was driving away the flies with his handkerchief. One can imagine what he felt seeing the fatherly love of the giant of his generation.

[Page 270]

Receiving his ordination as a rabbi, he was hired as a *dayan* [religious judge] in Goniadz. This was his first rabbinical position and his last. My father, may he rest in peace, was a refined scholar, quiet and modest and a great peacemaker. He always tried to calm things with good and clever words and when a couple came to him for a *get* [religious divorce]. His tall figure, his pale face with the beautiful beard and rabbinical frock coat, strolling across the room with an open book in his hand remains in my memory from my childhood.

He died very young at the age of 36 of pneumonia, on the 19th of *Tishrei* (*Khol HaMoed Sukkous* [intervening days of the Feast of Tabernacles]) 5651 [3 October 1890], when I was still a young child. I was later told that one of the cheerfully argumentative, embittered Hasidim in Goniadz, a scholar, who was a vindictive person, threatened to pour a dipper of cold water on him on *erev* [eve of] Yom Kippur at the steam bath. In order to avoid the grave disgrace and the quarrels, he [my father] went away to the river for the ritual immersion for purification – and the *erev* Yom Kippur immersion led him to the grave.

Thus a noble scholar was annihilated before his time by a sorrowful joke by a fanatic. May his soul be bound in the bond of life.

[Pages 271-276]

The Rabbi Tzvi Wolf z"l
by Josef Hertzig, Tel Aviv
Translated by Gloria Berkenstat Freund

Rabbi Tzvi Wolf   **The *Rebbitzen* Blume Wolf**

The Kovnicer Rabbi, Reb Tzvi Wolf, was chosen to occupy the rabbinical chair in Goniadz in 1907 after the death of the old rabbi, Reb Gedalia *Hakhohan*, may he rest in peace. The Rabbi Wolf was a lively, active personality. The middle class in Goniadz understood that it was not enough that the rabbi be a scholar; he had to know how to administer the *kehile* [religious community] and, in addition, to represent it vis-à-vis the state organs. These two traits were possessed by the Rabbi Wolf: he was a great scholar, an exceptional speaker and representative figure. His wife Blume was a true woman of valor and a helpmate to whom all related with respect.

Both the rabbi and the *rebbitzen* [rabbi's wife] threw themselves with life and soul into the activities of charity with good Jewish hearts. There was no lack of needy people in Goniadz who always struggled for their livelihood. The new rabbi's home became a communal Jewish center where one would come not only with a religious question or a *Din-Torah* [case brought to a religious court], but also for good advice in family and business matters. Before the loan office was created, the rabbi's house took care of many of the needs with interest-free loans. Not a rich man himself, the rabbi would borrow from others and give loans. The borrowers were usually not punctual in repaying the loans. The rabbi had to take a second and a third loan. All members of the family helped and, particularly, the *rebbitzen*. The *rebbitzen* also knew well who was in need of immediate help, a sick poor man needed a piece of meat, a baby a little soup or milk, or only a little jam for a delight. And if a needy woman lay in childbirth, linens or sheets were taken out of the cabinet and sent as a secret gift.

[Page 272-273]

In general, the rabbi's home was open for everyone "who is hungry" – whoever entered hungry left satiated. Visitors, who always had enjoyment from the homey and friendly attitude, often sat at the table.

Rabbi Wolf sensed that which he had traced in his first sermon at his welcome in the synagogue that was as overflowing as at *Kol Nidre* [prayer opening the evening service] on Yom Kippur:

"A rabbi in a city must be a *city clock*; *placed high* and *in the middle of the city. Placed high*, in order that no one can steer him as he wishes... And in the *middle* of the city in order that all can see him and be guided by him at all times..."

Rabbi Wolf did not treat the political powers in the city with partiality, but he was always on the side of the just and the weak and therefore he had opponents with whom he carried on a struggle.

He was well known as a good arbitrator and they turned to him from other cities with the most complicated disputes and religious court cases. He possessed a sharp mind and a phenomenal memory. He did not have to turn pages in a religious book to find the necessary law or answer to a religious question; but he knew exactly where and how to handle the matter. He did not need to take notes about the arguments of both sides at a religious trial because he remembered all of the details exactly. In addition, the "school of life" which he had gone through before assuming the rabbinical seat helped him; he was a merchant and a textile manufacturer in Bialystok for a time. His system was – to let the person who brought the case speak and argue as much as his heart wished without interruption, and then pose questions to the point.

Rabbi Wolf was an exceptional speaker. He directed the Khevre Mishnayus [Mishnah – compilation of early Torah commentary – Society], Khevrve Shulkhan Orech [Shulkhan Orech – code of Jewish law – Society] and for a time also the Khevre Shas [Talmud Society], in which Yakov Rudski had the privilege of leader. The Khevre Mishnayus was actually democratic and consisted of a large number of old and young Jews from various strata – businessmen, traders and artisans.

[Page 274]

There was no yeshiva [religious secondary school stressing Torah studies] in Goniadz, but Rabbi Wolf was interested in the0 young men from the yeshiva, who would study "away from home." The rabbi gave a lesson in Talmud several days a week for the capable young men who could not travel "away from home." (His students were: Zelig Niewadowski, Yehuda'l the son of the shoykhet [ritual slaughterer], Meirim Welwl Zodczak's son, Idl the watchmaker, Khuna Machai, Sender's son Avraham'l and so on). He exhibited a warm interest in the unfamiliar young men who would come to Goniadz to study ritual slaughter (Goniadz contractors would slaughter many cows for the Russian military in the Osowiec Fortress and there was no fear of a cow becoming unkosher. Therefore, Goniadz was a suitable place to practice ritual slaughtering.)

Before the outbreak of the First World War the rabbi would make an appearance to intervene with the Russian regime on behalf of Jewish soldiers or reservists who came to Osowiec for several weeks' exercises. Once, *Erev* [eve of] Rosh Hashanah, the rabbi delayed the praying until 11 o'clock at night, until the Warsaw reservists arrived from Osowiec. It was a group of several hundred Jews. They did not start praying until every reservist was taken care of in an inn and with meals for the two days of Rosh Hashanah.

At that time high ranking military men would come to the synagogue hill in connection with defense plans. The rabbi would come to greet them and receive the assurance that Russian soldiers would not disturb the calm in the city.

[Page 275]

When the war broke out, a group of staff officers with the War Minister [Vladimir] Suchomlinov at the head once came to the synagogue hill in the morning. Rabbi Wolf accompanied by Reb Benyamin the scribe came to the synagogue hill and opened the synagogue for them. When Suchomlinov observed, "It is dark and it is difficult to see the horizon" – Rabbi Wolf responded – "Therefore there will be light in all of Russia." And the War Minister offered him his hand with a thank you for his good wish (several years later, after the collapse of the Czarist regime, Reb Meir the watchmaker said that the rabbi's blessing had come true...)

At the expulsion of the Jewish population from the front lines in 1914, the rabbi and his family traveled to Bialystok, which was flooded with refugees from the surrounding *shtetlekh*. He occupied himself with work on behalf of the homeless and particularly with the poor people from the town – the Goniadzer.

Rabbi Wolf received a high office in the Bialystok rabbinate and could have lived esteemed in the large city, but an opportunity arose to return to Goniadz and he returned with others. Then a misfortune happened and his devoted wife died. She was brought for burial in the Goniadz cemetery. From that day, the rabbi's health became severely worse. He suffered from diabetes for a long time and during a visit to his brother in Bialystok he became very sick and died. He died on the 18 Sivan [20 June] 5684 (1924) at the age of 58 and was buried in Bialystok.

[Page 276]

Goniadz Jews mourned him deeply as their spiritual representative, the sage and worldly man. His handsome appearance, his neatness and purity, his energetic walk and worthy way of speaking remain unforgettable for everyone who knew him.

Blessed be his memory.

The Synagogue Hill

[Pages 277-280]

The Rabbi Yisroel Shlomowitz z"l
Translated by Gloria Berkenstat Freund

Our father, the Rabbi, Reb Yisroel Shlomowitz, of blessed memory, was born in 5641 [1881] in Yanow [Yanaveh], near Kovno. He was descended from the esteemed families of the *shtetl* [town]. While still in his young years, our father traveled to study in the world famous *yeshiva, Knesset Yisroel,* in Slobodka, where he was immediately recognized as one of the pillars of the *yeshiva.*

He excelled with varied expertise and intelligence so that he received the nickname, "the small *Ketzot haChoshen**". He also had a good reputation because of his good traits.

My father studied in the *yeshiva* until his wedding. Widely known as a giant of Torah and *musar* [Jewish ethical movement], he received rabbinical ordination from the Rabbi, the *Gaon* Reb Eli Borukh Kamay, Mirer Rabbi and head of the *yeshiva;* from the Rabbi, the *Gaon,* Reb Iser Zalman Melcer, Slucker Rabbi; from the outstanding rabbi of his generation, the Telcer Rabbi and head of the *yeshiva,* Reb Eliezer Gordon (Reb Leizer Telcer).

My father was married in 5669 [1908 or 1909]. Our mother was a daughter of the Horodok *shoykhet* [ritual slaughterer], Reb Eli Rapoport, a distinguished scholar in Torah and a God-fearing person. After the wedding, my father spent time in Horodok and studied with an extraordinary zeal, as in the *yeshiva,* for approximately 16-18 hours a day. He traveled to Grodno from Horodok to study.

Later our father, may the memory of a righteous man be blessed, occupied the rabbinical seat in Amstibowe. After a short time, he arrived in Meyshegole [Maišiagala], near Vilna.

[Page 278]

He would study a page of *Gemara* at the Ramailes *Yeshiva* and at the same time published the book, *Beit Yisroel* [*House of Israel*], part one (published in 5686 [1926]). The book quickly was accepted by all Torah sages and *yeshiva* members.

In 1924, following the advice of the leader of his generation, the *Gaon,* Reb Chaim Ozer Grodzinski, he chose Goniadz from several towns that had invited him.

There were many good merchants, scholars and esteemed Jews in Goniadz at that time among whom my father became beloved.

Rabbi Yisroel Shlomowitz

In Goniadz, my father immediately began to create and revive various institutions, such as the *gmiles khesed kase* [interest free loan found], *khevre kadishe* [burial society] and so on. My father also renewed the *linas hatzadek* [society that cared for the sick] that really blossomed and helped very many poor and sick families.

In general, my father would spend a great deal of time helping all of the needy.

[Page 279]

There was no one who needed something who was left without help. He often did not leave the *beis-hamedrash* until he had made arrangements for all of the visitors and poor.

I find it necessary to remember that in all needs of the *shtetl*, the dear, generous Reb Benyamin *Sofer* [scribe], of blessed memory helped a great deal. He did good things for everyone throughout his life. My father would work together with him, as well as with the "Ladies Auxilary" of the Goniadz *Landsleit* [people from the same city] in New York.

My father did much in the realm of religious-cultural life. He created and studied with many societies: Talmud Society, *Mishnius* [Oral Law] Society, *Mishneh Torah* [*Repetition of the Torah* by Maimonides, also known as Rambam] Society and *Chafetz-Chaim* [*Seeker of Life*]. He created his *khederim* [religious primary schools] and hired teachers from other cities because the school in Goniadz, according to his understanding, was too liberal.

[Page 280]

But our father always strove to create a *yeshiva* in Goniadz, which, alas, he did not live to see.

In 1938-1939 my father printed the book *Beis Yisroel*, part two which, alas, remained in the printing establishment and was not published because of the war and his manuscript, a work of several treatises, was lost.

At the beginning of the war, 1939, before the Nazis entered and everyone ran from the city, my entire family also left for Horodok. My father returned when the Russians entered, even though we were opposed to this, because he believed that one must not leave the *shtetl* neglected. We escaped to Vilna, which had been given to Lithuania and we wanted everyone to travel together. But my father did not agree to this at first; then it was too late.

The family of Rabbi Shlomowitz

*Translator's Note: Ketzot haChosen [*End of the Breastplate*] is the title of a book by Aryeh Leib Hacohen Heller. He was known as *Ketzos*, a name derived from the title of the book.] While in the *yeshiva* he opened his own *Gemiles Khesed* Fund [interest free-loan fund] and every evening after *Maariv* [the evening prayers] he gave loans to the *yeshiva* members. He would himself make loans of money for this purpose.

[Pages 281-284]

Moshe Levin – Pioneer of Hebrew Schooling in Poland
by Moshe Bachrach
Translated by Gloria Berkenstat Freund

Moshe Levin

It has happened more than once that I have heard from a non-Goniadzer that there was a greater abundance of idealism in Goniadz than in other *shtetlekh* [towns] – and I am inclined to agree with them on the basis of my own experience. I will only add that there was a spiritual and communal climate in Goniadz that made it possible to collaborate; mutual respect among scholars and simple Jews, Orthodox and free [secular] and between intellectuals and artisans. One met pious intellectuals in Goniadz who helped plan and carry out in practice the principle of modern education, both in content and in form – and equally for girls and boys. We also had "freethinkers" who strongly valued the pious and tolerant scholars and discussed Jewish matters with them with mutual respect.

For a provincial *shtetl* this was surely a rare phenomenon. I think that we have to remember here certain individuals who, with a kind of tolerant spiritual relationship to people and ideas, had an effect upon us.

I will record in the book of memories of Goniadz one person who represented a rare combination: practical idealism. This is Moshe Levin, who we would familiarly call: Moshe Klewianker [Klewianka is village near Goniadz].

Moshe Levin has been identified with Hebrew education for more than a half century. First we know him as a private teacher, then as a founder and leader of Hebrew schools, as a teacher of teachers, as a writer of text books and – as a result of all of this – as an educator of two generations of cultural Jews in the Hebrew and Zionist spirit.

[Page 282]

Like every self-educated man, Moshe Levin always studied and never "graduated" from anywhere – when the frame became too narrow for his widened horizon he would expand, and as an educator he adhered to the precept that "Because this people has rejected the gently flowing water of Shiloah..." [Isaiah 8:6].

He was quiet and industrious for all the years, first as a pioneer of modern, Hebrew education in Goniadz, later as the most recognized pedagogue in Bialystok, then in Canada and now, in 1957, in Israel, where he is the author of text books at the ripe age of more than 70.

But the crown of creation of Moshe Levin was without any doubt the Goniadz Hebrew School for Jewish and general education.

[Page 283]

This was during the time of the First World War in the autumn of 1915, right at the beginning of the German occupation. The military commandant still had not gotten his bearings in the life of the partially shot up *shtetl* and Moshe Levin, the *practical idealist* immediately planned and began to organize a Hebrew school – with the material that he found or decided to create on the spot.

Ephraim Halpern, of blessed memory, found favor with the commandant of the fortress in Osowiec and he probably persuaded the *yekie* [German Jew] that he [the *yekie* commandant] would be doing a "civilized" thing if he would permit the taking of the school chairs for the *shtetl* from the "*skole*" [public school] that the Russians earlier had for their children. Perhaps Ephraim had bought him off with what he said, that German would be taught in the school...

Right from the start Moshe Levin had one experienced teacher in Yoal Meir Khahan (son of Fayge Ruchl) and he trained two young intelligent young men in the work itself. This was Shimeon Halpern and Yohnatan Nejman, who were annihilated too young. Luck favored Levin and, among the Jews evacuated to the *shtetl* from the Brisk region, exiled behind the front by the German military regime, an experienced Hebrew teacher just happened to arrive in Goniadz – an instructor from the Grodno Hebrew pedagogical course who in addition could lead a choir. This was Shmuel Skliut.

[Page 284]

As if through a spell, in a relatively reasonable short time, the *shtetl* became filled with the ring and melody of Hebrew, under Moshe Levin's leadership. Over a period of several years, Hebrew became a fluently spoken language among the school youth of Goniadz. The level of general education continually rose.

The Hebrew school was the "darling of the *shtetl*" and the influence of the new spirit that the school introduced had an effect on young and old. I cannot forget how once in the middle of praying in the house of prayer, I was called to the side by a Jew in a *talis* and *tefilin* [prayer shawl and phylacteries] and he roared a song for me that his children had "brought home" from the school…

The Goniadz school became a pattern for the entire area and years later earned recognition when it was declared to be the best *Tarbot* [network of secular Hebrew schools] school in all of Poland!

Rarely does a man live to see an ideal so fulfilled as Moshe Levin saw in the Goniadz Hebrew School, of which he was both the founder and the administrator.

[Pages 285-288]

Binyamin the Scribe z"l
by Moshe Bachrach
Translated by Lazer Mishulovin
Donated by Bradley and Kathy Fisher

Benjamin the scribe

Anyone who grew up in Goniadz in the days of Binyamin the scribe, cannot be objective when writing about Binyamin. Willingly or not, the writer will touch upon moments of his own life that are bonded to Binyamin *with chords of love.* This assertion explains how when the synagogue was the grandeur of Goniadz, Binyamin was the key to its splendor.

God blessed Binyamin with the skill to ignite candles of holiness. For decades he sparked festive and ecstatic joy in the hearts of an entire community of Jews. He was at that time the "minister" of religious-celebrative moments in the supernal Goniadz, of which the synagogue was her corridor. It is, therefore, not a wonder that already during his lifetime Binyamin was a national hero and a legend.

In his poem, The Shul," Eidel Treshtchansky poetically expressed the sentiments of many Goniadz Jews towards the synagogue: "withy her thousand charms – where rests Godliness himself." But the man, who with the skill and enthusiasm of an inspired artist, made the poem "one thousand charms" vibrate and flutter in the synagogue – was Binyamin. Under his influence, the entire "ensemble" – the prayer leaders, the cantor, along with the choir and the holy congregation of worshippers – very impressively played the religious-Jewish symphony in the Goniadz synagogue.

Certainly, there were synagogue wardens and "remarkable bourgeois" who voiced their opinion to Binyamin. Binyamin, however, invested so much of his personality in the minutest detail pertaining to the synagogue that the wardens and the bourgeois were totally eclipsed. Everyone in the synagogue was happy to be Binyamin's "subject."

The slim livelihood Binyamin earned working for the synagogue, was compensated by the productive moments that he experienced. This is the case with every authentic artist, whose true profit is the mere creation.

I remember the pogrom at the Goniadz synagogue by the local Polish pranksters in the year 1912. The scene of a torn Torah scroll on the ground, where nearby elderly Jews stood weeping like children, will never leave my mind. But the most unfortunate one of all was Binyamin; his synagogue, his Torah scrolls and holy accessories to be so lowly desecrated!

Binyamin demonstrated another virtue for which he earned the love and reverence of many of the Goniadz's Jews. He, literally, felt a paternal love for everything and everyone that had a connection to Goniadz; and to Binyamin, all of the surrounding towns belonged to Goniadz's parish, including Bialostock...

Through the red-kerchief-method of gathering and sending help to the needy in Goniadz and its vicinity, Binyamin, from America, helped and cheered up many people between the two world-wars. In the Vale of Tears on the other side of the Atlantic Ocean, where there were so many people who did not have any contact with relatives in America – he became their "relative."

Binyamin managed a precise, although primitive, bookkeeping of the collected money and the money that was distributes on the other side of the Atlantic – understandably, according to his instructions. He would, literally, experience the complaint-letters as well as the thank-you letters from his correspondence. With time, Binyamin became a legend to those who were suffering on the other side of the Atlantic, and for us Americans – a national hero.

Binyamin spent his last years in the Bialostock nursing home on East Broadway in New York, where he was honorably cared for. For many years, he was a great patriot of the institution, as well as a frequent visitor. On the nineteenth of Kislev, 5754 (November 26, 1953) Binyamin passed away. Binyamin's physical body was redeemed from the institution, but his memory lives on.

Binyamin the scribe and his family

[Pages 289-291]

Rabbi Ephraim Halpern z"l
by Yeruham Levine z"l
Translated by Selwyn Rose

Rabbi Ephraim Halpern

Even though the town had considerable economic difficulties, Goniadz had a group of residents who strenuously concerned themselves with the welfare of the public and Zionist activities without any consideration of personal gain or prestige.

The time: – the days of the German conquest during the First World War. For political and administrative considerations, the German authorities transferred Goniadz from the district of Grodno in the county of Bialystok (southern Lithuania in the German view) and attached it to the Warsaw zone (under von Beseler's General Government). The Warsaw zone was, from the beginning programmed for independence of the hoped–for future Polish government.

In Goniadz it was seen as an opportunity to exploit the pseudo–independence of the situation to found a Hebrew school, while in the Lithuanian zone such schools were forbidden. Shortly after the conquest the German authorities chose Rabbi Ephraim Halpern, a highly respected businessman in Goniadz and named him Burgomaster. A teacher and the son of a teacher, a close friend of Dr. Matman–Cohen, founder of the Hertzlia Gymnasium in Jaffa and Ramat–Gan, near Tel–Aviv, he sent his eldest son Joseph Halpern to study at the Gymnasium in 1912.

[Page 290]

It was his intention to send his second son, Shimon as well but the 1914–1918 war broke out and delayed his plans. Rabbi Ephraim was dedicated heart and soul to the idea of a completely independent, fully Hebrew school in the Diaspora for the experimental educational methods of the teacher Gedaliahu Kozlowski who founded the school in Goniadz in 1903 through the instigation and efforts of Rabbi Ephraim.

[Page 291]

After a concerted effort lasting some months trying to deal with the problems of "What shall we eat?" on the 1st January 1916, the Jewish Burgomaster dared to open the first Jewish Public School in Poland where all subjects are taught in Hebrew.

Yaakov Rudeski's brewery temporarily housed the school. At that time, the Germans demolished the Osowiec Castle and Rabbi Ephraim requested permission to use the rubble and furniture to construct and furnish the school from the Russian schools that had previously existed, and received in writing authority to do so, at no cost.

The first Hebrew school in Goniadz existed throughout the German occupation together with all its instructors. The manager, Mr. Moshe Levine, a veteran teacher of Hebrew, authored the school's first Hebrew text-book in geography. He was assisted by teachers who had been his pupils and one teacher who had been trapped in Goniadz by the blocking of the roads at the outbreak of war.

The manager of the first Hebrew school in Goniadz and Poland, Mr. Moshe Levine, and together with him, two other teachers, Joel Meir Cohen z"l and Shmuel Skalyt subsequently transferred to the Jewish Public school that had been founded in Bialystok in 5769 (1918–9) and there, too, were among the pioneers of Hebrew education.

One of the most accomplished and erudite of teachers, Shimon Halpern, the son of Rabbi Ephraim Halpern, was taken from us in the springtime of his life at the end of the First World War in the Typhus epidemic. Rabbi Ephraim Halpern immigrated to Palestine with his children in 5681 (1921) and resided in Tel-Aviv. He lived to enjoy happiness among the ranks of the population, dancing the Hora in the streets which were at the heart of his life's desire. All his life Rabbi Ephraim mourned over the sacrifice of the Jewish people and the Land of Israel, living to a ripe old age. He was killed on 29th Tevet 5708 (29th January 1948), one of the nights Tel-Aviv suffered an attack, when he fell victim to a volley of shots fired from the Hassan Bek mosque.

May He Be Remembered for a Blessing.

[Pages 291-292]

Yaakov Rudski
by Moishe Bachrach
Translated from Yiddish to English by Dr. Isaac Fine

Yaakov Rudski

Yaakov Rudski was a Talmud scholar. He was also a man of worldly achievement. He was clever in dealing with the world, but not with himself and his family. Yaakov was a handsome man. He had a keen intellect and a charismatic personality. Yaakov was from the stock which gives rise to leaders and diplomats. He brought prestige to Goniondz. He was competent to serve as spokesperson for the Jewish community with the Tzarist government.

Yaakov traveled from Goniondz to attend the Fourth Zionist Congress in Basel, Switzerland. He had a momentous experience there, a face-to-face encounter with Teador Herzl, during which he received a greeting from this distinguished person. Yaakov built and destroyed worlds in Goniondz. In doing so, he exhausted his strength and his ability. He built the Osowiec fortress. He also destroyed the hill and built a beer brewery on its site. He was however not successful in this enterprise. Yaakov spent a fortune on the brewery project, and the hill lost its face.

His enterprise was phenomenal in scope. In the illustrious phase of Goniondz history during the Tzarist occupation, he served as leader of the Talmudic study group. Later, when Goniondz was in decline under the Polish regime, he wished to be town rabbi. However, he was not considered an appropriate candidate for this position.

He was a brilliant entrepreneur, but he did not acquire wealth. It always seemed that, for Yaakov, the scope of the enterprise was more important than the profits which might result. The town considered him a rich man. However, his demeanor was not that of a wealthy person. He had neither the time nor the patience to behave in such a fashion.

In 1914, his world was completely overturned by financial reversal as a result of the events of the First World War. He was left penniless. Yaakov left Goniondz, and was not heard of again until the War ended. When he returned to town, he was like an eagle whose wings had been clipped. He again became involved in public affairs. But it was not as it had been before. He had become a poor man, and was dependent on the community for economic support. Yaakov Rudski ended his years in poverty and loneliness, even before the Jewish community of Goniondz was destroyed.

[Pages 293-294]

Gedaliah (G'dlake) Seid z"l
Moshe Bachrach
Translated by Gloria Berkenstat Freund

Gedaliah Seid

We in New York knew G'dlake Seid as a quiet man who was not active in communal affairs. He was a capable businessman and a sociable man, but he could not utter a word at a meeting. It seems that the shocking news of the death of all of Goniadz gave him a push to throw himself into the aid work on behalf of the individual Goniadzers who survived. Evidently as he needed a great deal of help to be able to organize an aid committee.

At the Goniadzer Ladies Auxiliary (New York Ladies Union), which excelled with aid for Goniadz in its time of need, Seid easily agreed that they [the Ladies Auxiliary] should incorporate as an organization in the planned committee and when he turned to me for "technical" help I promised to place myself in the service of the task without delay, on the condition that this not be bound with too many "parliamentary" idle words. I meant by this that the aid committee should be declared as a fact and to then draw people to something that exists and is already functioning. (Here it is necessary to mention that the Goniadz-Trestiner *Landsmanschaft* could not, as an association, join an aid committee only for Goniadzer. Therefore, they [the new committee] had to think of Goniadzer Jewry - wherever they would be located.)

[Pages 295-296]

**The[se] two pictures were taken during the visit of
Gedaliah Seid (of blessed memory) and his wife in Israel, 1951**

[Page 297]

Seid truly from the start was afraid of "public meetings" that could yet ask, "who authorized you" to organize a Goniadzer aid committee? But the circumstances demanded bold activity; we began to do the work ourselves. And as usual - people did not frown when someone else freed them from heavy work. And right from the start, the work was varied and difficult, although the call was admirable. Seid received courage; the thought was constantly in terms of doing and not of meetings.

[Page 298]

"There are those whose who acquire the World to Come in numerous years, and there are those who acquire the World to Come in an instant."* It happens that a person repays himself - and the community - with one sacred work for an entire life of daily work. G'dlake Seid achieved this in full measure through his great accomplishment with the aid committee.

*Translator's Note: This quote comes from the Talmudic tractate, *Avodah Zarah*.

[Pages 297-300]

Yaakov Tucker, a Hero of Tel–Hai
by Joseph ben Ephraim Halpern, Tel–Aviv
Translated by Selwyn Rose

Yaakov Tucker, the son of Avraham Kalman and Haya–Gittel, and a son of Goniadz, fell heroically defending the main entrance gate to the Tel–Hai compound with his rifle in his hand.

Yaakov was a dear friend of mine; our memories go back to our earliest childhood recollections as members of the town's Cantor Rabbi Nahum's z"l choir. Yaakov was blessed with a clear alto voice, light and pleasant to listen to. He was always the one upon whom rested the role of the solo in recitative passages, on the High Holy Days and the three pilgrimage festivals. His good–looks and delicate features captured everyone's heart and soul.

Tel–Hai memorial

[Page 299]

Our ways parted while we were still young; he left Goniadz and went to live with his older brother in America, and I immigrated to Palestine. From then we never met or even wrote to each other.

After the First World war of 1914–1918 the 38th and 39th Battalions of the Royal Fusiliers – Yaakov Tucker served with them – were demobilized and Colonel Margolin z"l was in charge of their dispersal. I returned from Egypt to Jaffa from where I made my way to Jerusalem. In those days, we would travel as far as Lod by a narrow gauge railroad. At Lod we would have to walk about two kilometers to the station where the regular gauge railroad station was situated. The tracks were occupied by hundreds of wagons loaded with military equipment and heavy and light ammunition. Walking on my own, deep in thought, between the rows of wagons I suddenly became aware of a Jewish soldier, in British uniform striding towards me.

We both stood rooted to the spot – I in mine, he in his and after a brief glance one startled word sprang from my lips: "Yankov!" – as we used to call him when we were youngsters – and the soldier standing in front of me cried in disbelief: "Joseph!" It was our first meeting in Palestine.

We hugged and kissed each other and told each other everything that had befallen us in the years we had been apart. From that day onwards we never lost close touch with each other. He frequently visited us in our home in Neve Shalom and would spend days – months, even – in the company of my family. This was at the end of 1919 and Palestine was still closed with restricted entry and referred to officially as "Enemy Territory"; no one could come in and no one could leave. Representatives of the demobilized soldiers were seen throughout the country and Trumpledor* was active among the released Battalions. His voice was heard and listened to throughout their ranks; his fame preceded him. He was already on the lips of all our comrades in arms – the remnants of the "Zion Mule Corps" of 1915 – who fought under the command of Colonel Patterson.

The time: the days of Tel–Hai – Trumpledor, alarmed, was stuck in Tel–Hai – a weak spot. A call went out from there to all released soldiers dispersed throughout the country, to take up their arms and come to the defense of Tel–Hai, to defend it with their lives.

Leaving my home in Neve Shalom our dear Yaakov walked to the railroad station in town in order to travel to the Galilee in response to "Josef the Galilean's" (Trumpledor) call as he was nicknamed by everyone. Early Sunday morning Yaakov parted from us all with much warmth and affection, his haversack on his back and his rifle in his hand. We accompanied him as far as the railroad station. At four o'clock he returned to our house together with his equipment and ammunition.

[Page 300]

We were stunned with surprise. Yaakov calmed us and explained that he together with others waiting to travel to the Galilee, were forced to return because the stormy rains that had fallen overnight had caused serious flooding and erosion along the tracks between Kfar Gigis and Rosh Ha–Ayin and the connection with Haifa broken. The situation continued through Monday and Tuesday and each day he went out and returned. Only on Thursday was the connection restored between Judea and the Galilee and Yaakov was on his last journey – to Tel–Hai.

There he fell, the hero's death. His name is engraved on Tel–Hai's memorial for eternity.

*Translator's Note: Joseph Trumpeldor, was an early Zionist activist. He helped organize the Zion Mule Corps and bring Jewish immigrants to Palestine.

A letter from a Goniadz fellow-resident, Aharon Friedman, on the death of Yaakov Tucker z"l

Mahanayim 19th Adar 5680 (1920).

Mr. Joseph Halpern,

I am writing this letter in deep sorrow. You certainly know from our town's newspapers that a son of our town, Yaakov Tucker was killed while defending Tel-Hai. Our responsibility now lies on us to arrange for the money due to him from the camp should be sent home. I have spoken about this with E. Golomb and he tells me that he sees no problem with doing so but since I am in Mahanayim I am unable to act – will you please take over this project? Please tell Golomb (if you agree to act), that I have asked you to act for me. I think Goniadz should be informed, taking care that his mother should not be informed.

Maybe this news will awaken in the youth of Goniadz the impetus to immigrate to Palestine.

I have not received any other letters from home.

Yours truly and in friendship, (–) A. Friedman

[Pages 301-304]

Yakov Tuker z"l
by Dovid Bachrach, Petach Tikvah
Translated by Gloria Berkenstat Freund

(A garland of memories to the memory of my childhood friend, who fell among the heroes of Tel-Hai,* 11 of Adar, 5680 [1 March 1920].)

I remember Moshe-Kalman, his father, the turner. Sick, always coughed and wiped his face with a red handkerchief. He was an *Ein Yakov* [Ein Yakov is the ethical and inspirational section of the Talmud] Jew, one of Nisen the tailor's students. He coughed out his soul and his son, Yakov, was left as an orphan [The word for orphan in Yiddish can apply to a person who has lost one parent] at a very young age. He became the provider of food for his family - a mother and two sisters.

We studied together in Motye's *kheder* [religious primary school]. He had a beautiful voice and he was one of the best choir boys with the *khazan* [cantor], Reb. Nakhum, of blessed memory. He was the long-standing solo singer and he would "turn" his melodies with a fine sense of music. His resounding voice would be heard during the study of *Gemara* [Talmud] and younger children would pay him a *kopike* for going over a section of *Gemara* with them.

Once Idel Meir, the watchmaker's son, brought a chess set to *kheder*. The *kheder* students were very happy playing and decided to make their own chess set. Who would make it? Yakov Tuker, naturally. *Kopikes* were collected for Yakov, who little by little turned all of the pieces on his lathe. This would be done in the evening by the glow of a small lamp. The cold in the room was unbearable. The windowpanes were covered with frost. The poor turner's wife did not have the money to heat [the room]. But Yakov turned the chess set with his own hands and everyone was proud of their friend, the "artist."

* * *

Goniadz started a new occupation, matzo baking, between Purim and Passover and it was called *podriad* [enterprise].

[Page 302]

I remember three such "enterprises": at [the house of] Gershon the orphan, the Sotnik's relative; at [the house of] Gershon the cabinetmaker near the *beis- medrash* [house of prayer]; and in Josl Sayke's house where Yoske's [wife or daughter] Nekhame's old bakery was located. The bakery was run by Majczuk's [wife or daughter] Mirke Feywl and Mashe [wife or daughter of] Shimon Yankl... Mirke stood at the market the entire summer with a trough of fruit. In winter she would sell lampshades. And there was no income from this - and the "enterprise" came after Purim. Yakov Tuker was employed there [the matzo bakery] as a matzo roller. His work hours were from six in the morning until late in the evening. And he never could be absent. I was then studying in the *kheder* of Uncle Shlomo Moshe, Shimeon's son, who lived in Saike's house. I would drop in to see Yakov rolling and, at the same time, learn the trade. - Yakov was interested in teaching it to me so that he could catch his breath for several minutes... I would work in fear that my father would learn that I had slipped out from *kheder* and also that the supervisors - the rabbi and Gershon Borukh - would catch me. But I learned on the condition that my work would be added to Yakov's account.

* * *

Our friend, Yankl Szmerke's son, died in the spring of 1920. The *khevre kadishe* [burial society] approved that we, his friends, would carry the *mite* [board on which the deceased is placed or carried] to the cemetery. On the way back, Sender Miltshon told us that the turner's wife received a letter from the Zionist Organization that her son Yakov fell in the fight

[Page 303]

in *Eretz-Yisroel* along with Josef Trumpeldor and six other comrades defending the solitary settlement of Tel-Hai in the Upper Galilee.

* * *

Dear, dear Yakov! You fell a hero, defending the Jewish land and Jewish honor!

In your merit and in the merit of your fallen comrades, who defended a solitary Jewish settlement, the entire Upper Galilee was saved and remained in Jewish hands.

Your death is a worthy one and full of consolation_[Although the literal translation of the Yiddish is "full of consolation," it is possible the author meant "sorrowful."] like the death of our millions of brothers, sisters, who were tortured in the concentration camps and gas chambers. Your comrade, Trumpeldor's last words, "Never mind; it is good to die for our country," was also said in your name. You were the first to fall in Tel-Hai, running to block the gate against the wild Arab bands. You were a model of self sacrifice and heroism and we will always remember your name with reverence.

[Page 304]

And Goniadzers are proud: the fine choir boy, the chess turner-artist, the matzo roller grew into a great Jewish hero of the entire people and land of Israel.

*Translator's Note: Tel-Hai is the site of a battle between the residents of Tel-Hai, an agricultural village, and Arabs searching for French troops. Eight Jews were killed during the fight, including Josef Trumpeldor, a Zionist activist. His final words, "Never mind, it is good to die for our country," are well known.

[Pages 303-306]

Yaakov Tucker z"l
by Yisroel David Yardeni (Yarushevski)
Translated by Selwyn Rose

From the depths of my memories a ghostly figure rises up before me; standing before me is a young boy – seven or eight years old, red–cheeked, a crumpled hat stuck on his head, his head slightly bowed with a faint smile on his face. I take one or two steps forward and I am in his house – one long, broad room. A beam was place across the ceiling rafters to which was tied a length of rope and below, just above the floor a second beam. Between the two beams were two logs of wood into which were stuck sharp iron teasers. In the center of the room a wooden tree–stump with an axe or two stuck in it – this was his father's workshop for manufacturing spindles. Among the tangle of wood–shavings and wheels his father worked, making spindles in time for the beginning of the weaving season of autumn.

The house was full of adults and children and Yaakov, the youngest. His father, Avraham Kalman was a sick man with a serious lung complaint spending many weeks in bed during the winter. Yaakov began working at a young age and even during the few months of the year when he learned in the "Heder", I would see him standing next to his father in the afternoon, winding the thread onto spindles.

[Page 304]

As an adult he became the provider for the family and when his mother became a "milkmaid", I often saw him carrying two full milk urns. I knew that he regularly rose up early in the morning with his mother to walk four or five kilometers at milking–time to the Christian farmer to buy milk from him and then sell it to householders at their door.

Once he came to me with a proposition: he would always assist me on condition that I taught him some Torah, some Rashi and a little Hebrew. From then on he would come to my paint–shop and help me with my work and afterwards I would teach him; we were happy to see how he advanced in his studies.

I recall the long passageway along which he had to walk in order to get to David Shmerl, "the tutor". On the left was a bakery – the bakery of "Pascha and her Daughters" and the tempting aroma of fresh bread that awoke the appetite. His compliments and praise for Pascha and her daughters saved him on more than once from hunger.

– "Give me some fresh bread for a kopek"

– Pascha weighed some bread – and gave it to him.

– ...and for a kopek! Says Yaakov, a little shame–faced and feeling qualms of conscience.

And the following morning he waited at the open door of the bakery and not Pascha but Bilka was standing there at the counter and from her, too, he bought a kopek's worth of bread.

[Page 305]

Yaakov's father died when Yaakov was fifteen years old and before he was fully competent at making a complete spindle in all its aspects and so one day he traveled to the nearest town – Korycin to finish learning the trade.

From then on I hardly saw him because he came back only very rarely to see his mother and his home and when he was due to join the army he went to America. Once, when I was sitting in the railroad station in Lod, waiting for my train to Jerusalem, here striding towards me was a soldier. He fell on my shoulders.

Yaakov!

He had come from America with the Jewish Brigade.

[Page 306]

He spoke to me about the possibilities of finding work in his trade in Jerusalem. He was not going to leave Palestine. What had moved him so? I remembered: His father had a brother in Jerusalem. Twice he had visited the town as a doctor. On one of the evenings, I had gone to Tucker's house and saw there an old man with bushy eyebrows shielding his eyes, his white beard sticking out from his face like lowered spears. He was talking about the Western Wall with the children sitting round the table listening. Yaakov's mouth was agape and his eyes fixed immovably on the old man's face, the peak of his cap to one side.

Yaakov fell heroically in defense of Tel–Hai 11th Adar 1920.

Indeed – he never left Palestine.

[Pages 305-306]

Yonatan Neiman z"l
by A. Ben-Meir
Translated from Yiddish to English by Gloria Berkenstat Freund

A beautiful, bright soul. Who does not remember him? A grandson of the old rabbi, a genteel, sensitive one, rich spiritually.

Yonatan Neiman

His rabbinical pedigree did not create any luxury for him - not in his orphaned childhood years and not in his youth, when, during the World War [One] years, he lived as a refugee in Bialystok and later - as a teacher at the Hebrew public school in Goniadz, where he occupied a respected place and was beloved by everyone.

His delicate body could not long endure and during the difficult war years he became ill with tuberculosis.

His devoted sisters applied every means to save him, sent him to sanatoria in Germany and to Switzerland and then, in 1921, brought him to America. He was in treatment for several years at the best sanatoria, first the *Arbeter-Ring* sanatoria around New York, later in Denver, Colorado and in California, hovering between "better" and "worse".

[Page 306]

Yonatan knew that his days were numbered and he accepted his fate with resignation. He died in full consciousness on the 25th of March, 1933 (27 Adar, 5693) in the Denver sanatorium.

[Pages 307-308]

On the Grave of Natan Noyman (Yonatan Neiman)
(Sonnet)
by H. Leivik
Translated from Yiddish to English by Gloria Berkenstat Freund

The days and years pass, pass, Natan Neiman.

And I stand again at your burial garden bed.

The blue Rocky Mountains in their timelessness - -

They do not speak today - they are all still.

Are they happy that I have come? - -

I take a handful of your grains of sand and I spread them apart - -

The silence immediately becomes bright, delighted

As if it has heard a reawakened voice.

Through a ballad I made your death known,

And through it people grew to love you

And yet I do not avoid asking you now: forgive me

For leaving you at the end of the world in Colorado.

Forgive me, too, that I wake you unexpectedly from your rest,

And take my 14 lines with approval.

H. Leyvik*

Denver, May 5, 1948

[Page 307]

The famous poet, H. Leyvik [Halpern Leyvik], long may he live, who in 1932 started a friendship with Yonatan, was with him during the agony of his death and took part in his funeral and burial. He then created the unique "Ballad of the Denver Sanatorium" - a pearl of Yiddish poetry that has been published many times and also translated into Hebrew by A. Shlonsky.

Leyvik visited Yonatan's grave in 1948 and immortalized him impressively in a sonnet entitled, *On the Grave of Natan Noyman* [Yonatan Neiman].

Yonatan left a diary - a small notebook where he recorded his great experiences: family memories from his childhood, impressions of friends, copies of touching, content-rich letters to his devoted sisters, opinions about Yiddish and Hebraic works and writers, moods from his sick bed and also several original lyrical poems and free translations.

[Page 308]

From his diary, written in a fine, restrained style with a deep feeling and clear understanding, radiates the bright personality of a young, smart man who loved life and who approached his end stoically calm, without complaints to God and to the world.

"I did not go to visit your brother out of pity," - the poet, H. Leyvik, said at the time to Yonatan's sisters - "I came to him to learn how a person can be purified through suffering."

We bow our heads to his spiritual strength. Neiman's purified soul was united in a great and elevated work of a world famous Yiddish poet. With the deepest recognition, and with the friendly consent of the author, we include the fine, touching sonnet in our Yizkor Book.

*Translator's Note: Halpern Leyvik, the Yiddish poet, contracted tuberculosis and spent four years at a sanatorium in Denver, where he met Yonatan Neiman

[Page 309]

As At Night...
(Poem)
by Yonatan Neiman
Translated from Yiddish to English by Gloria Berkenstat Freund

As at night, the stars fall

Become still and quickly lost

Thus fall my sparks

By now for years and years.

Letters and moans, quiet tears,

Insufficient, drop quietly.

Children will not hear them.

* * *

My windows are open

Only to the west and to the north,

Only from darkness, sunset, cold

My world only exists from them.

(Written in the dark after a hemorrhage)

[Pages 309-310]

My Grandfather z"l
(Excerpts from Yonatan Neiman's notebook)
by Yonatan Neiman
Translated from Yiddish to English by Gloria Berkenstat Freund

What a bright personality he was! I remove the negative side - his intolerance to Jewish *apikorsim* [literally, heretics] - he was entirely fair. Christians are what they are, but... Jews, sons of the covenant, to whom God revealed himself, and they would sin? - this cannot be tolerated...

* * *

A Din Torah [law suit before a rabbinical court] before my grandfather: A Jew sold his "holiness" to another one for two *gildn*. He arrived home and his wife shouted that she would rather have the holiness... However, the customer would not take back the money. They came to the rabbi. My grandfather ruled that the customer is not really a customer and scolded both Jews, "One does not trade in Godly things!"

* * *

My grandfather's sense of humor: With honey cake and whisky in the house of a rich man of the *shtetl*; the rich man says to my grandfather: "Rabbi, I am still a *godl* [prominent man]." - My grandfather answers: "In Lithuania a *groshn* [small coin or penny] is called a *godl*."

* * *

...Welwl and Zalman play chess, my grandfather sits and studies. Suddenly he raises his head, looks at the chess board and shows one of them a move. The brother protests: "Father, why, why?" My grandfather answers: "Never mind, never mind, we need to help someone who is weak..."

* * *

When I came to Motya the *Melamed* [teacher in a religious school] in kheder [religious primary school], Motya said to me this: "Your grandfather, of blessed memory, warned me: 'Motya, do you hear me, we do not hit children in my home.'"

* * *

In his boyish years my grandfather was a great brat. He liked to ride on a he-goat. Therefore, he did not grieve when my brother, Khone, often did not want to go to kheder.

* * *

My mother adored my grandfather. When she was a small girl she wanted to learn to read and write Russian. A small book cost 15 kopikes; my grandmother was stubborn: it is not needed. My grandfather finally asked my grandmother to give the 15 *kopikes*. He told my mother that in his young years one "learned to write Russian" on the floor with chalk. And when the floor was covered with writing, it would be wiped with a wet rag and he would again write.

* * *

My grandfather was very well respected by the Christian gentlemen. They trusted me because they knew that I was a grandson of the old rabbi. Apparently they believed that a grandson of such a rabbi must be an honest young man...

[Pages 311-312]

Yehoshua (Alter) Supraski z"l
by Avraham Yaffe, (Tel–Aviv)
Translated by Selwyn Rose

Yehoshua Supraski

He was born in Goniadz the son of Eliyahu Supraski. He received a traditional "Heder" education, became enamored of the "Ha–haskela" [Enlightenment] movement and began to learn Hebrew and Russian. He was self–educated and a voracious reader both of literature and the Russian and Hebrew Press of those days. From his intense studying began to feel pain in his chest. The town's doctor, Dr. Kanpinski, advised him to exercise by walking and running in the fields around the town during the winter when the fields were covered in snow.

Supraski belonged to the younger generation of the town – the first among the adherents of the Haskala and Zionists, like: Ze'ev Kaminski, an active Zionist and orator at meetings, or Shimon Louis, scholar and academic, organizer of Zionist and Haskala propaganda in the Beit Ha–Midrash where spent many hours studying, teaching and commenting on the Torah and Midrash.

Later, he made his way to the Russian town of Kursk where he quickly became a central figure in Zionist activity. His aptness and suitability for the position found expression in his being elected as a delegate to the Basel Congress and also to the All–Russian Zionist meeting in Minsk. In the Memorial Book for Dr. Yehiel Czelnov there is a photograph of the Minsk meeting in which he appears as the delegate from Kursk together with Yaakov Rudenski, the delegate from Goniadz. After his marriage to one of his acquaintances from among the girls of Kursk, he rarely came to Goniadz, visiting only occasionally. He became an active citizen in the Jewish community of Kursk devoting himself to the Zionist cause. With the Russian revolution, at the time of Kerensky, he was very active with speeches in public and local political institutions. In recognition of his personality and public activities for the good of the town, he was delegated as a representative by the temporary authorities for the entire Kursk area, With the outbreak of the Bolshevik Revolution, He left Kursk and moved to Berlin with the rest of the Russian refugees who found asylum in Germany in general and Berlin in particular. There he remained for a short time and then moved to his final place of refuge, for the rest of his life, his personal and national refuge – the land for which his soul yearned – the Land of Israel.

He remained idealistic and multi–active all his days in Palestine. He succeeded in his commercial ventures and also consolidated his social standing. He acquired properties both for himself and also for his acquaintances in Goniadz as settlements for them. Later he opened a successful credit bank that achieved a respectable standing in the banking community. His public works brought him further recognition and he was elected vice–chairman of the Tel Aviv–Jaffa community. In multi–national meetings dealing with Zionist interests he was one of the leading speakers. He rose to the top of General Zionist party and was one the founding activists of *"Ha–Boker"* ["The Morning"] journal. He achieved his highest post when elected to the board of the Sochnut management.

Yehoshua Supraski was the bridge who, from his modest "nest" in Goniadz, rose to the heights of public works in Palestine. He took part in the temporary government meetings of David Ben Gurion at the time of the Declaration of Independence in 1948. A few weeks after that he died at the age of sixty–eight – years full of splendid activity for the good of the people and the country.

May his memory be blessed forever.

[Pages 313-315]

Dovid Ben Yaakov Rudski z"l
by Avrom Yaffe
Translated from Yiddish to English by Dr. Isaac Fine

His first education was in the traditional religious elementary school of his Jewish town. However, he did not continue his studies in the House Of Study, as did the children of other merchants in town. At the beginning of the twentieth century, some young Goniondz men journeyed to known centers of Torah learning, such as yeshivas and torah centers in other cities. Dovid Rudski was among those who pursued secular culture. He went to Lodz, where the German language prevailed. There he succeeded in acquiring a smattering of German language and culture. Since he did not receive economic support from home at that time, he was forced to return to Goniondz.

When he came home he suffered from pulmonary problems. His family very actively sought a cure for him, and a cure was found. He continued to improve his competence in the German language and later in French as well. He wanted to travel to France and study there. Meanwhile, the time came for him to present himself to the Russian Army for induction. His parents were suppliers to the Osowiec fortress. He had learned how to make a certain kind of hatband worn by the army in summer from a Goniondz hat maker.

He was recruited into the army and sent to Moscow, where Russian physicians conducted pulmonary exams for recruits. After a time, he was given a medical certificate stating that he was cured from pulmonary disease and fit for military duty. After being declared fit for duty, he went to Paris with neither parental approval nor their assurance that they would provide him with economic support. He hoped to achieve economic independence by his own efforts. He did indeed succeed in achieving this goal by means of the hat maker trade he had learned. Later, however, he did receive financial support from his family in Goniondz.

At first he concentrated on philosophic studies and passed the baccalaureate exam. Dovid at that time transferred to the Faculty of Medicine. He completed his medical studies shortly before the outbreak of World War One, and was granted the title of Doctor of Medicine. In Goniondz, Dovid had been very involved with a group of friends who were immersed in Zionism and secular culture. He very much enjoyed their discussions. Dovid also participated in the foundation of the Goniondz Zionist Library, later called "The Dawn", after the Dawn group of young Zionists in town. In Paris he participated in Zionist meetings with Dr. Max Nordau. The Paris Zionists recognized this very competent Jew from Russia. They fully accepted him into their group.

When World War One broke out, he volunteered for service as a military physician with the French Army, with the approval of the Russian Embassy.

France, England and Russia were at that time allies against the German Empire. He fulfilled this role with distinction. In a weekly edition of the Russian periodical Rivya Vidanosti Ogonoyed, his photo appeared with the inscription "A son of our land, doctor of medicine, now on the French front in charge of a medical detachment." He was once wounded on the front line. After his recovery, he again returned to the front to assist in providing medical care for the wounded both in hospitals and in the field.

At the time of his return to active duty, the typhus epidemic was spreading among the troops like wildfire. Dovid's devotion to curing the ill moved him to labor tirelessly day and night. He finally succumbed to the disease and perished. In his life and in his death, he distinguished himself by his dedication to duty.

May his memory be for a blessing.

[Pages 313-316]

Yehoshua Rosenbloom z"l
by Avraham Yaffe, (Tel–Aviv)
Translated by Selwyn Rose

Yehoshua Rosenbloom was born in the late 80's of the nineteenth century. During his childhood he grew up in the home of his mother and step–father, Eliyahu, Asher Bikowski. His mother had two other older boys from her first marriage. Yehoshua – the youngest – differed from them: he was talented and very studious, continuing to be so for the whole of his short life. After completing his studies at the "Heder" under Yudel the teacher, he went to the Yeshiva at Lomza.

After about a year returned to Goniadz as a senior graduate. A year later he joined the yeshiva in Novogrudok. There he underwent a spiritual transformation: Enlightenment. He became one of the major workers in Zionist activities in the Yeshiva. When a Zionist Congress took place in the Yeshiva of Lida, from its foundation under the management of the leader of "Mizrachi" [Religious Zionist Movement] Rabbi Y. Y. Reines z"l., the young Yehoshua was present. Yehoshua, with a very ebullient and vibrant personality, was very excited with the congress and when he returned to Novogrudok from there, he leapt enthusiastically from the train to join the few colleagues who had come to greet him, falling heavily on the platform and breaking a leg. He lay many weeks until his leg healed but even so not completely.

When he returned home, exhausted and ill, his mother devoted herself to caring for his health. And indeed after a few months he was well enough to return his "evil ways" – his ambition for a general education and knowledge. His main ambition now was to be examined in Russian and four years' gymnasium. When he came to visit me at the synagogue he told me what he had read in "Moreh Nevuchei Ha–Z'maneh" [Guide to the Perplexed of the Time] by Nachman Krochmal, "Paradoxes" by Max Nordau, which we read to each other our own writings – poems – originals and translations.

Yehoshua was also a very talented speaker and with great courage was not deterred from approaching the somewhat older "Young Zionists" in Goniadz and was active in the Zionist meeting and in the Zionist Library Council. However, on his return from Germany it was discovered that he was suffering from well–established tuberculosis. In the last year of his life he managed to publish a Yiddish poem in the "Der Shtral" periodical. From time to time he would come to the library and talk to those gathered there on culture and Zionism.

In the last few months of his life his illness intensified and confined him to his bed from which he did not rise again. For a few weeks he lingered on in pain with a high temperature and breathing difficulties and died at the age of twenty–five.

"His life's song was cut short in the midst thereof"

[Pages 315-318]

Aryeh-Leib Bachrach z"l
by Moishe Bachrach
Translated by Marvin Galper

Aryeh-Leib Bachrach

Leibel was born and raised in the town of Grajewo. He acquired distinguished competence in Hebrew language and grammar, the Bible, and the Talmud through a program of personal self-directed studies. He studied Hebrew language and grammar in the seclusion of his attic. He also acquired knowledge of Russian and Polish as well as calligraphic script. When his time arrived for active duty with the Russian Army, he was assigned to serve as a regimental headquarters scribe. This duty spared him from many strenuous military drills and maneuvers. When the time came for him to stand watch with his rifle on his shoulder, he would memorize the 618 commandments from the book "Commandments Of The Lord", whether by day or by night, in intense heat or in bitter cold. He observed these commandments throughout his life, but the law of the rifle, never. This is the sort of soldier Leibel Bachrach was in the town of Saratow on the Volga River in the late eighteen hundreds of the nineteenth century.

He was an iron merchant in Goniondz. Leibel was always immersed in his studies at home during his leisure time. His wife Shayne Belke facilitated his freedom for solitary studies to a considerable extent. He often studied late through half the night while very quietly humming a Gemora tune, so as to not awaken the family from sleep. If any of us awakened during the night we would witness a remarkable sight. The house would be enveloped in darkness and sleep, except for father immersed in his Talmudic studies, with a small kerosene lamp by his side. The sweet melody which accompanied his studies was wonderful to hear.

He never relied on the classroom teachers of his children or their private tutors. He often had talks with teachers and tutors about the most effective methods for bible instruction and childhood education in general, as well as education of his own children in particular. His first step was to teach his children Hebrew with the proper intonation, so their teachers could then continue on in the same fashion using the appropriate word stresses. With his talent as an educator, he allowed his children to pray according to the Ashkenazi tradition. Goniadz was very immersed in traditional Judaism. He, however, was a Chassid, and prayed in the Sephardic fashion of the Chassidim.

Leibel Bachrach was the first in Goniondz to advocate the principle of equal education for boys and girls. His vision embraced not only German, Polish and Russian, which were then in fashion, but also the Hebrew language, the Prophets, a special book of bible commentaries, and the "Introduction To The Talmud" as well. He was a gifted educator and completely lacking in self-consciousness in his approach to teaching. He could explain the first problems encountered in Talmudic study with such clarity that even a child could comprehend. All his students found it a pleasure to learn from him.

When the First World War broke out in 1914, the German Army bombarded the Russian fortress of Osowiec. While this bombing created devastation among the homes of Goniadz, Leibel Bachrach remained immersed in Talmudic studies in the tiny apartment of Yehuda the cap maker, surrounded by a group of refugees from Grajewo. The assembled group seemed oblivious to the surrounding bombardment.

Leibel Bachrach was also a prolific writer in both Hebrew and Yiddish. He was interested in both secular and spiritual matters. He communicated with both merchants and yeshiva directors. When he sensed that a merchant in Warsaw or Brisk, for example, was an educated man, he would add on a few sentences on biblical matters or other Jewish topics to the end of each business letter.

He was a long time subscriber to Yiddish and Hebrew periodicals such as "The Time", "The Friend", "The Life" or "The Moment." Russian newspapers from St. Petersburg also arrived at our home on a regular basis. The Russian newspapers were intended only for us children to learn Russian, and certainly not for absorption of the Russian spirit. Leibel Bachrach established a well-balanced Jewish education for his sons and daughters. In November 1917, when the news of the Balfour Declaration reached Goniondz, he advised the town youth, including his daughter Chaske who now lives in Israel, "Children, learn a trade and be in the land of Israel."

Arye Leib Bachrach died in Goniondz in 1919. His bones remained in Goniondz and it seems that not a trace of his grave remains. But his name lives as a perpetual memory, engraved on the tombstone of his wife Shayne Belke in a Tel Aviv cemetery.

[Pages 319-324]

Chaim Aryeh Pekarski z"l
by Kalman Bachrach
Translated by Gloria Berkenstat Freund

Chaim Aryeh Pekarski

He was called Leibl Mushke's [Mushke's son] or Leibl [Aryeh is Hebrew for "lion" and Leib is its Yiddish equivalent.] Pekarski. To me he was Chaim Aryeh. This is because we studied together in the same class in the Goniadzer Hebrew School. There, everything was in Hebrew, our names, too.

I remember the name in Hebrew because this was characteristic of our acquaintance, our comradeship and, perhaps, for our entire life. Both of our ideologies and strivings were the same through all the years, built on Hebrew and Zionism, although we were almost always physically apart since our parting in Goniadz, he in the distant city in Canada and I in New York, thousands of miles apart each from the other. We were together only one more year and worked in the same school in Montreal, Canada.

Our friendship was deep and strong. True, we did not correspond because Chaim Aryeh was not a letter writer, but we were bound together emotionally and we could never forget one another. When he suddenly left us, a wound remained in my heart.

When I begin to think of our young period, the word "zealot" comes immediately to my mind. Chaim Aryeh was a modern, zealous man, that means not for studying *Gemara* [Torah commentaries] like a [poet Chaim Nahman] Bialik's zealot, but for modern subjects: Hebrew language, literature and several sciences, all subjects that we studied together. His zeal was natural and elemental. He had the strength of pulling along everyone around him like the force of a terrible rainstorm. When we prepared ourselves for examinations, he could study 18 hours a day. Sleeping or playing, all of the things that play a great role in a young person's life, did not exist for him. He had one purpose - to study. And he studied with persistence and a strong will that broke through all difficulties.

Chaim Aryeh loved to talk of that period: incidentally, he possessed the ability to tell stories. Everyone already knew the story of the string when I returned to Montreal and I met Chaim Aryeh there.

The story is from the last days of our Gordz exams from the Gordz school. Chaim Aryeh was then constantly studying and repeating, truly as it is written: "While you sit in your home, while you walk on the way, when you retire and when you arise," before eating, in the middle of eating, during the day, at night - without measure and boundary. I do not know how many hours a night he slept then; I was afraid that he even studied in his sleep. And also I with him - as much as possible, as much as I could help him. When he arose early, I had to arise early, earlier than anyone in the house. How does one arise earlier than everyone? I did not have an alarm clock and he did not want to bang on the shutters because this would wake up other people in the house. It was decided to bore a small hole under the window, draw through a string and to bind the string to my hand. And so it was. Chaim Aryeh came in the morning, pulled the string and woke me from sleep.

[Page 321]

The same story was repeated in Montreal, but a little more intensively. There, I have to confess, I could no longer keep up with him. His zeal and determination were even stronger than before, at a time when the differences in our character traits were more distinct and stronger. I let myself be influenced by the environment and went along slowly. He stormed with his entire strength and wanted to take in everything around him. His energy had no boundary. Perhaps this actually was his misfortune, his energy burned out too quickly.

We were then newly arrived in America and learned to read, write and speak English. The goal was to prepare ourselves for university. Chaim Aryeh threw himself into English with fervor. English, as is known, is not a phonetic language and "speln," that is, the laying out of the words, is an entire education. Chaim Aryeh developed his own theory about how to learn "speln." He wrote each word 10, 20, 50 times; it depended on the difficulty of the word. And as he began to write, there was not enough paper. He wrote on everything, the calendar, on the walls, both sides of envelopes, all paper bags and all sorts of wrapping paper. There truly remained no paper in the house on which there was no writing.

[Page 322]

I was told that he acted the same way later when he was in the Canadian Far West. He reached the goal that he had set for himself. He graduated from the university there, became a lawyer and one of the most important Jewish leaders in Western Canada. There he also married and built a family.

Chaim Aryeh was an immigrant who was newly arrived in a country where he was strange and where the language and the customs were strange. He had to make his way in the country with his own 10 fingers, adapt himself to new circumstances and establish himself. This was not easy. First, he needed to support himself and at the same time study. Secondly, he needed to begin his career as a lawyer when he already had a family with children. He achieved both, thanks to his stubbornness and enormous driving force.

Earlier he had maintained himself and supported his family as a Hebrew teacher. As such, he did a great deal in the area. He founded a day school in Edmonton, one of the first in the country, which made a great name for itself in the history of education in Canada. He was a very capable teacher and administrator. It is a shame he did not remain in the profession.

And as a lawyer he achieved great esteem in the province in which he lived. There he became the greatest in his field among Jews and non-Jews. At his death, he was mourned by all of his colleagues and the flag over the courthouse hung at half-staff for his funeral as an expression of sorrow.

[Page 323]

Our sages have said that a man does not leave the world with half of what he wanted to achieve. This was particularly true about Chaim Aryeh. He achieved wealth and fame; he created a beautiful family. He was a leader in Canadian Jewish life. But he did not achieve one thing, settling in *Eretz-Yisroel*.

There is no doubt at all that this was one of the main goals of his life. He wanted to transplant his family to our homeland as we once dreamed in our youth. He hoped to raise his children in the land of which we dreamed, in our revived language. This he did not achieve. He tried. He especially traveled to *Eretz- Yisroel* in the 1930's, knocked on the doors of the Mandate Government and tried to find a new soil and foundation for his family. However, he returned in a grave mood. I saw him then for the last time. Traveling through New York he stayed with us in our house and spent several days with us.

[Page 324]

Yes, if he had been 15 years younger, he certainly would have achieved it with his stubbornness and diligence. But a man is only young once. Even he did not have enough energy for a second time.

Chaim Aryeh, my friend, you went through Goniadz, the small *shtetele*, to Edmonton, the capital city of the province of Alberta, like a storm. Your tempest lived its life somewhere in the distant emptiness of Canada and disappeared. Chaim Aryeh, the friend of my youth, your illustrious memory will always live in my heart.

[Pages 324-326]

The Dearest of Men
by Dr Josef Karmin
Translated by Selwyn Rose
In memory of my father, Rabbi Yehoshua z"l

Few were the years that I can recall visiting my father's house because already as a child I was moved from one Torah location to another at my father's behest and the store of memories of that dearest of men is sparse indeed although I know, and am witness to the deep love he had for me, his eldest son. I recall many walks had with my father on Shabbat afternoons outside the town as far as the Sabbath limits allowed. I wondered what it was that brought my father to take these strolls. His love for me? His wish to give me pleasure and to chat with me in Nature's bosom? That was more than fifty years ago in a small forgotten little town in hostile Christian surroundings!

He had his own way of educating his children:

[Page 324]

Intense love, understanding and consideration, and thus he was with thousands of his pupils, educating and guiding them from their earliest childhood and continuing to maintain contact with them throughout their lives until they immigrated to Palestine. He had the pleasure of seeing hundreds of his protégées immigrate until in his latter days he, too immigrated.

My father didn't want to make of the Torah a pick–axe for digging: he distanced himself from the Rabbinical authorities and sought for himself many ways of sustaining himself: he opened a shop; he indulged in various business ventures such as the manufacture of shoe polish, inks, and many other ideas. Only when all hope failed he became a teacher – and with remarkable success, for he loved the task and made many improvements.

[Page 325]

He was one of the first to create a "studio" that became known, in time, as the "Heder Metukan" ["Improved Heder"]. Apart from the "regular" subjects of the "Heder", the "Heder Metukan" taught Hebrew and Hebrew grammar and arithmetic, festival tractates, plays in Hebrew and introductions to National Zionism. The Heder was spotlessly clean, thanks to my mother who saw it as Holy work. The government inspectors always left in stunned silence at the order and capabilities of my father.

My father was active in all the town's various institutions: Hostel for the homeless, Talmud Torah, Accommodation for the traveler and all the rest of the town's institutions. He was the first among the leaders in matters concerning Zionism in town and when Zionist workers organizations began to appear, it was he who found them and brought them to town; he it was who organized and paid for the room, organized the library, gave lectures and established dialogues and conversations. In spite of being an orthodox Jew with a pure spirit, he refrained from joining the "Mizrachi" movement and remained close to those movements. His hand was in everything "and everyman's hand was against him" [Genesis XVI v 12]] there were even threats against him...he knew no fear to the end of his life. In Palestine as well, he would walk alone at night even when there was shooting in his neighborhood. While still in the Diaspora he was not deterred by anyone among the powerful non–Jews whom he faced as an equal. He was an intelligent Jew and as such he was called in Polish "Storozom" ["genius"] a man of endless information. Many came to him for advice and counseling on an infinity of topics and he always knew to give the correct advice. Because of this he won many, many friends. It seemed to me that the whole population of the town was his friend.

My father loved books and he had an extensive library in which were to be seen side–by–side, not only the "six orders of the Mishna", the Haggada and all the regular religious works but also all the books on "Enlightenment" from those days: Mapu, J. L. Gordon, Smolenskin and others. He was extremely knowledgeable as a scholar of Hebrew grammar, of the Tanach and its interpretations and even the Talmud itself had felt his touch. On more than one occasion he had been invited to take part in discussions, clarifications and debates together with the leading rabbis of the area. He was a subscriber to the Hebrew papers of the day –"Ha–Tzfira" and "Ha–Melitz" and also "Olam Katan", a children's Hebrew journal of the day for us and for his pupils. And with what great interest and warmth and deep penetration he would read all these children's stories. He was a faithful colleague of Avraham Mordecai Fiorka, one of the Enlightenment era's most conspicuous writers who wrote also for children. He loved children, understood their outlook and their souls.

All of us – all his children, he taught foreign languages and tried, as hard as he could to provide us with a broad education and found us, undeterred, revolutionary students, many of them in hiding in the town from the authorities chasing them, trying to find whatever work they could giving private lessons. Still as a child I recall him teaching me Russian (which he himself commanded), German and French and other secular subjects, and thus he was towards my sisters as well.

He was totally confident of himself with complete faith in his methods and when the "Herzliah" gymnasium opened in Jaffa he didn't hesitate for one moment before sending our mother there with all the "baggage" (six children). I remember all of us sleeping on the floor in one room in Neve Tzedek – and caught a fever. Our mother took us all home. A year later my father sent me back again alone, when I was only twelve–years old, to the same gymnasium "Herzlia". He accompanied me as far as the ship in Odessa. He saw me aboard and parted from me. It is easy to imagine how much courage and faith that took to do so. I recall when I reached thirteen he sent me a gold watch that I sold and bought a pistol. I can still remember my father's moralistic comments to me after someone had informed him of what I had done. He wrote: "You can't be a writer and a fencer*" and so on. And thus, always, he guided me from a distance with a smile and so much love even if, sometimes, he disagreed with my choices in life that very often were strange to him.

Already as a child I wanted to be a writer or a compiler of books and I remember "A Nature book teaching the Children of Israel to Grow Wheat" with the help of articles printed in Russian of popular science magazines of the time – and sent it to "Toshiya", a publisher of Hebrew books at the period. I didn't have any money and sent the manuscript without postage stamps. "Toshiya" declined to pay the postage and it was returned to me. Of course this became known to my father and he paid for the double fee. He delayed the manuscript for a couple of days and looked over the material and afterwards returned it to me with a smile saying not a word. That was my father in everything he did.

Often when he returned from meetings of one sort or another, he would bring one or two guests from among visitors to town on public business, or even drunks and paupers whom he had found on the way home. He would wake our mother up and she would prepare food and beds for them.

And mother, like every wife, wanted our father to sit at home with her and the children and refrain from public affairs and would try to let him know by subtle clues or a word here and there; more than that she didn't dare to his face. She respected him enormously and there was always peace and goodwill; however, none of this came to his attention and he maintained his actions. My mother grumbled a little but continued to be the dutiful wife and mother to her husband and children until her dying breath.

*Translator's Note: from a commentary in the Babylonian Talmud Tractate 18 on idolatry.

[Pages 327-330]

Yitzhak Yaffe z"l
Avraham Yaffe. Tel-Aviv
Translated by Selwyn Rose

Our father, Rabbi Mordecai Yaffe (z"l), came from a long dynasty of rabbis, descendants of the Gaon, Rabbi Mordecai Yaffe "The Lavush" (z"l). My brother, Yitzhak was born in Kovrin (Grodno Province), in 5640. When he was about ten years old he already knew by heart several portions of the Tractate Berachot from the Talmud. When our father passed away in only the 33rd year of his life, Yitzhak was eleven. In the town of Goniadz, where our father had moved to be the town Rabbi in the last years of his life, the spirit of the Enlightenment movement had begun to infiltrate and my brother, wearing the long caftan of the orthodox Haredi movement, began to visit the school that had opened in the town. He diligently pursued his studies both at school and in the Beit Hamidrash. During the daytime at school and at night until well after midnight he was intensely involved with his studies. He was tireless in his studies of Hebrew grammar, Russian and other subjects.

With the first awakening of the work of cultural Zionism in town my brother became involved deeply in that also and took part in the establishment of the town's reading-room and library and other branches of Zionist activities of the period.

While still young he already began to work as a teacher, in the beginning privately, and afterwards, in the "Heder-Metukan". He became teacher and mentor to his younger brothers and acted as father to them.

When "Pedagogical Courses" opened in Grodno in 1907, he was immediately accepted and shone in his speciality of the Tanach and grammar, as well as in his studies of geography and history. When I was in the final year of my studies of these courses the seniors were still talking of the diligence and learning of my brother whose statements and comments were quoted as the words of a professional authority. When he completed his studies he was appointed teacher at the modern Talmud-Torah in Kovno which was supported by the "Dissemination of Enlightenment" movement in St. Petersburg. His work at the Talmud-Torah reflected his devotion and capabilities as a teacher and instructor, which in his eyes he saw as Holy work. To a great extent that was the fruit of the efforts and influence of the excellent course instructor A. Kohnstamm (z"l) who was the director of the Grodno courses.

Page 328]

My brother would get up very early before going to school to prepare his daily lessons. As a student at the Talmud Torah he intended to set a good example from the beginning. At the same time he completed his nature studies and created a small garden at his lodgings and planted and grew various plants tending them until the garden became an example of excellence. Tenants saw him day after day, sleeves rolled-up, carrying buckets of water from the well to water his garden. In Grodno, he married a woman, the daughter of the loyal teacher and writer, Menahem Mordecai Silman (z"l). She too excelled in her studies and was gifted as a teacher.

The quality of his work in Kovno was recognised by the members of the "Disseminators of Enlightenment", Kohnstamm, Pialkov and others, but the young couple intended to immigrate to Palestine, the land of their desires, and of the people to whom they belonged, and to which they wanted dedicate their talents.

They were aided in achieving this. Dr. Nissan Turov who was head of the Teachers' center in Jaffa in those days had contacted the course management in Grodno and requested a good manager for the school in the settlement of Rehovot and the management thought of Yitzhak Yaffe and suggested the name to Dr Turov. My brother accepted the offer with joy and pleasure and at the end of 1912 they immigrated to Palestine.

[Page 329]

There he found happiness. He was director of the school in Rehovot for eleven years and devoted all his energies strengthening the school, and raising its standard to that of the Settlement's school par excellence.

His knowledge and love of nature aided him greatly.

However, while living in Rehovot he became ill with rheumatism and moved to Jerusalem to teach there at the school for boys under the directorship of Joseph Meyouhas, and lived in Beit Ha-Kerem where he built himself a house. Here also his dedication and love of his life's work of teaching added to his reputation.

[Page 330]

Here, in Beit Ha-Kerem, he brought to fruition the results of his knowledge and research of the geography of Palestine.

After a hard day's work of teaching in school, he would sit until late hours, reading books, both in Hebrew and foreign languages, examining and investigating, evaluating and digging deeper into earlier obscurity until he had raised his investigation to a level surprising many.

"If a man that dieth in a tent"... in the tent of his work of teaching and investigation. The weakness of his heart did its work; from day to day he grew weaker and on the 17th of Av, 5688, my brother passed away.

What matters if we conquer the world? Both life and death are a puzzle for the world; the soul that mourns refuses to be consoled. The loss was great for the family and also for education and investigation of the country.

[Pages 329-331]

Nakhum Zakai z"l
Translated by Gloria Berkenstat Freund

Nakhum Zakai

Nakhum, the son of Eliezer and Rywka Zakimowicz, and brother of Moshe, Shaul and Mashe Gitl, was born in Goniadz on the 4th of September 1911. He studied in a *kheder* [religious elementary school] until he was seven years old. From age seven on, he attended the Goniadz Hebrew Tarbut School [Zionist, Hebrew language school]. At age 12, he became a member of *Hahalutz HaTzair* [the Young Pioneers]. From then on, he was active in the youth movement. At age 16 he went to *Hakhsharah* [preparation for emigration to *Eretz-Yisroel*] by himself and he worked in various locations as he prepared to become a *halutz* [pioneer who emigrated to *Eretz-Yisroel*]. He already showed his writing abilities then.

He emigrated to *Eretz-Yisroel* in 1929 and settled in the *Kibbutz Ayelet ha-Shahar* in the Galilee. He was drawn to the Galilee while still at home. There he met his friend, Genya, and he brought his parents and sister there. In 1935, his first son, Nemrod, was born.

He did every kind of work in the *Kibbutz*, simple fieldwork as well as with the tractor.

[Page 330]

He was connected with Haganah [the defense - underground military organization from 1920-1948] throughout the years and always was ready to defend the country, particularly during the time of Arab unrest. During the Second World War he demanded that he be permitted to join the "brigade" (in which his two brothers served).

[Page 332]

The Land of Our Forefathers
Nahum Zakai (Zakimovitch)
Translated by Selwyn Rose

Blessed be thou to me for a possession for eternity

A safe haven you were for me when I arrived from the Land of Nod. In your breast I absorbed for the first time, the scent of the fields and the taste of the land of our forefathers. Walking in the wake of the horses behind the plowshare, my blood was rejuvenated: Earth. Mother-earth! Solid earth lies beneath my feet. A foundation; mountains, endless forests surround me. Every day I hew hidden treasures from the Galilee scenery. I felt empowered in its presence by its strength and its magnificence – I drank it all in thirstily but my thirst was not quenched.

With you I learned a new prayer, the summer prayer for dew. And the curse of Genesis "with the sweat of thy brow thou shalt eat bread" – you became for me a blessing. How did I love in the Canaanite nights to roam with the breeze, open-chest and wild hair, among the fields of wheat and orchards and to split the silence of the night with song.

(From the book "Scrolls of Fire": The chronicles and writings
of those who fell in the War of Liberation.)

[Pages 332-334]

Nahum Zakai (Zakimovitch)
Translated by Selwyn Rose

26.3.43.
To a Friend

– – – Outside it is raining ceaselessly. The floodgates of heaven have opened and it seems as if the sun was stolen this winter; and the mud – Oh, my, the mud! – was an inseparable part of our lives. It also snowed, soft snow–flakes like feathers, and how happily the little children welcomed Nature's gift. Eyes sparkled and legs danced: "How it caresses, tickles; cold, hot, burning"… and even I, myself: my eyes for an instant and I will see pure, shining–white snowy fields, like the bright, pure innocence of our childhood… the snow melts and with it – all the imagined fantasies of that childhood. Blood–stained snow, the blood of magnificent European Jewry, trampled on and pillaged to the clarion–sound of the jack–boots of wild animals; and the whispered secret prayers of the messenger who only recently visited us, and only a short while ago broke out of the ghetto walls, still ring in my ears: A people slaughtered will remember the millions trampled under the jack–booted heel of defiled legs and the hundreds of thousands shamefully exterminated. A people slaughtered like sheep and no strength to resist – and the argument continues…European Jewry destroyed and none to save it…and Yehezkiel, Eliyahu, Ze'ev, Prisoners of Zion – in round figures: 8, 6, 5, 18 years of building and effort. They are our guilty ones!… You are not alone! As you are, so are all of us. It is the law of life – to forge ahead and arrive at the end without retreating. A people condemned to the fire will not be consumed by the fire. No edict and no law, dry and modish – will stand in our way. Our justification we will ask from no one. One fate for all of us. Our hearts are with you, friends, and we will continue on our way, the road of pioneering soldiers in the Homeland. We will not rest until we see you all again among us at home. We know that "the entire world is a gallows for me". We will not deceive ourselves for one moment but with determined stubbornness and increased courage we will continue. "Seven times we fall and yet rise again*." The guilty ones know who they are – and their helpers. "Zion, Will you not enquire after your prisoners"?

(From "Scrolls of Fire….Part B").

Translator's Note: Translator's paraphrase of Proverbs 24:16

[Pages 333-334]

Hagai Zakai z"l
Gideon K.
Translated by Selwyn Rose

Hagai Zakai

Hagai Zakai, the son of Nahum Zakai, was born on 13th Shevat 5698 in Ayelet Hashahar. Exceptional qualities, which became clearer with the years, were noticed in him from his youth, especially in his personality: pleasant with people, good-hearted, likeable and smiling. It was possible occasionally to anger him but with the first contact with him the anger subsided and dissipated and an apology was forthcoming. Thus we knew him throughout his school years, in the kibbutz society and at work.

Two years have passed since, together with his age-group, he was mobilised for his national army service. Every leave, whether long or short, he would change his uniform for his work clothes, without hesitation and report for work, happy with the anticipation.

On Monday, 26th Tishri 5718, Hagai fell fulfilling his duty. In our hearts the sense of loss remains of the dear, likeable young man, pure as a child, the greater part of whose life lay before him.

May His Soul Be Bound up in the Bond of Eternal Life

[Pages 335-336]

Moshe Biali z"l
(Born 25 Shevat 5681 Died 8 Nisan 5716)
Sarah B. & Elimelech S.
Translated by Selwyn Rose

Moshe Biali (z"l)

Moshe was born and grew up in Godniondz. Very early in his childhood he absorbed from his Zionist parents and town, together with his mother's milk, the love of Zionism. In the "Tarbut" school Moshe was one of the he was a new immigrant. And Moshe indeed very quickly accustomed himself to the country, took part in all phases of the War of Independence, from Latrun, via Sodom and up to the Galilee.

But he was determined to finish the war, to be released and to join Kibbutz Kfar Blum and add his contribution to the Kibbutz.

Very quickly, as was his way, he became integrated into the life –style of the Kibbutz and stood out with his abilities and endless dedication to the task in hand. Always in a hurry, he never had time for private matters. With difficulty, he would drop-in occasionally to see his family and friends. Every task to which he was assigned he filled to his utmost ability. More than once we thought to ourselves: "Is it right to lay yet another, heavy burden on this one man?" His self-confidence and his concern for others allowed him to fulfil all his responsibilities with notable success. He was always calm and at peace with himself and he welcomed all who came to see him with a smile on his face. His good-heartedness and intelligence convinced everyone who came into contact with him, and as a result always achieved his aims in completing successfully whatever public appointments were laid upon him.

It is difficult to come to terms with the bitter and cruel fate that Moshe – the refreshing, powerful and ever-smiling – was plucked from our midst so suddenly and cruelly while still only at the beginning of his journey.

We, his family and friends, have lost the very best from among us because he was the very basis of our pride.

His memory will never fade…

[Pages 337-340]

In Memory of My Brother z"l
Yona Levinshal-Mali
Translated by Selwyn Rose

Liezer (Lazer) Mali

Together with the youth movements of "He-Halutz" and the "Bund", there existed in our town a small branch of the Communist Party. The social relationship between the various parties was not influenced by the differing political opinions and whenever festivities of the one took place, the other would come and vise-versa.

I remember the First of May 1924. The first of the speakers – Zaidel Altschuld, good-looking, graceful like a palm-tree, dark with long sleek hair, fire-spitting in his speech: "The handkerchiefs of the rich, their soaked in perfume and they themselves smelling of expensive intoxicating drinks, while our handkerchiefs are soaked in blood and sweat!" His words made a deep impression on me. For a long time afterwards I would "ambush" him in the hopes of seeing him take a handkerchief from his pocket stained with blood and sweat...

[Page 338]

Among the pupils of the school who inserted herself into communism was Heshka, the Rabbi's daughter. She had a fiery and tempestuous personality. Wherever she appeared, her hair tightly curled like a sheep, refusing to succumb to a comb, there everything seethed and bubbled. She was of medium height, a little tubby, round-faced and a large area of her face was marked with a dark red tinge. That big red mark, that would undoubtedly mar the face of anyone else, seemed to add grace and harmony to her appearance, perhaps create a doubt in someone concerning her fiery nature – and the mark was a witness to that...

That girl was gifted with the logic of a man, blended with a sensitivity of a woman. With her persuasive strength and personal charm she conquered the hearts of the boys: Yankele, Asher - and finally Lazer.

When the boys grew up and matured they rejected all their youthful opinions and together with their childhood dreams, they dropped away from them with the passage of the years. Not so with Lazer. The Movement was the axis of his life from his childhood until his last day, and lead eventually to his death.

He was a quiet, introspective boy, of medium height and slightly stooped, with wavy, chestnut hair with a sharply angled, high forehead, under which peeped two dreamy brown eyes that always had a hint of sadness in them. In contrast to the soft and good-hearted expression in his face his lips showed a certain stubbornness. And, indeed, with that stubbornness he fought for his ideal.

[Page 339]

In 1927 he immigrated to Palestine with his parents but the Homeland being rebuilt seemed strange to him, the smell of the midden failed to charm him and he found no roots there. In 1931 he was exiled from Palestine for belonging to the Communist Party and returned to Goniadz.

Desolation and silence spread throughout the few streets of the town. With a heavy beating heart he neared "Alte Markt" the street where he had grown up. Here also was the house where he had lived with his family, a big wooden house, old and gloomy, all cracked with age. Here, he spent his happiest early years. Such warmth, gaiety, and childhood noise once pealed from that house and how neglected and dark it was now.

Lazer found an escape from the boredom at the home of the Hazan family. That was the place where the group of Communists from the town met together. The life and soul of the group was Racheleh Hazan, the youngest and most gifted of them all, small, pink-faced graced with two dimples and decorated with two long black plaits that reached down to her hips. She immediately won Lazer's heart.

[Page 340]

After a while many of them were caught and imprisoned, among them Lazer.

Throughout all the stormy period of the Great World War, only faint echoes penetrated through the dense stone walls of the prison until suddenly one bright day in 1939 the iron gates opened before them – The Russian Army had conquered that part of Poland. Lazer fell as if into a seething cauldron. All the energy that had been pent up inside him for years burst out of him in a flood. He jumped from one field of endeavour to another, like a butterfly flitting from one flower to another tasting their nectar. Then he married Racheleh and their happiness was complete – but only for a short while. Two years had not passed before Lazer together with the rest of the six-million Jews, was exterminated.

[Pages 339-342]

Yosef Bobrowski z"l
by Moshe Bachrach
Translated from Yiddish to English by Gloria Berkenstat Freund

Yosef Bobrowski

Yosef Bobrowski, or Yosef Mendele's [son of Mendel], as he familiarly was called, belonged to the older generation of "Young Goniadz." This was a generation of "pioneers" who began a new chapter of history in marking the completion of the yearly reading of the Torah] (where pledges were made to donate to *Keren Kayemet LeYisroel* [Jewish National Fund]) and emigration to *Eretz-Yisroel.* As small as the group was and as modest its start, their accomplishments were of important significance for the increase in Zionist strength in Goniadz and for the founding in 1915 of the Hebrew Folks-School [public school] with which its founder and the *yeshiva* director, Moshe Lewin, won over Goniadz.

The library was created by the same group of idealists. This was a Folks [public] Library in which reigned a Zionist atmosphere.

As usual there were both dreamers and doers among the young people - Yosef Bobrowski was among the dreamers. As a former *yeshiva* [religious secondary school stressing the teaching of Torah] student, as well as a Hasid, he was the pious one amidst the group. He even prayed wearing a *gartl* [a belt signifying the separation of the sacred from the profane] and let his beard grow.

Yosef emigrated to America before the First World War. Here, he worked in a "shop*" until he succeeded in [starting] his own small factory for women's clothing. However, he was not swallowed up by the factory. His spiritual and communal ideals and interests remained - [he was a] Goniadzer.

Based on the size of his [monetary] donations for all purposes and institutions in which he believed - and he was by nature a passionate believer - one would think that he was a very wealthy man, although he was very far from being one.

[Page 342]

Yosef was one of the pillars of the Goniadzer Aid Committee after the destruction of Goniadz. He also was slender [frail]; things were difficult for him physically. At that time, Yosef already was gravely ill - and at the same time he worked for the United Jewish Appeal with self-sacrifice. In his characteristic manner, he once said to me: "What should I do - leave everything in chaos?"

Yosef's heart would yearn with longing to just once be able to meet the friends from his youth who were living in Israel. However, his wish did not come true. He died in Norwalk, Connecticut on the 3rd of November 1950.

*Translator's Note: In American Yiddish, a "shop" was a small factory making clothing

[Pages 341-344]

Nissan the Tailor z"l
by David Bachrach
Translated from Yiddish to English by Gloria Berkenstat Freund

When I want to evoke a tzadek [righteous man] in my memory, I recall the image of Nisan the tailor. He was short, hunchbacked, with a blond beard. He always wore a long talis-koton [fringed garment usually worn under a man's clothing] that was very visible when he stood and worked with a needle or iron. His thoughts always were dedicated to God. His wife was a tall, thick and simple Jewish woman like most of the women in the shtetl [town]; however, he was sensitive and gentle. No coarse word ever came out of his mouth because his thoughts were in Ein Yakov [book of Talmudic commentaries] or in another sacred book. He barely drew an income from his work.

I remember a Shabbos [Sabbath] when my father, of blessed memory, and Reb Nisan came together from the synagogue; we lived next to each other. Reb Nisan described how he had seen the Beis HaMikdash [Temple in Jerusalem] and heard the singing and playing [of music] of the Leviim [descendents of tribe of Levi]. His description of the ceremonies and music of the Beis HaMikdash that he witnessed in his dream lasted for a long time and we stood for a considerable time and listened to him until the end.

I loved to listen to his teaching of Ein Yakov. He studied with a group of Jews in the house of prayer at a table that was close to the tile oven. There he explained the interesting stories in Ein Yakov with great insight and love. His regular "students" were Avraham'ke the glazier, his brother Arke, Khackl the water-carrier and still other poor Jews.

He never went home on Yom Kippur after Shir HaYichud [Song of Unity], but he remained overnight in the synagogue. He would lie on straw under a bench for an hour or two.

He would recite Psalms during the remaining hours.

This is how he remained in my memory – a man of perfect saintliness in his relationship to God and to people.

[Pages 343-344]

Avraham Szwarc z"l
by A. Ben-Meir
Translated by Gloria Berkenstat Freund

Avraham Szwarc

Avraham Szwarc, or as we called him, "Avraham'l Sender's" [Sender's son Avraham'l], was born in Goniadz in 1895 into a fine family. His father, "Sender the writer," who died young, made a living by giving lessons (*urakn* [private lessons]) in Russian, Yiddish and Hebrew. Avraham'l, who studied for a time in a *yeshiva* [religious secondary school that emphasizes the study of Torah], knew Hebrew marveled at him. He had a strong love of music: he was the best member of the choir of the *khazan* [cantor], Reb Nakhum, and a distinguished mandolin player. A dreamer and a searching spirit, he came to the ideas of *Paolei-Zion* [Workers of Zion - Marxist-Zionist workers movement] and to Yiddish literature when he was very young. He published a number of lyrical poems of a social character and was a co-worker at the *Bialystoker Shtime* [*Bialystok Voice*]. He had a difficult life as a Hebrew teacher, as he was the one who provided food for a poor, sick mother, a widow.

Avraham'l lived in Trestiny [Trzcianne] before the last war. After Trestiny was occupied by the Nazis, heavy shooting broke out in the *shtetl* on Wednesday, the 24th of June, 1941, due to a false accusation by Poles. The Nazis dropped incendiary bombs on the houses, which caught fire lightning fast and a number of Jews perished in the hellish fire. The entire *shtetl* was burned and the Jews ran to the meadow in panic.

As Tsipora Braverman tells it (in the *Goniadzer-Trestiner Jubilee Journal*), Avraham'l, Sender's son, was among the first victims to fall in the meadow. "He received a bullet in the stomach and died after a night of suffering" (exactly like his heroic friend Yakov Taker in *Tel Hai* [former Jewish settlement in the northern Galilee, where eight Jews were killed during Arab attacks on the settlement in 1920.]). The memory of the tragic fatality of our talented dreamer was memorialized in our book by one of his best poems.

[Pages 345-346]

Yankl the Doctor
Translated from Yiddish to English by Dr. Isaac Fine

In actuality he was no more than a doctor's assistant (feldscher), but like all doctor's assistants in Jewish towns, he carried the honored title of doctor (roife). In Tsarist Russia, feldschers played a significant role. Russia was not able to supply the giant nation with physicians, and the bulk of the public's medical needs were met by feldschers.

The mission of the feldscher was to heal wounds and also minor ailments. They were not trained to deal with any more serious medical problems than that, nor were they permitted to do so. However, there were able men among them who, through practice and experience, had earned the confidence of the people and had been permitted to deal with more serious problems. Yankl the roife was this kind of feldscher.

I recall him from my childhood as an older man. Goniondz Jews rarely went to the Polish Dr. Knapinsky, although he was a quite competent physician. One needed to converse with him in Polish, and one needed to treat him with reverence. In addition, a visit to his office cost twenty kopecks. Also, it was required to buy the medicine for his prescriptions from the Polish pharmacy of Lintchevsky, which again was quite expensive. In contrast, the expenses with Yankl the roife were much more modest. This was in large part because he prepared the medicines himself. By seeing him, one was able at the same time to save money and also avoid the gentiles.

The whole town used to buy common remedies, such as zinc ointment, from him. He mixed the ingredients himself. For stomachaches he would first prescribe castor oil and then an enema. Even though the roife was very much respected, there were rascals who used to tease him about conducting this sort of unclean business. One time, for example, when one of the wilder young men met him at night in the darkness, he cried out to Yankl from the distance, "Rabbi Yaakov, make me an enema." This comment affected Yankl's dignity. He ran after the youngster as fast as he could, but could not catch him. After this incident, he came to Gedalke's classroom, where I was a student, and asked where was Shimon Abramsky. The latter was a youth from Grayve who was studying with Gedalke. When the youth was pointed out to him, Yankl wanted to hit him with a stick. The boy swore that he knew nothing of the matter, and was overcome with fear.

When Yankl the roife recommended that an ill person be brought to Dr. Knapinsky for a consultation, one knew that the matter was quite serious. Yankl would accompany the patient to the physician, and Knapinsky would obtain a detailed report from Yankl. It was quite clear that the doctor respected his opinions.

Yankel the roife was quite successful in his professional career. On Sundays, when the Christians would come to church, and on Mondays, which was market day, many of them would come to "Pan Yankl."

In the winter of the great fire, Pesach of 1906, he married off his youngest daughter to a wealthy young man from Krinik. He didn't invite in the orchestra from Stutchin, which was ordinarily invited. The Stutchin orchestra consisted of a fiddle, a flute, and a drum. Rather, he brought in the military orchestra from Osoviec. The whole shtetl was in a very festive mood. Everyone stood in the old marketplace and sang and danced along with the music. Goniondz had never had this kind of attraction before.

Immediately after the fire he built a magnificent wooden house next to Schloime-Yossel the fisherman, and did not require any loan in order to do so. During the three bitter years of the German occupation during the First World War, Goniondz did not have a physician. The German military doctor from Osoviec was very rarely brought in. For those reasons, during that time period Yankl was the only healer of the sick in town. Many people died of weakness, simply because they did not eat enough, and Yankl's remedies could not help them.

During the winter of 1918/19 "Rabbi Yaakov" was very busy. He cured the first of those who were struck with the typhus plague at that time, including Cheikel Yevreisky and me, and thank God we were restored to health. Later, when the epidemic had spread in a very dramatic fashion and there were many critically ill, a physician from Kniesin was brought into town, but he was not able to help very much.

In 1923 the Polish government sent the roife a medal as a reward for his meritorious actions in the past. In 1863, the second Polish uprising against the Tsarist regime broke out and the Russian regime threatened the death penalty for any person who provided the slightest assistance to the rebels. Yankl the roife, who at that time was living in Sapatzkin, which was located near Grodno, had given medical assistance to those who participated in the uprising. Yet years later, when Poland achieved its independence, they recalled his deeds and rewarded him with great honor.

He was very much loved by all. When one met another townsman in the greater world, the first question was about the synagogue hill, and the second, "What do you hear about Yankl the roife?" He lived out his years in honor and generosity. He left this world in 1926, at which time he was more than ninety years of age.

[Pages 347-350]

Max Schwartz z"l
(1884-1955)
by Dovid Forman
Translated by Gloria Berkenstat Freund

I feel it as a debt to immortalize in our book the memory of our *landsman* [man from the same town] who occupied a respected place in Jewish communal life in America. Max (Mendl) Schwartz truly was one of the children of the poor, who thanks to his abilities and strong will grew up to be a well-educated man going along a difficult road through life.

His mother was Khashke, the fish seller. He lost his father when he was three years old. He studied in *khederim* [religious primary schools] and in a *yeshiva* [religious secondary school], wandered to various countries in Europe – Sweden, Denmark and England – and came to New York when he was 19 years old. His goal was to study. He had a sharp mind, studied languages and showed a particular interest in political economy. In New York, he joined the anarchist movement – and was an active speaker and writer. His articles on various themes were published in the *Freie Arbeiter Shtime* [*The Free Voice of Labor*]. He translated the works of the German scholar, Ludwig Büchner, and also was active as a correspondent to the letters section of *The New York Times*.

In possession of good Yiddish and a worldly education and a fine character, he became beloved and respected by everyone. After the loss of his devoted life's companion, which greatly damaged him, his young comrades invited him to join them in Detroit.

After the Second World War, he organized the Goniadz aid committee in Detroit under the name "Goniadzer Friends." About 20 Goniadz families are located in the city, but under his influence, great activity is shown in gathering large sums on behalf of those from Goniadz. He also had a great influence on the Goniadz *landsleit* [people from the same town] in Chicago. He died of a heart attack on the 18th of November 1955.

Honor his memory.

[Pages 349-352]

Dr. Josef Chazanowicz z"l
by D.B.
Translated by Gloria Berkenstat Freund

The famous doctor, Josef Chazanowicz of Bialystok, was born in Goniadz and descended from Feywl Grodzinak's family. I do not know how a young man from a not well–to–do family could make his way to a university that at that time, over 90 years ago, was connected with great cost and much difficulty. Perhaps one of his relatives who now live in New York can clarify the matter.

Chazanowicz was a well–known doctor and had a good reputation throughout the area. There was a very good doctor in our *shtetl* [town], a Pole named Knapinski, but when someone was seriously ill and he was well–to–do, he would bring a great doctor from Bialystok and it usually was Chazanowicz. When Moshe Kramkower was gravely ill and actually died of his illness, they had brought Chazanowicz. I saw him for the first time then.

Chazanowicz was a very nervous man and many curious things are said about him. A patient could not repeat a question to him about something because it was no problem for him to show him to the door... His office was on the second floor over Wilbuszewicze's apothecary at the market place, after the city clock.

When giving the patient his written prescription, he would often use a short, laconic ritual: "With Wilbuszewicz in bed." This was to signify that the patient should buy the medicine from none other than Wilbuszewicz in the apothecary (he had no trust in any ordinary apothecary), and he should lie in bed for a certain time... In general, he would speak very quickly, with short cut–off phrases and this language had to be understood because as already mentioned, asking was not permitted. With all his renown, he remained a typical man of the people both in his conduct and in his relationship with people. He loved the common man, poor toilers. He healed them without payment and often also added a prescription on his own account. In contrast, he could not bear any rich men. He believed that their illnesses and diseases come from comfort and luxury. "They ceaselessly overeat and they guzzle!"... It is no surprise that he was very well accepted and became very admired among the widespread strata of people and the sick were drawn to him from far and near.

He was a dedicated Zionist, an ardent follower of [Theodor] Herzl and traveled to the First [Zionist] Congress in Basel. He was very inspired by Zionist thought and immediately began to collect books as well as old Jewish antiques for the future university and museum in Jerusalem. It required a strong belief in this dream, just as in the idea of a Jewish land would be accomplished some day. One really also had to be a great lofty dreamer and he truly was.

I do not know if Chazanowicz had a family: but it is known that he used his entire income for the acquisition of valuable books. Zionists from the entire area were his "agents" and would send him many books. He packed the books in crates and sent them to Jerusalem. This matter cost him a huge sum of money, but he continued it until the First World War when contact with *Eretz–Yisroel* ceased. Later, as his dream became a reality and Hebrew University was erected in 1925 on *Har ha–Tsofim* [Mount Scopus],his books served as the basis for the large National Library.

The old [volumes] of Rambam with pages greenish–yellow from age bound in wooden covers suddenly disappeared from the synagogue. After much investigation it was shown that Josef Halpern had taken them out one morning and sent them to Chazanowicz, certainly with the agreement of his father Ephraim, of blessed memory, an ardent Zionist, as well as of other Goniadz Zionists. It is entirely possible that this is the only book surviving from the Goniadz synagogue...

It also was said that once when Dr. Ch. was in Goniadz he proposed that the *gabbai* [sexton] of the synagogue sell him certain antique vessels from the synagogue. However, the *gabbai* could not be persuaded to part with such beloved antiques and refused him. These vessels disappeared in fire along with the synagogue, which the Nazis – the name of the wicked will rot [Proverbs 10:7] – burned.

In memory of his name the library was named *Beit Yosef* [house of Joseph] *al shem Yosef Chazanowicz* [in memory of Josef Chazanowicz].

At the end of the summer 1915, when the Russian Army withdrew from our area, he, already an old man, escaped to Russia and perished forlorn and alone from hunger and want in an old age home in Yekaterinoslav [Dnipropetrovsk, Ukraine] during the civil war after the World War.

Honor his memory!

[Pages 353-354]

M. Sh. Ben–Meir z"l
[an obituary]
Translated by Gloria Berkenstat Freund

The sudden death of the Hebrew–Yiddish poet and essayist, M. Sh. Ben–Meir (Treszczanski), evoked great sadness in the deceased in Yiddish, in the name of the teaching personnel of the synagogue scholars from the Reb Yitzhak Elkhanan *Yeshiva* [religious secondary school], of which the deceased was a member.

The pedagogue, Josef Eisberg, spoke in the name of the Ussishkin branch of the Jewish National Workers Union. The community, and a sister, Chava.

(Der Tog Morgen Zhurnal [The Day], New York, 20/1/1959)

[Pages 353-360]

Idl Treszczanski (M.Sh. Ben-Meir) z"l
by Dovid Bachrach
Translated by Gloria Berkenstat Freund

It is very difficult to write about Idl as someone who is no longer here. We had just been in contact with him; he edited a part of our book; we sent complaints to him. He answered, [we] again wrote to him and suddenly he is gone, died and the end. It is difficult to get accustomed to the idea, but what do the Sages say: "If you hear that thy friend has died, believe it." "Every death has its reproach." And I think that if his wife had been alive and he had had proper supervision, he would not have died.

I remember Idl (Idl is a pet name, like Zeydke, Alter; his real name is Moshe Shlomo) from when I remember myself. Our families lived as neighbors, one door next to the other, we grew to feel at home with each other and were as close to each other as family members. He and his sister Chaya (lives in Antwerp) found friends in our house. We played together in childhood and grew up [together].

We did not study together with Gdalka at the Hebrew school. I was then six years old, he four, or perhaps three. I do not remember him either at Leibl Wajnsztajn's, the Suchowola teacher, who took over the school when Gdalka went to serve the Russian czar and we did not study together later in the *khederim* [religious primary schools]. When he studied with Shlomo Welwl, I studied with Motya the *melamed* [religious school teacher] and when he came to Motya, I moved to study with my uncle, Shlomo Moshe, Shimeon's son. But because we were very close, I would go to their house quickly every morning and [we would] go to *kheder* together. Often, very often, he would not be in the best of health, his throat wrapped in a shawl and he looked pale. "Today, I am not going to *kheder*," he would say, and his grandmother, his mother's mother, would add: "In any case, he will not be a rabbi." I thought: he is missing so much learning, what will happen to him. But he lost nothing; he was a very capable young boy with a good head and caught up with everything.

He was the "*muzhinek*" (youngest] of the family; they spoiled him greatly. In addition, he was weak and frail and they gave into him with everything, and he grew to be an overly sensitive man, a trait that remained for his entire life. He was a timid man by nature, was afraid of a dog when he saw it from a mile off; to him a worm was a snake and he trembled [when he saw one]. The boys, sensing his physical weakness, would badger him, so I was his constant protector. He clung to me.

He has his parents to thank for his rich spiritual life. When I would visit in the evenings after *kheder*, when he did not feel well and sat at home, I always would find him playing chess with his mother. Idl grew up to be a good chess player and even died in the middle of a chess game. Where did one see a woman who played chess and fifty years ago in Goniadz? However, Chaya Beyla was a very intelligent woman, had mastered the German language and read a great deal during her youth. She also was knowledgeable about our old religious books and in her daily conversations, and people still speak about her letters in which she made use of expressions from the *Midrash* [Talmud], *Menoyres haMoer* [*The Lighter of Light*] and other religious texts. Where did she [learn] this? Every *Shabbos* our mothers read the *Tsene-rene* [Yiddish adaptation of Biblical texts], but for her the words of the *Taytsh-Khumish* [Torah translated into Yiddish] went deep into her brain and she made use of them. He inherited much from her. He immortalized her in his poem, *Meyn Mame* [*My Mother*]. I think that the poem is one of his strongest creations. Our family in Tel Aviv would receive letters from her from Antwerp where she lived during her last years with all four of her children. She died in deep old age during the Second World War. His father died in the 1920s in Jasionówka.

Idl also inherited much from his father, Meir the watchmaker. Meir made a poor living from his work, watchmaking, until his two older sons, Leyzer Zelig and Kalman were grown up and subsidized [the income]. Thanks to his friend Yankl Rudski, who was a large supplier to the government at the Osowiec Fortress and had many acquaintanceships with officers, Meir received employment. Every Tuesday morning he would travel there to wind and regulate the clocks in the government buildings. He received a monthly salary for this and also would fall into a little work. However, income was an afterthought for him; the main thing was the spiritual life. He sat reading a *Gemara* [Talmudic commentaries] every *Shabbos* evening, studying with enthusiasm. Jews did not read books from the Enlightenment; Torah study was the quintessence of life and Idl, being very gentle and impressionable, absorbed much from him.

We grew older and left *kheder*. In my house they began to talk about a purpose for me, what is the point of being idle? A decision was reached to send me away to study in a *yeshiva* [religious secondary school with an emphasis on the study of religious texts]. This was the true purpose. Because of Idl's weak state of health, he could not even think of it. The first two years of the *yeshiva ketana* [small religious secondary school] I would come home for the holidays; the last three years from the Raduner *Yeshiva* – rarely. Idl always was my first visitor. He had much to tell of the books that he read. He read a great deal and was proficient in Hebrew and Yiddish literature. Idl did not receive any academic education. But he acquired a very good comprehension of everything himself and what he read was [placed in his memory] as if placed in a box.

We separated during the First World War when we had to leave Goniadz. His family went to Jasionówka, a little farther from the front, where Meir's sister lived and never returned to Goniadz. Idl would come to visit the *shtetl* [town] and usually was our guest. In August 1920 I left Poland and our connection was interrupted. However, in 1934, when I emigrated from America, I began to correspond with him in Antwerp until the Hitler invasion when he succeeded in reaching Portugal and from there, America.

I am not in a position to write about Idl's literary work. He was far from me for so long, but visiting in Israel several years ago, he published a very beautiful poem about the *RaMHal* (acronym for Rabbi Moshe Chaim Luzzato) in *Dvar Hashavua* [*Word of the Week*]. The poet and kabbalist fled Padua, Italy, the city of his birth, for Amsterdam because he was persecuted by the rabbis and there fed himself as a diamond polisher. Idl also studied the same trade of diamond polishing in Antwerp. His poem about the *RaMHal* was very successful. Idl's poems would be published from time to time in *Hadoar* [*The Post*], the Hebrew journal published in New York that I would read with pleasure. Recently he collected his poems and they were published in a book, *Tzlil va-Tzel* [*Sound and Shadow*]. The book was published in Tel Aviv and sent to New York. Idl left this world one day before the book left the bindery and he did not live to see his life's wish accomplished.

Idl's wife died suddenly two years ago and he was left with two children. His daughter already was a grown girl. But, his son was a recent *Bar-Mitzvah*. In any case, it was a difficult situation. But he was completely lost. He complained strongly of his loneliness in his letters to us; friends and acquaintances were not taking an interest in him and he was alone. The truth was that daily life in New York was difficult, friends and acquaintances were spread across the large city and everyone was busy with himself. Idl worked hard himself, beyond his strength. But one needs to live, maintain a home and raise children, one makes an effort. In the mornings he gave lessons at a teacher's training school in the Bronx, where he lived, and in the afternoons he held a position as a teacher in distant Brooklyn. The long daily trip on the subway exhausts a strong person, so what about him? In addition, he also suffered from diabetes. While his wife lived, she watched over him. He could not endure remaining alone and collapsed.

This is a great loss for we from Goniadz and a strong ache for me personally.

[Pages 359-362]

Master of Sound and Shadow
(Spoken at a Gathering of Mourners)
by Kalman Bachrach, New York
Translated by Selwyn Rose

Kalman Bachrach

Moshe S. Ben–Meir was an honorable and honored member of the Ussishkin Chapter [of the Jewish National Workers' Union]. Our Chapter is known for its pre–eminence in Jewish cultural activities and our members show great respect and admiration for Hebrew poets and lyricists; clearly, then, we respected Ben–Meir as being one who stood head and shoulders speeches and speakers who were to take part in the celebration. And now, instead of a happy celebratory event, we are taking part in an act of mourning. "The night of pleasure he hath turned into fear unto me." We weep over the death of our dear friend. His passing is a loss to the Chapter and to Hebrew culture never to be replaced.

Moshe S. Ben–Meir was a son of my home town and a friend of my family from the days of his youth. I feel, therefore, that I am permitted to say a few words in the name of the town. In our town of Goniadz we never knew him as Moshe S. Ben–Meir: we called him Idel Ben–Meir, the watchmaker's son and hence the name Ben–Meir. The family name was Tershansky. His father Meir, the watchmaker was a true artist in his profession. It was said of him in town that he was busy inventing a machine and nobody knew what it was. The clocks and watches that were brought to him for repair were of all shapes, types and sizes. On the walls were hung pendulum clocks, large and small, with heavy weights and light weights. The swinging of the different pendulums, the different rate of swing of all of them, the different chimes – harsh or clarion–like, small or tall, spread an air of mystery throughout the house. Behind his work–bench sat Meir the watchmaker, completely silent and confident, immersed in his work. When the door opened and someone entered the house, he would raise his head and gaze at the visitor – his eyes were large, thick–lidded and filled with curiosity.

They displayed both seriousness and mischievousness and the visitor would never know whether he would be welcomed by Reb Meir the watchmaker with a joke or something more serious. In his free time, Reb Meir read "The Time" and studied the Holy Books. In the room behind his work–room the Babylonian and Vilna Talmuds were displayed on the shelves in their glory. Ben–Meir's mother was a rare type – perhaps the only one of her kind in town, praying three times a day, just like the men–folk, understanding everything she read. Thus it was with her general conversation – everything she said was clear and reasonable.

Nevertheless, the house of Meir the watchmaker was free of all religious and educational pressure and coercion. The older sons (Idel had two brothers), left the town and settled in the wide world, one in Warsaw and the other in Switzerland. When they came to visit their parents there was never any friction between them. On the contrary, freedom reigned – even something of the small village atmosphere. On Sabbath Eve, after dinner, they would play chess and discuss political issues.

Idel himself was somewhat sensitive. Every experience, light or intense left its mark on him and every minor change was mirrored in his face and his mood. As a result his every mood could change within seconds; as it was with the father so it was with the son – a sense of humor and mischievousness, an impish smile hovering over his lips although his sensitivity was such that his mood could change instantly to one of sadness. The border–line between laughter and sadness was thin indeed, much like the name of his book "Sound and Shadow". With time, after his encounters with day–to–day life and especially after drinking of the cup of sorrows – both his own and those of the Jewish world, the hovering smile disappeared from his lips and his face displayed only endless sadness. During the latter years of his life, he walked as a shadow. And the "shadow" vanquished the "sound"...

His talent for poetry was discovered early in life, during his youth. He loved to create rhymes and compose tunes, mostly humorous. He especially liked parodies in the style of classical Russian lyricists and poets; his rhymes were in either Russian or Yiddish but when he turned to Hebrew they took on a more serious and respectful note. His first songs that were published in "The Times" during the twenties were devoid of humor to the astonishment of his acquaintances. Only towards the end of his life, with the establishment of the State of Israel, his natural tendency towards humor was reawakened somewhat and he wrote poems such as "The Red Burden", "Celebration", "Circus Informer". In "Celebration" he expresses scorn regarding the matching of Esau with the sickness of Ishmael's daughter – in other words, between Soviet Russia and Egypt...

Thus we of his town knew him, and he was much loved by us. His last activity benefitting his home town was editing "Book of Remembrance", which will appear this year, in Israel.

May He be Remembered for a Blessing.

[Pages 361-362]

M. S. Ben–Meir
by M. Meizlish
Translated by Yocheved Klausner

It was only a few days ago that his book of poems, "Sound and Shadow" [*Tzlil Vetzel*] arrived from Israel; a book that was as modest and pure as its author. But he barely had time to set his eyes on his completed work and unfolded through the book, in the lines and between the lines, the humility of a person who is convinced that his pain does not deserve to be discussed in high style or even made public; his worries he relates only to himself, in a low voice, in order not to disturb others – in life as in literature. But this very whisper is what impresses the reader and touches his heart. In one of the poems in the book, a poem on a surprising subject – "a memorial to the poems that were born dead," poems that the poet had not succeeded in clothing them with silk and purple – he prays: "May the Prince of Poetry remember these naked souls – – – an echo of a stifled prayer, a shadow-sound melted in tenderness, a fetus from the seed of sorrow that sprouted from a barren phrase – in the place of a song a sigh poured out and the fruit dissolved in tears. May the God of Poetry remember." This is what makes Ben–Meir's modest poetry unique and dear. In it, we shall forever hear the voice of prayer, forever the seed of sorrow shall sprout, the whispering sigh rise and the dampness of the tears be preserved.

[Pages 363-364]

The book is small, modest in its form as well, but in the tears of its poems the destiny of man is reflected, the destiny of a generation – and what generation was tried harder than ours, a generation sentenced to fire, to burning of soul and body? In the section of the book named "Nightmares," the descriptions of war and holocaust, flight and survival, in their simplicity of colors bring to life the frightful sights in all their horror, and we almost feel their touch and are burned by it. A sharp yearning for faith is reflected in many of his poems, which mourn the loss of so many souls, of a generation that "an evil wind has blown away the illusions of their adolescence and curbed the sources of innocence and mercy." And also "Doubt has locked the gates of prayer, and the key was thrown into the deep." A cry like: "Please be with me even when I am denying You, even when I reject You... so as I shall not hide my face from You, oh my Father, my Father in Heaven!" – deserves to head every prayer–book in our days of confusion and perplexity, not having any guides for the perplexed*.

M. S. Meir trod along the edges of the roads, in life as in literature, as if his very existence was not significant enough to project its presence, its reality, upon others. But this walking of his was very pure, as was his poetry – unsoiled and true. We can trust his own testimony in one of his poems, *Tefillin* [phylacteries]:

> *The mark on my hand*
> *Is always with me –*
> *On both my hands,*
> *On my ten fingers,*
> *And a hidden band*
> *Passes and connects*
> *My thumb with my little finger.*
> *I am innocent:*
> *In my fury*
> *I have not raised a criminal hand,*
> *I have not shown a clenched fist,*
> *Never shut my hand to a brother.*
> *Never did I shake a hand*
> *In an untrue shake,*
>
> *Never raised it in a pledge*
> *Under false pretenses.*
> *I did not take what was not mine,*
> *Or show an accusing finger*
> *In a false hint.*
> *Not in vain, not in vain*
> *Is the mark on my hand.*
> *The phylacteries between my eyes*
> *Are deep inside my eyes*
> *In them and in back of them,*
> *In the cells of my brain.*

Pure of eyes am I:

I have never perceived evil

Out of my own desire.

have never stared with wrath,

Nor with despise or scorn.

I did not rest

When my fellow was in danger

I did not gloat

On the shame of my fellow –

I did not stare at him

To humiliate him.

Not in vain, not in vain

Is the mark

With me always.

The phylacteries

Are mine

This is how he walked among us, one with his sorrow, alone in his seclusion. Only from time to time did his loneliness shed one tear – in the form of a poem; at times – but not often – the poem was a legend, full of simple charm and consolation, and at times it was heavy in form and thought and brought to life figures from the past. Even his occupation – diamond cutting – was sometimes reflected in his poetry, as in the poem "The Vision of RAMCHAL [Rabbi Moshe Chaim Luzzatto] the Polisher," a song of great beauty that mirrors both its theme and its author. He had hoped, and with him his friends, that perhaps the collection of his poems in one volume would ease his pain a little, would bring some light into his solitude. But lo, his loneliness closed upon itself and the song became an orphan.

May His Soul be Bound in the Bond of the Living Jewish Literature.

(Hado'ar ["The Post"], New–York, 14 Shevat 5719 [1959])

*Translator's Note: An allusion to "The Guide for the Perplexed" by Maimonides

[Pages 365-368]

A Man and his Book
**Remarks on M.S. Ben–Meir's Book of Poems *Tzlil Vetzel* [Sound and Shadow],
Tel Aviv, 5718 (1958)
by Aharon Zeitlin
Translated by Yocheved Klausner**

A Hebrew man lived in New–York, and the man had a great love for God. He did not feign righteousness; he truly lived through the purity of his soul and its pains. And as for his love of God – he described this feeling with the words "sick with God[1]" and this phrase remained engraved in my memory.

He was a man who was obsessed with the problem of "leadership of the world" – it was like an illness that demanded resolution at once. He was sick with God – and just as a sick man is tossed between hot fever and cold shivering, he was caught in the fervor of seeking closeness and intimacy with God – in turn finding and losing this nearness, finding and losing again and again. The feeling was like the sun in autumn, disappearing behind the clouds and appearing anew, in and out.

"The greater the effort" – he complains in one of his poems – "the greater the confusion. The eye that sought hope, trying to find a key to the secret of the valley of tears, was smitten with blindness." On the other hand, when a moment of intimacy was indeed uncovered, it brought remedy on its wings: all the questions and problems were solved. And with that, it brought to life the melody of "A shapeless violin"... also "In the blindness of my soul an eye shall open..." or: "In the wasteland of my soul a spring shall flow / that soothes, as a good wine, my suffering / and I shall believe – there is a law and there is a judge / and I shall not fear my death"...

Further, from another poem: "one by one they shall wander, alone in the forests of faith." Let us pay attention: in the forests of faith. For, on the backdrop of the explicit faith, on the basis of the inner knowledge that transcendence does exist, that is where the problems begin – the great quest for a hiding God, a God that is near and far; the nearer He is the farther one has to look for Him. The questions and the answers are intertwined; the prayer becomes a question and the question – a prayer. So was this man: he wondered while believing and believed – wondering further. He never ceased asking and never ceased praying. This never–ending prayer is expressed in the poem "...Neither Morning nor Evening Prayer" (page 33). The prayer prevails even when it turns into weeping: "You demand sacrifice as well as massacre" (page 58). Moreover, out of a desperate denial, after the great fire of the European Jewry, he prays and pleads with the Almighty "Be with me even when I deny You, even when I reject You" (ibid.). Logically this is an obvious contradiction. In faith it is not; on the contrary

– it is the truth of the special experience of fusion of opposites. Truth is achieved through agony of the soul that finds and loses, loses and recovers, falls and rises again. "I lift the wings of dawn; I dwell at the end of the sea." This is the polarity of religious experience.

Far from saying that all this is conveyed in his poems, I shall admit that the course has been set. The man did not cut into the rocks of poetry with the insatiable desire of the possessed; he was like a visitor in the front yard of poetry, not always being able to give form to basic inspiration. "May the Prince of Poetry remember / the naked souls – / the sparks of poetry lacking the dressing of words. Aborted songs / not clothed in verse; / spirit sparkled in them, but the flesh of words has not grown upon them." Unassuming, of a timid soul, the man gave up lofty words, too shy to rise to the heights of the poem or to reach its depths. In song as in life, he walked the margin of the road, tenderly, modest in creativity as in suffering and prayer – the man Moshe Shlomo Ben Meir, "the teacher and friend of small children," himself a forlorn child, vibrating between the "blindness of the deep" (page 26) and "an anchor of faith" (page 32, the poem "Rescue"). The same "anchor of faith" is described elsewhere as "missing its hook," the mast of the ship is "the final mast" and a trembling hand is hoisting "torn sails, a miraculous banner of rescue.2" The flag of rescue, raised by an anxious hand, is a torn flag, like the torn soul. But Ben Meir is grasping the miracle, which is the miracle of the State of Israel, the miracle that followed the Holocaust. Again we are reminded of "A shapeless violin." Again a fusion of opposites.

On the one hand, he writes "My soul is sad in your midst, my homeland Israel" – asking "Does the reward measure up to the destruction;" on the other hand, "The heart recovers from its illness... a nation returns to its borders... and the world advances toward recovery." The banner, both torn and miraculous, is the banner of rescue.

The heart barely recovered, and a sudden blow struck – again. The sun darkened at noon – his devoted wife and friend, his only support in time of distress was taken by God. When mourning was over, he stood up, his face pale, his eyes dark and his lips quivering as if arguing with a secret figure. When I tried to comfort him, saying that his wife only passed from this to another life, from one existence to a different one, he would listen with both trust and wondering, with a pale face and dark eyes – whiteness and darkness, darkness and whiteness together. When I would show him, in conversation, para–psychological facts that proved the immortality of the soul, his eyes would clear up, as if a distant light shone on them through the cloud. He would read, then, para–psychological literature, discuss it with me, accept it and yet wonder.

One year after the death of his wife, he followed her, anxious to join her. As she left this world suddenly, so did he; but he did not fall down – he rose and followed her path.

He left a legacy – a book of poems, a book modest as its author, bound in black and upon the black golden–shining letters, a hint to the light of salvation. Letters of light in the darkness: M. S. Ben–Meir – Sound and Shadow.

The poems are reciting the *Kadish* and the heart answers *Amen.* And "the rest is silence" – in the words of the Prince Hamlet.

("*Hadoar*" [The Post], New–York)

Translator's Notes:
1. Based on The Song of Songs 2:5 "for I am sick with love."
2. Based on the two meanings of the words in Hebrew: 1. flag, banner, 2. miracle.

[Page 371]

Part III

Memoirs and Portraits

We Will Remain the Eternal Dreamers...
by A. Szwarc, of blessed memory
Translated by Gloria Berkenstat Freund

We will remain the eternal dreamers,
Who cannot find any rest on the way;
The sunny days of youth
Once intoxicated our blood, like wine.

Like experienced hands in the field,
They sowed an unease in our beliefs,
And a longing for heaven, for the strange, for the far-off world
Penetrated us like the sun.

Like white small clouds in the blueness of heaven
Desire after desire quietly took shape,
There ripened in our hearts
A constant pizmen [liturgical poem] an eternal sound,

That wriggles terrified in a net of dreams
And is not forgotten, not silenced for a second,
That still becomes enchanted with every spring
Ripens in the rays of light, blooms in the brightness.

We will remain the eternal dreamers
Who will never come to shore,
Flying even more with new desires
Ever further as we trudge on the way.

[Pages 373-390]

Goniadz Dances Before My Eyes
by Arieh Khativa
Translated by Selwyn Rose

In every man's heart is hidden a certain special measure of love for the house in which he was born, his town or his village, the place in which he grew and took his first steps. However, that is the attachment and the special affection that the people of Goniadz have for the town where they were born, refined, without a doubt, by the magic of the passage of time: her forests, river, her fields and meadows, her hills and gardens. It is seemly, therefore, to place a memorial–stone to our pleasant childhood's cradle whose earth has been sanctified with the blood of our loved ones and it will also be a kind of memorial to those of our martyrs whose pure souls breathed their last far from her borders in a land of blood and whose burial place is not known.

***

In my mind's eye, my spirit flies to the distant days of my childhood, through the streets of Goniadz, looking in the homes, wandering through her lanes and scenery. Here I stand on top of the hill by the synagogue and face north. On the horizon is stretched a thick black line, neither its beginning, nor its end can be seen. A veil of mystery is spread over the mass of that forest. Perhaps beyond there are "The Dark Mountains" the location of the exiled ten–tribes. For sure the River Sambotion[1] also rushes there although no sound reaches to here.

My eyes probe between the tall pine trees before me. On the hill yellow sand shining in the distance, I see the straw roofs of parts of the town; isn't that the dwelling–place of the giants? Or perhaps that is where Nimrod the Mighty Hunter lives.

Beneath the black line a green carpet – a grassy wilderness, with no beginning and no end. When the eye stops, it sees herds of cows, sheep and horses, wandering freely at their pleasure. Carts, laden with fresh–mown hay, move across the scene towards the river.

Two at a time they cross the river by ferry to the other side of the river and from there they make their way to town.

That's the river Bober at the foot of the hill – the joy of every child. Every "rebellious child" found shelter there, on the boats that plied upon it here and there, in the long twilight hours of the hot, summer days its banks next to the house of Bohanky* the fisherman, were crowded with bathers.

Fleets of rafts weaved like snakes between the curving course of the river and would disappear downstream when only their lanterns in the distance could be seen. At night they could be seen from the town center twinkling like stars, as if lost on the face of the earth.

[Page 374]

The youth on a boat on the river Bober – on the hill in the background the synagogue and the brewery of Yaakov Rudeski.

[Page 375]

"The River Bober, at the foot of the hill…"

The Bober wasn't just a river for us: surely it was none other than the Nile itself and an many occasions we went searching for the little ark of reeds in which we expected to find the little Moses...and among the bushes of Kalutczki's garden, not far from the bath–house, I imagined finding his sister, Miriam, watching over him, her eyes full of tears as the little craft drifted away to the middle of the river.

We were very proud of our river in spring–time, with the melting snow. Its water reached as far as the first barns, wooden fences could be seen sticking up out of the flood, and on the other side, the waters just reach far enough to kiss the edge of the endless forests on the horizon.

[Page 376]

I feast my eyes and soul on the sight and set forth on the dirt road which rises and climbs beyond the silos of the farm buildings and I arrive at the crossroads: to my left an unmade road of deep sand leading to the slaughter–house – my short–cut, the Shabbat road along which my feet had trodden down a pathway to the village of Klewianka. There was an orchard there that I guarded during the school holiday months – the Fritz farm, and just before the High Holy Days we picked the fruit: piles of apples, pears and plums that were transported to the town by wagons for the festivals.

The right–hand road is the Christian road and at the end, living alone among the Christians, Yankel the blacksmith. Birch trees line the road and at the gate of every house cherry trees. All the houses were made mainly of wood with thatched roofs on a few of them. A pleasant lane, straight but unpaved; there is something of a city quality, fastidiousness – about it. Pigs rarely scavenge round here. Only rarely the "forbidden animal" happens by, it can be heard squealing from the boiling water that was thrown over it. Hearing the noisy commotion only awakened the anger of the Christians at the "Jewish impertinence". To "help" their anger they uncaringly allowed their pigs to scrabble around in the Jewish courtyards.

The house of Yankel the blacksmith, "The Iron Plow", is a wooden house with a small veranda attached to the side facing the street. It is unusual and not from the time of the original construction and I always remember it covered in moss. Just a few paces from the house, along the row of houses, is the smithy itself. Smoke swirls out through the cracks in the walls and the open window. The regular tempo of the squeaking bellows can be heard from afar. Yankel stands with his back to the bellows with the eternal cigarette dangling from his lips. Tailoring, shoe–repairing and the work of the blacksmith were the three most important trades in our town and these last, as if by design, placed themselves at the edge of town and the suburbs – at the main road leading to all the nearby villages. The smithy of Yankel the blacksmith was the furthest of all from the center of town and in my imagination I see him as if making weapons for the Messiah: "The smithy there / light as a horseman / performing there his work / with his bellows he strengthens the flame / whuff, whuff, whuff, whuff / he strengthens the flames."[2]

And from there just a few steps and we are at Dolistowa Street. This is the road – the highway to the big surrounding country: the silos, the flocks of sheep, and all the fruit of the earth. This was the road along which, on market days, came all the wagons and

carts laden with all the produce of field and garden and in the evening the last of the drunkards dragged themselves noisily along. If one turns left this part of the road passes through a suburb of the town that is not built and is unpaved and after a very few minutes one gets to the end. From here and onwards only fields until it meets the road coming from the south and down the hill to the north east. The avenue is lined with willow trees for its entire length. Through the trees one can glimpse the forest of Kolkowoczyzna* which is some distance from the road at this point but a little further along the road turns eastwards and crosses it. The riot of trees and copses encircled the town and we, the children, the pupils of the school, would make our way there at Lag B'Omer in a festive parade, with the blue and white flag waving before us, singing "To the forest, the forest with bow and arrow".[3]

[Page 378]

Proud and full of strength, the children march on, two–by–two, singing Hebrew songs of spring–time, holidays and freedom.

In the forest are many mighty ancient oaks with wide spaces filled with many tree–stumps showing that the hand of Man had been here, and beyond them many young birch trees and bushes and shrubs all tangled together. Narrow paths lead to no one knows where. Indeed it is very easy to find hiding places here during games of hide–and–seek. Hanging above our heads, like the tassels on a table–cloth dangled the clusters of fruit on the birch trees while the pollen dusts all our clothes. The joy of the world around us infects not only us but also the adults who accompany us. The leaders of the singing and the happiness are our first teachers: Shimon Halpern, the effervescent and happy, ready for any prank perpetrated by his pupils, his second–in–command, Joel–Meir Cohen "The Tall", introspective, his face always expressing seriousness. Even when laughing his lips remain closed, a forced laugh, as if he is listening to the constant sound of music and heaven forbid that you should trouble him. Nevertheless, he is indeed pleasant and friendly to his pupils. We like his good taste and choice of music. When he picks up his tuning-fork complete silence reigns. The audience of children at last cease to skip and jump and are still, the heart listening to the song and the story of the deeds of heroism of our forefathers of long ago, in their wars against the Romans, the Bar Kokhba Revolt, and from the recent past: the heroism of Hashomer and their defense of the Moshavim in Palestine against the Arabs.

The introduction of the school's Lag B'Omer parade to the forest became the start of many such hikes to the forest. Groups of friends would wander through the forest afterwards and meet at the forest rangers hut and dine royally on dark rye bread liberally spread with cheese and yoghurt.

The cabin of the ranger is in the middle of the forest, near the road that crosses between the old forest and the new one, close to the well that has a low wall covered in

moss surrounding it. Resting on top is a beam from which is suspended a large wooden bucket.

However, if one turns right from that section of Dolistowa Street one arrives very soon at the paved section of the street. The section of the street as far as the pavement is empty on the south side facing the windmill.

[Page 379]

On the other side of the street, stood just one white–washed house, without any shade tree at the side. This was once the house of the postman.

The start of the paving marked the entrance to the town – as apart the suburbs. From this point, the homes of the Jewish residents begin one after the other. Except that in contrast to other streets, whose houses are mostly duplexes, here, in Dolistowa Street, the houses are detached and separate from each other and a few of them have a small patch of land behind them.

I remember Dolistowa Street when all the houses were still intact. The wooden houses had verandas with wooden decorations on the beams, and red brick houses with steps leading up to them. On summer evenings, the residents gathered on the stoops splitting and eating seeds and conversing in loud voices so that passers–by could hear them from afar.

The fenced–in enclosure of "Old Yisrael" wood–store breaks the continuous building–line of houses on the south side of the street and destroys the orderly row. But that didn't stop the children; they find a use for all the logs and beams of wood stored there, climbing on the logs without losing their balance. They make see–saws out of planks balancing them on logs. It was here that we saw our first automobile which had come from the Osowiec Castle in the days of "Ponia the Thief".

Just a few paces away is the town square, rectangular in shape. From its four corners four streets radiate outwards. In its center had stood for many years a large wooden building – the fire department's station and all its machines. Next door to it is an adjoining room which is the temporary jail–house for all the drunks and street brawlers arrested on market days and Christian festivals. The opposite side of the square – the west side – is composed of a row of almost continuous houses with no gap between them. Starting with Motke Kaliap as far as the house of Navoddowski (the watch–repairer), and from there as far as the street leading to the old market place. In that row are two two–storied conspicuous houses: from the veranda of the first one it is possible to see the entire market square. The upper floor of that house was always used as a hostel for different officials.

However, our memories transport us from here to the second of the two houses – the lime–washed one. An arched passage – a tunnel – serves as a quick route from one house to the other for the residents of the courtyard. This is the house of the Nimoy family. Many people remember the upper floor: It was used as a temporary hostel by the school, a reading–room and a meeting–place for lectures and party–debates. Later it was taken over by haters of Zion among our brethren of the Children of Israel who ensconced themselves there. From among a string of memories one stands out starkly, etched into my memory: during a lesson on literature, into the classroom walked the poet Idel Tershansky from our town, who was due to sail beyond the seas to distant lands, asking to read to us as a parting gesture one of the poems of Tchernichovski. He reads with deep emphasis "On the Wide Blue Sea" while we all sit enchanted and in front of us spread the endless sea with its waves constantly moving, coming and going, not like those waves that "...in their separation sadden the heart and destroy the soul of the stranger", we feel, as youngsters with sensitive emotions, a great sadness when separating from Tershansky. At the time many youngsters took the "staff of the wanderer" and left, a feeling of tearing apart spread among those who remained.

[Page 380]

The parallel row of houses on the east side of the square, begins with the brownstone house of the Bourak–Breski* family. It has two frontages – one facing onto Dolistowska Street and the other onto the market square. Stuck to it is a wooden house belonging to old man Pandrei*. At the end of this row is the house of Moshe Dubcek and the opening to "Death Alley". Here there is nothing worth mentioning. Perhaps just to recall that those who are pupils of Diyudka the teacher A: the "Heder" of Diyudka is in the courtyard of Moshe Dubcek B: in the center of the row is the shop of Marie and in the yard of her house, a factory for making soda–water that is operated by Shlomo "Kijak" (the nickname he was given because he loves to play the fool to the amusement of all). In this corner of town, in the depths of winter when the river is frozen solid and fishing is impossible, they sell "stinky–fish" – fish that has been brought from some distance. They have a smell all their own and when I recall that smell, I see before my eyes the snow–storms at the end of the winter month Tevet, deep drifts of snow pile up at the front of the houses and against the fences. The streets are empty of people. Passers–by hurry along, pushed sometimes by the wind; while those who have used up all the water from the barrel or is frozen, where will they find the water–carrier in this weather? With no other option, they take a yoke and two buckets and go down to the spring or the water–wheel at Dolko*. To leave the warmth of the stove in that weather is the least desirable of all activities. However, the exercise and the work of going and fetching the water makes you twice as warm!

[Page 381]

The third side of the square is a row of buildings the first of which is a church and as far as the house of Berl–Leib at the beginning of "Death Alley", this row, unlike the others, is broken at two places by two alleys. One, the access to the house of Yitzhak Foreman a dealer in leather and opposite was the house of Moshe–Lazar, the watchmaker. The exits join up with the alley from the other side near the "Empress's House" as far as the home of Gedalia Mondrim*, bordering the churchyard. On its other side, at the corner of the street, the house of Cherniak* and beyond the churchyard fence continues.

In the first alley there are only a few houses. By the way, for the first half there are houses only on the right of the street and beyond that only on the left.

In contrast to that the second alley is empty of structures that draw the attention. It is virtually one large empty square, to all appearances, the result of a fire which occurred at one time, leaving behind a number of empty lots. In fact, the empty areas are in direct contrast to those that are built up with house after house, block after block, crowded and pressed, one against the other. Usually, the homes of the Jewish people in towns and villages were built cozily close to each other, in each other's shadow, maybe because of the fear of the Christian neighbors, rather like sheep surrounded by a pack of wolves...

For the tots of the town, there was good reason for that. Indeed there are no pleasant houses here and important institutions are not situated here either. But doves there are aplenty – lots of them all sorts of shapes and shades. Just between us, where will you find a child who's soul doesn't hunger after a puppy, and who's soul doesn't pine for that pleasing bird? That's why we stand for hour after hour pressed against the high wooden fence in order to feed our eyes on the flock of doves of the priest pecking around on the ground and flying up to the red– tiled roof of the warehouse where they had their nests.

That same street with the church is the street where we stroll on Shabbat and festivals. Almost half its length is taken up with the garden fence of the church. The continuation leads to Dolko*, the location of the water–wheel and the weir , next to which is a path used as a short–cut to the road. On hearing the name "Dolko"[4] many people will immediately recall the smell of black–bread with the aromatic weeds that grow there in the shallow water. This is also the habitat of large flocks of ducks here. Even the storks, who make their nests here at the nearby granaries, find plenty of prey for their mouths. Their slow, stately strut is an expression of their calmness and self–importance.

[Page 382]

A little to the right, on the way to the road, it is possible to discern the tower of the Catholic cemetery and the entrance gate. Willow trees alongside the road form an archway casting their shadows over the gates although they are readily visible because the path from the road below to the entrance climbs upwards. After saying the prayer of acceptance: "...And thou shalt utterly detest it"[5] we sneak a look as we pass by the surrounding low wall at the sight of so many crosses and inside, row upon row of beautifully cared–for flowers between the tall pine trees, their trimmed trunks affording a wider field of vision. Nevertheless, above, the treetops merge together forming a canopy of evergreens that casts a shadow of gloom and depression from both the desolation and the rustle of the wind among the trees. A few minutes' walk from here, along the same road, is the Jewish cemetery in the center of the fields on the main road to the village of Downary, alongside the road to the county capital Bialystok.

The stone wall surrounding the cemetery can be seen by people moving along the road on the east side. Inside – high weeds, thorns and thistles and much neglect. The scattered pines are not very tall. It seems that our departed fathers (Z"L), devoted to their faith and beliefs, considered that the future of the dead in any case, at the coming of the Messiah, will be transported to the Promised Land and that there was no point in caring for the "half–way house".

The row of houses on the other side of the street, parallel to the churchyard fence comes to a stop with the Russian school building, only the walls of which remain standing, a reminder of the destruction. No luxurious mansions are found here and no business houses. All the residents are laborers and artisans. Plots of land behind their homes are vegetable gardens, a safety–net for the family income. The paved roadway reaches as far as the entry gate and then stops.

[Page 383]

The weir of the water–wheel of Meir Nuzar* (Palaskovski*)

It is also the extreme limit of the casual strollers. This far they come, gaze upon the thatched roofs of the houses and at the barns and silos of the village of

Guzy, and then retrace their steps. Guzy is a suburban village only a short distance westward from here but can be clearly seen.

The road down towards it from the Russian school is discernable without having to search for a vantage point. The tracks of cart–wheels stretch in a straight line between the staked fences on both sides of the road.

Seemingly a street in the town center, peace and serenity reign during the early–afternoon hours. As such, there is no better place for a friendly conversation, debates, arguments, a brief stroll with a guest in town or to hold forth in public with his opinions.

On the Sabbaths and festivals the street was jammed with people. The youngsters milling around in the street with only the starlight to illuminate the scene: in those days there was no street–lighting and only the heavens lit the world.

Now, just for a moment we will turn our attention to the lane we have called "Death Alley". Isn't the strange, expressive nickname not justifiable? Surely it has to be the only fitting name for the path taken by our town's departed on their way to their eternal resting place?

[Page 384]

The entire lane is composed of two rows of houses and the residents are mostly artisans and small traders and businessmen. There is just one shop here...that of Yashak Ulshavski, who lives at the end on the left. Whenever I remember this, I am full of wonder: his perfect Yiddish is liberally seasoned with the sayings of our rabbis and wise men of old and his speech more pleasant than some of our own brothers...his Jewish neighbors.

If you are stuck here around noon–time on a hot summer day, with an hour or so to spare, you should turn left, towards the top of the hill where two windmills stand, their sails rotating. At the beginning of the street there are houses on both sides in which Christians live; towards the end there is a row of barns built on one side.

The top of the hill is bare and exposed to the winds from all directions. A cool refreshing wind always greets your face. The constant noise of groaning and creaking from the turning sails is nearly deafening. The giant sails, in the shape of a cross turning, turning, turning.

[Page 385]

But if your soul seeks serenity, silence and solitude, to lie and wonder and nourish your soul with the beauty of the scenery – then you had better retrace your footsteps to your starting point, to Yashak Ulshavski's home and from there make a detour to the right and wend your way through the plowed and sown fields because there is no prepared path, as if by intention, so that those who wish for solitude from prying eyes, may be alone. There at the top of the hill is where you will find a stone–built chapel, filled with icons.

***

The stretch of road ahead of us that passes close by the weir at Dolko on the left, seems to stop at the crossing to Rawe, but from here onwards it disappears behind the rise which hides its continuation on its way to Suchawola and Goniadz. This part of the route is cut by a small tributary of the Bober which eventually flows into the Narew. There are two other water–wheels: of Dolko and Guzy. The second is maintained by Meir Guzi (Plasktowski).

The willow trees planted on both sides of the roadway for its entire length, are swallowed up between the trees and bushes that sprang up from the soaked surrounding ground. On hot days, during the twilight hours, the road swarms with people out for a stroll. The green trees and the grassy areas between them imbue the area with the grace of an urban park. Couples stroll to and fro. Not so the Halutzim ["Pioneers"]: they get every new song from Palestine brought by the missionaries and from them to all the towns and villages. They come here in organized ranks taking up the entire roadway singing loudly, from the time of the founding of the "He–Halutz" [Pioneer] movement by the teacher, Mordecai Nolobitzki and while we were still pupils at school, without compromising the spirit pervading the town. The question of respect for one's elders was pushed aside, and not heard of again: "We are all equal under the sun[6]".

The discharge of these earlier judgments spread over us a small measure of pride. The children of families began to interest themselves in acquiring an education in a profession or trade. Some of them went to various training institutions of "He–Halutz". Business houses of some of the members of "He–Halutz" were defined as "temporary business". The most respected employment was that of farm–worker. The vision of being a farmer in Palestine, "…who bringeth forth bread from the earth"[7] alluring for all of us. Our mothers and fathers pester us and drive us mad with warnings about the life of toil and difficulties of the farmer as sons of the earth. Privately, however, in their hearts, they, too, are caught up in the enchanting idea of working the land at peace, in our land in our state. Therefore they place no obstacles in our path. We are quite sure that the major and principal work of the land was plowing. So we spread ourselves over the local fields surrounding the town and ask the farmers to teach us the work of plowing. There were those who agree and the satisfaction we have at grasping the plow and watching the ground turn into long, black parallel rows of freshly turned earth, was great. Although there were also those who hate the Jews and would make the usual Christian comment: "Jews have never plowed the fields and never will plow." The sneering comment meted out to us by the Christians and our own brethren who agreed with them, doesn't deter us one little bit from our path and the idle dream is the beginning of the road that led a small group of youngsters – boys and girls – to become, in time, the way of life for thousands.

The last side of the rectangle contains a row of houses, starting with the street crossing the old market and ending at Dolistowa Street with the house of Sarah the pastry–cook. That row, with its six two–storied houses is like a "sandwich" to the town. The row, like its parallel, is broken by two lanes that lead from it. One starts from the lime–washed house of the Luria family. That spot is the lowest in the town square and the rainwater always collects here and pours noisily down the steep slope of the lane until it reaches the river. It's a wonderful place for sledding in the winter. The whole right–hand side is covered with broken bricks and the remains of walls. The place has remained desolate since the time of the great fire, apart from the wooden home of the tailor, a fixture on the synagogue hill, where the flames failed to reach. In contrast to that the left–hand side is fully built up to the point where the slope downwards becomes too steep. I am often reminded of the expression: "Between two mountains" and I saw myself as standing as if in a deep Wadi with the synagogue on top of one steep hill like a wall and the hill facing it which is also fairly steep.

At the foot of that hill, on the side facing north, facing the river – was the brewery of Yaakov Rudeski. For many years the town theater was here. There would be amateur performances by local enthusiasts and groups who occasionally visited the town.

The River Street

[Page 388]

At the entrance to the second lane on the right stands the home of Mania Tsukert*. On the second floor of that house the Hebrew school was established. With its establishment a new era began in town and a fresh spring–like fresh spiritual breeze blew and was felt by everyone. A new tempo was given to the life of the town and the youth from all sectors of the community met together and were revived, in the classroom framework, sitting together.

School excursions outside the town for entertainment were arranged to teach visually something of the flora and fauna and awaken in the children a love of the scenery of the country. We also learned to examine and know the scenery especially of the town itself. A love of our people and our renewing homeland was nursed diligently within the school walls. The spirit of the festivals and performances brought together the many and breathed the spirit of life into the town.

The Hebrew school impressed everyone and its founders were blessed, especially their leader Mr. Moshe Levine.

In that lane stands the Yeshiva, a building constructed of wooden beams with many windows looking out on every side. A large stove serves as a screen for the women's section. It is a prayer–house, for Torah–study and a meeting–room for the community, whose doors are open every day and every evening. Our fathers, who toil every day to sustain their families, business–men, traders and workers alike, find here a relief from their yokes: through prayer, or study of the holy books – either alone or in groups. Here we are reminded three times daily: "...and may our eyes behold Thy return to Zion."[8]

The house of Benjamin Sofer separates the Yeshiva from the court–yard of the synagogue. It is a low house, made of wood and in the front a garden with fruit trees and behind it is the slope downwards to the river. Those who go down this way take a flight of wooden steps into the valley and can easily see what is happening in the garden from the point of view as a locked and "Inclosed Garden[9]". The red cherries on the trees are a source of temptation when ripe and the appetite of the Yeshiva students, peeping through the windows facing that direction. The image of Rabbi Benjamin remains in the heart of many. Rabbi Benjamin, the Cantor and a good hearted man, lover of children "sophisticates" the children with sips of Kiddush wine...

The people Goniadz, in foreign lands, when speaking of Goniadz will recall instantly the synagogue. It is doubtful if they will recall every small detail, but you can be sure they will see in their mind's eye every little detail of the synagogue's design and décor.

[Page 389]

The synagogue is situated on its own on a generous plot of land surrounded by a fence with willow trees planted alongside the fence except for the side facing the lane. The land became ours by a sort of "independent territory" separated from strangers. The two lanes on either side, left and right of the hill, and the level area of waste–land in front, facing the river, seem like a rocky cliff on the sea–shore with two inlets of water bursting through into the land. The synagogue building which stood near the edge of the lot allows one to see a great distance. The entire exciting scenery cannot be seen from within the building because of the high windows, as if deliberately constructed so as not to distract the attention of the worshippers to "...how pleasant the trees and the plowed field"[10]. And indeed, only the sky can be seen. The largest congregation attends the synagogue during the New Year and the Day of Atonement and already at the Feast of Tabernacles with the early frosts, the number of attendees drops off noticeably. Only one or two quorums remain constant and faithful to the synagogue even on the days of hard frost. These are generally young scholars, among whom are also some non– orthodox youngsters, but who keep the tradition who enjoy from music of the liturgy.

The new market square was broadened from the old one by the addition of a short crossing lane, with shops on both sides. Nothing is found here to bear witness to the age of the place except the wooden house of the Wilamovski family. The square served as a parking place for the farmers from the other side of the river and a crossing point to the railroad station at the Osowiec station.

On this route, the gateway to the wide world, travelers and guests arrive from afar and it is a departure point for those leaving their home–town for distant parts.

Entrance to the square of the New Market

[Page 390]

For many people, the sound of the wagon wheels on the cobbled streets is the last sound they hear and remember on their way to the railroad station, on leaving Goniadz through the village of Guzy* as far as the hill up to weir and water–wheel of Meir Guzi and the entry to the castle through the iron gate – who didn't throw one last glance – even at night – towards the deep canal on the left. Its waters were always quiet and dark and all the surroundings: trees, bushes and the steep banks express and stir up mystery in the hearts of the travelers – and also the drivers.

Please use these chapters of Goniadz and its tragic end as an example for all her sons and daughters who are scattered throughout the world, unable to re– erect other " Goniadz's" in strange lands. As for that, it was good for us there, in our home, and our home still stands still ready and the waves of the blue sea lick its shores with love.

Translator's Footnotes:

1. "In rabbinical literature the river across which the ten tribes were transported by Shalmaneser, King of Assyria" from JewishEncyclopedia.com.
2. David Frishman "For the Messiah".
3. From a song possibly attributed to Shmuel Leib Gordon.
4. A low barrier which is built across a river in order to control or direct the flow of water.
5. Deuteronomy Chap 7 v. 26.
6. Free translation and paraphrase of the original text.
7. A direct reference to the blessing said over bread.
8. From the daily services.
9. From the Song of Solomon.
10. From the Mishna.

[Pages 391-410]

The Goniondz Landscape
by Aryeh Khativah, Tel Aviv, Israel
Translated from Hebrew to Yiddish: Alf
Translated from Yiddish to English by Dr. Isaac Fine

A special love lies within each person's heart for the house in which he was born, for the town or city in which he took his first steps and in which he was reared. But the special love of the Goniondzer for the town of his birth surely has its root in the place's entrancing landscape: its woods, fields, hill, river, pastures and gardens. Thus it is fitting for us to establish a memorial for our town, the cradle of our childhood.

People in boats on the river

I transport myself in thought to the shtetl of my youth, and pass through its streets, stroll along its paths and out to the surrounding landscape. I stand on the synagogue hill and turn my face towards the north. On the edge of the horizon one can see an endless thick bluish black line. A mysterious veil covers that clump of forest. My eyes see through the high pine trees directly across from me. I see the straw roofs of Dolke village glistening from afar, on a hill of yellow sand. Perhaps the nymphs live there, or perhaps Nimrod, the hunting hero. A green carpet spreads forth under the black line, an unending grassy plain. One's glance falls on flocks of sheep, herds of cattle, and many contentedly grazing horses. Wagons laden with sweet smelling hay are seen over a broad expanse at the river's bank. From there, the hay will be carried by barge to the other side of the river, and then transported along the road leading to town.

This is the river Bober, flowing by at the foot of the hill, and the joy of every child. Every rascal found a welcome place on the boats which floated along the currents of its waters. In the long summer evenings, the river shore was filled with crowds of bathers. Fleets of lumber barges glided along the twists and turns of the riverbed, and disappeared in the downward course to the west, with their lanterns twinkling in the distance. From the town square, at night when it was dark, the lights seemed like stars that had become lost on the earth. The Bober was not just a river for us. We scanned its waters looking for the papyrus box of little Moses. From the thicket of Klitsky's orchard, not far from the bathhouse, we thought we saw Miriam, Moses' sister, as she sought with weeping eyes the little box which moved increasingly further towards the middle of the river. We were especially proud of our river in springtime, when, with the melting snows, its waters overflowed up to the first barns. Wooden fences protruded above the surface of the water. On the other side, its waters licked the edges of the forest.

I shift my view from the scene, and move forward on the earthen path which passes behind the barns. I arrive at a fork. To the left, a sandy trail leads to the slaughterhouse. This is my shortcut, the Sabbath route, where my feet have trodden to the village of Klevyanke. During summer vacations I guarded an orchard there, which belonged to a wealthy landowner. The fruit was harvested during the Days of Awe . Piles of apples, pears and plums from the orchard were transported to town during the High Holy Days.

The way that leads to the right is the Christian street. On the corner one solitary Jew, Yankel the blacksmith, lived there among them. There were birch trees by every gate, and cherry trees encircling the houses. They were wooden houses throughout, some of them with straw roofs. It was a beautiful straight street, unpaved, and it had somewhat of an urban flavor. Pigs foraged there, and one heard their squealing from time to time. When they appeared in a Jewish backyard these creatures would be scalded with hot water. When Christians heard the pigs squealing at such moments, they would boil with anger at "Jewish nerve." They believed the pigs should be allowed to roam freely in Jewish yards. Yankel the blacksmith's house was built before his time, an old moss covered wooden structure with a little porch on its street side. A few steps beyond, one finds his smith with smoke seeping out through the cracks in its walls. Through the open windows one hears the rhythmic wheezing of his bellows. Yankel stands at the door with his back to the bellows, always with a cigarette in his mouth. Tailors, cobblers and smiths were the most important tradesmen in town. Smiths established themselves on street corners and in the outskirts of town, on all the routes leading to the outlying villages. Yankel's smithy was the furthest from the center of town. In my fantasies I saw him as the smith who forged weapons for the Messiah, as described in a poem by David Frischman.

A few steps further on, and I am already on Dolistover Street. This street is the gateway to the greater outlying areas of Goniondz - to the granaries, to the herds of cattle, and flocks of sheep, and so on. On a market day, hundreds of wagons could be seen on that route, laden with fruit from field and garden. At night a late drunkard could be found staggering there, shouting and making a commotion. One turns left, and finds oneself in the path of the street which cuts through the suburbs, partially built up, and uncobbled. In a few minutes we come to the corner of the street. There and further ahead there are only fields, through which passes the highway coming from the west and descending towards the northeast. A row of poplars accompanies the highway along its entire length. Through the trees one can see a forest - Kolkovechisner Forest, which is located a little beyond the highway cutoff. In its continuation, the highway passes through it.

The houses around the old market

Of all the forests and little roads which surround the town, this forest is actually looked upon as the town forest. On Lag B'Omer , we students of the Hebrew School marched through it in a festive parade. With a white and blue flag in the lead, we children marched in pairs, strong and proud, singing Hebrew songs of spring and freedom. In the forest there were many old oak trees, and, in the space between them, many cut stumps and trunks, bearing witness to the intrusion of human hands. Further along are many birches, with wild bushes entangled between them. Little paths lead out from here, and no one knows where they lead. It's not difficult to find hiding places for playing here. The flowers hang overhead like tablecloth fringes, and dust from them sprays out over one's clothing.

This scene evoked a happy mood, even in our adult guides. These leaders of fun and song were our first teachers. There was Shimon Halpern, a dynamic and happy man who was ready for any mischief, just like his students. Accompanying him was "the long one", Yoel-Mayer Cohen, self concentrated, with an ever-serious face. When he laughed he didn't open his lips. He was always humming a melody within himself, and God forbid you should disturb him! He was loved by his students for his fine voice and the joy he took in singing. When he took his tuning fork in hand, they were always quiet and attentive. We cavorted around and loved to hear his songs of the battles between our ancestors and the Romans during the time of Bar Kochba's uprising. From our more recent past, there were also melodies about the battles of our warriors with the Arabs in Eretz Yisroel. The Lag B'Omer march in the woods, sponsored by the school, served as an introduction for frequent wood walks. Groups of friends were accustomed to stroll around in the woods. They would pause at the forest warden's table to nourish themselves with black corn bread, cheese, and sour cream. The forest warden's house stood in the center of the forest, next to the path which separated the old woods from the new woods. The structure was near the well, which was built with moss covered stones. A pump stood over it, with an attached wooden bucket.

When one goes from the previous place onto Dolistover Street towards the right, one comes to the beginning of the cobbled street. This section of the street is empty on the south side, which is in the direction of the windmill. On the other side stands only one house, whitewashed and without any surrounding shade. That house had, at one time, been the post office. The beginning of the cobbled street heralds the beginning of the town, and marks its separation from the suburbs. Here one finds Jewish homes, one after the other. It was not as in other streets, though, where the houses are usually connected one to another. Here the houses stand separate, some with a small lot. I remember Dolistover Street with its wooden houses and their balconies and carved beams. The inhabitants were accustomed to sitting on their steps on summer evenings, shelling pumpkinseeds and conversing in loud voices. Alter-Yisroel's lumberyard, on the south side of the street, interrupted the continuity of homes on that side, and flawed its appearance. We children weren't concerned about that. We found a great fascination there, climbing on the boards without losing our balance, and swinging on boards which rode on the beams. There I saw an automobile for the first time, which was arriving at the Osoviec Fort when we were under the rule of "Fonya the Thief" (the Tzarist government).

A few steps further from there and the marketplace lies before us, in the shape of a long quadrangle. Four streets lead out from each of its four corners. In former times, a wooden building stood in the center of the marketplace, and it had served as a warehouse for fire brigade equipment. The adjacent building had been a temporary jail for street fighters and drunkards on a market day or Christian holy day. The western side of the marketplace forms almost a closed row of houses without any intervening space - beginning from Motke Kliap's home, up to the house of Nyevodovsky the watchmaker, and from there, to the access street which leads to the old marketplace. In that row, one finds two storied houses. In the first house from the right, with a balcony, various government officials had been quartered on the second floor. From its balcony, one had a view of the entire marketplace. My memory, however, quickly leads me to the second, whitewashed house. It was penetrated by a vaulted tunnel, which served as access for the dwellers in the yard. This was the home of the Nemoy family. Many of us recall its second floor. A school, reading room, and a meeting place for political discussions had been temporarily quartered there.

Later, the club for Jewish Zion haters was established there. From the cluster of memories attached to that building, one surfaces which is deeply etched in my memory. During a lecture on literature, our townsman the young writer Yudl Treschansky suddenly appeared in our class. He had decided to migrate to foreign lands, and wanted, as a farewell, to read us children the poem "Al Mio Rechov Yam Hatchelet" by Saul Tchernikovsky. He read, and we listened entranced. He laid out before us an endless ocean with countless waves "whose separation is without sadness and longing", and whose waves moved in a rhythmic fashion. But we impressionable children felt a deep sorrow arising from Treschansky's departure. During that time many young people had taken the wandering stick in their hands. A feeling of loneliness and uprootedness would overwhelm those of us who remained.

The parallel row of houses, on the eastern side of the triangle, starts with the brick house owned by the Burak-Barsky family. It has two fronts, one to Dolistover Street, and the other to the marketplace. The wooden house of old Pandre was attached to it. On the other corner of that side, is Moshe Dobchak's house, which runs near the entrance to Dead Man's Alley. There one finds nothing particularly noteworthy.

I still remember the students of Diotke the teacher. Diotke's classroom was located in Moshe Dobchak's yard. In the center of that row was Mary's shop. "Schlomo the Colt's" little hand-operated soda water factory was located in her yard. Schlomo got his nickname from entertaining the children by neighing like a colt.

In winter, when a thick sheet of ice covered the river and fishing was impossible, in that corner of town one could buy smelts, brought from afar. These fish had a special aroma. When I remember that aroma, the snowstorms at the end of the month of Tevet arise before my vision. Piles of snow towered up before the passerby, and lay against the fences. The streets were deserted and pedestrians went running, impelled by the wind. When the water barrel was empty or frozen over, who could find the water carrier in such weather? Without any choice, one would take up a shoulder pole with two buckets and go up to the spring, or to the watermill in Dolke. To tear oneself away from the hearth in such weather was certainly not pleasant, yet one could nonetheless enjoy the warmth that came from activity and movement.

The row of houses beginning with Church Street is on the third side of the triangle continues up to the house of Beryl-Leib at the entrance to Dead Man's Alley. This row, unlike the previous one, is separated at three places by three alleys. One is at the entrance to the house that belonged to Yitzhak Furman the leather merchant, opposite the house of Moishe-Laizer the watchmaker. At its end, it meets with an alley which runs perpendicular to it, which begins with "The Tzarinas' House", and continues to the home of Gedaliah Mondres, near the

Church Street fence. On one side, at the corner, is located the house of Cherniak (Haskel Peretz). On the other side, the fence from the churchyard extends forward.

There were few houses in the first alley. Along the first half of its length, houses are found only on the right side. Further on, there are houses only on the left. Across, in the second alley, one finds not a single building that might attract the attention. One finds there a big empty lot which remained from a previous fire, after which there had not been reconstruction, leaving behind a few free and deserted places. In actuality, this openness was a contrast to the "house on house" architectural style of closed blocks of dwellings. Perhaps the Jewish homes in town clung one to the other in fear of the Christians, like a flock of sheep surrounded by a pack of wolves.

The children in town found the spot quite interesting, even though there was no construction there. There were pigeons, though, and of varying appearance and color. Just between ourselves, where will you find a youngster who isn't attracted to these delicate birds? We stood there many hours pressed against the high wooden fence pickets, to gratify our view of the priest's covey of pigeons. They would coo, hop on the ground, and then would suddenly fly in the air over our heads, circle in the air, and land on the red shingles of the church storehouse, where they had built a nest.

Church Street is the street of Sabbath walkers. The church fence takes up nearly half of its length. The continuation of the street leads to Dolke, where the watermill and the pond are found. Near it is a path that serves as shortcut to the highway. Hearing the name Dolke, the aroma of fresh pumpernickel bread wafts forth, intertwined with these fragrant leaves, which grows in Dolke. There, where the water is shallow, large flocks of storks found ample living space. They found abundant nourishment there and nested on nearby barns. These creatures would step quietly, conveying an impression of dignity and self worth.

A little further on, by the broad path which leads to the highway, one notices the tower of the Christian cemetery, and the gate which leads to it. The willows on both sides of the highway cover them, yet one sees them clearly, since the way from the highway to the cemetery gradually ascends. In seeing the many crosses within we would always say, "Sheketz Tischektseno" (Deuteronomy Ch 27). We passersby would look in, over the not very high stone wall that encircled it. Inside, well-cultivated beds of flowers between rows of high pines, with pine needles cleared away from the path, greeted the view. Above, the pine tree branches were clumped together in a dark mass, which conveyed a sense of sadness, both in their stillness and by their waving in the wind.

A short distance further on the same road is located the Jewish cemetery, in the midst of fields on the main road to the village of Dovnari and which lies near the highway leading to the provincial capital of Bialystok. The stone wall, which surrounds it, is visible to the passerby on the right, easterly side, bordering the road. Within, its high grass, thorns, and weeds give an overall appearance of neglect. The pine trees, which grow on its periphery, are very low. Perhaps our ancestors, may their memory be for a blessing, observant and faithful, felt that since the dead will rise and come to the Promised Land when the Messiah comes, it is therefore not worthwhile to occupy oneself with this temporary earthly station.

The row of houses on the second side of the street, parallel with the churchyard fence, end with the building of the "skole" - the Russian school. Only its walls remain, a remembrance of the great destruction. There one finds no large homes or any businesses. The inhabitants of the homes here are workers, and manual labor is their calling. They have green gardens behind their homes, an auxiliary to making a livelihood. The cobblestones lead up to the church gate and end there. This is also the boundary for town strollers. They walk to that area, remain standing for a while gazing at the houses and barns of Guzi, and then return. The village of Guzi lies to the west, further on, and is clearly seen. The road to it descends from the Russian school, and lies open before the eyes, unobscured by any structures. One can hear the scraping wheels of the wagons, as they move in a straight line between the fence poles on both sides of that road. Although Church Street is a street in the center of town, in the early afternoon hours one could not find a better place for a friendly chat, a discussion, or a stroll with a guest who has come to town to give a lecture. On Sabbath and High Holy Day evenings, the street is full of youths, strolling by starlight. There were no lanterns on these streets.

Now I step forth, and in a few minutes, arrive at Dead Man's Alley. It surely was not proper to attach such a horrible, frightening name to this street. Simply because the town corpses were transported through there, was it needful to give it such a melancholy title? In all, this little street consists of two very short rows of houses. Its inhabitants are Jewish manual laborers and small businessmen. Only one shop is found there, the shop of Yashe Kolshevsky, on the corner of the left row. When I recall this Christian, I never cease to wonder. His pure Yiddish was intermingled with Talmud words, and his diction was superior to that of many of his Jewish neighbors.

If you find yourself here on a warm summer day, and you have leisure time, it's worth the while to turn left. Moving in this direction, you'll arrive at the top of the hill on which two windmills stand. At the start of this route there are only a few houses on either side, inhabited by Christians. Further on, one passes by a row of barns built on only one side of the street. The hill itself is bare and open on all directions. A cool refreshing breeze meets one while grating and scraping sounds emerge from the mill. Giant, cross-shaped wings revolve from one place. If one wishes quietness and solitude, however, and to gratify oneself with a view of the beautiful landscape, it is better to turn back to the departure point, to the house of Yashe Kolshevsky. From there, turn aside on the path to the right. You will find yourself in a cultivated field, in which there is a path leading to the hill with the little Catholic shrine. There is no trodden path to the top of the hill, seemingly designed for the taste of those that take pleasure in solitude. There, one feels no glance of a strange eye.

The same highway shortcut is intersected by a brook which comes from Rave. From that point and further on it is hidden behind the highland through which it continues in the direction of Sochovole and Grodno. The brook currents move forward on their way to the Bober River into which it flows, after passing by two windmills, one in Dolke and the other in Guzi. The latter belongs to Mayer Guzer of the Plaskovsky family. The willows on both sides of the highway are swallowed up between the trees and bushes that grow in the water-rich soil of the area. During summer evenings, the highway was noisy with crowds of strollers, just as one might find on a city street. The trees and the intermingled growth gave the place the attractiveness of a city park. Couples ambled back and forth there. Zionist pioneers (chalutzim) used to walk there in closed ranks, and took up the whole breadth of the highway while singing with vigor. Every new song, which arrived from Eretz Yisroel by messengers, first came to them and then was passed on from them to the whole shtetl. After the pioneer organization was established by the Hebrew school teacher Mordechai Nielovitsky on the synagogue hill, a marked change took place in the atmosphere of the town. Concerns about family prestige became outdated. We no longer heard the comment "It's proper to associate with this one, but not with that other one." This elimination of class prejudice filled us with pride. Youngsters from prosperous families began to take an interest in learning a trade. Some moved away to the pioneer preparation station. Agricultural labor was considered the most highly esteemed trade.

The vision of being a farmer in Eretz Yisroel, and wresting your own sustenance from the earth, had entranced us all. Our fathers and mothers were concerned for us, and showed us the strenuous labor of the local farmers. In the hidden places of their hearts, though, they also had been caught up by the wonderful dream of being a tranquil agricultural worker, tilling his own soil in his own nation. Therefore, they didn't place any obstacles in our paths. We believed that plowing was the most important aspect of agricultural work. We'd go out to the surrounding fields and ask the farmers if they would show us how to do this kind of work.

The last side of the rectangle, which makes up the town-square, includes the row of houses from the transit street of the old marketplace up to the beginning of Dolistover Street, by Sarah the baker's house. That same row, with six two storied homes, gives the shtetl the appearance of a real city. But that same row, just as its opposite, is interrupted by two alleys which open out from it. One alley starts with the whitewashed house of the Luria family. That spot is the lowest ground in the marketplace. Rainwater flowed noisily through that area on its steep descent down to the river. It's an especially good place for sliding with a sled in wintertime. Its whole right side is covered with rubbish and segments of bricks. The entire place has been deserted since the great fire, and remains empty with the exception of the tailor's wooden house, which clung to the synagogue hill and was not reached by the flames. Across, on the left side, there is dense construction up to the place where the hill descends sharply. When I encounter the phrase "between two mountains", I see myself standing in the deep valley between the steep brush of the synagogue hill and its opposing hill -which is also quite steep. Beneath that hill, on its western cliff, the brewery of Yankel Rudsky stands. For many years, it served as a sort of temporary theater for performances of local amateur groups, and also occasional traveling theater companies.

At the entrance of the second alley from the right stands the house of Manye Tsukert. The Hebrew School was founded on the second floor of that same house. A new epoch was begun in town with the establishment of that school. A fresh springtime wind passed through the town's atmosphere. Life took on a new rhythm. Youngsters from all social ranks intermingled within the boundaries of the classroom, sitting on one school bench. The school sponsored walks outside of town for fun and for learning about the vegetation in the area. These walks awakened a love for the flowers and landscape of the region in us children. Later, in these walks, we learned about the landscape of our own nation. Within the classroom walls, our diligent studies awakened in us a love for our people and for the rebirth of our fatherland. Happy evenings and presentations drew out

crowds of people, and brought refreshment and new vitality to the shtetl. The imprint of the Hebrew School was felt everywhere. Thanks and blessings go to the founder, Moshe Levine.

The House of Study stands in the same little street, a wooden building with many windows on all sides. Within, an enormous oven served as separation between the men's and women's section. This place was a house for prayer, learning and community meeting. Its doors stood open all day and evening. Our parents, who worked hard to make a living for their families, found rest and refreshment there in praying and in studying, either alone or with the community. There we would say three times a day "May our eyes see the return to Zion."

The house of Benjamin the scribe separated the House of Study from the synagogue yard. It was a low wooden building with an orchard behind it that ran down the hill. On the side, wooden steps descended to the valley, from which one's view of the orchard is blocked. The red cherries on top of the trees would stimulate the appetite of those studying in the House of Study when they glanced out of the windows facing in that direction. The image of Benjamin is etched in the hearts of many of us. Benjamin, the good-natured scribe, the lover of children, who used to kid with us and befriend us with a sip of kiddush wine.

A Goniondzer living in a foreign land remembers the synagogue when he remembers his home-town. Perhaps he will not remember every detail of his own house. But he recalls every aspect of the synagogue decoration. The synagogue stood in a broad open place, with willows planted near the fence, except for the side in the direction of the street. This community area was a sort of "independent territory" for us, separated from the Christian parts of town. The slopes on the right and left sides of the hill, combined with the broad flatland in front (across from the river) gave the place the appearance of a boulder on the shore of the sea, with two arms of water reaching out on the two sides of the dry land. The synagogue building, which stood near the corner of the open area, was visible from quite a distance. The impressive surrounding vista could not be seen from within the building, since the windows were high. Perhaps the building was constructed in this way so that the worshippers could pray in concentration, free of distraction from the beautiful surroundings. From the windows within, one could see only the heavens. The entire body of worshippers would seek out the synagogue for Rosh Hashana and Yom Kippur. From Succos on, with the beginning of the cold weather, the group of attending congregants diminished. Only a minyan or two remained faithful to the synagogue without any break in continuity during the great frosts. These were mainly young folk, including the non-observant who had a feeling for tradition and loved the loved songs of prayer.

The new marketplace was connected to the old marketplace by a short little transit street with shops on both sides. There one finds nothing that bears witness to the antiquity of the place, except for the wooden house of extraordinary appearance which belonged to the Viliamasky family. This place served as station for the village folk from the other side of the river, and to the train station at the Osoviec fort.

On the road, which serves as doorway to the greater world, guests and travelers from outside come to us, and by the same way, sons and daughters have leave the shtetl to go out to the entire world. On their last ride to the train station, the rattling of the wagon wheels against the stone cobbles of the street continues to echo in their ears, through the village of Guzi up to the shortcut to the highway, near the pond of Meyer Guzers' watermill. Entering the fort one passes through iron towers and casts a backward glance at the deep-water canal which passes on the left side. Its water is always black and still. All around it, the trees, bushes and steep hill convey a sense of mystery akin to the feelings of he who is departing -and later to those who were deported to the concentration camps.

Let us hope that the story of the shtetl of Goniondz, and the tragic epilogue of that story, will convey a lesson to our sons and daughters who are scattered throughout the world, not to reconstruct such Goniondzes in foreign lands. For our home is where our heritage lies and where the waves of the blue Mediterranean lick its shores with love.

[Pages 411-422 - Hebrew] [Pages 423-436 - Yiddish]

Long Ago in Goniondz;
A Bundle of Memories
by Avraham Yaffe, Tel Aviv, Israel
Translated from Hebrew to Yiddish by M. Goelman
Translated from Yiddish to English by Dr. Isaac Fine and Gloria Berkenstat Freund

Avraham Yaffe

Entertainment in the Shtetl

Our shtetl had no knowledge of the theaters and concerts of the greater world. We did have a group of town youth, though, who enjoyed presenting, from time to time, a theatrical piece such as Goldfadden's "David and Goliath," "Bar Kochba," and many others. I remember the role of Saul's daughter, Michal, in "David and Goliath". It was enacted by Dorach-Sheimash Vikotsky, and he took the role of a young woman. In those days, women were not allowed to take part in dramatic presentations. The theater season was generally Purim time, and the location was Itshe Anshel's great storage structure, which was to be found in the alley across from the priest's garden. There were also entertainments put on by the Zionists, who presented Zionist melodies as well as folk songs. The lead singers were the son of Sheimash, Yossel, Zorach, and Pesach.

A Moral

One house in the shtetl was the center for song throughout the entire year, particularly during religious festivals. This was the residence of Cantor Nochum Amdurer. His dwelling was located in Avram- Moishe's house, across from the post office on the corner of Dolistover Street. The Cantor Nochum Amdurer was a beardless man of average stature. He was always seen with a hat and a long coat. Nochum was a schochet, a ritual slaughterer. Day by day he and Yankel, the other schochet would go to the slaughterhouse. On the evening before Yom Kippur, everyone would bring the chickens for slinging to their home. In the fall, when geese and calves were in season at the market, the two men would go to various homes in the town and slaughter them in the prescribed kosher manner. From my childhood years, I remember being with Avram-Moishe, the son of Yankel the schochet, along with his father in the slaughterhouse. During our return back home afterwards, we met a Christian on the path along the way. We clung to our patron, Yankel for protection, being frightened of Christians at that time. As he passed, Yankel bowed down to him and greeted him with a very submissive "Good morning!" The Christian was willing to answer but glanced in our direction. Immediately afterwards, Yankel gave us a lesson. When a Jew passes a Christian, he must greet him. That way he can be sure that he hasn't slighted him. The image of spilled blood in the slaughterhouse and that encounter with the Christian man saddened our childlike mood.

The Shtetl and the Cantor's Residence During the Month of Elul

During the month of Elul, prior to the Days of Awe, when even the fish were trembling in the water, the Cantor's residence was transformed into a temple of music. It drew the attention of everyone, great and small. Each day the Cantor and his choir would be preparing themselves for the prayers of the High Holy Days, singing new as well as familiar melodies. The cool winds of Elul and the voice of the shofar (ram's horn) all contributed to the seriousness of the Jewish mood during that particular time period. At this time, world Jewry is held accountable for the condition of their souls. One must prepare oneself for the Day of Judgment and it is well, indeed, for he who is prepared. The Days of Awe began with the first night of slichos of Rosh Hashana. The introduction was the Sabbath evening, when by tradition the Cantor and his choir sang the chapter from Psalms, "Lamnatzeiyach bin ginos mizmor shir." It continued with "Elohim, yoducho omim kulom (All nations will praise the Lord all nations in unison)" and then, "Eretz nosno yevulo, yivorcheinu Elohim eloheinu (The earth gives of its bounty, bless us Lord our God.)" A sense of awe would overcome over the assembled congregants in the dark Sabbath night, "Gilu B'rodo (Rejoice in trembling)."

The House of Prayer Street and the House of Prayer

From my childhood years, I remember the alley which led from the marketplace to the House of Study and the synagogue hill. It was between the shop of Gershon-Leib and Chayim Koppelman on one side, and the store of Yente Chaya-Feigel's on the other (this was at the beginning of the twentieth century). During the time of the great winter rains, the alley was transformed into a muddy swamp. One dark evening at that time of year, while I was walking, plopping through the mud, to the House of Study for a Torah lesson, I tripped over some wooden boards which were lying in front of Moishe Dinge's house. I fell and was covered with mud. Entering the House of Study, black as a Negro, I was seen by Mordche, the assistant sexton, of whom the children were frightened to death. At that moment, he was adding fuel to the great oven which covered one third of the House of Study wall. His custom was to fill it with large pieces of wood, shut the oven doors, lock them, and then go home. After he left, the boys who were studying there used to bake hot potatoes on the oven. Sometimes one of them would bring along a herring, and baking it there was a great joy. Seeing me, Mordche grabbed the wet towel which hung by the basin and remained there from one Sabbath evening to the next. The worshippers always dried their hands with it, after saying, "Asher yotzar" the prayer traditionally said in the European shtetl after leaving the bathroom: "Baruch atoh Adonai Elohainu melech ho'olom asher yatzar et ha'adam b'chachma, nikavim, chalulim, chalulim, galui ..." translation: Blessed art Thou O God, king of the universe who has formed man in wisdom making within him a system of ducts and tubes. It is well known that before Thy glorious throne that if one of those be opened, or if one of those would be closed, it would be impossible to exist in Thy presence. Blessed art Thou, O Lord, who healeth all creatures and does wonders.

A lighting system for the road to the synagogue hill was installed at the same time that cobblestones were put in the alley of the House of Study. The energetic sexton, Eleizer-Laishke Neivodovski, who had made many improvements in the interior of the synagogue, had sawed a series of large poles from which hung big petroleum lamps, which lit the way to the synagogue hill and the synagogue. On the first night of Slichos, the scribe, Benjamin, would kindle the lantern lights for half of the entire night. Throughout the year, generally speaking, the lanterns were lit only on the evening of Sabbath on religious festivals.

The First Night of Slikhos in the House of Prayer and in the Synagogue

In those days, it was the only lighted street in the entire shtetl. The night of Slichos was an all night event in the residence of Reb Nochum, the cantor. The choir members remained there rehearsing Slichos songs from the end of the Sabbath, until midnight. The Cantor's wife would strengthen them with tea and milk, which promoted a clear voice. After rehearsal was over, the choir would climb up on the large oven in the kitchen, and catch a nap until it was almost time for Slichos. From the distance, one could see the bright light coming from the windows of the House of Study. The community gathered together and the wealthy man of the town, Yahatzkel Bialototsky, would appear with his son Chayim. Chayim was a student at the high school in Grodno, and wore his school uniform with its shiny brass buttons. They would arrive from their house, which was near the lumber mill by the river. Mordche, the assistant sexton, would be running around the House of Study very excitedly, seeing that everything was in order. Yehatzkel would give a wink to Motke, the teacher, that he should come forward to the lectern. Ische- Leib, the main sexton, would be standing on the altar with his assistant, Mordche. A loud knock was then heard from the wooden clapper resounding against the table and all was still. Motke, the teacher, with his prayer shawl covering his head, moved forward with a serious step to the lectern and with his powerful voice broke forth in the traditional "Yiskadal, yiskadash." The entire House of Study became filled with holy awe. The Jews prayed the Slichos service with great fervor. An hour after the conclusion of the Slichos service in the House of Study, a movement began in the Cantor's residence. The

Cantor awakened his choir and went out with them to the road leading to the main synagogue. A light was shining out from the windows of the synagogue where the Slichos service would be held somewhat later. We pass by the House of Study, which was already darkened again, but the lights from the synagogue's windows and from the lanterns along the way brightened the path.

The synagogue was filled. The sexton, Benjamin the scribe, stood on the altar after lighting all the candles and lamps. The Cantor was with his choir by the lectern, and thus began Slichos. Song filled the entire large room, and all the congregants joined in. After a while, one would go outside and stand on the synagogue hill. In the evening stillness, stars would winkle and twinkle from on high. Not far from the foot of the hill, the river Bober passed by with a quiet whisper. On the other side of the river the forests were dark, enveloped in the darkness of the night. Only from the northwest direction, towards the Osoviec Fort, a dim light could be seen emerging from some of the houses in the village of Dolke. Perhaps a Jew who lived out there in the outlying suburbs was rising for Slichos. A deep stillness was conveyed from the distant forests and marshes. A bird twittered in his nest. From behind the red bricked, red-roofed bathhouse the frogs had silenced their croaking. One stood intoxicated, encountering the dark horizon in the night stillness. Yes, this was the first Slichos night for a faithful Jewish community. All was quiet for that community, in holy stillness.

The Morning After *Slikhos*

The morning after Slichos, the congregation prayed in its usual fashion. Leaving the synagogue, the whole shtetl was enveloped in a grayish-white fog. The fog began to lift and separate like the holy smoke from the altar incense. During the morning services the blowing of the shofar reached to the loftiest realms of Heaven. In the alley of the House of Study, which lead to the main marketplace, a shop door opens here and there. A crowd of Christians thronged to the church on Tifle (Church) Street. A weekday has come to the shtetl.

The Days Before Rosh Hashanah

All the seven days prior to Rosh Hashana , people arose early to say Slichos and then to blow the shofar after morning prayers. In the shtetl marketplace, the glances of customers were especially drawn to the watermelons cut in halves, quarters and eighths. There were also, of course, the grapes. These last two items were brought from afar, and were quite expensive. They were only available for purchase for Rosh Hashana so that one could make the "shecheyonu" blessing on the second night of Rosh Hashana.

The Synagogue and House of Prayer in the Days of Awe

All these activities heralded the approaching Days of Awe. In the House of Study, there was much preparation. The gabbayim were busy selling seats. Among those who came to the House of Study at this time were some who added an additional Psalm or an additional chapter from Prophets or the Mishna to their study after the morning service, in reverence for the special days which lay ahead.

One needed to mobilize oneself. The Day of Judgment approached. There were ten miracles which our ancestors experienced in the Temple. One of them was when they were standing clustered together for prayer. When it was time to kneel, there was enough space for all. This miracle did not happen in our House of Study during the Days of Awe. All the small minyans which met in the shtetl throughout the year were closed and locked during the Days of Awe.

There were two exceptions to this pattern. One was the minyan of Moshe Lemborg Kramkover. The other was a little shtibl , Nimas Tsdek, which met in the house of Gershon-Lieb. At this time, all the others came to the House of Study or the Synagogue. In addition, many Jews who lived in outlying areas came to town with their families, to pray with the communities. Unlike the House of Study, the Synagogue had a very high roof, which eliminated any feeling of overcrowding among the congregants. But within the House of Study, the main room and the hallway filled up with those sitting and standing so that it was almost impossible to move. The air was stuffy and uncomfortable, and there was a great deal of perspiration. The square skylights were opened, in order to improve the free flow of fresh air. There were a few, who, unable to tolerate the discomfort, would change their place of prayer and pray at the Synagogue during the High Holy Days. Reb Nochum, the cantor, prayed alternately at the House of Study and the Synagogue during Rosh Hashana. For evening services, Yankel the schochet prayed once in the House of Study and once in the Synagogue, seated to the right of the Holy Ark. During the Days of Awe, he prayed in the Synagogue. On these occasions, Yankel's place in the House of Study was taken by Yehatzkel Bialototsky, who was a wealthy townsman and owned the lumber mill. Yehatzkel also was the primary advocate for the Jewish community of the town with the local Russian government authorities. His nickname in town was Yehatzkel- Moishe's.

The Cantor, Reb Nakhum and Yankl the Shoykhet As Prayer Readers

How did the prayer of Yankel the shochet and Reb Nochum differ? When Yankel would begin his praying "Borchu" of the evening service, one felt the passion in his voice as he hummed. He was a Chassid. His white overgarment, beard, and earlocks added a further sense of intensity to his appearance. His thin voice shrieked out like the sound of a bleating little lamb. Listening to him would remind us that Israel is like a lost lamb. The warmth coming from him warmed the hearts of the worshippers present. It was different with the cantor, Reb Nochum. He was a competent reader of music, and had a choir wherein one simultaneously heard four voices - a soprano, an alto, a tenor, and a bass. His special talent, though, was for singing prayers which moved one to tears.

The stamp of the Gabai of the Synagogue

Inside the Shul

[This photo replaces the less detailed version in the original book and was provided by Yad Vashem, Jerusalem, Israel]

The Cantor's Choir

Among the youth who sang in the choir, I remember Peisach-Shammesh and Moishke, the son of the cantor. They were sopranos. Eliyahu, the oldest son of the Chassid, and Zaitke, the son of Koppel the teacher were the altos. The altos were Avramel Schmuel's and Achi Sender, the writer. The tenors and basses were all apprentices in ritual slaughter to the Chassid who was also a schochet. Most of the week, they sat in the House of Study and learned Gemara . Between them were the two sons of the Cantor's daughters, as well as the man who later became the Chassid's son-in-law, Nochum Vilkomersky. Nochum later became the father of the singer, Avram Vilkomersky. Nochum was an intelligent and studious youngster. He usually could be found learning diligently in the House of Study. He also regularly read a Jewish periodical, and often chatted with those in the House of Study about this topic or that. Later on, Vilkomersky relocated to Germany to complete his studies in music and singing - especially religious music. Later, he became famous as a great cantor. In keeping with the requests of those among the worshippers who particularly enjoyed singing, the choir youths, during weekdays, would repeat certain holiday prayers and songs in the shtibl. On the Sabbath of the New Moon, the appreciative congregation would shower them with compliments and praises, which were their reward.

Mayer Bodner – Bel Musaf

Mayer Bodner enjoyed the traditional prerogative of praying the Musaf services on Rosh Hashana. He was called Bodner because he came from the small village of the same name. Mayer was a Jew of quite diminutive stature, with a long white beard. The congregation suffered from this traditional prerogative, but no one dared to challenge him. It is said that he who would lead the congregation in prayer is required to wear a beard, have a pleasant manner, and in addition, a sweet voice. Mayer Bodner did not meet the last of these three requirements. From my youth, I recall that his voice would emerge from him as something coming forth from the ground. One could only hear the air from his mouth and his "oy, oy, oy!". His voice was neither powerful nor sweet. He could only moan, "oy, oy, oy!" I recall one occasion during Musaf of Rosh Hashana when Velvel Kaminetzky was standing at the right of the lectern where the Cantor prayed. Velvel sat across from his father, Gedaliah Kaminetzky (whose place was in the east corner, to the right side of the Holy Ark) and was singing to the prayer, "How Shall One Die?" with "Who By Fire ...". Mayer Bodner excitedly spread out his hands as he prayed. Velvel got a fiery slap on his head, and his hat went flying. The entire congregation couldn't keep from laughing, even though this occurred in the middle of "Uktsaneh Tokef", one of the most solemn prayers of that day.

Reb Nakhum's Musaf on Yom Kippur

The Cantor Reb Nochum wore a kittel, a white gown, with his tallis over his shoulders. His tenor voice was not particularly powerful. He would begin "Hineni" with a loud voice, walking forward towards the Synagogue altar. His voice brought forth tears from the congregation while the choir responded to him in unison with

"Hineni m' maas". One felt that this prayer had the power to open the gates of Heaven, and that the gates of Mercy had not closed. In my youth, I would see the Cantor on his knees on the floor, praying in a loud voice and then falling on the floor with his head and feet stretched out, completely covered with his long prayer shawl. I heard sounds of crying from under his tallis. The choir standing behind him in the lectern would be rhythmically crying out "ay, ay, ay!" I was completely enthralled. At times I feared the Cantor had fainted. Weakness caused by fasting was not unusual. With a thumping heart, I waited until they picked up the Chassid by his elbows and helped him to stand again. When he arose and continued on with his praying I breathed a sigh of relief. Now, when I hear the leader of a congregation praying at such moments during the service, and he is not having a world-shaking effect on those present, I become caught up again in these childhood memories.

Cantors and Ritual Slaughterers
Sitting from right to left:
Reb Nakhum the khazan (cantor), Reb Yankl the shoykhet (ritual slaughterer).

I was young and I have become old – and from then until today I feel the chills of the past when the cantor comes to *Vehakohanim* ["and when the *kohanim...*" – priestly class] and *koyrim* [bending the knees during certain prayers] (although cantors today do not create a sensation with their crying nor with their bending of the knees).

Reb Nukhem showed wonder with his choir in *Unetanneh Tokef* ["Let us speak of the awesomeness..."]. The "...like a shepherd pasturing his flock..." captivated the worshippers who would sing along quietly and forget their weakness from fasting (on Rosh Hashanah the worshippers would be delighted with his march and dance melodies of *Melekh Elyon* [the Most High King] and *V'ye'etayu khol l'ovdekha* ["...everyone will arrive to serve]...". They would be particularly taken with the longing-filled, heart-stopping melody of *Haben-yakir-li-Efraim* [*Is Ephraim My Favorite son?*].

Neilah

The floor of the synagogue and anteroom would be covered with fresh straw on Yom Kippur to ease the standing without shoes all day. There was a pause after *Musaf* [additional holiday morning prayers] during which the congregation rested, some in their seats and some outside the synagogue, in the anteroom. In good weather they would go out to the hill to lie on the grass and breathe fresh air. I remember that as a child of 12 I decided to fast the entire day. At the pause Mordekhai Kliap, the rabbi's son Zalman, and my older brother Yitzhak (may the memory of all of them be blessed) sat in the anteroom to rest. When my brother told them about my decision to fast, they began to try to persuade me to go home and end the fast, but I did not listen to them. I was very weak when it came time for *Neilah* [the concluding Yom Kippur prayer], but as soon as the cantor began the *Kaddish* [mourner's prayer] during the *Neilah* service with the traditional melody of prayer, exaltation and encouragement, the entire congregation became refreshed. We sang along with the cantor with exaltation and the elevation of the soul. And I along with all of the other children forgot our hunger, tiredness and weakness. The entire synagogue filled with the exalted, magnificent melody of *Neilah*.

The Conclusion of Yom Kippur

After *Maariv* [the evening prayer] many still remained on the hill to recite the blessing for the new moon. A pale, dreamy moon looked out from the river just as if it had fasted with the congregation. As if staggering I went home to break the fast. I encountered Yudl Dolistower when passing the market; he was walking rapidly to his inn to break the fast. When he saw me he greeted me with a smile: "Have a good appetite!..."

End

Much water has flowed from the Bober [River] to the Narev [River] since then. I have been through two world wars, revolutions and wandering; I have lived to emigrate to *Eretz-Yisroel* and became a citizen of the Land of Israel. But those homey Days of Awe still are fresh and new in my memories as I lived them then in my old home.

[Pages 437-444]

Three *Beli-Tefillos*
[Prayer Leaders]
by Moshe Bachrach
Translated by Gloria Berkenstat Freund

Forward

Our Jewish way of life was once very rich in distinctive music. An abundance of musical sounds accompanied the Jews from cradle to the "gutn ort" [good earth – the cemetery]. Everyone was influenced by the Jewish singing – cheerful and sad, serious and humorous, religious and secular (weekday [not Shabbos]). A good preacher, for example, would sing out his sermon, and the gemara [rabbinical commentaries on the oral law] melody was well known. However, the collective musical experiences in the synagogue and in the Beis-haMedrash [house of prayer] made a particularly strong impression. And lucky was the shtetl that had a talented khazan [cantor], sensitive beli-Tefillos [prayer leaders] and musical beli-koyres [Torah readers].

In the thinking of the majority of us – the generation that lived in Goniadz until around 1920 – three men had a very large part in the musical life of our *shtetl*, through the synagogue and the *Beis-haMedrash*: The *khazan* Reb Nakhum, Yankl the *shoykhet* [ritual slaughterer] and Eliezer Zakimovitch.

[Page 438]

The Khazan

Reb Nakhum, the *khazan*, was an educated musician with a "sweet" voice and with a talent for fusing prayers with music in such a manner that it would transport an entire congregation of Jews as if everyone under his spell would be elevated and profit greatly from the religiosity in the music and from the music in the religion.

In order to express the full beauty of the style – of the commonplace melodies with which every Jew is familiar – requires a mastery. Because with ordinary *beli tefillos* it emerged mechanically, as "correct" – they would not sing. It was also the style that the *khazan* was a sincere musician. But he was a true artist in singing special cantorial compositions and, indeed, from "a sheet of paper" (notes)... The *El Melech Yoshev* [the King sits] at *Neilah* [concluding prayer on Yom Kippur] was, for example, such a composition, which he would sing solemnly and "dramatically." The synagogue, fully packed with Jews who were already feeble from the fast, would truly be revived. All of the worshippers would receive fresh strength and faith that - - - *Mokhel avonot amo* [God forgives the sins of his people]. Everything was disregarded and forgiven...

Eliyahu haNavi [Prophet Elijah]
As a child I heard this melody from Beniamin the *Sofer* [scribe] at the locking up of the synagogue on a
Shabbos night. – M. B.

[Page 439]

And who of us does not remember how sincere and moving Reb Nakhum would
perform the prayer, *Hineni Heni Mimas* ["Here I stand before You"], going through
the entire length of the synagogue from the door to the cantor's desk with prayer
and song, dressed in a white *kitl* [white robe worn during Yom Kippur services] and
his face covered with a *talis* [pray shawl]? Who did not feel with him, the
representative of the *kehile* [organized Jewish community] who had taken upon
himself such mighty responsibilities – to open the heavens for an entire
congregation of Jews?!

During the war, in 1914, we realized that the Goniadz *khazan* could occupy a
position in a large city, when because of the nearness of the "front," we ran from
the *shtetl* after Rosh Hashanah and the *khazan* was also among the Goniadz
"homeless" in Bialystok.

Probably arrangements had been made earlier for a *ba'al Shakhris* [person who
recites the morning prayer] for Yom Kippur in the large Bialystok synagogue.
However, when they learned of Reb Nakhum, the plan was changed at the last
minute and it was suggested that he *daven* [pray] *Shakhris*. It should be understood
that the *khazan* was happy with this and that Goniadz was proud at the honor
which Bialystok gave to our *khazan*.

When Reb Nakhum died in 1915, his nearest and dearest went to the funeral. The *mite* [board on which the deceased is laid] with his remains was taken into the *Beis-haMedrash* and placed on the *bimah* [platform on which the table holding the Torah during readings is located] and when the Goniadz Rabbi, Reb Tzvi Hirsh Wolf, eulogized the *khazan*, he, himself, cried like a child – and the entire congregation with him.

[Page 440]

Yankl the *Shoykhet*

"A still, thin sound" – that is how I would characterize the praying of Yankl the *shoykhet* [ritual slaughter]. He would not approach the lectern the entire year, only in the Days of Awe he would *daven* [pray] *musef* [extension of the morning prayers].

The *shoykhet* was a *ba'al-Tefillah* who did not act as a cantor... He prayed with feeling, but he was not a *ba'al bekhi* [one who likes to cry], not a crier. He would keep to his version and only in the liturgical songs, for which there was no Skarbower melody, he sang the melody that he had learned somewhere. He was not a great "fastidious man" in this respect. So, for example, he sang "*Veyativ kol lavdekha*" [and you will accept everything of your servant (Israel)] with a "Piechotnem" [infantry] march – and all of the worshippers "marched" to the beat with him...

Yankl the *shoykhet* was a dear person, a scholar and he had a sense of humor. Once, on *Shimkhas-Torah*, he brought humorous joy to the *shtetl* when he went up to the *ahron koydesh* [ark holding the Torah scrolls], at close of prayer, stood facing the congregation in a pose for *dukhn'en* [giving the priestly blessing] and with the melody of *Yevarechecha* [From Psalm 128:5 – bless - "May God bless you from Zion..."] went into *She-hakol nih'ye bidvaro* [blessing said before eating or drinking certain foods – "...through Whose word everything comes into being."]... It should be understood that this was not a benediction given in vain; he immediately drew out a bottle of whisky from under his *talis* [prayer shawl] and took a good sip.

There was an idyllic friendship between Reb Nakhum the *khazan* and Yankl the *shoykhet*. Both of them were *shoykhetim*, but absolutely not competitors. It could be that one *shoykhet* would have been enough for Goniadz for all of the days of the year, but *erev yom-tov* [on the eve of holidays] and particularly before Yom Kippur for *kaparot** there was indeed a need for having two. We children were very surprised at how such gentle men could grab a slaughtering knife so quickly in their mouth – for the hands, it should be understood - turn over a hen with its neck up, flick a few feathers, "*Khik*" [sound made when cutting the hen's throat] – and throw it to the ground...

[Page 441]

Yankl the *shoykhet* was loved and honored in Goniadz as only a Jewish *shtetl* can love and honor a sincere person who is an affable man and a well known and respected figure in the religious life of the community.

In 1933, Yankl the *shoykhet,* passed through New York on the way from Chicago to *Eretz-Yisroel,* where he went to live out his last years. He achieved his wish; shortly after his arrival in the Holy Land, and the city of the Kabalists – Tsfat [Safed] – he died. And as if sent by Providence, he first met – and then "accompanied" – the third Goniadz *ba'al-Tefillah* – Eliezer Zakimovitsh, who had been living in *Kibbutz Ayelet HaShahar* [a communal settlement in the Upper Galilee], which is very near Tsfat.

Eliezer Zakimovitsh

Eliezer, my uncle, was a *ba'al-Tefillah* who was enamored of the cantorial art. He "made a living" from a "spice store" where, by the way, one could buy – – herring, gauze and even pitch tar to rub on boots. But he *maintained* his life at the synagogue lectern – in the synagogue. Eliezer was the greatest *nosher* [person with a sweet tooth] of cantorial pieces. And his memory for the thing was truly astonishing. It is correct to say that if he heard something from a *khazan* or from one who repeated something once – it was already his, forever and ever.

[Page 442]

Eliezer Zakimovitsh

If we all loved the *khazan* very much and valued him, Eliezer was truly idolized. Everything that the *khazan* sang in Goniadz could be heard first from Eliezer at the same lectern – in the synagogue and years later – in the *Kibbutz Ayelet HaShahar* in *Eretz-Yisroel* where Eliezer and his wife, Rywka (daughter of Ruchl's son Moshe) lived in honor, as the parents of the settlers.

[Page 443]

The order was that the *khazan* would only pray in the *Beis-haMedrash* during the winter. This left the cantor's desk completely free in the synagogue for Eliezer; he was the "substitute *khazan*' there for the *minyon* of half-frozen synagogue-patriots. After the *khazan* died, he became his "successor," both at the cantor's desk in the synagogue and with the *khazan's* entire "repertoire." Thus the *khazan's* spirit still hovered in the synagogue for a number of years until Eliezer emigrated to *Eretz-Yisroel*.

As an older person, Eliezer did not have the responsibility of working in the *kibbutz*, but he was very interested in making himself useful – he was given easy tasks to carry out. This greatly satisfied him.

As is known, the parents are held in great respect in the *kibbutzim*. They have the same privileges there as the children – in regard to food and comfortable facilities; in the *kibbutz* you could find Eliezer in the middle of the day at a *sefer* [religious book] and, a little later, giving his attention to the large pump, taking a nap at the same time... Once when he woke from such a "watch," he saw a snake in front of him who was looking right into his eyes – he then *gebentsht goylm* [said the blessing for escaping from danger]...

[Page 444]

To pray in a *kibbutz*, after the Goniadz synagogue, surely was a decline for Eliezer the *ba'al Tefillah*, but without a doubt he had great satisfaction in that in a non-religious *kibbutz* he was the one who held a pious-Jewish position. And he upheld it in such a manner that everyone respected him for it because even in the *kibbutzim* they were delighted with the familiar melodies and cantorial pieces.

Eliezer died on the 28 of Khesvan 5710 [20 November 1949] and his wife, Rywka, died on the 18 of Shevat 5717 [20 January 1957].

*Translator's Note: From I Kings, 19:12 ;*Kaparot* is a ritual performed during the days before Yom Kippur involving the waving of a white rooster [for a male] or a hen [for a female] over the head in expiation of one's sins and the transfer of those sins to the chicken.

[Pages 443-450]

My Grandfather Reb Gedaliah
By Khannah Neiman, New York
Translated from Yiddish to English by Dr. Isaac Fine

I remember well the old community-owned house where my grandfather's father sat in the rabbi's chair. The house stood next to the House of Study. It was such a palace that the Russian government decreed that it be demolished. I remember that during heavy rains the water would drip down through the roof, and grandfather would move the books from one place to another. From there, they moved to Dovid Shilevsky's house where they lived until grandfather's death.

The family consisted of Bobe, our mother, and her four brothers: Pinchas, Velvel, Zalman, and Moishe-Meier. I still see my grandfather in my mind's eye. He was a tall erect man with a noble face, blue eyes, and a long gray beard. He was always dressed very neatly and cleanly, often with his coat slung over his shoulders. In my view, his appearance was always majestic. In the house, I never saw him other than with a book, except on Christmas night.

Bobe never called him by name. After all, he wasn't an ordinary man such that she could appropriately call him "Gedaliah." At the same time, she had too much of a connection with him to call him "rabbi." Her solution was to say to him "Listen." For example she might say, "Listen, do you want to eat now?" or "Listen, have you heard what happened?" As for himself, my grandfather rarely called her Rivke.

Grandfather was accustomed to arise quite early in the morning. Soon after he would open the door, in case someone should wish to enter. He made tea for himself, so as not to disturb those still sleeping in the house. Men often came in the morning for a glass of tea, and also later, in the afternoon. He would leave for prayer in the House of Study with a heavy tallis bag filled with books, and would arrive back home around twelve noon. He was accustomed to eat only twice a day. The first meal was around noon. If he had a little chicken, he wouldn't eat any dairy products whatsoever for the rest of the day. For other Jews, a six-hour wait was sufficient. His own personal self-imposed restrictions, however, were more severe. He would only eat meat which was "glatt kosher". I remember how the butcher would come in and tell my Bobe, "Rebbitzin, this is a glatt kosher one." In those days I didn't know what that phrase meant. I recall also my mother having told me that, in his earlier years, Grandfather would fast intermittently on Mondays and again on Thursdays. From the point of view of religious observance, he was strict with regard to himself, and lenient with regard to others.

Their income came from the monopoly to sell yeast in the shtetl. This was Bobe's responsibility, since Grandfather couldn't recognize the shape of a coin. At times, however, a Christian would arrive at the door quite early in the morning to purchase a few ounces of yeast. He didn't want to wake Grandmother from her sleep to assist him, and would handle the matter on his own. When Bobe awoke she would soon realize what happened and good-naturedly tell him, "My businessman, it looks like you made a deal this morning.". Incidentally, I recall one occasion, on the evening prior to a Christian holy day, when some Christians came to buy yeast. We children used to come and help Grandmother. It happened that, after the clients left, my brother Chonan found a three-ruble piece on the floor. He almost immediately gave it to Bobe. Grandfather heard of this from a distance. He called out that they should immediately go out in the streets and announce what had happened, asking who had lost the cash. Grandmother doubted that one could trust the moral integrity of the townfolk so completely. She said that it would be wiser to wait until he who had lost the money returned to claim it. A half hour later, the Christian man who had lost the money arrived at the door, and grandmother gave it to him. Grandmother asked him, "If I had followed your suggestion, would I have the three rubles now to give this man?" Grandfather answered calmly, "No one would have falsely claimed that it was his own." This anecdote illustrates not only his own sense of honor, but also his belief in the moral integrity of others.

With regard to tsedekah (charity) it was his custom that, in a transaction, he would never accept small change from a poor man. When he had small change in his pockets and other occasions, he would give it to a poor man. What would happen if he afterwards encountered a second poor man, he would either ask for more small change from Bobe, or would borrow some small change for the second person. Also there were times when a guest arrived in town and grandfather sent him to the local inn, arranging for payment of his lodgings.

The tradition of contributing money to the plates for charitable organizations on the evening prior to Yom Kippur is well known. He frequently wanted to give more than he possessed. He would borrow from someone else in order to make the contribution, and then repay the lender in installments over the course of the year.

With regard to education, he was advanced in his outlook. He held the view that one should not hit school children. Our father held a position far from Goniondz. Grandfather used to tell our teacher that he shouldn't hit his little ones. He also used to say that one should not send children to an angry teacher for education, because one cannot trust an angry man. I recall a case where a mother complained to him about her son, that he was too much of a rascal. Grandfather answered her, "A boy that doesn't fool around can't learn!"

One of the aspects of his character, which is most deeply engraved in my memory, was his constant concern not to trouble anyone in general, and most particularly the family. I remember one time when he was walking to the House of Study. It was slippery and he fell. There were a few men with him at the time. The first thing that he said, after they helped him to stand again, was, "Don't tell the family, they would worry." One of the men was Berl Rudsky. He came to us at home and very discretely told my brother Pinchas what had happened. Pinchas became concerned that it was a serious matter and that a physician was needed. This was how the rest of us learned of his fall. For Grandfather the main thing always was not to worry people.

My mother almost deified him. She ascribed supernatural powers to him, believing that he didn't need to use them. In that connection she told us about an incident which had occurred when the great dispute broke out in Goniondz. At that time she was still a young girl. Grandfather had said, "The dispute will last five years. Five years I have taken bread from others, and for five years others will have to take bread from me." What did he mean, that he had taken bread from others? At one time in the past, he had been wanted as new rabbi in the city of Vishneve. Grandfather did not want to take the position unless he was accepted as substitute by the rabbi who was leaving. The other rabbi felt that no such interchange was needed and suggested he simply take the position. Nonetheless, Grandfather still felt that by coming to Vishneve he would be taking the bread from another, which was the basis of his prediction. Indeed there was a five-year delay. Would our mother need a better example?

The truth is that the shtetl itself used to ascribe wonders to him. Once a fire broke out in town and my grandfather said, "I believe that it won't go any further than the house of Gershon the carpenter, which is near the House of Study." And that is how it was. I also recall a comment which was made about him after his death. He died Friday night, the evening prior to Shevuos. The funeral took place on the Sabbath night of Shevuos. One of the town-folk who were present told Pinchas, my brother, that the heavens had split open at his father's death. When Pinchas, who was involved in a secular enlightenment, did not accept this as a factual account, the Jew became angry with him.

He was a very humble man. He truly believed in the saying, "He who seeks honor, honor flees from that person." He also lived out his daily day in a manner consistent with this belief.

I recall one occasion when it was necessary to call in a rabbi from another town for consultation in resolving a dispute. The particular matter at hand was extraordinarily complex. The second rabbi was not willing to travel to our town unless accompanied by his sexton. Grandfather's comment, in hearing this news, was "It is not proper for a Jew to be served." With regard to his humility, my mother had said after his death, "As it was during his lifetime, so it is after his death. If his funeral had taken place in midweek, the townsfolk would have closed their shops in order to bestow this final honor upon him. However since it took place on a holy day, the shops were closed anyway, and this saved him from having to receive that special distinction." In connection with the great dispute I have already spoken about the loss of bread. Actually, this was not an exaggeration. We were truly in hunger. Our grandmother was a very proud woman and didn't want others to be aware of the extent of our suffering. Fridays during the day she would heat up the oven thinking that perhaps one of grandfather's allies in the dispute might come to the house to see if we had enough provisions for the Sabbath. The hot oven would give them the impression that she was about to heat up chulent. The pots, however, were empty.

I remember a story told to me by my uncle, Moishe-Meier, in connection with the dispute. The leaders of the opposition group were from the strata of society referred to as "the upper crust." When some dirty work needed to be done, however, they sent out common folk. One Sabbath, Grandfather was saying Shmoneh Esrei. prayers in the House of Study. The community was accustomed to wait until he was finished. A sharp-tongued shoe repairman spoke out and said to the assembled congregation, "Who are you waiting for?" Hearing this, Grandfather was filled with pain and shame. It was perhaps the first time in his life that he had cried on the Sabbath. Years later, when the dispute had become a matter of the past, the children of that same shoemaker died. The cause was clear. This was a punishment from God for having humiliated the rabbi. He came to Grandfather to ask forgiveness and to ask my grandfather to pray for him. Grandfather's answer was, "Surely, I forgive you. You want me to pray for you, of course, I will say a chapter of Psalms if you like. But do you think I have some sort of special connection with the heavens?"

There was another who also came years later to ask forgiveness from grandfather. He was the owner of a yard goods shop. He wanted to bring Grandfather a lounge chair called a fauteuil in French. Also, in this case, the answer was, "I forgive you, I forgive you, but I don't need a lounge chair. My father didn't sit in a lounge chair and I don't need one either."

Although Grandfather was always concerned that grandmother should not worry, she was nonetheless constantly preoccupied with the needs and responsibilities of daily life. Hers was the responsibility to see that the children had enough to eat, that they had proper garments and when they were a little older, that books were available for them, etc. I remember many scenes when Grandmother would be at home sitting with an obviously anxious appearance. Grandfather would turn to her and ask, "What are you worried about?" "What am I worried about?" Grandmother responds, "I've lived a magnificent life," and then went on to convey a concern to him. Grandfather would answer, "As far as the past is concerned, you should think that we have lived in wealth. As far as the future is concerned I have faith that we will make it through."

There were cases when even Christians who had a dispute with the Jews would come to Grandfather for a judicial decision, rather than take the matter to a civil court. There were cases when the decision fell to the favor of the Christian, and the Jew was very unhappy.

My Grandfather was pleased that during the approximately thirty years during which he had been rabbi in Goniondz, he did not have to give many divorces. Incidentally, couples came from other shtetls where there was no flowing river to seek a divorce from him. According to Jewish legal requirements, the divorce document needed to list the name of a flowing river near which the divorce was awarded. Speaking of divorces, I remember situations when, as a child I would sit at Grandfather's side in the house when a couple would come to him seeking a divorce. Grandfather always tried to arbitrate and make peace between them. As a girl, it annoyed me that he would do so, and I would think, "They want to get a divorce - let them divorce!" During those tender years I was too young and immature to understand what dissolution of a marriage meant. Actually I was fascinated with the procedures, the volume in which the divorce decrees were written, the witnesses, and the questions.

Once a couple came for a divorce. As usual, Grandfather tried to arrange a reconciliation. However, they were not willing to consider this option. When he found that all of his arguments were of no avail, Grandfather told them, "I don't divorce on Thursdays." He was hoping that perhaps over the Sabbath they would have second thoughts. The result was that the couple lived out the rest of their lives together, had children and also grandchildren as well.

When he became afflicted with the cancer from which he eventually died, I had the privilege of watching over him one night. During that period, cancer victims were not given medication to alleviate their pain. The poor thing had to go on in suffering. He would ask me to put the cushions down on the sofa, and from the sofa on the bed. When I would ask him, "Grandfather, are you suffering pain?" He would answer, "No, thank God." Everything he did was to avoid giving concern to others. A few weeks later he emitted his last breath and departed from the world. It would be difficult to find a man like him in his generation.

He was in full possession of his mental faculties up to the last minute of his life. During the day on Friday, several hours before his death, a man came to the house with a question. Pinchas wanted to know what grandfather's position would be and he led the man into the room where grandfather was lying. My grandfather answered the question. Several minutes before he died he muttered the name "Krapniak." We didn't understand his meaning at that moment. During the week of sitting shivah , Krapniak came to the house to comfort us. The family wanted to know whether mentioning this man's name had a significance. In response to our inquiry, this man explained that Grandfather was accustomed to borrow several rubles from him each year prior to the Days of Awe, in order to have more to contribute for the plates which received donations to charitable organizations. During the year the rabbi would repay Krapniak in installments. Since Grandfather had died in the middle of the year, he wanted the family to know about this financial obligation so that they could fulfill it. We, of course, paid his debt.

[Pages 451-456]

Family Memories
By Chana Neiman
Translated by Gloria Berkenstat Freund

My grandmother was a woman of valor. She carried the responsibility of providing the family with all necessities.

My mother was the only daughter. She was given in marriage when she was 16 years old. My father had a leather store for the first 10 years after the marriage. But the business went from bad to worse and they had to give it up.

[Page 452]

In as much as my father was, as Sholem Aleichem would say, a Jew who could hold a pen in his hand, my father took a position as a bookkeeper. Actually, it was with a nephew of my grandfather, far from Goniadz. I was three years old when he left home. He held this position for the last 10 years of his life. He would come [home] only twice a year on Passover and on *Sukkous* [Feast of Tabernacles in the autumn]. My father called it a "paper life" because every day of the year we would [be in contact] with letters. Be that as it may, I barely have memories of him. All that I remember is that when he would come home from afar for the holiday and tell stories, the uncles would laugh heartily. Apparently he had a good sense of humor. My Uncle Moshe Meir told me this in passing here in America. He [my father] died at the age of 42. My mother was left a widow with six children at the age of 36. This is the reason we had to leave our home so young and go to America. First, Yakov Yehosha, my oldest brother; later, me and then Khonen and Malka. My mother remained in Goniadz only with Yonatan.

[Page 453]

My mother was one of the quiet types, but a deeply emotional person. One can imagine what it meant for her to send away her young children across oceans. She did not want to come here for religious reasons and she obviously could not be without us. She wanted us to return. Therefore, Khonen actually did return and arrived just at the outbreak of the First World War. My mother was never happy with herself. She could not make peace with the fact that she could not read the *Tanakh* [Hebrew Bible] in the original [language]. She knew a little Hebrew, but not enough to read *Tanakh* in the original; during the years of the First World War, when there really was not enough to eat, she perfected her Hebrew. I was told this by Yonatan. He said to me that she asked him to help her.

After the First World War, when Benyamin the *soyfer* [scribe] came to America, he told me that my mother was the city nurse. She actually was infected with typhus and died *erev Pesakh* [eve of Passover] 5679 [1919] at the age of 51. She was fully aware and her last words were: I thank God that my children are not now helpless as when their father died. Benyamin the *soyfer* also told me this. Yonatan was not in Goniadz then. He had to run away.

[Page 454]

Pinkhas, the oldest of the sons, was a student in the Volozhin [Belarus] *yeshiva* [religious secondary school]. As Moshe Meir told me, it was during the time when [Jewish poet Chaim Nakhman] Bialik studied there. Returning, he [Pinkhas] began to study Russian and other languages. He mastered the Russian language perfectly and also knew German very well. Incidentally, none of them attended the Russian school because they would have had to sit without a hat. The grandchildren did go to the Russian school. My Uncle Moshe Meir told me that when Pinkhas returned from the Volozhin *yeshiva* he tried to establish a library in Goniadz. In general, he was interested in communal matters. For example, after the fire in 1906, he saw to the obtaining of a 10–year loan to be paid back with low interest, so that those who lost property in the fire could rebuild and have a roof over their heads. Later he also founded a loan fund. Incidentally, he was one of the first Zionists in Goniadz. At the time of the First World War he was carried off at least to Rostov–on–Don. When I was in Russia in 1937 I had the opportunity to see him and his family. It was a sorrow to see that a Jew such as he was severed from religious books, from Hebrew books and Jewish communal life in general. His son was an engineer and at that time had a very responsible position. The daughter is a bacteriologist. At that time, she worked in a hospital. My uncle and aunt are no longer here. It should be understood that I do not hear from the children.

[Page 455]

Welwl, long may he live, is in Israel with his family. He also was an active Zionist, would go around selling *shekels* [memberships in the World Zionist Organization]. However, things are good for him; he and his family accomplished their life's dream.

Zalman wanted to go even further; he wanted to go to America, hoping that he would study there. With his capabilities and his diligence he could surely be a professor. He left his home and simply did not tell his parents that he was going to America. Alas, grandfather died not long after his [Kalman's] departure and he felt guilty. Meanwhile his brothers at home began to ask him to come back. Not being satisfied with his achievements here, he and my brother Khonen returned and arrived right on the eve of the First World War. Zalman was taken for forced labor during wartime, went through the seven levels of hell, but later returned to Goniadz and accompanied our mother to her eternal rest. He, himself, became infected with typhus and died a lonely man. His fate was to accompany both our father and our mother.

[Page 456]

Moshe Meir, the youngest, left for America as a young boy along with Moshe Rudski. He went through all the difficulties of immigrant life here; with great effort he became a dentist, but he was not happy with this profession. He himself always said: " A trade – making holes in teeth and then filling them." By nature he was more a poet. Standing at the dentist chair he would hum parts of musical creations under his breath; he loved to quote Bialik and [Jewish poet Shaul] Tchernichovsky. He was also a Zionist. He bought land in *Eretz–Yisroel* and hoped to see it one day. However it was not destined for him [to do so].

Goniadz – Snow in June 1918

[Pages 455-459]

Torah in Goniondz
By David Bachrach
Translated from Yiddish to English by Dr. Isaac Fine

Goniondz did not give rise to any scholars of great reputation, but the shtetl at all times had its Torah students, scholars, and sons in yeshivas. At the beginning of the twentieth century, Goniondz was drawn into the stream of the enlightenment, both in Hebrew and in Russian. During that period, the voice of Torah became weaker. As a fire, which does not burn out immediately but smolders for a lengthy time period, so was it with Torah-yiddishkeit. in our town. Goniondz experienced a major intellectual and spiritual revolution during the 1900 - 1920 time period, from traditional to modern yiddishkeit. Since Torah- yiddishkeit is the foundation upon which the second stage was built, it is proper to delineate that phase of our shtetl life here in the memorial book.

Reb Gedaliah

Reb Gedaliah Kamenitzky was also known as "the old rabbi." He was a classical example of the older generation both in his stature in Torah and in his patriarchal appearance. He was continually studying, yes, even living Torah. He had little use for the "vanities of this world." For him, the main thing was "the next world." One should prepare oneself.

In the last year of Reb Gedaliah's life (1907), I prayed with him as part of the minyan. in his house. I recall that he was always sitting at the table learning by memory. Once my father told me that he was studying the tractate Nedorim , which is a Kamenitzky family tradition. Years later, in the book "Knowledge of the Holy" I read the following anecdote with regard to this family. Reb. Pinchas-Leib Hacohen, the father of Reb Gedaliah Kamenitzky (both, in their time, rabbis in Goniondz) told how his grandfather Reb Schloime Hacohen was in great danger on the sea when the ship on which he was traveling threatened to go under. He dreamed that the ship would survive the storm because of the merit of his son Tavye, who had just that day completed his study of the Talmud tractate Nedorim. And that is indeed what happened. He noted the day of his dream and, returning home, he discovered that his son Tayve had indeed ended the tractate on that day.

Reb Gedaliah's four sons all were able students, but they were all caught up in the enlightenment.

Harav Tzvi Hirsch Volf

Reb Tzvi-Hirsch Volf arrived in Goniondz as rabbi after the death of Reb Gedaliah. He was in tune with the new spirit which reigned in Goniondz and with modern times. He was an energetic young man of distinguished appearance. He spoke and read Russian fluently, and knew who to approach in the Tsarist government when a problem needed to be resolved.

Harav Volf did not fulfill the commandment to "study day and night." Nonetheless, he was at the same time, an accomplished student. His daughters were enrolled in the high school in Grodno. Later, he had a youngster who studied in the modern Hebrew school in town. Reb Volf was at the same time a pious Jew and a modern rabbi.

Harav Volf was accustomed to study Mishna Brura. between early afternoon and sundown prayer services. After the sundown prayer service, he studied Mishna . When Yaakov Rudsky stumbled and allowed construction to be done on his brewery on the Sabbath, which was a profanation of the Divine Name, Harav Volf withdrew his permission to conduct a regular study session in Gemara , which previously had been Yaakov Rudsky's privilege.

Harav Volf accomplished his greatest act of statesmanship during the First World War in 1915, as a refugee in Bialystok. This was in connection with the order given by Nikolai Nikoliavitch that all Jews should evacuate their homes, which lay along the entire battlefront, within forty-eight hours. Harav Volf, together with leaders of the Bialystok community, arranged to have the decree lifted for the entire Bialystok region for a certain time - until the Russians themselves later had to evacuate.

Krapuniak

Old Krapuniak was a distinguished student. He was from Reb Gedaliah's generation and was always steeped in Torah. His son-in-law, a young rabbi who was waiting for a position, studied at his side for several years in the House of Study. Both he and his son-in-law died one after the other around 1909, and the House of Study became still.

Itze-Lieb

One did not hear Itze-Lieb the shamash. when he was studying Torah. In my time he was almost blind. He was accustomed to study Mishna by memory alone and quietly, standing on the bimeh.

Zelig Issac's

He was the father of the Rudskis and a brilliant Talmudic scholar. There were legends told about him and about his life. He was accustomed to study day and night in a solitary fashion in his brick home, and was almost never seen in the House of Study, even on the Sabbath and the High Holy Days. He would, however, visit with his rabbi in Kotzk during the Days of Awe.

Zelig Issac's was a fervent Chassid. During an earlier time, he was a leader in the great dispute which took place in Goniondz, toward the end of the 1880's, with regard to the rabbi - ritual slaughterer - cantor. When the misnagdim won the dispute, he withdrew from the world. Children used to hear Zelig Issac's Gemara nigun. coming out from the window of his home, though they would not see him. When he took a stroll on the synagogue hill to catch a breath of fresh air, the children would ask themselves, "Who is that?"

The remainder of this article was translated from Yiddish to English by Gloria Berkenstat Freund.

[Pages 459-464]

Two Quiet Talmud Students

There were two Jews, great Talmudic students, in Goniadz, whose sounds of Torah study were not heard in the synagogue. That was not because they had a falling out with the community... They were just quiet men who loved to study in their homes...

Meir-Ayzik's [son] (Idl Treszczanski's father)

...was one of them. He was a *yeshiva* [religious secondary school] student in Bialystok during his youth and then he studied by himself his entire life. He had natural mechanical abilities and he was a "self-taught" master watchmaker. He had a meager income, but his great "wealth" was in the Vilna Talmud. Because of my friend Idl, I was a frequent visitor in their house and every evening I would see him reading his Talmudic lesson.

Meir-Ayzik's [son] was an intelligent man, full of humor and insight. He would delight adults and children with his talks on worldly matters in the synagogue and at the workshop.

He called all of the scholars in the *shtetl* [town] to his house for the celebration of the completion of the group study of a Talmudic tractate and his *seudat mitzvah* [celebratory meal for the fulfillment of a *mitzvah* – a commandment] was an event in Goniadz.

Arya-Leib Bachrach

The second quiet Talmud student in Goniadz was my father, Arya-Leib Bachrach (Leibl the iron-shopkeeper). In general, Leibl Bachrach was a person who devoted his time to study, not taking part in any kehile [organized Jewish community] activities. The raising of his children, his studying alone and worry about making a living filled his life. And he studied every free minute – during the day, in the evening and late in the night. He studied the Gemara and Mishnah [Talmudic commentary] "methodically" on the weekdays and on Shabosism [Sabbaths] [he studied] Kabalah [Jewish mysticism] and other religious texts. In addition he was an avid reader of the Hebrew and Yiddish press.

Societies

Talmud Society

The Talmud Society studied a page of *Gemara* every evening after *Maariv* [evening prayers] at a long table along the southern wall in the house of prayer. The "rebbe" [teacher] was Ayzyk's son Yankl-Zelik (Rudski). By nature, Yankl Rudski was a modest person and his presence in the house of prayers was almost unfelt, but he was something different when he recited a Talmudic lesson. Then he revealed his insight and made himself heard.

Ayzyk's son Yankl-Zelik had a large family, ran a large business with the [Russian] exchequer and had a "clear head" for learning Talmud with a group at night.

Among other constant members [of the Talmud Society] I remember Pinkhas the rabbi's son, Moshe Klewianker (Lewin), Gdalke (Gdeliah) the teacher, Tovya Motl Kohn, Gnendl's son Avraham and, finally, Yehoshua, Chaim Dinke's son-in- law.

Mishnah Society

– The rebbe – Avraham Moshe Mekhaber. A tall Jew with a strong voice that could be heard from one corner of the house of prayer to the other even on *Shabbos* before *Minkhah* [afternoon prayers], when the house of prayer was full of children who made a great deal of noise... The routine of his teaching a chapter of *Mishnais* [Talmudic commentary] was: every day before the *minyon* [organized prayer service] and on *Shabbos* before *Minkhah*. Of the students I remember: Yoske Murajnski, Chaim Velvl the dyer, my father Yisroel Yitzhak, Yankl Elia the blacksmith, Berl Dalker and Alter and Hershl, the owners of the windmill.

Avraham Moshe would also recite Psalms on *Shabbos* between the afternoon and evening prayers and we children would zealously sing *LeDovid Borukh* [Psalm 144 – Of David, Blessed be the Lord] along with him.

The yearly *Siyum* [completion of the reading of a Talmudic tractate] by the *Mishnah* Society was on *Simkhas-Torah* [holiday in celebration of the annual cycle of Torah readings and the start of a new cycle]. On this holiday Avraham Moshe really moved heaven and earth... Yankl the *shoykhet* [ritual slaughterer] helped him in this, after which they both recited the *Shehakl* [blessing of food and drink, but not of wine]. And which Goniadzer does not remember Avraham Moshe's spiritual singing and his merry-making on this day of all days – *Simkhas-Torah!*

Ein-Yaakov Society

The rebbe of the *Ein-Yaakov* Society [*Ein-Yaakov* is a compilation of the ethical and inspirational sections of the Talmud.] was Gershon-Borukh Krawiec. He was a Jew, a gifted person, but without a [strong] body... So that it was thought that the wind blew him away. He always had a ready answer for every question. Gershon-Borukh was not a great explainer; he interpreted and went on, interpreted and went further. However, the Jews who sat around the table absorbed his words and were delighted with the beautiful stories and parables.

He was a fervid Russian patriot and although it [Russia] shamelessly lost to the old Philistine during the Russian-Japanese War, he was certain again that the Russians would win in the First World War. In this case, at least, it [Russia] went [to fight] "equal" [to its opponent], taking it in its stride...

Nisen the Tailor

Nisen the tailor led a smaller *Ein-Yaakov* Society.

Nisen sat at a table with his usual few students, toiling Jews, unhurriedly explaining each article and each example. He simply chewed it over and spoke about it... They left his table "satisfied." They studied every day before the first *minyon* and on *Shabbos* before the afternoon prayers. (Incidentally, Nisen "had tenure" at the reader's desk on *Shabbos* for the afternoon prayers and his *Atah Echad* [Thou art One] was a pleasure to hear).

Velvl Rawer

Every Friday night after eating, Velvl Rawer (Sajd) would study a chapter of Torah with a number of artisans who had their *Shabbos minyon* in Itshe Francoizl's house.

Yeshiva Students

Yehoshua Rozenblum

The "old man" of the *yeshiva* [religious secondary school] students in Goniadz was Yehoshua Rozenblum (Golda [and] Elya-Asher's son). He was once a child prodigy as well as an adherent of the *Musar* [moral discipline] movement in Novaredok and Reb Yosl's *yeshiva*. Later, he studied in Konigsberg. The young were drawn to him as to a spiritual leader. When he died in 1910, the entire *shtetl* [town] accompanied him to the *gutn ort* [good earth – the cemetery]. The *mite* [board for carrying a corpse] was carried around the house of study...

Yosl Hercik

Yosl Yehuda, the furrier's son, studied in Trestine with Rabbi Biszko. Later, when he became a follower of the Enlightenment, he rarely was seen in the house of prayer... (Now, incidentally, he is one of the oldest Goniadzers in Tel Aviv.)

A Son of Hershl Yosl Zorakh's. – (a cousin of Sender Mitlszan's)

Very few Goniadzers know of him. His family emigrated to America (in 1903). However, he did not go with them and spent his entire life in *yeshivus*. He was a great scholar and God-fearing.

Yosef Bobrowski

Mendele's son Yosef also studied in Trestine. He remained a Hasid even after he stopped studying and praying... He lived in America for many years; he was a patron of scholars, a generous supporter of Torah institutions and a great contributor to *Eretz-Yisroel.*

Yeshiva Students of My Generation

The *shoykhet*'s son Itshe Yankl, Leyzer-Ayzyk's son Yitzhak-Lieb, Mordekhai Kaplan (a son of the Kuliav *melamed* [teacher at religious school], (the blacksmith) Elya-Shlom's son Zeydke, Chana-Dina's son Dovid and Yehosha the shoemaker's son Avraham-Yitzhak studied in Lomza, Brisk and other *yeshivus*.

I, myself, first studied in the Wizner *Yeshiva Ketana* [junior *yeshiva*] and then in Radin for three years. At the start of the summer of 1914, shortly before I left Radin, Meirim Rubin (Velvl Zodjok's son) came to study there. Meirim was the last Goniadz *yeshiva* student in my memory. He is now the rabbi and *shoykhet* in a town in Argentina.

In the middle of Elul 5680 (1920) I left Goniadz and never saw our *shtetl* again. It can be said that the house of prayer already had lost its glory: there were few Talmudic students and even fewer young ones, but the influence of the earlier years remained.

Petah Tikvah Elul 5718 (September 1958)

[Pages 463-468]

Reb Binyamin Yosef son of Reb Tzvi Boyer
A. Miltshan
Translated by Lazer Mishulovin
Donated by Bradley and Kathy Fisher

Binyamin the scribe accompanied the Goniadz Jew from the cradle to the grave, as they used to say in Goniadz. That is how, for example, already before a Goniadz Jew came into the world, Reb Binyamin provided the mother in the labor room, a "Shir Hamalos" for all of the four walls [It is customary to post psalm 121 on the walls in the labor room], written in his beautiful scribal handwriting, so that, Heaven forbid, ghosts or evil sprits could not harm the newborn. In the synagogue, prior to the circumcision, Reb Binyamin led the prayer, "Shira Chadasha Shibchu G'ulim," and during the circumcision, he was the chief host of the celebration, bestowing all the honors and taking care of all the arrangements. When the child had grown up just a bit, the father would bring him to the synagogue, where Reb Binyamin would call him by name and give him to taste from the wine of the Kidush and Havdala. Anyone with ancestral merits, would have the honor to hold the thick woven Havdala-candle, which Reb Binyamin himself had woven and provided for the synagogue.

Later, when the child had just started to babble, Reb Binyamin would provide a printed Hebrew Alphabet on a big tablet with all the vowels and letters from long and shorthand. When a child would enter chader [Traditional religious school] to the melamed [teacher of children] , the first turn would be to Reb Binyamin, as the Jewish book vender who supplied the prayer book with large letters; later on, a Pentateuch and then the whole twenty-four scriptures. When, God helped, and the young boy grew to his Bar Mitzvah, then began the process of ordering from Reb Binyamin a pair of nice Tefilin (phylacteries) from the best of the best, as it is written in Shulchan Aruch [The Book of Jewish Law]: finely polished with see- through leather, (i.e. that the parchment should be visible from below the Tefilin), with a nice wide "shin"[Twenty-first letter of the Hebrew Alphabet that is engraved on the Teffilin] from both sides and a maroon velvet Tefilin bag on which was sewn the name of the Bar Mitzva boy with the Jewish date and a big gold embroidered Star of David. Reb Binyamin arranged the entire Bar Mitzvah celebration: Prepared the Bar Mitzvah boy for his Haftora and the blessings; on Shabbos, called up to the Torah all of the friends, relatives and the bar mitzvah boy himself for his Haftorah, and simultaneously partook in the Bar Mitzvah celebration.

Besides for all of the aforementioned functions, and the actual administration of the big synagogue of which he was the unofficial manager, he sat entire days "learning and praying" in the full sense of the word. When one passed his house, which was located between the synagogue and the study house, through the window they would notice Reb Binyamin, sitting hunched over large scrolls of parchment, inscribing the Holy Torah with great holy-awe and encircling every letter with peculiar crowning and embellishments.

The greatest joy that Reb Binyamin created for us children was in the month of Adar, as the Talmud says: "As Adar arrives one increases in joy." It was then, when in the second window of his so-called salon, appeared an exhibit of all types of Megilla scrolls, rolled and folded, small and large, with various decorations; a large collection of various gragers (rattles), tinned Haman-rattles, engraved colorful toy-hammers, richly painted; a whole collection of different Purim masks: Haman, his wife Zeresh and their brat Vayizasa. But the main attraction was Haman and his ten sons on the gallows, in gaudy oriental colors. This was so skilfully crafted, that when one pulled a little string, Haman jerked and wriggled his hands and feet as if a spirit possessed him, and the little Hamans would accompany him with the quivers. When we, chader boys, on our way home for dinner would pass Reb Binyamin's window and stop, wondering at the beautiful exhibit, Reb Binyamin would send over his youngest daughter to pull the string. The wriggling of the Jew-haters would let loose our enthusiasm and joy of revenge. We would stand this way for hours at the window and even forget about dinner.

The day before the holiday of Shevous [Pentecost, an early summer holiday celebrating the gathering of the first fruits and the giving of the Torah to the Jews], Reb Binyamin would call us from Motye's chader to help him spread out the grass and roses on the street of B'neymke the tailor all the way to the Synagogue and in the Synagogue as well – in honor of the Festival of the First Fruits. On the eve before Simchat Torah [The last day of the Holiday of Suckot which marks the completion of the annual Torah reading], it was the task of the chader-boys to climb up to the highest balcony of the Synagogue, to kindle the candles in the clay pits that Reb Binyamin would prepare there. On Simchat Torah eve, Reb Binyamin would conduct from the almemar the Hakafos and hand out the children's flags. On Simchat Torah morning, he would take us young boys, "holy sheep," under his Talis like under the Chupa (canopy), for "Kol Hane'arim" [The prayer recited when calling up the Children for the Torah on Simchat Torah].

We would often come to the Synagogue to catch a smile from Reb Binyamin, a lovely glance, or a joke with a rhyme, which he always had prepared for us. Across from Reb Binyamin sat a Jew by the name Chatzkel Burak. He was a town tailor by profession, who throughout the week would sew fur coats for the peasants of the surrounding region and come home for the Shabbos. He is the pedigree of the Blum family in America, and the father of Dr. Blum in New York. While he was observing how Reb Binyamin would sit entire days writing Torah scrolls, he came up with an idea:.For the few hundred rouble which he put aside throughout the long years of his work in the village, as well as for the accumulated money his son sent him from America, he would begin writing a Torah scroll in the name of him and his wife and place it in the Holy Ark for the future generations, while serving as a memory for him, his wife, children and grandchildren. He discussed his idea with Reb Binyamin and they put together a plan, travelled to Bialostock, purchased the best parchment and approached to actualise the plan.

It took a few years to write the Torah scroll. When it was completed, they celebrated the Completion of the Torah at Zerach Miltshan in the center of the market place. The director of the whole ceremony was, naturally, Reb Binyamin the scribe. The whole façade of the homes and all of the shopwindows were hung with colored lanterns on which were sketched different animals, such as: Weasels, dragons and scorpions, which no zoo ever saw its equal. Inside, on clothed tables, were spread out the snow-white Torah Scroll, and Reb Binyamin was dressed up in a black silk suit with a snow white bowtie, a velvet hat and was selling letters. The people were buying; one for himself and one for his wife, one for a daughter who reached her time, so that she should find her mate, or for a son who has to stand for the military draft, he should be free of Fonye's [The Yiddish word for Russia or Russians] hands. After inscribing the letters in the scroll, Toba Tzivke would honor everyone with liquor and biscuits. For the conclusion celebration, the whole family has gathered; starting with Shlomo Yosel's large household, Yoel Chana-Chaya's and all the rest of the relatives and friends, no one was missing. Our Reb Binyamin is sweating pitifully as he is announcing everyone by name and the amount each one contributed for the conclusion of the scroll, or the letter, which word and of which verse in the Torah he bought for his maiden, Miss Elke, or for his son, the groom Shmerl. So it went, the entire evening, until the people stopped coming and there were no more letters. Only then was the completion. The scroll was rolled up, clothed with the beautiful, shiny red velvet, gold embodied jacket, with a dedication to Chatzkel Burak as the sponsor. They carry the canopy with the four sticks from the synagogue, and under it they escort the elderly Chatzkel Burak with the Torah Scroll. Near him stands his wife Toba Tzivke, who supports him with her hand, surrounded by the whole family with candles in their hands. Following them, the whole group marches to the study house, skipping the puddles along the market lane; holding the lanterns, candles and torches. Yehuda the Kirzshener dances before them backwards, claps with his hands, sings a happy song, a melody, or dances in a kazaske.

So marches the whole train under the command of Reb Binyamin until the little lane of the study house. At this time a delegation of all of the neighbors, relatives and ordinary good friends appear and attach themselves to the train. They march in a pressed crowd until the anteroom of the study house. Chatzkel Burak's cheeks are flaming and joyous tears roll down his cheeks. The crowd yells out loud "This is the Torah and this is the reward.". "Let us be joyous and festive with this Torah for it is our strength and light," as the masses enter the study house. They take out all of the Torah Scrolls from the Holy Arch and they perform the Hakofos around the almemar.

After all the honors are allotted, the Safer Torah is placed in its position in the Holy Arch, one wishes each other life and health until one-hundred-and-twenty and the crowd disperses. Our Reb Binyamin, dead tired, barely crawls home....

[Pages 469-472]

My Synagogue and the Synagogue Hill
Feigal Rubin (Daughter of Reb Binyamin the Scribe)
Translated by Lazer Mishulovin
Donated by Bradley and Kathy Fisher

The Synagogue and the Synagogue hill meant a lot to us, Goniadz's, and it is important to record the agony and the ecstasy, the joy and the worries that occurred at the Synagogue hill – my Synagogue hill.

I am saying "my," because as a young girl I thought that the synagogue and the Synagogue hill is the property of my father and my mother. The Torah Scrolls that were in the Synagogue were naturally my fathers, in fact I see him writing them.

The memory of my childhood and youth are tightly bonded with the synagogue and the Synagogue hill. I was brought up at the Synagogue hill, dreamt dreams of joy at the Synagogue hill.

How great was the pain and suffering when we learnt that the Polish hooligans desecrated our holiness and tore a Torah Scroll. The impression is unforgettable, engraved deep into my memory. This happened after the Holidays in the year 1912. Scraps of torn parchment of a Torah Scroll were scattered at the Synagogue hill, dirty and trampled. The ritual washstand was broken and scattered with torn muddy towels. The entire Goniadz was drenched in sadness, full of pain, resembling depressed mourners. My father cried so much, similarly as when my mother passed away in that same year. Rabbi Wolf, the town Rabbi, came out with an order that we should fast, and the grief was very great. They brought down snuff-dogs, who sniffed and ran around the Synagogue hill and down the Synagogue hill. However, since it was after a rain, the dogs were unable to discover the footprints of the criminals. .

Heart wrenching scenes would take place, when a mother with a heartbreaking lament would devolve upon the Holy Torahs in the synagogue, pleading from them to make an effort on behalf of her ill child. Children as well, would beg mercy in the synagogue before the Torah Scrolls for the sake of their ill father or mother, that they should not remain lonely orphans.

The synagogue and Synagogue hill were soaked with lots of tears, however, also joy.

A wedding in Goniadz!. The entire city, old and young, take part in the joy. The bride and groom are being escorted to the Chupa [wedding canopy]. Where? Naturally – At the Synagogue hill. The music is playing. The windows are illuminated with lanterns or candles in all of the homes that lead to the synagogue avenue. The young couple, full of happiness and hope for a new life and a happy future, experience their happiest moments on the Synagogue hill.

Summertime, the Synagogue hill was full of children, happy, worry-free, playful; the air resounding with their chatter and laughter, playing in little horses, games like the *"devil," "fifty fifty"* or military manoeuvres. After a hot summer-day on a choking summer evening, we would go to cool off at the Synagogue hill. We would take along pillows to lie on, or to sit and schmooze.

And who can forget the Holidays? The Synagogue would be packed with people, old and young and the Synagogue hill with children, who would, with din and hurly-burly, run in and out and fill the air with happy worriless cacophony.

Another picture swims before me. The year 1911, it was on the last day of Passover. A fire breaks out in my Uncle Gershon Leib's shop. Screams and alarms. They rescue the children, the bag and baggage, property and goods. Where is the securest place?. On the Synagogue hill. A cry from the children. A lament from fathers and mothers; blankets and pillows, furniture etc. The synagogue and the Synagogue hill is their safe haven – my Synagogue hill.

The year 1916 – The world renowned Cantor Sirota comes to us in Goniadz. Goniadz is in a holiday spirit. We, children of the Hebrew school, march with our teachers (Moshe Levin, Yoal-Meir Kohen, Yonoson Neiman and Shimon Halperin) singing Hebrew melodies into the synagogue, where we listen to the songs of Cantor Sirota.

Boys and girls, students of the Hebrew school, would do their assignments; learn Bible verses by heart at the Synagogue hill.

Over there, we built towers in the air, hoped and dreamt of a nicer and better world, a world of fairness and justice. We dreamt of the Land of Israel.

My town Goniadz and its people were massacred by murderous hands; desolate and destroyed are my synagogue and my Synagogue hill.

The Gabaim, Shamosim and ordinary Jews in front of the synagogue building
[Translator's note: Gabaim and Shamosim are synagogue officials.
The words are often translated as "sexton or "beadle"]

[Pages 473-474]

Sketches of Goniondz
(A Bundle of Memories from an Old Goniondzer – Nisan the tailor's son)
By Dovid Forman
Translated by Gloria Berkenstat Freund

Dovid Forman

Although not a historian, I understand from the name "old market" that Goniondz began to build on the river side. As the city spread, the "old market" remained for the annual fairs and markets to sell horses and cattle and Kalin to singe his pigs.

The new, larger market already had a semblance of a large city, as if planned by a master craftsman, divided into a privileged side and an unprivileged side, as ostensibly, the great world cities – New York or London with an "east" and a "west"...

I will describe the large market a little, beginning from the eastern side with the *Meysim* [dead men's] Alley: Avraham Tshudak's house, unfortunately a ruin almost sunken into the earth, an indication of *thkises haMeysim*...[resurrection of the dead] Avraham had dressed his "house" in a large hat, that is, a roof much larger than the house itself. This "hat" stood on poles. In general, this hat was not "permanent," but it was not enough simply to complete the house, so he made the hat so that no water would pour on his head...

After his house – a brick one – Yoske's son Yitzhak. On the south side – Moshe's Ruchl [either Moshe's wife or daughter] and several wooden houses and then several brick ones up to Peshe, the baker and Chaim Dinke's brick one.

Farther, Zelig-Ayzik's brick house was a complete "center" for him. First of all – Malka-Reyzl's "office" and the second story a center for medicine: there was the pharmacy and also the doctor, although Yankl the *refuah* [healer – old time doctor] had a large practice at the old market.

On the west side (Respect!) two wooden houses of Meirke's Reyzel [Meirke's daughter or wife] and Shimeon Maranc – and the entire side of brick houses – up to Moshe-Gershon and Markowski. I remember when the brick house was finished, Markowski and his family would sit on the little bridge on *Shabbos* in the evening and throw nuts and sweets for the Jewish children.

The south side as with the east side – one brick building, Zarah's son Leizer's and only a few wooden houses.

Goniondzer "mountain" – three continuous mountains, Beyle-Ite's, the *Shul* synagogue] mountain and the T-mountain with the large, deep valley in the middle. If one looks carefully with a good eye, it is evident that all three mountains were one mountain from the beginning of time. And, to be truthful, they are only half mountains because they level off to the street on the south side.

And the *dol* as it is known, a Hebrew word that means "poor," because the Jewish poverty settled there.

So Mendele Moykhet Sforim [pen name of Yiddish writer, Sholem Yankev Abramovich] can describe the *shwitz-bod* [steam bath] and the *mikvah* [ritual bath] better. And, *lehavdil,* [word used to separate the sacred from the profane or secular] Sholem Aleichem has already described the beautiful synagogue with the old *beis-medrash* [house of prayer] before me... But I remember the *rathoyz* [city hall] that stood in the middle of the market as if it was the municipal *duma* [Russian Parliament] or *uprawa* [building of agriculture] . And I still remember the *turme* [jail] that stood not far from the city hall, because of an actual incident:

Yehuda the shoemaker had a feud with a *katsap*, namely, he, Yehuda made a pair of boots for him. The *katsap* [derogatory nickname for a Russian] put them on and did not want to pay. Sheyne-Feigl's son, Yisroel-Moshe, his worker, a strong youth, pulled the boots off of the *katsap's* feet and gave him a push so that he flew into Zelig-Ayzik's wall. The frightened *katsap* brought the *uriadnik* [constable] and Yisroel-Moshe was put in jail – near the city hall. When the constable left, Yisroel-Moshe gave the door a push and – the youth was gone! Later the constable met him in the street: "How is that possible? What right did you have to break out of jail?" Yisroel-Moshe answered him: "If you talk a great deal, I will make a *danos* [constable denunciation] of you, that you put people in a broken jail".... The constable became quiet and then the ruin was taken down.

[Pages 475-476]

My Town Long Ago
By Yitzhak Ellen, New York
Translated from Yiddish to English by Sherry Warman

When I close my eyes, I see before me Goniondz with her old-new market. I see the constant mud of Dead Man's Alley, that never dried itself out and the deep mud in the other streets after every rain. I remember the Zdroi and the Dolke [streams], where we used to go to refresh ourselves with cold water every Sabbath afternoon, and the fear that the gentiles would beat us.

I remember, also, the great historical argument that continued in the city for many years. When "Amcha" ["one of ours"] or as we called him, Buzi, wanted only Mr. Shmuel Kantor (who now lives in New York) as cantor-ritual slaughterer and the synagogue elders, with Zelig-Isaac at their head, didn't want him. I remember also how that argument led to the formation of a gang, in Goniondz, led by Yehuda Katz and his brother Shimon, of whom it was said, "He is so strong, that he has metal bands for muscles." I also remember that the same gang held the gentiles around the adjacent towns in fear, and when, on a Sunday, a tall, healthy gentile from the village Guzi, pushed him around, little Aaron Puzman knocked him down with one blow. And I saw the same Puzman years later here in New York, where he had been punched about the eyes by an American bum and had not even had the chance to return one blow.

I remember, also, the old priest who, on Sabbath afternoon, would gather Jewish boys near the gate of his orchard and would learn Ethics of the Fathers with them. Later, they said he was one of the true righteous gentiles. It reminds me of a fire on a Sabbath that burned a lot of gentile shacks around the town, and Jewish houses escaped, and even the windmill that stood exactly in the way of the fire wasn't singed. Being mere children then, we believed the fire listened to the Jews.

I recall many, many things that awaken in me a memory of the town where I rarely had enough bread to eat, but where I dreamed my unfulfilled childhood dreams. I remember the synagogue hill, and the other hill (with its charming name), where we would dig yellow sand to spread on the wooden floors in honor of the Sabbath, and the Bober River, and the lawns and fields, and the soldiers who would muster in the market and the slaps they used to get from the under-officer or from Diodka - all these things implanted in that generation a feeling of nature's beauty, a love of Torah and culture, a hatred of tyranny and despotism, and a pioneering spirit that tore us out of that corner and brought us to a new free land where we became a part of its life and raised our children.

Yes, our children probably didn't hear too much about Goniondz, but for us, whose cradles were in that town, it remains, the town, with its synagogue-hill, river, fields and woods, a part of our dearest memories.

[Pages 477-484 - Hebrew] [Pages 485-492 - Yiddish]

The Great Fire in Goniondz
and the Pogrom in Bialystok
By Avraham Yaffe, Tel-Aviv, Israel
Translated from Hebrew to Yiddish by M. Goelman
Translated from Yiddish to English by Dr. Isaac Fine

Our shtetl Goniondz, like all other shtetl in Russia, suffered from a special summer plague: Fires! Every fire placed the entire town in danger since the houses were mostly made of wood, although a few dwellings in the marketplace were brick homes with shingled roofs. The majority of dwellings had roofs either of shingle or of straw, a light material which burned easily.

In those days articles would frequently appear in the press from correspondents from smaller towns with the title "The Red Rooster Is Back Again!" Towards the end of the nineteenth century and the beginning of the twentieth century, a fire battalion was organized in Goniondz founded by a Jew named Bulbe, who was a spice shop owner, and later an industrialist. He lived in the second house from Dovid Shilevsky.

A wooden building stood in the center of the new marketplace, in which the fire equipment was quartered. The equipment consisted of a large barrel with wheels on both sides. The barrel had one pole on each side, with which to pump the water through a rubber hose, which would be attached. When a fire broke out somewhere, the leader of the fireman group would immediately appear with his horse, open the building's doors, connect up the horse to the fire machine - which unfortunately was not always filled with water. Young men would run along its side as he moved out in the direction of the conflagration. The runners would accompany him with noise and shouts which brought to mind a quote from the prophet Nochum, "A snapping of the whip, noise of the wheels, galloping horses, and lunging chariots."

Arriving at the place, they would attach the rubber hose to the barrel. Then they would place the wooden poles in position on both sides of the barrel. One group of boys and young men would push down on the pole from one side, while another group would pull up on it from the other side. In this manner they would pump the water out through the pipe and the water would then be poured out over the fire. Unfortunately, they were not always successful. At times the barrel was empty, and on such occasions there might be a considerable delay until such time as it was filled; sometimes the hose was not operating properly and it would require time for repair. Meanwhile the fire would be blazing with full power.

There were times when, in the middle of the night, one would hear the outcry "Fire!" The residents of town would run out into the streets half dressed. Seeing the red skies, they would immediately run to the place of the fire. One would bring a bucket, another an iron pole. For the most part, they would stand helplessly in front of the flames which, by this time, usually would have reached up to the roof of the house. The roof would fall with a crash; the walls would break and crumble. The tongues of smoke and sparks of fire would be carried by the wind to all of the houses in the shtetl. People would then run home as quickly as they could to save whatever was possible.

Goniondz was fortunate in that the Osoviec Fort was only seven kilometers from town. As soon as the commander became aware of the fire, the military fire battalion would come into town. With their modern equipment and special uniforms, which included bronze hats, they would extinguish the fire with rapid and expert hands ("The hands are the hands of Esau"), and the domestic fire battalion would assist them with supportive shouts ("The voice is the voice of Jacob"). So Goniondz was very fortunate in that this work was effectively done by means of others.

Fire Fighting Volunteers of Goniadz

In the first years of this century, when the Zionist ideal and the associated self awareness became powerful among our youth, the young men formed a modern voluntary fireman's group, well organized and trained, and equipped with sophisticated equipment. From that point forward, when a fire would break out in the shtetl, the sound of the bell and the trumpet was heard and we felt as if there was someone there to rely upon.

Of all the fires in my times, I particularly remember two. The first one took place at the lumberyard which was attached to Chatzkel Bialitotsky's steam mill, and it destroyed all of the nearby houses and structures. Even more vividly etched in my memory is the blaze which destroyed a large portion of town - the fire which took place on Sabbath evening Hol Hamoed of Pesach in the year 1906.

That fire broke out in the afternoon hours. The town-square was full of businessmen and of buyers and sellers. Suddenly, an anguished cry was heard, "Fire! Fire!" Everyone ran out from the shops. From behind Dead Man's Alley, in the direction of the windmill, a cloud of black smoke was seen rising to the heavens. The wind carried the sparks to the center of town. Smoke arose from the barns and the great silos which were in the rear of Zorach Miltzchan's great brick house, and from the houses which stood in the corner of the square - Dead Man's Alley, Berel-Leib Nochum the smith's house, and Yitzhok Yoske's the leather merchant's house. At first they tried to extinguish the fire but when it began to spread in various directions, the town folk were helpless and despairing. We ran home to save whatever we could, that is, whatever was possible to take from the houses, silos, and shops.

The fire raged for four hours and moved from place to place and from house to house. Everything was in flames from the corner of Dead Man's Alley to Church Street and from the old marketplace alley to the Vigotsky's house. The military fire battalion arrived from the fort, and first of all attempted to save the church, under orders from their commander, and they succeeded. Returning to the marketplace, they met Zorach-Chaya Yossel's and his neighbor Litman. Zorach and Litman gave the military commander a substantial donation and asked him to save their homes. And indeed, their homes were rescued. But the homes which were further out, from Moishe Kramkovkers' house to the alley leading to the old marketplace, and the Vigotsky's house were caught up in the fire. Yankel Rudsky went to the commandant and notified him that there were inflammatory materials in Vigotsky's cellar (Vigotsky was a military supplier to the fortress), which endangered the entire town and human lives. Hearing this, the commandant immediately centered all of his men's activities at Vigotsky's house. The house itself could not be saved, but the cellar, and all that was within it, remained intact.

When the fire had diminished somewhat, the homeowners whose houses had not burned, began to return home and bring back the possessions which they had earlier removed. It was just a few hours before sundown and only two hours remained before the lighting of the Sabbath candles. The situation of the fire victims was terrible. For example, Moishe Kramkovker, one of the wealthiest businessmen in the shtetl (and owner of a great house in the town-square with smaller houses in the rear) went to the marketplace crying over his new-found poverty. He went to sleep in a stable of a Christian in a corner of town.

Friday night arrived. The Sabbath candles were twinkling from the windows of the homes which remained intact. On the far side of the marketplace, the fire was smoldering, emerging from under the ruins. In the morning, the fire was still rising from the piles of ashes, which remained from the burned out homes. All of the homeowners gathered in the square to think about the destruction and the situation in which they now found themselves. At that time, the commander of the construction battalion from the fort arrived and offered to have his troops build barracks for the fire victims in the town-square. They rejected his proposal, stating that they would make housing arrangements for the unfortunate on their own. They had a suspected that the town council might later use the barracks to establish Christian shops, which would be competition for those of the Jews.

Later in the afternoon, the fire battalion returned again to totally extinguish the remains of the fire, which were still burning under the ruins. They remained quite a few hours, pouring out water until the embers were completely stilled. The fire was so great and destructive that the high commander of the fort came to town, himself, to secure a report from the fire battalion commander regarding the extent to which the blaze had been localized and extinguished.

A few months later the fire victims began to get themselves together and to seek to rebuild their destroyed homes. The first were those who owned fire insurance. Also, those who had saved a little money were able to begin a little reconstruction with the assistance of loans. Construction activity began in all corners of town. Learning from their bitter lesson, they built brick homes only and no longer wooden structures. To accomplish this, they brought down laborers and bricklayers from Bialystok.

[note from editor: this last section appears to be the second part of "Yehuda the furrier", from the article "Goniondzers in Israel" and was placed here for continuity by the translator.]

After the great fire, the Goniondz police chief did not permit residents to rebuild their homes without first submitting an official construction plan. One day, Yehuda the capmaker went to Grodno in the hope of resolving this problem. He was able to arrange a personal meeting with the provincial governor. During the course of a brief conversation, the governor granted his request (to eliminate the need for official plans - ed.). Even before Yehuda had arrived back in Goniondz, the police chief received a telegram from Grodno stating that all the townsfolk were given blanket permission to rebuild their houses. Pinchas Kaminetzky, the son of Reb Gedaliah, also helped the victims of this catastrophe. He was able to secure a ten-year loan at modest interest rates for the impoverished town-folk so that they could rebuild their houses and have a roof over their heads.

[Pages 491-493]

[continuation of The Great Fire in Goniondz and the Pogrom in Bialystok]]
Translated from Yiddish to English by Gloria Berkenstat Freund

June 1906, in the middle of a clear day, in the very fervor of the building work, the *shtetl* [town] became terrified by the news that a pogrom had broken out in Bialystok with the participation of *katsapes* [derogatory name for Russians], who were brought from distant Russia for various government work near the Bialystok train lines. The Bialystok brick-layers and artisans immediately interrupted their work and ran to the train station, went to Bialystok to protect their own (Jewish self defense groups were organized in various cities of the Pale of Settlement after the Kishinev pogrom). They did not know, poor things, that the pogrom was mixed in with the Russian military regime and as soon as the Jewish workers went out into the streets in defense (in Bialystok there were large textile factories in which thousands of Jewish workers were employed, organized in unions: Bund [secular, Jewish socialists] and *Poalei-Zion* [Workers of Zion, Marxist Zionists], the troops would come to help the hooligans and open fire on the Jewish self defense group.

When they arrived in the Bialystok train station they were attacked by hooligans who killed and wounded many before the eyes of the soldiers who stood there, ostensibly to protect those attacked. But two of them were saved by various circumstances. One, who had an award from the Russo-Japanese War, put on his medal before leaving the wagon [train car]. The army commandant noticed him and immediately ordered the soldiers to protect the "Georgievsky* Cavalier." The soldiers removed him from the hands of the hooligans and saved him.

The second, a middle aged Jew with a long grey beard, traveled in a wagon with a *podpolkovnik* (lieutenant colonel) from the *polk* (regiment) that camped in Monki and entered the wagon at this station. The lieutenant colonel, seeing what was happening in the train station, placed the Jew in a wagon, locked it and ordered two soldiers to guard the wagon until the train departed. Thus he was saved.

When the news reached the *shtetl*, a fear fell on everyone, particularly the families whose own had left this morning on the train to Bialystok or who had traveled there earlier. Many telegrams were sent and replies received. The telegram carrier of the *shtetl*, a non-Jew, had a cheerful day. He was paid very well for bringing a telegram. My mother, may she rest in peace, who had that day traveled to my sister in Warsaw, successfully passed through the Bialystok train station an hour before the pogrom began.

Several weeks later, when the construction work in the *shtetl* had resumed, a horse cab once stopped in the market and that lieutenant colonel and his wife got out of it and inquired about the worker whom he had saved. The worker fell to their feet and thanked them with tears in his eyes. The lieutenant colonel and his wife were also moved and had eyes filled with tears.

*

For a long time, the fear from the Bialystok pogrom reigned over all of the *shtetlekh* in the area. At that time a Christian religious precession was supposed to pass through our *shtetl* in which many gentiles from the surrounding area would take part. Such a march could end in a pogrom. They turned to the regime and a military division was sent that day which met the procession outside the city. The *shtetl* Jews took comfort: now after the large fire that had wiped out Jewish property, it did not pay the *pogromshtshikes* [those who carried out a progrom] to carry out a pogrom here!... As Sholem Alecheim's Motl Peyse the *Khazan's* [son of the cantor] says: "Lucky me, I am an orphan"...

A short time after the pogrom the commander of the Bialystok military was shot by a Bundist and the police chief was seriously wounded in the lower part of his body and had to walk with crutches.

Yona'khe's son, Moshe Khatskl, who lived across from the synagogue, was denounced as belonging to the group, *Kramolnikes* [revolutionaries]. A search was made of his home and a small Bund library was found there. He was lucky; he was sentenced to only a few months in jail in Bialystok.

When he was freed, he told me with joy how he had seen in court the police chief, who was called as a witness there in a trial of revolutionaries, how he stood resting on his crutches. The police chief, who was the terror of the Bialystoker revolutionary party, now looked so wretched and pitiful that Moshe had forgotten his troubles and rejoiced at the defeat of this "hero."

In the bitter end of the two tyrants, the organizers of the Bialystoker pogrom, the Jewish workers found consolation after the casualties and encouragement to continue to struggle against the Czar and his devoted servants.

*Translator's Note: Georgievsky refers to the Cross of St. George, a medal awarded by the Czar for bravery in battle

[Pages 493-500]

Goniondz's Firemen
By Moshe Bachrach
Translated from Yiddish to English by Dr. Isaac Fine

Every Jewish town in Europe experienced fires to some extent. Our shtetl Goniondz, however, was known for its great conflagrations. We were much admired by neighboring towns such as Trestine, Yashinovke and Sochovole. Their jealousy arose from the fact that Goniondz became more modern and more beautiful after every fire. Impressive brick homes took the place of wooden dwellings, and shops with showcases appeared. Due to this reconstruction, Goniondz took on a distinctly urban appearance near to the time of the First World War.

A few of the surrounding communities had their own fire battalions. Goniondz had two of them, one civilian and the other military. The military fire battalion was stationed in the Osoviec fort, several viorsts from the shtetl. They put out fires in Goniondz as well. It was an alliance. Goniondz provided the fires, and the Tsarist government provided the fire battalion.

You might ask, why two fire battalions? There is an explanation. The domestic firemen provided the town with entertainment in the interim periods between fires. The military battalion brought drama and color on the occasion of an actual blaze. The potency of the domestic firemen was centered in their shiny bronze hats. Their helmets with sharp edges in front conveyed the impression of fantastic heroes. The soldier-firemen were pure heroism, from head to foot. The domestic firemen drills consisted primarily of various acrobatics. They quickly climbed up a ladder and immediately climbed back down. They would pull themselves up with a rope, and slowly let themselves down again. Also they climbed the underside of a ladder which stood against the wall, and practiced other similar arts. To this day, I am not entirely clear as to how these fascinating activities could help extinguish a blaze.

The equipment of the domestic fire battalion consisted of several red colored barrels, each attached to an axle with two wheels; a small pump placed on low wheels, together with a hose; also, a long wagon on which was placed ladders spades, and axes. The domestic firemen were responsible for transporting the water barrels and the pump to the scene of the fire, like an arrow shot from a bow. A pair of horses were needed to move the long wagon. However usually there were no horses near to hand when needed. Half the boys in town would push the wagon to the location of the fire, while a few firemen would sit on top. On route, some water usually spilled out of the barrels. When they got there, the rusted pump pushed out the water through the dried up hose.

The military fire battalion from Osoviec, by contrast, was the real thing. They, too, had bronze hats, but under the hats were soldiers. They were heroic Russians who worked under military discipline under the direction of the fire commander, who wore a two-tiered bronze hat. Their equipment was the most modern available, and their horses were really horses.

The domestic fire crew brought entertainment to town with their brass band, which was active until a few years just prior to World War I. The bandleader from the Fort would come to town just to train them, and after the rehearsal he'd get drunk. One of the most popular numbers in the brass band repertoire was a military march, during which the public, at a certain moment, would join in with, "One! Two! Three!" in unison with the drum which was given three raps. The most colorful figure in the domestic fire battalion was "Mr. Commander", Tevye the chimney sweeper. Every performance was a spectacle. Tevye was decked out in a uniform with bronze buttons and epaulets. His chest was decorated with many medals. The medals were given to him by Mayer the watch repairman, and added to the distinction of his overall appearance. When he marched in at the beginning of a concert, his chest would protrude so all could have a view of the medals. When someone in town asked him if he had earned the medals serving in the "prisoner battalion" of the Russian Army he answered, "Certainly, the Tsarina sent them to me!"

Once, Natschalstva gave a big party in Tiebe's orchard, which later became the property of Motke Kliap. They had a buffet with ice cream. They also had a high pole, bets to win a prize, and paper tickets to sell. The military orchestra was brought in from Osoviec especially for the occasion, and they played the most beautiful melodies Goniondz had ever heard. The pole climb, however, was a big swindle. The pole was high and very smooth. To make it even more slick, the party organizers coated it with soap so that climbing it with bare hands would be very difficult. What did that roughneck Pesache-Schmuel Leizer do? Before the betting actually started, he quickly pulled himself up to the top of the pole. When the organizers found out that he had already done this, they canceled the entire event.

Fires were always, of course, a surprise. Because of the speed the domestic firemen displayed in their practice drills, we school boys were convinced that they were ready to move very fast when needed and that they were only waiting for the signal to move into action. This was the sequence of events when a fire broke out in Goniondz. When a blaze broke out somewhere, everyone would shout, "Fire! Fire! Fire!" After, when we arrived to where it was burning, men would run to the fire while the women packed bedding, books and other moveable property. Those who were close to the fire would carry the full packs to the center of the marketplace. For the children it was fun. Every family had its own pile of possessions in the street. The kids would sit on the bundles and between the bundles. Before too long, we would be playing hide and seek among the bundles. The bedding was just the beginning. Soon afterwards, they would be carrying everything out of the house, tables, beds, noodle boards, kneading troughs, and the utensils for Passover - if there was enough time. Everyone helped each other in taking merchandise out of the shops.

We had a hardware shop. Our merchandise was the most difficult to save, not only because the hardware is heavy in weight, but also because metal bends and breaks. We were always dead broke after a fire, even when the fire passed us by, if only from the damage we used to suffer from the "rescuing". When the confusion is so great, how are you going to teach friends and relatives to tell the difference between an article which you can throw and another one, which has to be handled as delicately as an esrog ? One time, my uncle Schloime, the son of Moishe-Shimon, ran from his burning apartment carrying a pot of beets. He ran with it onto the synagogue hill. He didn't save anything except the pot with beets.

Where is the local fire battalion when a real fire breaks out? They also were rescuers. Their skills were acquired entirely through practice sessions. They hadn't learned from actual fires, and the equipment of the local fire brigade were really no more than toys. The local fire brigade would also shout "Fire", and carried out bundles from houses which the fire had not yet reached. Someone sends a telegram to the Fort, sending for the military firemen to come and extinguish the blaze. But why do they delay so long? Half the shtetl is already in flames!

Quiet! Can't you hear the clattering of their wagon wheels on the cobblestones of the road from Guzi, leading into town? And don't you hear from nearby the clanging of the bell on their wagons? They're here! They gallop in! And right to the fire! No one needs to tell them where the flames are. The horses are like wizards! And they bring with them wondrous equipment: iron barrels with water, a giant pump with endless coils of hose, and tools with which one could demolish a house to the count of one and then two. The soldiers themselves are remarkable, all giants, warriors, and fast as deer.

The military fire commander takes over and puts all the manpower of town under his orders, even school-boys, and the domestic fire brigade as well. One works the pump while another runs on foot with a barrel to the well in the priest's courtyard. Some help the soldiers demolish burning houses. The bundles of the fire victims are meanwhile transported by powerful horses galloping back and forth, to the ringing of the bell. We small children used to jump back on one side when someone pulled on the pump from the other side. That was a lot of fun for us. This would last a whole day until we all were tired, and the fire too.

When the firemen were all finished with a blaze in Goniondz, half the shtetl was burned down and the other half had provided help for those affected by the catastrophe. Then the military fire commander would arrange to have his battalion's own fire extinguished with vodka; and their hunger too, with delicious Jewish dishes. After that they would receive a hundred rubles for their efforts. Then they would slowly head back to the fort. Before returning, their custom was to give the shtetl a salute by making a circuit around the marketplace, slowly and with a sense of majesty. Then, their bells would ring very slowly.

[Pages 501-502]

A Wedding in the Shtetl
By Avraham Yaffe, Tel Aviv, Israel
Translated from Yiddish to English by Dr. Isaac Fine

A wedding was one of those joyous happenings which caused a great stirring in the shtetl and brought everyone to his feet, young and old, little and big. It would be announced in town by the sounds of the klezmers' (musicians') instruments. At these special festive occasions, the group of musicians from Trestine, the neighboring village, were brought in. One heard the drummer with his clanging brass cymbals, and the fiddler at the front of the group. At the wedding of a wealthy family, the klezmers from Stuchin were brought in. They were better caliber musicians, and had finer instruments.

The wedding hall was usually located in Chaya Yossel's' brick house located in the corner of the main market place, in Kliap's house, or in the first brick house on the corner of Church Street, which belonged to Moishe Gershon, the shoe repairman.

The bridal chair was white velvet and there was always the master of ceremonies (badchun) with his jokes, rhymes, and song. He also had plenty of predictions to offer about the life which lay ahead for the new married couple. The melodies and lyrics of the badchun used to bring forth tears from the assembled guests, especially when the bride happened to be an orphan. On such occasions, the tears could become quite apparent and the singer's voice might become transformed from a wedding tune to a tune of the eve of the Yom Kippur . Such a bride could even fall into a melancholy mood from which her girlfriends and relatives would revive her. The bride and her coterie would dance - polkas, mazurkas, waltzes, and various others.

At the same time, a welcoming would be arranged for the bridegroom, by the men, at another home distant from the wedding hall. Then, the bridegroom would be led to the bride, wearing a white robe and his new wedding clothes while the musicians played a march or a happy song. When the bridegroom arrived in the wedding hall, everyone would shout, "Make way, here comes the bridegroom!" He would be covered totally with confetti, thrown at him in fistfuls, like a many colored snow. In this way, the assembled crowd would make the bridegroom feel like royalty.

The waiting badchun would greet him with a song about how he should appreciate the great joy of the occasion since life is fleeting and one's time on earth passes rapidly. As it is written in Psalms, "Man is like the grass that fades, like the smoke that vanishes." He therefore needs to be an observant and honorable man, leading a life of worthy actions. The musical accompaniment during this song would create somewhat of a sad mood among the assembled group temporarily, and then the bride and bridegroom would be led forward to the bridal canopy. They were surrounded by lit candles to symbolize that the couple should have glowing good fortune in the years that lie before them. Then the musicians would strike up a march and the whole wedding procession would move forward along the road which led to the great synagogue.

In snowy winter weather, the wedding canopy would be set up near the House of Study (Beys Hamedresh), and friends of the couple, very often, would throw snowballs at them. Led by the in-laws, from both sides, the whole shtetl would accompany the bride and bridegroom to the wedding place with an atmosphere as if the entire shtetl were their friends. The main "in-laws" were children of many ages, who moved forward in front of the band of musicians, very excitedly, keeping pace with the rhythm of the music. There's a wedding in shtetl, joy and gladness to the Jewish world.

[Pages 503-506]

Reb Gershon Boruch and the Senate Decision
By Khatzkl Peretz Tsherniak
Translated from Yiddish to English by Dr. Isaac Fine

Reb Gershon Boruch lived in poverty and misery with his sister Faygel and son in law Yankel Tschudak, who was a wedding cake baker. He himself, though, never partook of these cakes.

They lived on the old town square, next door to Moishe Mendel the tailor on one side and old Yankel Laibkes the wagonner on the other side. Reb Gershon Boruch was a scholar. He was quite competent in the Russian language. He had memorized the entire Russian law code as a result of solitary study. Mr. Gershon Boruch had a tremor in both hands and could not write. He dictated his petitions to a scribe, one of the young men with excellent handwriting who came to his home for this purpose.

He would buy the Senate Journal with the few pennies he earned. This was a periodical which he received on a monthly basis. In each journal issue, there was a section that reported unresolved legal cases in which the Senate had not been able to arrive at a final judgment. This section contained the opinions of legal experts from throughout the breadth of the Russian Empire. The submitted opinion which eventually was viewed as the best resolution of the problem would then become the Senate judgment. Mr. Gershon Boruch took part in these controversies and forwarded his opinions to the Senate.

About sixty years ago, on a summer day, the town was astonished when the Provincial Attorney General from Bialystok arrived in Goniondz. It was an extraordinary occasion, and everyone speculated about the reason for his visit to town. People began to clean their courtyards, the shop merchandise and the streets out of concern that something might be criticized. The police and the constable ran around like poisoned mice. Everyone began to examine his deeds. There was plenty to examine. In the afternoon, a carriage arrived led by two horses, approaching from the direction of the village Guzi. The Attorney General and his secretary were seated in the carriage. Another carriage followed them carrying the mayor and the police chief. A crowd of children and very curious people accompanied them as they approached.

Arriving in the old town square, the Attorney General turned towards the mayor and asked, "Where does Gershon Boruch live?" The crowd led them to Tschudaks' house. The Attorney General opened the door and asked, "Where is Gershon Boruch Kravitz?" Faygele was frightened and stammered, "Gershon Boruch? He's in the House Of Study. Where else should he be, if not there?" The secretary conveyed this response to the Attorney General. He had the carriage turned around and proceeded with his train through the town to Deadman's Alley. When they arrived at the House Of Study, the Attorney General entered alone and called out "Reb Gershon Kravitz, please!" The frightened Gershon Boruch, accompanied by the curious, went out from the House Of Study, not understanding what was wanted of him.

The Attorney General gave him a wink as if to say that Gershon Boruch should approach closer. He had expected to find a distinguished person. Gershon Boruch, however, was a short little Jew with a small beard. The Attorney General asked, "Who is Gershon Boruch Kravitz?" The mayor gave Gershon Boruch a wink that he should approach nearer. At the same time he pointed at Gershon Boruch and said to the Attorney Gener, "This is him!"

The Attorney General smiled. He turned to Gershon Boruch and asked, "You are Gershon Boruch?" He answered, "It's me, Your Excellency." The Attorney General turned to his secretary standing at his side and directed this man to hand over his attache case. He removed a document from his attache case and turned again to Mr. Gershon Boruch, who all the while stood there in fear. He asked, "Did you forward a legal opinion to the Senate Journal?" "Yes, I did." answered the frightened Gershon Boruch. "I have been given a document from the Senate conveying their appreciation for your opinion in the Senate Journal. Your opinion was considered the best solution for the problem and will be the final judgment in that case. In addition to the letter of appreciation, I have also been told to ask in their behalf if there is anything you wish from them. It is also their wish that you continue to send your opinions on unsolved matters published in the journal."

Gershon Boruch did not delay long in answering. He said that, since he is a poor man, he would appreciate it if they would send him the monthly Senate Journal on a gratis basis. The Attorney General smiled and had this request written down. Then he asked, "Where did you learn the law, in which university?" Gershon Boruch answered with a stammer, "I learned by myself, from books." The Attorney General shrugged his shoulders. He repeated again that he would convey this request to the Senate, and bid farewell with "Goodbye, Mr. Kravitz." He then ascended his carriage and left town.

From that time forward, Gershon Boruch received issues of the Senate Journal each month on a regular basis. The town of Goniondz had been a little frightened on this occasion. At the same time, however, as a result of this event, Gershon's prestige had been firmly established with all.

[Pages 507-512]

Silhouettes from the Old Home
By D.B.
Translated from Yiddish to English by Dr. Isaac Fine and Marvin Galper

Koppel The Teacher

A year before his death, Isher-Leib became ill and was no longer able to carry out his duties. He was, however, not a particularly good shamash even before he became ill. He developed a vision problem, and could hardly see. As long as he could stand on his feet, he carried out his responsibilities with the help of Mordechai, the assistant shamash. After his death, the seeking for a new chief shamash for the House of Study (Beys Hamedresh) began. Mordechai was a simple Jew and was accustomed to simple work - cleaning the floor, fueling the oven, and going around town on Friday evenings announcing the arrival of Sabbath to the community. When he would call out "In Schul Arien" ("Come to the synagogue") through the streets of the town, the women would light the Sabbath candles and the men would, soon after, walk through the House of Study. Nonetheless, when Isher-Leib became ill, the situation was quite difficult since Mordechai did not want to allow a replacement. When it was necessary for Mordechai to make a public announcement, he had a ritualized manner for doing so: "It is announced and told ...". The community would hear him and smile good- naturedly. Also, he had stage fright, and his right leg would tremble from fear when he spoke in front of the congregation. When it was time for him to announce the New Moon, he had a great deal of difficulty. When it was time for the shamash to announce a new month, it was expected that Mordechai would announce the exact day and time of this occurrence, thirty-six hours in advance of when the New Moon was born. He couldn't remember, even when he read from the calendar. He would repeat the time information for the new month to himself for four weeks in advance in order to get it right.

Once, a Jew from Kniesin appeared in the House of Study between the afternoon and evening services. He was about forty years of age, and had a golden beard. He had traveled the road from Kniesin on foot. He sat down wearily, and gave everyone a little of the snuff from his pocket. There was quite a commotion around him. Some Jews, who had been in Kniesin during the war and had prayed in the new House of Study on Grodno Street in the summer of 1914, recognized him. He was a shamash and a leader of prayer in Kniesin. Since he had not been economically successful in Kniesin, he was interested in securing the position as shamash in Goniondz. The congregation whispered that there was a better candidate - more specifically, Koppel the teacher. He had fled from Goniondz, settled in Dubrove and had not returned. A few days later, Koppel arrived and expressed his interest in the position as shamash. Until the war, Koppel had been a Bible teacher. His little classroom had been on Dead Man's Alley. He was a good prayer leader and studied throughout the year in the House of Study. He participated regularly in the morning prayers and on Rosh Hashana and Yom Kippur he led the first Sliches . He had an impressive appearance and a long, gray beard, a Jew with all of the virtues. Each Sabbath, during reading of the Torah portion of the week, the gabbai was expected to stand up in the altar and call out those who would come up for an aliyah . In actuality, however, Koppel was the person who called up members of the congregation for the aliyahs. He knew the entire community. He could distribute first class, second class, and ordinary aliyahs. An important, substantial citizen would be called up by him for the third or the sixth reading. A congregation member, of lesser but some substance in the community, would receive the last reading. When there is no obligation to call up a particular individual on a specific Saturday, the Maftir , reading from the Prophets, is also a very fine aliyah. The fourth and the fifth aliyahs would go to the average person. The one just before the last would go to a commoner. The successful Jews in town would receive aliyahs quite often. Some simple townspeople, who sat on the back benches, might get an aliyah only once a year - on Simchas Torah . Once, Koppel called up Avramel the cobbler. He read three sentences, and that was it. He was very angry, said "Such a little section!" and went down from the altar without making a second blessing. Koppel was not disconcerted, he ran the show. He said, "This is the way it's always been, and this is the way it will stay." One Sabbath morning, there was a new face in the congregation, the bridegroom of Beryl, Gedaliah Lampert's daughter. It was the custom to give Maftir reading to a bridegroom, but somehow Koppel overlooked this and did not call him up. With Benjamin (the gabbai of the synagogue), this would not have happened. I was offended. I talked with Avrom-Yitzhok, son of Yeshua the shoemaker, and we decided to make a remark to Koppel about this after the service. When all the congregants had left for home and Koppel was rearranging the prayer books, which had been left about in disarray, we approached him and said, "Mr. Koppel, we know that there was a bridegroom in the House of Study today. He is married to Beryl, the shoemaker's daughter. He should have been given Maftir or least an aliyah. But you overlooked him. Is it proper to put a man to shame in that way?" Koppel began to shout at us with a voice which was not his own, "How dare you! To tell me how to give out the aliyahs! What a nerve you have - to mix into my business!" We didn't answer him, and quietly left the House of Study.

Tsatchuk The Orphan

Bobke Yehuda's had confided a secret to us: that Tsatchuk the orphan wanted to travel to Germany only he was lacking sufficient funds. The boy was sixteen years old, a son of Meilach Tsatchuk, who had died quite some time earlier. Meilach's wife also died, and left four sons behind. The oldest had been in Paris, since 1908, and the other two were somewhere outside of Goniondz. He wanted to reach his brother in Paris, but he did not have enough money to do so. He was staying with the cousin who lived next to the brick home of Leibel Schanes. Bobke lived there too. We were living in the brick home of Motke Gershon's.

In meeting the young man, I asked him if what I had heard was true, and he answered - yes. I told him that I was prepared to help him. I would loan him five hundred Polish marks, which was at that time a substantial sum. He thanked me very much, and told me that he would repay the loan when he arrived at his brother's. I also gave him a letter to my aunt in Grayve, asking her to find him a reliable person to escort him across the border at a reasonable cost, since he was very poor and also an orphan on both sides.

Several days later, I received a letter from my aunt. She wrote that the young man had been with her, stayed overnight, and the next day had crossed the border. All had been taken care of properly as I had asked.

A month passed, then two and then three, and I didn't hear from him. Then, I received a letter from him from France. Within the envelope was a photograph of his oldest brother. It was a photograph of Karasik, who had lived in Goniondz until the First World War in Veintraub's house, in the direction of the train station. In the letter he wrote that I should look at the photograph carefully on both sides. I looked at it carefully, as he had suggested, and found that it was a little "swollen", on the backside. I withdrew two hundred and fifty francs from the back of the photograph.

The money had been very useful to him in his immigration from Goniondz.

Avraham Yitzhok The Shoemaker

Starting from the summer of 1915, when the Russians left our region, the fortress was no longer a battle site. German soldiers and a commander were stationed there, but only for ordinary purposes such as carrying out orders in the area and requisitioning food from the villagers.

Avrom Rudski had befriended the German commander. He got permission from him to collect materials in the fortress such as copper, lead, etc., as well as all kinds of iron which lay around everywhere. Germany had always been accustomed to importing raw materials from other countries. Now, in wartime, when they were cut off from the rest of the world, they were in dire need of such supplies. Avrom employed many men in this project. He sent many wagons of merchandise to Germany. He made a lot of money as a result of this enterprise, and became rich.

At the end of the summer of 1917, Avrom bought wood from all the trenches which the Russians had constructed during the first year of the war. He assigned the labor of carrying the wood out of the ditches, cutting it up, and selling it to my uncle Yisroel Yitzhak. Yisroel had been a lumber merchant all his life. My uncle took my brother Moishe and me to supervise the work. We hired only Jews.

The work was very hard. A lot of digging was necessary before one could remove the boards. Realizing the economic hardship of Yehoshua the shoemaker, I recruited his son Avraham Yitzhok for the project. Yehoshua the shoemaker lived near the House of Study at the end of Dead Men's Alley. He was not an extraordinary workman, and made peasant boots only. This was the only type of work which came to him. He had weak eyes and poor vision.

His wife Chashke was a pathetic woman who looked for ways to make money. Between Purim and Passover we would see her completely speckled with lime. She would lime a cake for someone, and in that way earn something. It was a very strenuous life. They didn't have to pay tuition for their children. The Talmud Torah charitable agency covered their tuition expenses. This was an institution, like Visiting The Poor and Hospice For The Poor. On Sabbath in the House of Study, the collection box was passed. A little money would fall in for charitable donations for these purposes.

Only Bible teachers who did not have enough students would accept these children on scholarship. This was because the Talmud Torah paid very little, and they paid on an irregular basis. The teachers were, however, willing to accept Avraham Yitzhok's children since they had keen intellects. The Kuliaver teacher and also Schlomo the teacher were both very pleased with them.

We studied together in the Hebrew elementary school with my uncle Schlomo. He was in a lower class, because he was a few years younger than I. The teachers advised his mother to send him to study in the yeshiva. They predicted that he would develop into a distinguished scholar. She sent him to the Grajewo yeshiva. I always felt close to him, and for that reason I hired him for this project.

The project was located in the fortress, which was at a distance. It was quite a trip from home, particularly since we traveled back and forth by foot every day. One evening when the work was finished, Avraham Yitzhok took a thick piece of wood three meters long with him to bring home. Avrom Rudski had warned us strictly not to take anything. However, so be it, it's not the end of the world if he should have one less piece of wood. We laughed at Avraham Yitzhok because he couldn't carry it home even though he had decided to do so. During the entire trip home, he moved the board from one shoulder to another. He would rest, and then moved on until he finally got home. The joy that would be felt in his house when they had something to cook supper with gave him the courage and the strength to carry the board such a long distance.

Avraham Yitzhok now lives in Detroit, Michigan and is a wealthy man.

[Pages 513-520]

Passages and Episodes from World War I
By D.B.
Translated from Yiddish to English by Dr. Isaac Fine

After the assassination of the Austrian Crown Prince, the political situation in Europe became very tenuous. We read that a world war might break out. However, Nachum Sokolov, the editor of the periodical Hatzfirah , had written in political articles that war will not come, and that the world is not so foolish that people will slaughter one another. The Hatzfirah was read in our house, and my father had agreed with Nachum Sokolov.

Only on Sunday afternoon of the ninth of the month of Av, we knew that war had broken out. A terror fell upon all of us. The German border is near, and also the Russian fort of Osoviec. We were in the first line of fire. The Monker Regiment of the Russian Army had been garrisoned in Goniondz for the last two weeks. They dug trenches on Beile Itche's' hill, on the synagogue hill, and on every hill which overhung the river. They had commandeered the houses which stood on the lower ground by the bank of the river, such as Mordechai the sexton's new house and the big house of Chatzkel, the son of Moishe, so that they might have a clear view from the trenches over the marshes which lay on the far side of the river. Many families fled to the nearby towns of Yashinovke or Kniesin, in order to be a little further from the front. Men and older children remained on their property in order to guard their possessions. The situation deteriorated in general, and no one knew what tomorrow would bring. To alleviate the situation, the Russian governmental authorities had ordered a moratorium that no payment should be made on debt on a temporary basis.

Meanwhile, we became acclimated to the situation. This was especially the case when the Russian Army was within East Prussia, and we were at that time far behind the front. The families returned then, and life took on a normal character. Many troops arrived in the shtetl from deep Russia and even Siberia, on the way to the front. Once, several riders on horseback arrived passing through Dolistover Street and requisitioned quarters to prepare them for officer housing. They told us that a regiment of troops was arriving on foot from Grodno. The latter regiment had been mobilized in the Tzernigover district. Among them there were many Jewish men. Hearing the news, women of Goniondz began to prepare a kosher meal for the Jewish soldiers. The leaders were Mary, the daughter of Yetzel Issac's and Chaya Yerachmiel of the Bruztzak family. They bought a lamb, had it slaughtered in the correct ritual fashion, and cooked a great kettle of food. After noontime, when the regiment had arrived, all of the Jewish soldiers received a good warm lunch. They certainly had not expected such a welcome. The regiment then moved forward to the fort and remained garrisoned there.

Before Rosh Hashana , the situation worsened. The Russians suffered their first major defeat in East Prussia, and fell back. The remainder of the beaten army arrived in town. Jews from the town of Grayve had fled from their homes and also arrived in Goniondz. We received them warmly and provided each one with food and lodgings. They remained only briefly in town, and soon after moved on. The customary road from Grayve to Goniondz passes the fort, but now they were required to travel through the fields and marshes. The Russians had constructed a bridge over the river, not far from the mill of Chatzkel, the son of Moishe. Strict orders had been issued from the fort that Jews would not be permitted to cross over the bridge. It was distressing for us to see the Christians cross over the bridge back and forth freely while we had to hire the service of Michel the barge owner in order to cross by boat.

The situation deteriorated. We heard the sounds of bombardment of Osoviec. But we did not expect to discover that the army and the Polish peasantry had been exchanging rumors that we Jews were German spies, and that we had hidden telegraphs via which we were passing information to the Germans. We lived through difficult days. We also had the "privilege" of seeing the notorious anti-Semite, Nikolai Nikolavietsich, General Commander of the Russian Army and uncle of the Tsar, on the synagogue hill during the first week of the war.

On Rosh Hashana we all prayed in the House of Study. We didn't dare approach the synagogue. Soldiers were on the synagogue hill scrutinizing the marshes across the river with binoculars to detect any possible advancement of German infantry. Rabbi Volf, may his memory be for a blessing, had ordered that the shofar should not be blown. He didn't want the Poles to tell the Russians that these were secret signals sent by us Jews to the German Army. We said tashlich near Sake's place, which is near the synagogue hill. We could see the river from there. Since blowing the shofar is a great blessing, we took the risk. The shofar was quietly blown in the house of Yankel the old healer in the old marketplace. When my father came to his house with us three kids, the place was full. The Cantor Nochum quietly took the shofar out from his bosom and blew three blasts.

The second day of Rosh Hashana something happened in the House of Study which was totally new in our experience. When the congregation was saying afternoon prayers, a soldier entered and stepped up to the Holy Ark. He opened it, buried his head in the Sefer Toras , and wept aloud. All those present were also moved to tears. After he had quieted himself he told us this story: he had just come to us from the fort. He had very recently been in a spying expedition with his squadron. Arriving in Tschemnasye, a village on the road to Grayve, the sergeant had ordered him and a fellow soldier to climb the roof of a barn in order to scrutinize the surrounding area. At that moment, a piece of shrapnel fell in the straw of the barn roof and it began to burn. His friend fell from the roof and was burned, while he jumped from the roof and saved himself. He had come to the House of Study to thank God for the miracle.

The situation deteriorated even further. The Germans drew near to the fort. The Russians burned down the villages of Osoviec and Biyelogrande. On Shabbos Tshuvah during the day, the Russians began artillery fire from trenches on Dolistover Street, in a garden by the post office, towards the direction of the Germans who were on the far side of the river. We were very frightened. If the Germans advance we are lost. Sunday night we didn't sleep, and stayed with our Aunt Rivke on Dolistover Street, which was considered slightly safer. Early in the morning, when the bombardment of the fort became extraordinarily fierce, we left the shtetl and headed out for Yashinovke. We had an acquaintance there. It was raining heavily. People were saying that the fire from the front had disturbed the atmosphere and brought the rain.

In the evening before Yom Kippur in the House of Study, before Kol Nidrei , we heard happy news. A Yashinovke resident had arrived from Bialystok. He brought an announcement from the General Staff, that the Russians had defeated the Germans starting from the area of Yagustov, and that the Germans had been thrust back across the entire front. Hearing this, the fasting of the holy day became easier to bear for us. At the end of Yom Kippur, we hired a wagon to travel to Goniondz and find out what was happening there. We got started early in the morning. The road was very muddy.

When we were passing by Kusharke, a distance of about six viorsts from Goniondz, we saw a little bent over Jew from a distance, his hands in his sleeves. When he drew near to us, I recognized Dudschneilor, the teacher. He told us that he was on his way to inform the Goniondz Jews in Yashinovke that the Germans had been thrown back, and that we now can come home. I assured him that this news is already well known, and that he can turn around and come back to Goniondz with us.

Arriving back in Goniondz, a fear fell upon me: we had not seen a single living soul. The doors and gates were shut. Here and there, the Christians had broken a window, torn down a door, and plundered. The stillness was terrifying. Drawing near to the house of Tzerel, the son of Gittel Abe's, we saw a group of Poles. Seeing us three Jews they began to laugh loudly, which frightened me even further. I ran home through the interconnecting streets. At that time, we had been living near Yehudah the capmaker . I found our little home and shop completely intact. Yehudah, himself, had stayed at home, guarding his dwelling and ours. I met his son Yossel there, who in the morning had replaced him as guard. I stayed in Goniondz all of the month of Succos , and our entire family returned from Yashinovke.

The first evening of Succos, there were several minyans in the House of Study for the evening service, but Cantor Nochum had not wanted to ascend to the altar. At the beginning, his voice was not heard there. But after a Kaddish of Aleinu , he sang "Adon Olam" in a vigorous voice, with a festive holiday melody, and that was the last time that I heard his voice. Three months later, the Cantor died.

On the night of Simchas Torah between afternoon and evening services, we were sitting and eating in the House of Study at a long table, by the western wall. A soldier came from the fort. He told us an interesting story.

In the Russo-Japanese War, ten years earlier, a Jewish soldier had lost his left hand in the battle for Fort Arthur. When he recovered, he wrote a letter to the Commandant of the Russian military installation at Fort Arthur, General Stoessel, asking permission to return to the front. He didn't want to be considered an invalid. His request was accepted. He was issued a revolver, since he could not use a rifle with just one remaining hand. The General made the heroism of the Jewish soldier known throughout the Russian garrison. When the Russian military installation at Fort Arthur fell, and the troops were taken into Japanese captivity, he did not remain idle in the prison camp. He organized classes in reading and writing for the illiterate soldiers. He remained involved with this project until the end of the war. Later, he was invited to Tsarskoya Selo, the residence of the Tsar, where the Tsarina herself awarded him the "St. George's Cross", the greatest distinction in the Russian Army. At the same time, he was also promoted to the rank of officer. In 1911, he arrived at Tschernigover District for a visit. He had become a very good friend of the soldier telling us the story in the House of Study. The young hero was the son of a cantonist in Kafkaz, far from the Jewish communities. Nonetheless, a nationalist feeling had been awakened in him and he had decided to travel to Eretz Yisroel (Palestine). He wanted to learn plowing and his friend's family owned a great deal of farmland. Despite the fact that he had only one hand, he learned to plow and migrated to Eretz Yisroel. When we asked the soldier the young man's name, he answered Josef Trumpeldor.

During the period of Shuvos , when we were refugees again, this time in Kniesin, we read that Josef Trumpeldor and Vladimir Jabotronsky had organized a battalion of Jewish soldiers in Kahir, in Egypt, to join in the warfare against Turkey and free Eretz Yisroel. Trumpeldor's life story was in the newspaper article. But we in Goniondz already knew the story from earlier. In Petach Tikva, where I now live, my neighbor is from Tschernigover District. When we talked, I found out that he had been in the regiment garrisoned in our shtetl. To this day, he can't forget the friendly welcome and warm greeting he received from the Goniondz Jews. During his long years of wandering, he stated, he had not received such a reception in any place.

[Pages 521-524]

The First Bolshevik Regime in Goniohdz
By Meirim Rubin, New York
Translated from Yiddish to English by Dr. Isaac Fine

The Red Army captured Goniondz during the Russian-Polish War of 1920. During the second day of occupation, the Russians formed a revolutionary committee with the abbreviated title of "Revkam." Only laborers were members of "Revkam", primarily Bundists . Josef, the son of Teme-Raizel, was the committee chairman. Hanoch, the son of Itsche the water carrier was the education commissar. Moishe-Feivel, the son of Chaya Vitzes, was put in charge of sanitation. He was given the title "Minister". Several Christians and Zeidke Rubin constituted the militia. Hanoch used to give talks in conjunction with the Bolshevik commissar.

The "Revkam" had the authority to issue severe sentences and even the death penalty. None of them, however, could read or write Russian. They appointed Eli Dlugolensky as secretary. He exploited the ignorance of "Revkam" and issued documents as he wished. The commissar would sign each and every one. Eli would arrange for a farmer to come for a written acknowledgment that he had sold his horse. In actuality, the document would be a permit for someone from Grayve to transport several sacks of sugar and a few barrels of kerosene into town. Such an act was considered "speculation," and was punishable by the death penalty. A Jew from Bialystok had been shot for a similar violation.

The "Revkam" established a cooperative which would give notes to the grain merchants with which to purchase grain. Instead of one hundred thousand pounds of corn, the secretary would give a note for three hundred thousand pounds. The remaining two hundred thousand pounds he would sell in Bialystok for three times the price permitted by the cooperative. The farmers, naturally, charged higher prices, but it was worth it.

Once, transporting two wagons of grain from the village of Dolistover, the local commissar seized the horses and wagons as well as the merchandise. We rushed with protest to our "Revkam," which provided us with assistance, specifically Zeidke-Rubin Droks and his rifle. The Dolistover "Revkam" was not frightened. They maintained that, despite our permit, they had the right to confiscate the grain for consumption by the Red Army, who had priority over the civilian population. They confiscated not only the horses and wagon but also Rubin Droks' broken rifle.

Later on, the cooperative was disbanded. The Bolsheviks had actually confiscated very little in the shtetl. Mainly they made speeches in which they threatened they would confiscate the property of the wealthy and distribute it among the poor. But, since they were relatively few wealthy people in Goniondz, the town-folk had little to fear. Yoshua, the tinsmith, who lived in the valley next door to Chayim Kobrinsky (Chayim Polak's), took the Bolshevik speeches seriously. He came to Chayim Kobrinsky with the demand that he should make an exchange. Chayim would give him his brick house, and Kobrinsky should take Yoshua's little shack in the valley in its place. Yoshua went to the "Revkam" and asked their assistance in facilitating this revolutionary justice. The Russian commissar responded that there were higher priorities to arrange at the time, such as provision of medicine and food supplies to the Red Army at the Front. Later, he said, we will arrange redistribution of lodgings.

Yoshua, the tinsmith, was enormously disappointed when the Bolsheviks were defeated. He lost his mental balance. He ran over the hills in a confused mental state. A few weeks later, he was dead. His son Nochum was away with the Bolsheviks in Russia. He became an officer in the Red Army, and later fell at the front.

When the Red Army withdrew, all the participants in "Revkam" fled. Hanoch, the son of the water carrier, was captured by the Polish in Kniesin, and they beat him severely. Thanks to the Jews of Kniesin, who collected a substantial sum of ransom money, he was freed.

Then a great terror fell upon all of the Jews who had cooperated with the Bolsheviks. All the young men of military age fled to Lithuania and from there traveled to America and Canada.

When the Polish Army returned to Goniondz, the priest blocked their way with crosses. He asked the soldiers not to treat the Jews harshly because they had treated him well during the Bolshevik regime. The Jews put up large posters announcing that they were going to distribute bread without cost to the Polish military. The old Polish mayor established a new town council. He included some young Jewish men in the new council, who were provided with staffs for purposes of guard duty. There were four guards assigned to each street to prevent attacks and robbery. During that period the Polish had shot many Jews, for example two in Sochovole. In Goniondz, however, the critical transition took place without loss of life. In our shtetl, the Jews were subjected only to several robberies and assaults.

Group of Goniadz Refugees in Marianpol at the Time of the Russian-Polish War

From right to left, standing: Moshe Gershon's son Avraham'l, Shoshke's son Avraham'l, Zorekh, Gershon's son Motl, Gelia's son Yudl Itshe.

Sitting: Mulya the Osowcer [from Osowce], Gele's son Meir Itshe, Bliacher, Biale's son Motl Itshe, Tuvye-Motl's son Gdalye, Lipke's son Yankl, Nukhem Guzer (Flaskowski).

Lying: on the right: Tserale's Yankl; on the left: Meir Luria (Katshke).

[Pages 525-542]

Goniadz's Youth Consider the Exile...
(Memories)
by Dovid Bachrach
Translated by Gloria Berkenstat Freund

After the rise of the Polish nation in November 1918, the life of the Jews in Poland became very uncomfortable. The hatred of Jews that had been hidden until then, earlier with the Russians and in the end during the time of the German occupation, had now come out in public. The government in Warsaw set the tone and the priests in the churches spread hatred of Jews. The *Hallertichikes*[1] and *Poznantichikes*[2] threw Jews from moving trains, cut Jewish beards and there was no one to turn to for help.

America gave its large stocks of ammunition, which it had brought for its army in France, as a gift to the rising Poland. Now, after the war, it had no more need of them. Their worth reached many tens of millions of dollars. Poland permitted itself to serve as a barrier against communism and the entire capitalist world supported her and tended to overlook her "nice" deeds against the Jews. Poland celebrated its liberation. It organized a volunteer Polish army and began to expand.

We, in Goniadz, forgot the general troubles because a typhus epidemic broke out here during the winter. The first patient was Heikl Jewrejski. Later, I became ill. It was said in the *shtetl* that I caught it from Heikl at the *Linas* [*Linas haTzedek*, a charitable organization caring for the sick]. Yankl the *rufah* [old time doctor] had diagnosed me as having stomach typhus. He told me that Shimeon Halpern also had typhus. Two months later, when I went out into the street, I learned that it was a long time that Shimeon was no longer here. Josl Gopsztajn, Yehuda the furrier's son-in-law, was ill. He was a good friend of mine; I went to him and spent the day and night. When he recovered, my sister, Keyla, became sick. At that time there was a kind of hospital in Goniadz at the old market, where Wajntraub's house was once located. I tended to my sister and others who were ill. Zalman, the old rabbi's son, lay in a nearby room. I also tended to him. He died. Many people left the world in a very short time.

When the typhus epidemic ceased, a new affliction started. The Polish government began to mobilize the young people. They needed a great number of soldiers to pry loose even more land from Russia. From our family, my brother, Moshe'ke had to be recruited. The only way out for him was to escape to Germany. Shmuel Ber's son, Moshe, agreed with him. In Kolnya, neither Moshe was successful in smuggling himself across the border; we tried Raczki, a shtetl near Jagustow [Augustow] and here they succeeded. It did not take long and my brother, Kalman, was called. He was all of 16 years old, but he was tall and looked large to Tovya-Motl. Tovya-Motl was the scribe at the city hall and was a very influential person. Perhaps, if my father were alive, he would have been ashamed to do this. They were good friends. Now my mother was a widow and we had no strong "shoulders" to support us – Kalman had to run away. The road to Raczki was broken up. We met Moshe-Chaim Burak and Yonatan Neyman in Jagustow; they came out of their hiding place and gravitated towards the German side. We all traveled to Raczki; they went across the border safely. We were calm for a time. But then I received a notice; I was being called to the military. It is true that I had wanted to leave exile-Poland for a long time, particularly after the wild Poles murdered a large part of the *Tzeirei-Zion* [Young Zionists] in Pinsk, creating a blood libel about them, that they were "Bolsheviks." But my mother did not permit it. An iron business is a difficult business. It demands physical work. She said that without me, they would not be able to maintain the business. I remained at home. It cost us 100 dollars, a huge sum of money for us. For it I received a *swiadetstwo* [witness in Polish](certificate) that I was much older than those being called to the military. I was nervous because I was concerned that someone would denounce me. Several months before, Leibl Rejne's son went from house to house with the police with a list seeking those in hiding. He said, "What do you mean, I will go to serve the Poles and they not?" There was turmoil in the *shtetl* and whoever could ran away; others reported for service.

The Poles captured Vilna, although the city was promised to Lithuania. She also occupied White Russia [Belarus] and then tore off a piece of Ukraine and occupied Kiev. [Jozef] Pilsudski, the field marshal of the Polish army, stuck his sword in the earth in the center of the city of Kiev and solemnly swore that they would not move from there. He said, "It was ours and ours it will remain." (Before Chielmnicki's Rebellion, it had belonged to Poland.)

Russia was weak. Four White Russian armies with the aid of the Entente fought against the Bolsheviks. But when Trotsky conquered all of them, he turned to the Poles. The Poles retreated from Kiev with Pilsudski at the head. It was not long before Vilna was taken by the Bolsheviks. The goal was Warsaw. The Poles resisted near Grodno, but the Russians overcame them. The Polish army withdrew; the highway that passed Goniadz did not rest day and night. Soldiers and baggage trains went from Grodno to the fortress and farther to Lomza. When the police left Goniadz, we knew that the Russians were very close. We did not sleep that night. All of the young, around 50-60 young people, were on watch and protected the city. We wore white ribbons with a stamp from city hall that meant that we were policemen. In the middle of the night three Polish riders came running from Dolistower Street. They said that the Bolsheviks were near and that we could expect them in a few hours.

The night passed quietly. When it became light, I went to Tzalel's son Leibl's to rest in the attic. Tzalel's son Leibl lived on Tifle Street, not far from us. His house was on a courtyard away from the street. He had a large stall and a great deal of hay in the attic. I had just lain down; I heard that there was running and shouting: "The Bolsheviks are here." When I awoke from sleep several hours later, there were many soldiers in the city. I learned that I was late for a very important speech. Henokh, the tailor, the son of the mute Itshe, was giving a fiery speech on Chaya-Ruchl Lurie's small bridge. He said, "We have freed ourselves from anti-Semitic Poland. In Russia, there are not Russians, but people." He described the happy future that waited for us under Bolshevik leadership and ended by saying that today is a bright day for us. Henokh was then crowned with the nickname, "the bright day."

The Russian army was dressed very badly, simply in rags. Russia was greatly impoverished by six years of war. Several wore the clothing of prisoners or murdered Polish soldiers.

Hunger strode in with the Bolsheviks. They did not carry any food with them. Whatever food there was in the *shtetl* was used. The fruits in the orchards that were half ripe (it was 15 days into the month of Av – July or August) were ripped from the trees and eaten. They looked to buy watches, but there were none; everyone had sold their pocketknives. They paid in rubles, a ruble for a mark. We knew that their money had no worth, but it should be understood, we had to take it. One bit of luck was that they quickly moved farther and left in the direction of Lomza.

The *revkom* (revolutionary committee) built a sort of city hall in the *shtetl* to keep order and carry out the administration of the *shtetl*. The *revkom* was quartered at Chaya-Ruchl Lurie's on the second story. The commissar was Josef Winer, a son of Moshe the *sotnik* [Russian military rank]. Moshe was a shoemaker and lived up on Dol [Dolistower Street] where one went to the bath. His wife, Teme Rayzl, Josef's mother, sold fruit at the market. Josef, himself, was a tailor. That is, he was a man with a pedigree, a proletariat *ben* [son of] proletariat. Even more, he also had a certificate that he was a comrade in the Communist Party from when they were under Polish rule. So he was chosen as commissar. He aides were: Henokh, the son of Itshe the mute. He spoke very well, also for his father, for whom speaking was very difficult; Leizer the baker, himself from Szczuczyn, a son-in-law of Yitzhak Czejnku; Zelig, the son of Moshe-Mendl of the old market, a tailor; Leizer the son of Rywka-Dwoyra of the old market, a former Russian soldier who survived the World War. Leizer received a sword from the Bolsheviks. He rode on a horse like a Cossack, with the saber at his side and galloped through the streets like an arrow from a bow. Josef carried a revolver, but no one knew where or for what. He was some sort of commissar. There were also two Polish comrades in *revkom*. One of them, Bochenko the woodchopper and the other, a shoemaker, a tall gentile with blond hair.

There were two policemen: Ruwin Drak's son, Zeydke, and Moshe-Feywl the shoemaker. Zeydke held a rifle naturally. He was a former soldier. But with Moshe-Feywl it was like an ornament. Moshe-Feywl's son of around 10 years old danced in the street and sang: "Father is an engineer! Father is a gendarme." During the German occupation [during the First World War], they dreaded the gendarmes like a fire. Now, his father was a gendarme. Some kind of trifle?...

There was no income; the peasants did not come to the city. It was very difficult to get bread. They did not take Russian rubles in the villages. Give them dollars, but where did one get this? Merchants took Polish marks, although the Polish government had escaped and who knew what would happen. Salt was very important. But where could we get salt? Girls came on foot from Trestine to buy a few kilos of salt and they were happy if they got it. Moshe-Feywl, the policeman, lurked near the cemetery and caught five girls with illegal goods. They cried and they pleaded; they were poor and they would get a piece of bread for the salt. But he did not listen and took them to the *revkom*. There the salt was taken from them.

A sapper division arrived; their baggage stood at the old market until they built the bridge over the river. They had no wood. They went through the courtyards and searched. I brought several wagons of wood to our courtyard from Bojdener Woods. I was afraid that it would be taken. I brought Bochenko, the woodchopper to cut it. After cutting it, I asked that he split it later. The bridge was finished without our wood. The Bolsheviks built the bridge on the same spot that the Russian army had built it in 1914, not far from Moshe'ke's son, Chatskl's mill.

Bochenko was no longer a comrade in *revkom* because of an occurrence. Wagons from the surrounding villages were brought together for the military. The Bolsheviks did not have any military wagons. The civilian population had to provide them. He, Bochenko, told a peasant that for a sum of money he would be freed [of providing his wagon]. This information was brought to the *revkom*. A military division had just arrived. Lev Kopian embraced the officer. He knew him from Russia. When the officer heard the story of the bribe, he ruled on the spot: *"Dwad-tsat liet."* [twenty years]; Not more and not less than 20 years in jail. Bochenko was placed in *reshyotka* [locked up] and, as soon as the soldiers departed, he was let out. Now, he sawed our wood with great eagerness.

A transport of the wounded from the Lomza front arrived. They said that the fighting was very heavy there. Their arrival was entirely unexpected. The Hebrew school was above Chaya Josl's. They threw out the crude benches (*skamejkes*), brought straw from Guzy, spread it on the floor and lay the wounded there on the floor. Girls went to the gentiles to gather a little milk and they gave it to the wounded. There were no instruments to treat the sick and nothing with which to bind the lightly wounded. As the air there was not very fresh, the soldiers who could, dragged themselves to the surrounding neighbors, opened a door and crawled into a room and lay down on the ground. Two crawled to us. I served them, got a little milk and did whatever was possible for them. Early in the morning, wagons were brought and they were taken to Grodno. More transports of the wounded arrived, but they were not taken down from the wagons. They were given milk; the lightly wounded were wrapped up with *swojske* [homemade] linens that were collected from gentiles. The horses rested and then went farther to Grodno. Once, a transport of the wounded stopped opposite our store. I went onto the wagons and with difficulty gave a half glass of tea with milk to a very sick soldier. The three Lenczewskis from the pharmacy, the mother and both of her daughters, who lived next to us, stood in front of the pharmacy and watched how we were busy with the sick. Their eyes burned with hate.

The Bolsheviks were already here for three weeks. They had conquered Lomza and they were going to Warsaw. There were no newspapers and we had no exact information. An important man in the Red government arrived during the fourth week. He came from Moscow through Vilna, Grodno and was traveling to Warsaw. He was enraged at seeing that the stores were open. He went to the *revkom* and created a tumult. "What is this," he said, "permitting the businesses to operate!" Do you not know that in the Soviet Union free trade is forbidden? They should go out immediately and requisition the goods in all of the businesses. He left and the comrades from *revkom* began to transfer the goods. We read in a Bialystok leaflet that a new Polish Red Army had to be formed immediately to fight against the lords, the bloodsuckers and so on, according to the well known formula. We saw that we faced a mobilization.

Saturday night when we were in the synagogue for *Ma'ariv* [evening prayers], Leyzer, the rabbi's son, came in from the street with news. An officer of a very high rank was lodged at Chaya-Ruchl Lurie's. He was lodged with her on the first day when the Red Army entered. Now he came from outside Warsaw. We understood from his words that something was fishy. But we were not allowed to ask him. All sorts of suppositions were created. Sunday, early in the morning, the highway in Dolko was already full of wagons. They were moving in the direction of Grodno. It seems the Poles were returning... Our skin began to tremble. The local Poles would betray us and in that fiery minute we would pay. During the day several automobiles with officers came and looked for quarters. Several came into us. They sat at the table resting and the driver prepared food for them. My mother worried that they were making our pots and pans unkosher. It seemed that here was the headquarters of the Fourth Army. They came from the *revkom* with the announcement that they had found a good headquarters at the Christian clergyman; they left for there, moved in telephones and began to work. They would only come to us to sleep. One automobile stood in front of the house and the driver did not leave. We recognized that he was a Jew, but he did not say so. He spoke and many people stood around him and listened. He said that the Jews were guilty in that they were going back [to Poland]... the capitalists supported the Poles with money and weapons. Who were the capitalists if not the American Jews who had all of the wealth. Consequently, revenge needed to be taken against the Jews. Terrible, where is Henokh, "the bright day" who needs to hear this!...

Everyone was very troubled and frightened and decided to escape. I packed several pieces of underwear, my *tefilin* [phylacteries], a sack, took a piece of bread and went to Dolko to the highway. There I would go until Suchowola by wagon and from there to Jagustow, Suwalk and Lithuania. It was dangerous to go through Raczki; the Poles could catch up with us. Before I began to descend from the mountain to the highway in Dolko I heard voices and loud shouting. As I came to the highway I saw what was happening there. If three wagons would have gone in the width, they would have moved forward, but the wagons took the entire width of the highway, ensnared each other and remained standing. Go and stop. This one shouted, the other raged; all screamed and cursed and we did not move, only crept. And thus along the entire highway as far as the eye could see, a wagon train extended without an end... We crept. Suddenly a bang was heard, a wagon broke. The baggage was laid in other wagons. The wheel with the broken axle was thrown onto the side of the highway and we moved farther. Gentiles stood by the side of the highway and one grabbed a wheel, one an axle, one a board. They stood thus from very early and waited for something to be thrown down. I decided to go back home. No good could come from such tumult. But then I saw how the artillery was running along Monker Road, six horses hitched to each cannon. They came to the highway and stopped. The officer of the artillery shouted: "Stop the wagon train, the artillery is more important; I will give you to the court!" But no one heard him. The thick mass moved slowly forward with the voices and shouts as earlier. I took my sack and went back home.

My mother was very happy about my return. It was Sunday night. It was dark in the house; we turned on a small lamp. I went out to look for bread. The soldiers from the highway had emptied all of the bakeries. Gershon's son, Motke, entrusted me with a secret that his sister, Merke, had just taken a baked bread from the oven. I immediately ran there and she weighed out a very large piece for me. Merke lived at the old market on the street that led to Moshe'ke's son, Chatskl's mill. It was an out-of the-way place and no soldiers came there. There was no water in the house. The water carriers were afraid to appear in the street with horses. I took a pail and went to the well. Motke's daughter, Beylke, and her small sister, Grunye, also came with a pail. On the way we met many Jews with containers. The well water was cold and fresh, straight from the well. Summer, on the hot *Shabbosim* [Sabbaths] we would go there to drink cold water.

I woke up with the day and went to the synagogue to pray. There I heard that all of the young were leaving the *shtetl*. I came home and told my mother that I had decided to go away. Everyone was going; I wanted to go, too.

I went to the highway through Dolistower Street. My mother accompanied me to the end of *Krutka Ulica* [street].There were no longer wagon trains on the highway, only walkers, 25 of them from Goniadz. Young men and girls from Ostrowa, Ostrolenka and still other *shtetlekh* were walking. Individual Russian soldiers went like us, with a gun, without a gun – we went. A soldier came close to me, tapped my sack and asked me in Russian: "What do you have there, bread?" I did not need anything clearer. I would immediately have scores of soldiers around me. I told him to be quiet. I went down with him among the bushes, opened the sack, showed him how much bread I had, divided it with him and done. I went back to the highway and he followed me. I wanted to be farther from him, but then we heard shouting in the bushes: "*Govjandinu, govjandinu!*" [meat]. A few soldiers had caught a cow; killed it and they were dividing the meat. All of the soldiers on the highway ran to grab a piece of meat and I was rid of my companion.

About halfway to Suchowola we met a Jew who was sitting and crying by the side of the highway. We stopped near him. He told us that he was from Wizna. The Bolsheviks had dragged him to Grodno and abandoned him, but they took his boots; he was going home barefooted. His feet had received a drubbing and he could not go farther, so he sat and cried. Hearing the name, Wizna, interested me. I spent my first year of *yeshiva* study there in 1909. I looked closely and recognized him: this was Dovid the fisherman; I had eaten with him on *Shabbos*. I did not want him to recognize me; this would take too much time. I advised him that he should use all of his strength and go to a nearby village for a few days and then to go farther. He should not remain on the highway because the Polish Army was very near and his life was in danger.

Wagon trains stood in all of the villages along the highway. Riders ran back and forth, leading one wagon onto the highway, then another.

We arrived in Suchowola around one o'clock in the afternoon, went to a Jew and there received a glass of tea. We did not hear any good news in Suchowola. For the few weeks that the Bolsheviks were there, the *revkom*, which consisted of a Jewish majority, sentenced a gentile to death and shot him. Now the gentiles were saying very often: "If other brothers come in we will take revenge." We immediately decided to go farther to Sztabin. Mikhal, the husband of Feyge- Ruchl's daughter Tsirl, came with me. We were again on the highway. The wagon trains went without end, but only individual wagons. A young officer, of my age, invited me to go with him to Grodno, but I said no thank you. We left the highway on the left and went to Sztabin. We arrived there at night, but the *shtetl*, Sztabin, was a ruin. The houses had been burned five years ago during the war and had not been rebuilt. An older gentile stood by the side of the road, saw that we had arrived and screamed: *Zydkes* [Jews], communists, let our Poles come and we will slaughter you all! He cursed and berated us. We did not answer him. We went to the only Jew who lived there. We received enough dairy foods from him and a piece of bread. We ate; we went up to the loft to rest.

We slept for about an hour. I said to my neighbor, Mikhal: I think it is dangerous to stay here; if the Poles come they will burn us together with the barn. We must go farther to Jagustow. We immediately all went down from the loft. The Jew showed us the way to go. We tried to go very quietly, particularly when we went through a village. We were afraid that the Poles were already in Jagustow, from the Rajgrod side and then we would be lost. It was already light; we saw four riders coming towards us. Our hearts beat. Poles, maybe? No, they were Russians and they asked us where the Poles were. We told them that last night the Russians were still in Suchowola. They rode on farther. We now went with a light heart. Arriving in the city we separated. Mikhal and I went to Meir Grabower.

Years ago, this Meir was a *melamed* [teacher in a religious school] in Goniadz. Then he rented the farm in Klewianka and sold dairy products. Now he had a farm in the village of Grabowa, so he was called Grabower. He was a relative of

Feyge-Ruchl from Tifle Street and was pleased to know someone connected to her son-in-law.

The retreat of the Russian Army stretched through Grodner Street. Meir's house was on Suwalker Street; it was calm here. Meir came in from the street and related that a Cossack had broken in a door in a shop, murdered the shopkeeper and took whatever he wanted. We sat in the house and shook. In the morning Meir came in from the street and said that a company of Lithuanian soldiers had marched in from Sulwak and taken Jagustow. That is, Lithuania had come to us...

Jagustower Jews went out to the streets. The Bolsheviks left; the Poles were not here, let only the Lithuanians remain. We Goniadzers wanted to go deeper into Lithuania. We sent in Zeydka Sidranski (Chaya Wikhne's son) to the Lithuanian commandant, a former officer in the Russian Army who spoke Russian. Zeydka came back with nothing; he was not giving permits and without them the group would not go farther. On the third day, Friday, with great difficulty I found a wagon driver who agreed to drive without a permit. But none of the other Goniadzers wanted to go with me. Having no choice, I went alone. The road to Sulwak stretched to the forest and no people were seen. It rained very hard. [Water] ran from my head as from a roof and I became entirely soaked through. I had to change my underwear and clothes in a hotel in Sulwak.

I went to the synagogue to pray *Shabbos* morning. I knew that the *khazan* [cantor] was Ruwen Rosher (Rosh is a *shtetl* near Grodno) who had studied *skhite* [ritual slaughter of animals] in Goniadz with the *khazan*, Reb Nuchem, and led the choir after prayers. I went to him, but he did not recognize me. I told him that in 1908, 12 years ago, I was a choir boy with the *khazan*, Reb Nuchem, and he and Reb Nuchem had sung with us choir boys from Purim to Passover. On the first day of the holiday, in the *beis-medrash* [synagogue or house of prayer], I was ashamed to go to sing in the choir. All of the Goniadz young boys had run after me and laughed at me. On the second day of the holiday, in the synagogue, I stood on the steps of the *aron-kodesh* [ark or cabinet holding the Torah scrolls] and sang. Yes, he remembered this incident, but he did not remember me.

Sunday, I hired a wagon and went to Kalvaria, Lithuania. The road also passed through a thick forest. There was an inn half way to Kalvaria. We stopped to rest the horses and to eat something ourselves. There we met people from Lithuania who were returning to Poland. They said that it was very bad in Lithuania; there was no place to earn money, the police did not register people and if someone arrived with a horse and wagon from Poland, it was requisitioned. My wagon driver was afraid and returned to Sulwak, leaving me at the inn. It was night; I did not want to go into the woods alone. There I saw a wagon with passengers was starting to go. They were traveling to Kalvaria. Under no circumstances did the wagon driver want to take me. I hopped onto the back of the open-sided wagon and went along. The wagon driver did not know about this. The passengers smiled. It was very difficult for me to stay on the wagon, but getting off and remaining in the forest was less pleasurable... The wagon went very fast and when we went on to the wooden bridge, we were in Kalvaria. I came down off the wagon. The lamplight was homey in the windows and I was happy seeing it. On the bridge I met young men strolling. They were from Sulwak and I brought them fresh greetings from there. They took me away to a hotel to spend the night. I would be registered in the morning. I slept on the ground and my neighbor was Henokh Hirszfeld, Sholem Hirszfeld's brother. I remembered him from home when he studied watch making with his brother-in-law, Chaim Leshkes. Henokh opened a watch business in Jagustow and lived there. He asked me for a favor. He had a great deal of money with him, so I should take a few packages of Polish marks from him until the morning. He would sleep easier. In the morning, the owner [of the hotel] registered me with the police. Now, I went out to the street calmly. There I learned that the Poles had taken Sulwak.

I met a young man of my acquaintance from Grajewo. He was here for three months. He said that I do not have to pay any money for the bed. He slept on hay; it did not cost him any money. He also had arranged for his food. That night I slept on the hay and was satisfied. It was Tuesday morning. I stood in front of the house and saw how [people] were going to the market. Today was market day here. There had not been a market in Goniadz for a long time and here life was going on as before in the quiet years. I truly envied the Lithuanian Jews. I saw a wagon going with young men and after the wagon went another young man holding his hand to his face. His name was Chaim Arya Pekarski, but I did not recognize him at first because he was very covered with dust and his red hair was now sand colored. I shouted: Chaim Arya! He turned around to me. Yes, this was him! He came from Janova, Lithuania. On the road to Kalvaria, his nose started to bleed. Now in Kalvaria on the bridge, he could not sit in the shaking wagon; so he went on foot. He said that going through the border with the entire group was very difficult. I invited him to come with me, but he said he had an uncle named Bash in Kalvaria. We went to him. His relatives welcomed him very warmly and I left him there.

I traveled farther to the German border and stopped in Wierzbołowo [Virbalis]. The border was five kilometers from there. I went to the border, gave the soldier who was standing on guard 50 German marks and he let me go through. I was already in Aydkunen [now Chemyshevkoye, Russia; Eitkunai in Lithuanian], Germany, but when I traveled farther, a gendarme stopped me because I did not have any certificate.

At the gendarmerie I was searched very thoroughly. It was a miracle that I had left my 20 dollars and 250 francs with an honest Jew in Aydkunen. I was arrested in the county town, Stalavka. There was very little food; the jail overseer only bought a piece of bread for the German marks that I had with me. He said to me, if I could give bail he would free me until the tribunal. I asked him to telephone a relative of mine in Lik, an escapee from Grajewo and I knew his address.

It was the first day of Rosh-Hashanah; I lay on the plank cot and prayed from memory. I did not have a *Siddur* [prayer book] and there was no *Makhzor* [prayer book for Rosh Hashanah and Yom Kippur]. I prayed and thought: it is now *Musaf* time; at home, my Uncle Lazer stood before the reading desk and sang the prayers with his strong voice. I was moved emotionally from longing and the door opened and the jail overseer called out: Bachrach, bail had arrived.

Twenty minutes later I was free.

Translators Notes:

1. The army of General Haller, a Pole who lived in America. He came from there with many young Poles to help liberate Poland.

2. The Poznantichikes were Poles from Posen [Poznan] (German Poland) and who now had liberated themselves from the German regime.

[Pages 543-544]

As I Remember It
By Meirim Rubin, New York
Translated from Yiddish to English by Dr. Isaac Fine

I.

The Great Schism

In Goniondz, in the 1880's, a great schism occurred between the Chassidim and the misnagdim . Older folk in town used to reckon time using this event as a benchmark. This was one of the rare and extraordinary crises, which took place in the shtetl, such as the cholera or the great fire. During that time period, there was a Reb Berele who was very staunchly supported by the poorer folk in town. The successful Chassidic merchants in town, however, were not pleased with him, and brought in Rabbi Gedaliah Kaminetzky. A sharp division soon broke out between the two rival factions. The Chassidim persecuted Reb Berele. They broke his windows and didn't provide him with an income, since the local government franchise was in their hands.

The misnagdim mounted a counter attack. They went to the little Chassidic shtibl , which at that time was located in Chatzkel Babniak's house. They pulled out the Sefer Toras and other books, and broke the benches and tables. From time to time, a fist fight would break out in the House of Study. Once, after the Sabbath prayers, the Chassids fell on Yehuda the butcher. When the other butchers found that Yehuda was being beaten, they all ran to the House of Study to defend him. At the end, the Chassids won the battle and Reb Berele had to leave town. When he was leaving the shtetl, his allies went along to accompany him. The Chassid, Zelig-Isaac's' was standing in the street at the time, and yelled out at him, "Tsedokasakoh tatzil memoves", like at a funeral. Reb Berele yelled back at him, "Soon they should say it to you!" Two weeks later, Zelig Isaac's' only daughter died.

[p. 544-546]

II

The Dybbuk*

Translated by Gloria Berkenstat Freund

This happened in 1926.

The water-carrier's wife suddenly became melancholy and began speaking strangely. This happened after she gave birth. The doctor in the shtetl [town] could find no remedy for her, so her husband traveled with his wife to Bialystok to a specialist, a nerve doctor, but no doctor could help.

A Hasidic rabbi travelled through Goniadz at that time and many women went to him for a blessing. When they learned of the case of the woman they went to the water-carrier with the good advice that he go to the rabbi and ask him for a remedy. The water-carrier grasped at this and immediately went to the rabbi with his sick wife.

– Dear rabbi! Save my wife from the melancholy! He pleaded with tears in his eyes.

The rabbi observed the woman, spoke a few words to her and then said: – A dybbuk has entered the woman.

He asked the husband to find a minyon [10 men needed for prayer] of older Jews who were truly God-fearing. They should all immerse themselves in the mikvah [ritual bath] and fast and then come at 12 noon with their talisim and tefilin [prayer shawls and phylacteries].

And they did as the rabbi asked. The rabbi ordered that no one except the woman and the minyon be in the house. My father, may he rest in peace, was among the 10 virtuous Jews. At around 12 noon a curious crowd that had learned that a dybbuk was going to be driven out assembled around the house. However, the rabbi asked that the shutters be closed and the windows covered with curtains so that no one outside would see what was happening inside the house. No matter how much I asked and begged my father to tell me about what had happened, he did not tell me because the rabbi had sworn them in their talisim and tefilin to keep the entire matter very secret.

For a time afterwards the water-carrier's wife remained in the same condition, but the elancholy ended two months later as if on its own and the woman became normal.

I believe that it is worth recording the fact that such a case could happen in our Goniadz, which was progressive in every respect in 1926.

*Translator's Note: a dybbuk is a mythological evil spirit that enters a living person, taking control of the person's soul, speaking through the person and thought to be the cause of mental illness.

[Pages 545-546]

The Penitent
By Moshe Bachrach
Translated by Marvin Galper

On a winter evening of 1913, between the afternoon and the evening service, a Russian peasant walked into the House of Study dressed in a heavy coat with a fur hat on his head. He grabbed Mordechai the sexton and cried like a child. In broken Yiddish, he then asked aloud about many Goniondz folk from twenty years earlier. A commotion arose in the House of Study. The students arose from their long tables. The mischievous children ended their mischief. A circle of conversation formed around him. All formed in a great circle around this very odd Russian peasant. It was then discovered that he had been born in Goniondz. He had been a member of the notorious bandit gang which had operated in Goniondz twenty years ago. The they had terrorized both Jews and Christians in all the region. The gang had been composed primarily of Jewish young men. For us children, they were a legend. For the adults, they were a terrible memory. Later they were sentenced to Siberia for their "good deeds." Then they became lost, even to their own families.

The peasant introduced himself. Some of the older men recognized him. They embraced him like a long lost brother who has been found again. We all had the feeling that a "repentant one" was among us, and that he had paid a heavy price for the sins of his youth. He was treated with great tenderness. For us children, he was almost like a storybook hero whom our town had been worthy enough to produce.

After the evening service, the "good time fellows" invited him for a dinner at Chanon's house. There he told them that he had been living like a Russian peasant in Siberia. He had his own family there. In his older years he had felt powerfully drawn to see his hometown and his roots, which he still remembered from his childhood. Some of those present cried to hear him. A child captured by the nations, they felt, especially since he has now repented. They made one toast after another to him until late in the night and offered him their very best wishes. Soon after "the repentant one" had gone forth on his way, his secret was made known to them. He was traveling through the land selling counterfeit hundred ruble paper notes. He had stopped on this occasion in Goniondz.

[Pages 547-548]

A Goniondzer Remains a Goniondzer
By Dovid Bachrach
Translated by Gloria Berkenstat Freund

Tishre [usually September] 5687, 1926, I crossed into the United States from Canada and received employment there as a Hebrew teacher in Birmingham, Alabama, a city in the Deep South. The change from the cold, far west of Canada to the warm South was very physically difficult for me and spiritually even more difficult.

Birmingham is a large city with many factories and iron foundries, where many thousands of workers, white and black, work. The local Jews are, as usual, merchants, and commerce is concentrated in their hands. Jewish young people born there are doctors, lawyers, dentists and so on. The tempo of life is very quick; one runs and chases after the dollar with one's entire strength, day in and day out, until one falls down. The life in the Canadian cities, such as Winnipeg, Montreal and Toronto is much calmer and more leisurely.

Yiddishkeit [Jewish way of life] there was at a low ebb. The fathers with their best intentions could not devote themselves to the education of their children; life demanded much of them, they had to work a great deal. There was no quiet hour before work; they closed very late at night. The main educators were the mothers. The mother who brought something with her from the old home had a kosher kitchen, the recognition of the *Shabbos* with a white tablecloth and lit candles; she also saw that her son went to the *Talmud Torah* [in Poland, a religious elementary school for poor boys]. But as soon as he finished with his *Bar-mitzvah- maftir,** he is seen no more. A girl ends with her confirmation at age 12.p> Three days a year, *Rosh Hashanah* [Jewish New Year] and *Yom-Kippur* [Day of Atonement] the Jews close their businesses and come to the synagogue. If *Yom- Kippur* falls on a Sunday, the synagogue is full. Only a few Jews come to the synagogue on *Shabbos*, but they rush from the synagogue to their businesses because this is the day for earning money. During the week, a *minyon* [10 men necessary for communal prayer] of several Jews assembles with great difficulty. Therefore, it was a great wonder for me on one occasion to see the synagogue open in the afternoon on a regular day.

Entering the synagogue I saw a very old Jew sitting over a *sefer* [religious book] (his son had persuaded the *Shamas* – sexton – to open the synagogue for his old father, because he was bored in the house). I wanted to leave immediately, but the old man noticed me and called me to him. He asked me to sit near him and carried out a conversation with me. Mainly, he wanted me to tell him how Yehosha *ben* Nun [Joshua son of Nun] had brought the Jews across the Jordan. Because of his deep age he did not hear well and I had to shout into his ear. I cited the verse from the Book of Joshua to him, "...the waters descending from upstream stood still and they rose up in one column ..."[Joshua 3:16] that is, the water of the Jordan that flows to the Dead Sea remained calm, and appeared in its full height as a pillar and did not flow farther, but the lowest water flowed into the Dead Sea, as a matter of course, the spot became dry land and the Jews went through. This was a miraculous place like the Red Sea, as we learned in *kheder* [religious elementary school for boys].

This old man did not agree with my translation and explained to me that everything had happened in a natural way. I was very impatient. The entire conversation was a nuisance and I would have willingly left him, but this was not proper to me. He stopped for several minutes and asked if I understood the explanation. When he had at last finished, he again asked me if I had understood everything; if not, he was prepared to begin again... I thanked him and wanted to be underway. He asked me where I was from. I said: from Bialystok. He asked me: from Bialystok itself? I answered: from a nearby *shtetl*. However, he demanded that I tell him the name of the *shtetl* [town]. As Knyszyn is as near to Bialystok as Goniadz, I told him: Knyszyn. To this he said to me: you are not from Knyszyn, you are from Goniadz. I remained as if stupefied and asked him how he knew. He said to me: You do not speak like a Knyszyner, you speak like a Goniondzer. I asked him where he was from; he said that he came from Sapockin near Grodno, but he would happen to visit Goniondz very often. To my question of how long he had been here from his old home, he answered that he was in America for 40 plus years.

I calculated in my head that he had left our area 15 years before I was born. He had spent so many bitter years among the Blacks in the South and yet he recognized by my speech that I was certainly from Goniadz and not from Knyszyn. A rare occurrence.

I learned a moral from this - that a person cannot deny his origin and he needs to remain what he was.

A Goniondzer remains a Goniondzer.

*Translator's Note: The maftir is the concluding portion of the Torah reading at the Shabbos service, preceding the reading of the Haftarah – a reading from the Prophets linked in its theme to the weekly Torah portion. At a Bar-mitzvah – the religious rite at which a boy of 13 takes on the religious obligations of a man – the Bar-mitzvah boy follows his role as maftir with the reading of the the Haftarah.

[Page 550]

A Mother of Goniadz
(Elegy)
by Alter Rozen
Translated by Gloria Berkenstat Freund

Dedicated to the memory of my mother, Ruchl-Leah, may she rest in peace, born in Goniadz.
Died in Brooklyn on the 26th of Tishrei 5717 [1 October 1956].

Filled like silver cups
With sweet, frothy Kiddush wine;
Like a gold plated picture,
[Covered] with a gentle, loving glow –
As then, once, kindled thus,
In death as in life,
Doubled many times a hundred –
My mother floats before me.
Like the heart without God,
Like a dead city,
So bare-naked remained
The walls of our house;
As in a grave, a dark pit
Had grieving secluded one in the house.
No Shabbas [Sabbath] rest, no holiday joy,
No sacred enthusiasm
Since my mother separated from me –
A person's joy, a person's glory,
The endless treasures
Sail away from my shore...
The heavens fall on me
Every day like a heavy stone.
Oh, how lonely I am, alone,
How the mountain of sadness presses my tired head
And the wounds burn in my heart –
Since my mother disappeared from me!

———— ———— ———— ———— ————

My mother calls to me,
I hear her voice from there –
She says: "Throw open the door with courage,
Be free! Run from the valley of tears,
Sever yourself from the grey earth!"
My mother, I have heard your voice!

Alter Rozen, New York

[Pages 551-556]

Itshe Shtumak wins a strike
by Osher Schuchinsky
Translated from Yiddish to English by Martin Jacobs

One frosty Sunday the skin which covered her protruding bones collapsed, never again to rise up. The horse died at the hole in the ice just when its owner, Itshe Shtumak, (Itshe the Stammerer) was filling a barrel with water to bring to his customers, the good people of the town.

He stood for a while holding the empty bucket and thought: A foolish animal! She went a whole night without tasting the bit of straw that I gave her. If you had eaten, you would not have come to such a bad end. And if you did pass away, you could have died in your own stall and not come here to the ice hole pulling the sled and the barrel. Now who will drag them up the mountain to town?

Itshe took off the wet frozen bag which he wore over his torn trousers, threw it over the hole of the half filled barrel, and stared at the beast. I no longer have to worry about you. You're done with your world, but what am *I* to do now? You've left me five orphans, and I, Itshe Shtumak, am a sixth. It's good that my Chaye- Leye didn't live to see this.

Seeing that the collar was still on the horse's neck, it occurred to him that it might be choking him. He went over, bent down, and tried to take the collar off. Rest in peace, he thought to himself. For four years you dragged the water with me; if only you waited a couple of years, little Henekh would be earning money working for Shmuel-Ber the tailor. He's been learning the work altogether now for two years.

"Henekh is a dear child." A warmth went through Itshe's whole body. "And Yisekher, such a smart child. He can already say his prayers by heart. If I hadn't been a water-carrier I would have been – enough! I'm not a water-carrier any longer. Without a horse, with just a sled – what will I carry? What will I carry?" He went over to the carcass and gave it a kick. "Carry water! On your neck, with a couple of straps, up the mountain." He lifted his eyes to the mountain top, lost in thought, big tears moistening his frozen silent face.

"I have to notify the knacker, the buyer of carcasses, Yashek Kozhol. You can't leave a carcass lying at the ice hole." Itshe thought. He tightened the cord on his trousers, looked at the sled and barrel, and began his climb up the hill. At the top Chatskl the water-carrier's sled appeared. His big, blind horse shook his head, as though he was trying to feel his way in the dark. He knew the way down the mountain very well. Many a time had he fallen there and injured his old bones. These days Chatskl the water-carrier no longer held the reins; he relied completely on his blind horse. Coming to a ditch, the horse swerved to the right on its own. It would have occurred to no one that the horse was blind. For equine intelligence this was nothing. This is why Chatskl loved his horse.

Chatskl very much hated it when someone said to him, "Your blind horse rides well." Even if it was his best customer, the finest citizen, he became angry and answered with anger. "What does it have to do with you that the horse is blind? Aren't you getting your water?"

Chatskl saw from the mountain top that Itshe Shtumak's horse and sled were parked at the ice hole. But what happened? Why was the horse lying down? He asked himself that question, and, looking at the river, he gave himself the answer: "It's dead. What will Itshe Shumak do now, when he has five orphan children?" A feeling of pity enveloped him. He pushed back his astrakhan hat, revealing his wrinkled brow. He stroked his beard: "The Master of the Universe didn't have anyone's horse to kill, so he chose Itshe Shtumak's."

"How is Itshe Shtumak to blame? As far as I'm concerned his horse could have lived a hundred and twenty years. The townspeople are to blame! Bring them water in the coldest frost, in a blizzard, in rain, lie on the ice and open the ice hole, all for three groshen a trip."

Itshe Shtumak came up opposite Chatskl's sled. He turned his head away so as not to see him. He was embarrassed and heavy in his heart. He stood there out of breath. Chatskl looked at him and said, "Good morning." Itshe shook his head and pointed to the river. "Finished", he stammered to Chatskl (you could understand him, although since his tongue and palate were fused together it was hard for him to talk). "Dead! I'll go tell the knacker."

Chatskl the water-carrier got up from his seat. "Where are you going? To the knacker? On foot? Get on the sled. I'll drive you."

"No, Chatskl. You've got to deliver water for my customers too."

"Let them get it themselves. To deliver water for three groshen a trip! Let them get it themselves! Get on!" Chatskl called out. "Five groshen. Otherwise no water."

"You're right, *Reb* Chatskl. Five groshen a trip, otherwise no water. Now you can do it; you're the only carrier."

"Now and later! Don't be a fool, you'll deliver water too. But for five groshen a trip, do you hear? Otherwise we don't deliver."

"Itshe", Chatskl called out. "Tomorrow is Monday, market day. Tomorrow you'll buy a horse. But buy a good one. I have twenty rubles, I'll lend them to you; you'll pay me back a bit at a time. At five groshen a trip there will even be enough for you to do good deeds."

The sad news that Itshe Shtumak's horse had died spread through the town. The housewives began to look into how their water was holding out. Itshe Shtumak's customers were very much afraid and started thinking about what they would do. Chatskl the water-carrier's customers remained calm and confidant. "He will take care of his customers. . . no problem!", they thought.

When Chaye-Tsirl, the baker, heard of the misfortune, she wrung her hands and ran out from behind her counter onto the narrow wooden bridge Perhaps she might see Chatskl and talk to him, get him to see you can't run a bakery without water. "Well, we'll have to give a two gulden contribution to buy Shtumak a horse. It won't be the first time." she thought to herself.

Chatskl went out very early to the old market place. Itshe was already there, looking around at the horses tied to the railing.

"Good morning, *Reb* Chatskl."

"Itshe, come here a moment. Do you see this animal? This is a horse for a water-carrier. Look at his legs. Look at his chest. This is the one for you. Do you have to have eyes? What does it matter to you that he's blind? A horse doesn't need eyes; it needs legs! It needs strength! Itshe, listen to me."

"If you say so, *Reb* Chatskl, there's nothing to think about. Who knows better than you what a water-carrier needs."

Chatskl touched the pocket where his twenty rubles were. "Agree on a price, Itshe, and come, let's go inform the customers that from now on they'll be paying five groshen a trip. Good luck! Take its reins," Chatskl yelled. "This is an animal you must be able to lead."

The great chestnut horse shook its head, as though it was looking into the darkness, trying to find out who its new master was. There was something strange about his speech. When Itshe Shtumak pulled on the rope and stammered out: Doh! it followed him.

"Come, *Reb* Chatskl Let's doh drink *lekhayim*. I have a dulden; it's like simchi-teyre (Simchas Torah) for us today.

Chaye-Tsirl, the baker, went out onto the little wooden bridge; seeing Itshe Shtumak leading a big horse, her face lit up. "We'll soon have water, thank God. But how did Shtumak come up with the money to buy such a stallion? And he complains that the little Shtumaks have nothing to eat! He'll give me buckets full to the brim if he wants to deliver for me."

"Good morning." The three of them drew near the bridge with a heavy step. Itshe walked in front pulling the beast by the rope which hung from the bridle. At his side, between Itshe and the horse, came Chatskl the water-carrier.

"We've come to tell you that from now on the price is five groshen a trip and you. .. ." "Did you ever hear such a thing? Suddenly, out of nowhere, five groshen a trip! When he got three he had with what to buy a stallion like this, but he wants five!" She pointed at Itshe. "I'll stuff him full of five groshen a trip! Never in all my life have I heard such a thing! I won't bake! We hardly pay that for a sack of flour, so I should give them five groshen a trip for water?" Her breath failed her from talking so loud and she remained silent.

Itshe gave a pull on the bridle. "Come", he said to the horse. Chatskl followed them.

"Thieves!" Chaye-Tsirl shouted after them. "You're leaving me without water right in the middle of a Monday. Come back! I'll give you four groshen, alright?"

Itshe and the horse stopped; he turned to Chatskl and looked at him, waiting to see what he would tell him to do.

"Five groshen, the same for everyone! For the bakerman Dyadye, for Peshe the bakerwoman, for everyone the same. One price for the whole town." Chatskl stated clearly.

"So when will you start delivering? An end to this! Just don't leave me without water," Chaye-Tsirl yielded.

"If necessary we'll deliver all night. You won't be without water," Chatskl answered.

"Chatskl!" Itshe Shtumak stammering cried out. "Chatskl, I have a dulden, come, let's drink *lekhayim*. Today is our *simchi-teyri*. It's like moshiach arrived. If Chaye-Tsirl is divving five droshen a trip, everyone will div."

Simchi -teyri Chatskl ! Simchi- teyri!

Goniadz – Synagogue building on the right, Bober River in the background

[Pages 557-558]

Daydreams
by Miriam Ferber–Keren–Tzvi, Yagur
Translated by Selwyn Rose

Memories arise of my childhood days in my home town of Goniadz, day in which both reality and dreams are mixed up together.

I feel the need, in no small way, to save these memories from the flowing waves of time.

With a fleeting glance, my eye is carried to the valley beneath the hill on which stands the synagogue, spreading as far as the slowly–flowing river Bober. "Synagogue hill" – a magic word scattering early legends.

The Night of Tisha B'Av

We, the small children, on the day before, spread out across the slopes of the hill gathering "sticky–balls" for the traditional Tisha B'Av "war of the thorns" between the groups of boys and girls. The girls tie up their hair with kerchiefs so that the thorns don't become entangled in their hair. In the end the battle ends as winners and losers just like in the days of the destruction of the Temple...

In the evening, after reading of the book of The Lamentations of Jeremiah and the evening service, returning home with my father Z"L, he would regale me with many stories and legends about the Destruction and redemption, and the expected future coming of the Messiah for the People of Israel.

I would listen trembling to the stories being told and see before me, in my mind's eye, the River Bober transformed into the Jordan flowing at the foot of the hill and the fields of the Land of Israel – broad spacious meadows beyond the river far, far away on the horizon.

And who knows if it wasn't from here, because of these same stories and legends, told during the night of the Destruction weaving into the heart, that the dream of the revival and rebuilding of the Land of our Fathers, that the driving force to immigrate, to fulfill oneself and the Kibbutz movement in the rebuild Land of Israel.

[Pages 560-561]

To My Mother
(Chaya-Bayla, may she rest in peace)
by M. Sh. Ben-Meir, of blessed memory
Translated by Gloria Berkenstat Freund

You are, Mama, over 80, gray and old,

And like an esrog [citron] after its time – your face is shrunken, dry,

And just like it – your golden quality is hidden,

Your back is bent in the yoke of Yidishkeit [the Jewish way of life].

The parchment hands are wrinkled, yellow and feeble,

Like your sacred, faithful holy book-brothers:

The prayers and the Tkhine in its sweet translation and meaning,

The Tsenerene and Korbn Minkhe prayer books*.

An old person's vision requires rest.

From too much prayer, and crying, too,

One must take care of her – the doctor warns –You could lose her,

God forbid, he says.

Do you not understand, you royfe [a doctor, usually without medical

training], you clever man,

You answered with a smiling face,

There is a brightness in the Korbn Minkhe,

And the Tkhine makes my eyes clearer.

The day is short and the prayer is long,

For me, for my son who does not carry the yoke of prayer,

And the heart has such regret for the Jewish people,

For Jewish calamity – heaven even cries.

No respect for all the good advice,

Did not listen to what the children ask, argue,

You have brought a korbn [sacrifice] to your Korbn Minkhe,

The light from both of your eyes.

And when the sad hour tore the bond,

Of your combined family,

My face touched your trembling hand,

Like Father Yitzhak's hand at Yakov's blessing.

Crying, you blessed me and told me to go,

Today we part – distant days and heavy storms,

Yet I hear your quiet crying in the night

And I always hear you calling my by my name.

I see you sitting alone silent and blind,

Hunched over the Siddur [prayer book] with a beaming face.

*Translator's Note: A *Tkhine* is a woman's book of Yiddish prayers; a *Tsenerene* is a Yiddish translation of the Torah and legends and commentaries; and a *Korbn Minkhe* is a woman's prayer book translated or written in Yiddish

Shoah and

Part III

Destruction and Perishing

[Pages 573-576 - Hebrew] [Pages 577-580 - Yiddish]

In Memoriam
by Fishl Yitzhaki
Translated by Gloria Berkenstat Freund

The picture of our *shtetl* [town; plural: *shtetlekh*], before the destruction, where we were born and spent the best years of our lives stands before my eyes as if alive. Every street, every house, garden, orchard, forest and the entire environs stands before me. I see the *shul* [synagogue] on the *shul* hill and the river beneath the hill. I remember the *yomim-tovim* [religious holidays], joyous days and also the sad moments through which I lived in Goniadz.

Goniadz was a *shtetl* like other *shtetlekh* in exile Poland, with communal activities and institutions, in which the whole of Jewish life in Poland was reflected. It was soaked in *Torah* and tradition, idealism and the love of Israel, like all the *shtetlekh*.

Goniadz was a pioneer *shtetl* in one respect – modern Hebrew education. The Hebrew full day school where all general and Jewish subjects were taught in Hebrew, was the first of its kind in Poland. Those who stood by its cradle put their entire youthful fervor and idealism into it. The entire pioneer and Zionist work of the *shtetl* grew from the school.

The *Tarbut* [*Tarbut* was a Zionist network of educational institutions such as schools and libraries] library stands before me with its wide circle of readers. The communal activities in connection with elections to the *Sejm* [lower house of Polish parliament], to the Zionist Congress and so on, were centered around it.

I am reminded of *Hahalutz* [organization training agricultural workers before emigration to *Ertez Yisroel*] and *Halutz-Hatzeir* [Zionist Youth Movement], which prepared a great number of pioneers for *Eretz-Yisroel*; the Jewish school that was supported by the so-called proletariat element; the stormy gatherings and meetings where the various ideologies that reigned in the Jewish neighborhood were discussed.

I also remember the two benches at the *gemiles-khesid* [interest free loan society] which supported the shop owners and artisans during difficult times, when the taxes were high and oppressive. I also cannot forget the community institutions, *lines hatzedek* [poorhouse] and *bikur-holim* [organization for visiting the sick], which often kept the needy alive.

There were Jews here with warm hearts, compassion, community workers, scholars, simple people and also paupers.

All, all, without exception or discrimination, perished in the great devastation of Polish Jewry. It is difficult to find expression for this great pain and calamity. We can only say that they will live in our memory for eternity.

May this *Yizkor* [memorial] book be a living *matzevah* [headstone] and an eternal memorial for them and for the beloved and cherished *shtetl* of our birth.

[Pages 581-582 - Yiddish] [Pages 581-582 - Hebrew]

Six Candles
by Asher Shtshutshinski
Translated from Yiddish to English by Martin Jacobs

For the souls of the six million slain of our people (may the Lord avenge their blood)

I light six candles --

and bitter tears roll

down my sorrowful face.

-- you will never be forgotten.

Six candles which burn darkly

darkening the world,

putting it to shame;

knead your tallow with our blood

and in the fire

– seek revenge!

[Pages 583-590]

Goniadz Under Soviet Rule
by Zeydl (son of Note Dwoshke) Altshuld
Translated by Gloria Berkenstat Freund

To the eternal memory of my dear parents, Note and Dwoshe Altshuld

The Germans occupied Goniadz on the first of September, 1939. Immediately upon their arrival in the *shtetl* [town], the German vandals looted Jewish possessions and made a ruin of our beautiful, historic synagogue which had adorned our *shtetl* with its particularly local architectural style and also its distinct solitary position – on the highest point in the entire area.

The Germans withdrew from Goniadz after several weeks as a result of the Molotov-Ribbentrop Pact and Goniadz was occupied by the Russians in the month of September 1939. At first, the life of the Goniadz Jewish population, which numbered more than 1,000 souls, was difficult. They could not accustom themselves to the new way of life that the Bolsheviks brought to the *shtetl.*

But a short time later, life became a little easier. A special "office" was founded whose purpose was to provide the population with the necessary products for living. The "office" began to bake bread for the population. Several government store cooperatives were opened – at which Jews were employed in most cases. Jews were also employed in various institutions and institutes that were founded in the *shtetl.* The Jews also took a major role in the city council.

The Jewish artisans – tailors, shoemakers, capmakers, and the like – proceeded with their work from which they fed their families, but with relative quiet and stillness. Thus, the life of the Goniadz Jewish population proceeded for nearly a year and 10 months – until Sunday, the 22nd of June, 1941.

The Change

That Sunday, in the middle of the night, the residents of Goniadz suddenly awoke from their sleep, hearing powerful bombs exploding. The news spread quickly that the Germans had suddenly started a war against the Russians. An indescribable fear fell upon the entire Jewish population in Goniadz. The Russian soldiers also ran around confused by the sudden change.

On Sunday night the Russian military regime issued an order that all citizens, former military members, must appear for military service immediately. A large number of young men obeyed this order; only a small number hid.

The Situation in Goniadz at the Withdrawal of the Russians

Goniadz, in the early morning at 2:30 on Sunday, the 22nd of June, 1941. There is a heavy knock at my window. I think I am dreaming... No, I really do hear knocking at my window mixed with a Russian curse word... "Wake up, you! (I am in the military.) Report immediately to the headquarters of the 10th battalion. Be ready in 10 minutes and report there to the military official on duty, *ponial*?! (Understood?) If not – a bullet in the head!" My good friend, Djodje Dlugolenski (who I lived with) was near me and said to me with a distressed voice that he had heard a tumult the entire night and then also shooting and heavy bomb explosions. He believed, he said, that these were exercises, but his face expressed astonishment and strong agitation. Meanwhile, I finished getting dressed and was ready to leave my room. My good friend, Djodje Dlugolenski accompanied me to the door and asked with tears in his eyes: "What happened?"... It was quiet, calm in the street; no sound was heard, the *shtetl* was asleep... But from time to time, bombs were heard exploding far, far away... At the old market, in Chaim Kobrinski's house, a weak light was seen and soldiers went in and out in great haste (military personal had lately been quartered there). Coming to Zalmen Bialostacki's house (where the headquarters of the 10th battalion air observation and liaison was located), it did not feel that something hung in the air. Calm, quiet, as usual... Starting as always with the entire row of houses, from Chaya Ruckl Luria to Kloip, the shutters and doors were closed, their residents calmly asleep, alas, not knowing what the morning would bring...

Arriving at the headquarters, I reported to the commander on duty, whose appearance expressed disquiet and anger. I immediately received an order to take an auto from the N.Z [unknown abbreviation]. (that is, the autos that were used only in extraordinary cases such as, for example, war or other special occurrences). I had already gone through military exercises twice with the battalion (so that I already knew everything from earlier). The autos stood in Berl Rudski's courtyard. Upon arrival there I tried to start the autos, one after the other, but, alas, without success. Each vehicle was missing another part. It appeared that the earlier drivers had taken out the parts for other automobiles and these were left standing... Then the door opened in Grodjenski's house and the woman, Chinke, came out. She looked at me in amazement that I was working here in the middle of the night. But she did not ask me anything because I was guarded by a Red Army member with a gun. Seeing that I could not do anything, I announced to the commander that the vehicles could in no case be readied for departure because they were missing necessary parts. The commander became very excited and cursed: "*Eto sabotazh, svolochi. Rasstrelyat vas.* (This is sabotage; we need to shoot you, outsiders, scoundrels!)." In spite of the cursing by the commander, the vehicles would not move from the spot... After long labor and searching, we were successful in borrowing a part from another military formation. The commander praised my initiative and ordered me to go to the observation points and take the soldiers stationed there away. The points were in various nearby villages around Goniadz. Leaving I saw a group of Jews in discussion standing at the market; they accompanied me with astonished looks, not asking what had happened. Perhaps they still only believed that these were exercises, as many of the members of the Red Army also believed. The roads were bombed and were full of holes several meters long and wide. I had to drive through the fields because it was impossible to travel on the highway. There were broken pieces of machine guns, dead horses, cows and also members of the Red Army, who asked for help. But no one was concerned about them; everyone ran farther... My vehicle rocked as a ship on a turbulent sea, making my way through fields and forests, arriving at various points and giving them the orders from the headquarters – Retreat! The Red Army quickly left their positions leaving all of their military equipment abandoned.

In the evening I came back to Goniadz. A dead silence reigned in the *shtetl*. The streets were dead. No lights were seen in the houses. Darkness around and around. I was controlled by anxiety; I wanted very much to be among friends and acquaintances. I asked my commander for permission to go see my acquaintance, but after 10 minutes I, alas, received an order to remain in the vehicle because conditions were unusual and moving from the spot would result in "shooting." Despite this I was successful in dropping in for several minutes to my good friends, to the family of Moshe Leizer Grajenski while my vehicle stood in Berl Rudski's courtyard. Knocking quietly, Moshe Leizer's wife opened the door to me. Her facial expression expressed fear and despair. The same was also noticeable on the faces of the remaining people in the house. Quietly she told me that her son, Gdalke, had also been mobilized by the Russian military and several others with him: Asher Szirtes [the teacher], Zeidl Khazan [Chenye Peshe's son], Ahrele Reznicka (Beilke the baker's son), Leibl Brumer (Yehoshua the tinsmith's son). I spent about 10 minutes with the Grajenski family and I left them with a grieving heart, feeling that I would never see them again. Upon leaving, I heard a sad, heartbreaking, quiet cry... I stopped near my vehicle. A dead silence reigned in the entire *shtetl*. From afar was heard something exploding, which became louder and louder – apparently the danger was getting closer... A great compassion awoke in my heart for the desolate Goniadz Jews who were now apparently sleeping calmly, not having any idea about the great misfortune that would appear in the morning... A strong desire awoke in me to be with friends and acquaintances, who were so close to me and so far... It began to get light. My commander gave me 15 minutes. My first visit was with my friend, Ida Rudski, in her residence on Kaszcalne Street in Ruwin the shoemaker's house. The shutters were closed. A soft rap and Ida opened the door for me with fear and dispiritedness. After speaking several words, she asked: "What will be? And what will happen to Zeidl?

– "I cannot give an answer to your questions, Ida," I answered. "But I would advise you to go to Suchowola, to your friend, Kohn, because you have no one here in Goniadz and you feel lonely." Her answer to my advice was a sharp sigh and a quiet, bitter cry... Wanting to encourage her a little, I said at taking my leave that during a bad time one must not lose their courage. And it could be possible that when I quickly visit her a second time, we will speak with joy of the past suffering. She smiled and said: "*Halevay* [God grant it]."

Going out into the street, I encountered the butcher, Leibl Tikocki, asking: "What will be, Zeidl?" Immediately, Zeidl Sidanski, Chava Furman, Moshe Feiwl Bialosukenski and several other Jews also approached and we began to speak "politics." I crept away and went to my friend, Yankl Mankowski, who was full of worry and grief. We parted with the blessing, "See you again in our homeland," and I went to visit the wife of my dear friend, Zelig Newodowski, who had to leave Goniadz during the time of Soviet rule because of his Zionist activity. His son, Leizer, a talented student in the Hebrew *gymnazie* [secondary school] in Bialystok, was also not at home at that time. Only the wife, Fanya Newodowski, and their small daughters were at home. Mrs. Newodowski greeted me with a cry, asking what should she do? She was alone. She did not know where Zelig was and she also had no news from her son... Her crying tore my heart in pieces. I tried to calm her, but it was impossible. With a broken heart, I said goodbye to her and her small daughters and I quickly ran to headquarters. Entering headquarters, I received an order to drive in the direction of Bialystok. I left my *shtetl*, Goniadz, on Monday, the 23rd of June 1941 at 10 o'clock in the morning.

I stopped at the market for a while where many very sincere friends and acquaintances were gathered to take leave of me. One, an old Jew, called after me aloud: The Lord bless and preserve thee on the path on which you go." Peace! In that time of danger, it seemed to me that I heard the words of the old Jew clear and distinct. My vehicle started to move slowly. A cry was heard... Tears also poured from my eyes without stop. Even the commander was moved by what was happening around us... We drove past the cemetery in the direction of the Monki railroad station. The gates of the cemetery were half open. A strong desire was awoken in me to enter the cemetery and say goodbye to my parents. But the commander said that when life is in danger, one should not take one step in that direction. But in the depth of my heart, I parted from my parents and from all of my friends and acquaintances...

Thus I left my birthplace, Goniadz, and with her, also the friends of my youth with whom I spent my past years. With a broken heart and with great sorrow and pain I parted with you, my dear ones, knowing that great, very great, was the danger that stood before you. And who knew if we would again see each other. But your memory will be engraved in my heart for eternity...

Munich, 8 Sivan 5716 (18.5.56)

[Pages 591-676]

The Destruction of Goniondz
By Tuviah Ivri (Yevraiski)
Translated by Gloria Berkenstat Freund

Dedicated to:

The memory of my unforgettable father, Heikl Yevreiski. Thanks to whom my brother and sister and I lived through the Hitlerist horrors. He became very sick as a result of the frightful events and died in the Bialystok hospital on the 22nd of Shevat 5705 (the 5th of February 1945), already having been freed.

The memory of my unforgettable mother Chana Yevreiski (née Khtiva), who sacrificed throughout her life for her children and who was torn away from us forever, lonely and forlorn, on the 2nd of November 1942, during the liquidation of Goniadz Jewry,

Honor their memory!

Chana Yevreiski   **Heikl Yevreiski**

First Chapter

The frightening warning from the Hitlerist barbarian-like attack on Russia came to our attention in Goniadz immediately during the morning hours of Sunday the 22nd of June 1941. Chaos and panic engulfed the shtetl [town]: the Red Army ran around disorganized, young people prepared their bicycles to escape in the direction of Russia, wagon drivers drove out to the villages with their families and possessions. The wives and children of the Soviet command were evacuated to Russia on trucks. The lines at the cooperatives [government owned businesses] were long and wide. The population of the shtetl was confused and nervous... Others packed their possession and were ready to leave the shtetl.

German bomber squadrons circled all day and from time to time explosions of bombs being dropped were heard in the distance. The bombers mainly were concentrated over the Osowiec fortress, aiming one by one for the Bober bridge that connected the two forts with the third. Several bombers flying over Goniadz flew low and with their machine guns shot groups of people.

Sunday night the Goniadz city council issued an order for a heavy mobilization of all citizens who had completed military service. Most of those mentioned above departed with the Russian army; only a small number, seeing the great panic that reigned over the army, took a risk and did not leave.

On Monday, the 23rd of June, the German artillery shells exploded near the river; the shooting increased and the population began to leave the shtetl: one on a wagon that he was able to hire from a village Christian, one with a pack on his back, one with a smaller pack in his hand and one without anything on a bicycle. We ran and we went to the surrounding villages and colonies to hide from the shooting.

All of Goniadz was surrounded by members of the Red Army who lay hidden in the wheat fields in great heat, baking in the sun and asking the civilians escaping from the shtetl for a drink of water... Alas, no one had water; if someone was carrying a jug in his hand, it contained kerosene or oil.

The shooting in the shtetl increased at night. There was reciprocal shooting with machine guns. The Jews in the colonies and villages considered themselves fortunate that they had left the shtetl in time and were beyond the shooting.

The shooting stopped on Tuesday. The members of the Red Army began to withdraw from the shtetl. The Poles, seeing this situation, started to come from the surrounding area to the shtetl, half naked and barefoot – to loot. They dragged civilian and military clothing, shoes, textiles, food, sacks of sugar, flour and the like from the cooperative. The artillery shells that fell in the shtetl and exploded near them did not frighten them. They ran around back and forth ceaselessly like hungry wolves after prey. Finally, a small group from the Red Army went through the shtetl and, seeing the looting, opened fire at a group of looters. Several fell dead from the bullets and the majority succeeded in escaping with the stolen packs in their hands.

The shtetl looked as if it were after a pogrom. The doors and windows were broken, masses of various goods lay scattered around near the cooperative.

Clouds of smoke could be seen around the shtetl... The German artillery fire continued. The Osowiec Fortress burned.

The same situation persisted on Wednesday. At night the Red Army began to completely withdraw from the area. The withdrawal lasted the entire night and Thursday morning. Feeling that it had grown quieter in the shtetl and that the Red Army had withdrawn, little by little the Jews began to return home so that the Poles would not drag and rob everything that they had left in their homes.

A meeting at the Goniadz market on the day of Poland's liberation, November 11th, 1935

2nd Chapter

The Polish population "cleaned up" everything that was left in the former Soviet cooperative. They grabbed the doors and windows from the other Jewish residences where Poles had not appeared quickly to drag out the furniture and take it to the village... In a word: they made good use of the time of the Jews' absence. They became joyous and jubilant: "Thanks to God! We are finally rid of the Jewish communists, the Bolsheviks." In that mood and with those words, they accompanied the Jews who returned to Goniadz. Powerlessness and loss hung in the air in the shtetl. The Germans were expected at any hour.

A rumor started on Thursday the 26th of June that German motorcyclists had appeared in the courtyard of the priest. The dressed-up strolling Poles suddenly started to go to the priest en masse. The Jews all sat confined to their houses.

Not having time to pack, cook something to eat, they looked out of their windows with frightened expressions [on their faces] to see if they could see the Germans. Suddenly a German soldier on a motorcycle appeared in the street. All of the Poles, young and old, ran with all of their strength to be near him. It was only a few minutes and it already was dark with Poles around him. Two dressed up Polish girls, daughters of the old letter-carrier Soboski, carried bouquets of flower to him. All of those standing around him lifted the German in the air accompanied by great shouting: "May our liberator, Hitler, live!" "Down with the communists!" "Death to Stalin!" Right after, the majority of the young people went with hatchets and crowbars in their hands to the town's market where a Red Army stage stood. All of the holiday parades would be welcomed from it. The Poles tore it to pieces, then poured kerosene over it and set it on fire. Joy reigned among them: "May the memory of Bolshevism be burned!" The crowd grew larger and larger and there was laughter, ironic shouts and finally singing...

3rd Chapter

The Polish population immediately began to worry about creating a regime in the shtetl so that "anarchy and looting would not reign." A meeting was called in the former city hall that was located at the old market.

The Polish intelligentsia and leaders of the shtetl came to the meeting. A city council was elected at the head of which stood Jan Balonowski as mayor and Kempa as secretary.

Muca (Potocki Adas) was nominated as the police chief and he immediately built the city police out of a few dozen voluntary gangsters. They immediately put a white armband with a black swastika on their left arm and began their work... Dozens of policemen walked through the streets with white ribbons on their arms and clubs in their hands. The young Poles filled the streets and alleys and the

Jews sat in their houses in fear and dread and were afraid to stick their heads out of the windows. Rarely a Jew sneaked into a back alley and made his way to a village or to Guzy [a Goniadz suburb] to a Christian acquaintance for a piece of bread or a sack of potatoes for his hungry family. No Jews appeared at the market in the shtetl. Thursday also passed quietly.

Friday morning a large number of German soldiers marching through in the direction of Grodno, that is to the front, appeared at the market of the shtetl. The Poles separately stood around each soldier who was resting in the middle of the street from his long march. They carried water to them, polished their bicycles and pumped air into the tires. In a word: they made certain that, God forbid, no harm would come to them: they should be able to fight against the Bolsheviks. The German army march through [Goniadz] lasted without stop until Shabbos [Sabbath] afternoon.

It again became quiet in the shtetl. The regime again was in the hands of the Poles. They governed the shtetl.

As a considerable number of days had passed and the Poles had not seen any Zhidkes [derogatory Polish word for Jews], they wished to have a "meeting" with several Jews that day – in honor of Shabbos.

Entrance to the Goniadz market through Tiple Street

There was an order from the Goniadz city council to the police: bring several Jews who are considered to be communists to the city hall. They were severely beaten at the city hall and told to go home. In the morning of Sunday the 29th of

June 1941 the situation looked very different. The local "regime" sent out all of the policemen to bring a sizeable number of Jews to city hall using a provided list.

The policemen left lightning fast for the Jewish houses, courtyards and alleys and dragged the demanded Jews to city hall. These [Jews] were supposed to be communists and Soviet activists: Elihu's son Yankl (the old sexton of the house of prayer), Betsalel's son Leibl, Avrahamke the glazier with the grey beard, Henye the cantor, and others.

They gathered together about 30 such "communists" in the premises of the city hall. The police tortured them terribly and murderously beat them. After, they were all told to go home, except for several who were detained. The young people could somehow walk, but the old, bearded Jews had to walk with help from those closest to them who held them under their arms. Several of them were ill for a long time from the wounds from the terrible blows that they had received over their entire body. After the "little bit of work" the city council informed the Jewish population of the following:

"Every Jew must come three times a day to report to the city hall; they are threatened otherwise with a bullet in the head." Relief was provided for the heavily wounded: they could be represented [at city hall] by a close relative. In addition to this, it was ordered among other things that every Jew was obligated to go every day to forced labor. The concern and fear among the Jewish population began to grow even more and more. Several Jews tried to escape to a nearby shtetl where they were not known, others to the Bialystok ghetto although making one's way there also was perilous, and others, most often artisans, to the villages [to stay with] peasants.

Groups of young people went to work every day: to build highways, to clear ruins and to break stones under the supervision of Polish policemen with whips in their hands that they would often "stroll" over the Jewish heads.

This situation lasted for several days until the sorrowful "black Friday" (3 July 1941).

4th Chapter

On Thursday the Polish managing committee in Goniadz issued the following notice: "All Jews who are in the villages must immediately return to the city. If a peasant is found with a Jew, the peasant and the Jews will both be shot."

The order threw great fear into the peasants in the surrounding villages. They drove all of the Jews who were with them back to the city. Friday, on the morning of the 3rd of July, during the morning check of the Jews, the officials from the city council ordered: "Ten o'clock in the morning all of the Jews must go into the street, at the market of the shtetl.

The order immediately spread among the Jewish population and they began assembling in the street at a quarter to 10.

No one knew the purpose of this. Other Poles calmed the masses and said the German officer who had come with his accompaniment in two Mercedes automobiles wanted to give a speech to the Jews. A few people believed this and others said: "Alas, what kind of interest in us could the German officer have that he would want to give speeches to us?" Not a half an hour passed and all of the Jews already were gathered on the street. Whoever did not come of their own will were dragged by force by the police. A search for the Jews began through all of the Jewish houses, courtyards, places of employment, attics and the like. Men, women, every member of the Polish population went to each corner, to each small shop to search for Jews. When small, gentile boys noticed a Jewish child somewhere, they immediately ran to let the police know about it and the Jewish [child] was dragged to the crowd standing at the marketplace while being beaten along the way.

After 10 o'clock several German officers suddenly were seen leaving Zaboszcziche's restaurant near where the Mercedes automobiles stood.

Their first order to the Jews standing in the crowd was: "The Jewish women should isolate themselves from the men and stand on the side."

When the command was carried out immediately, the oldest officer ordered: "All of the men should stand in two rows, one behind the other." When two rows of men formed opposite him he told the barbers to leave [the rows].

Both Goniadz barbers responded immediately. The officer told them to cut off the beards of all of the old Jews as they stood in their places in the row and the long hairdos of the young ones. The barbers began to do the ordered work lightning fast.

A large crowd of Poles stood in groups prepared with clubs and whips in their hands opposite the two rows of Jews and dissolved in joy watching the Jews placed in the rows. The Gestapo officer then gave the Poles the following order: "Choose all of the communists and members of the Komsomol [All-Union Leninist Young Communist League] in the two rows and place them in a separate row." At these words, Kempa, the vice mayor and secretary of the city council, called out:

"Why do we have to choose; all Jews are communists; one is not better than another. They all [without exception] need to be driven into the river and drowned." He ended with a shout: "There is no way to choose."

The eyes of the entire Polish gang with the clubs in their hands turned to the Gestapo officer and waited for an answer. However, seeing that he did not change his order at Kempa's intervention, they began their "work."

The entire crowd of Poles attacked the assembled Jews and began to drag "members of the Komsomol." They had the best opportunity here to make use of their private and general anger at the Jews because every Pole was dependable. He had a personal hatred of whichever Jew; he went over to him and pulled him to the row of "members of the Komsomol and communists." [They were] murderously beaten by the German Gestapo officers while going the short distance to the new row. They let out their great anger at the newly arriving Jews whom the police had pulled out of hiding and brought at that moment to the [market] place. Clubs flew over their heads from all sides and the shouts and moaning from the unfortunate ones echoed through the marketplace. The Jews were shocked to see such a terrible picture.

The entreaties of the Jews to the Poles that they not bring them to the bad rows were heartrending. One could hear a young Jewish man ask a Christian: "Tell me, why are you dragging me? Did I ever do anything bad to you?" "Come psa krew" [bloody dog] The Pole answered: "YOU once did not let me pass through a gate in Ostowiec." "Where, when?" – the Jew asked in tears, "I never stood near a gate. How can you say that about me?" The Pole shouted, "Come! Do not ask why, psa krew!" and dragged him out of the row by his lapels and pushed him in the direction of the "bad" row. The young Jewish man was accompanied on his way by blows from other Poles and from the Gestapo officers. Beaten, bloodied, he was finally placed in the "communist" row. The distance between the rows was more and more moistened with Jewish blood that the murderers spilled separately leading each on through.

The selection ended in the course of two hours. In front of the entire gang stood two sections of Jews placed in rows. To the Gestapo officer's question to Mayor Balonowski's – who are the communists? – Balonowski answered: "All of the Jews are communists. Only these (pointing to those remaining) are unofficial. And these (pointing to those selected) – are official communists." Then the Gestapo officer said: "Send the unofficial communists to work and you can do what you want with the official communists." After this he immediately sat in the Mercedes automobiles with the remaining officers and left the shtetl.

The Poles also went to "work" – The "unofficial communists" were driven to work on the highway under the supervision of many young, healthy Poles with clubs and whips in their hands. When life on the street became freer, the crowd of Poles became enraged and attacked the Jewish women standing in a line, gave them photographs of prominent men: Lenin, Stalin and the like, and asked them to hold the photographs with their heads to the ground, march through the streets and sing Soviet songs. The Poles laughed with great joy. They had rarely had such great satisfaction and such a happy day in their lives. Finally they began with the row of "communists and members of Komsomol," which numbered around 200 men. After a short conversation among the "prominent men" of the shtetl, a large gang with clubs in their hands left for the smaller Beis-Medrash [House of Prayer] Street. There they stood in two lines on both sides of the alley.

The unfortunate Jews in the line, tortured and beaten, with eyes full of tears, were taken to the Beis-Medrash. Entering the Beis-Medrash Street according to the order of police chief Muca (Potocki Adam): "Bić Żydów! [Beat the Jews]. The gang of murderers attacked the Jews over their heads, shoulders, hands and feet, wherever it was possible, and beat them murderously with clubs and whips.

The Jews, seeing what was happening, began to run with their last strength to wherever their feet carried them. A significant number succeeded in escaping. However, there were more seizing them than those running away. Therefore, the majority of those escaping were brought back as they beat them on the way. Everyone who ran to the left over the hill to the old market or to the sawmill near the river was brought back by the murderers. A significant number of those who ran to the right to the house of prayer, that is to Dolistower Street and to the boyna [slaughterhouse for cattle], succeeded in disappearing. The Poles gathered the majority of those in the lines and drove them to the house of prayer. Many agile gentile boys immediately brought bales of straw to set fire to the house of prayer along with the Jews, as was the plan. However, here several Christian neighbors immediately ran to the mayor and his representative and pleaded for mercy that the house of prayer not be set on fire because their house could be consumed by the fire. The plea was taken into consideration and the plan was changed; the Jews were driven back from the house of prayer and arranged in the courtyard, each of them with their hands tied with wire behind them and simultaneously bound one to the other by their arms in groups of three. All of the bound groups of three were placed behind the other in a line. Then Kaminski the carpenter lifted his club in the air and gave the command; they should lead them back to the marketplace. The rows began to move... Half dead people, bound with downcast heads, inexpressive eyes, open wounds, blood flowing, ripped clothing and unsteady feet, dragged themselves through the Goniadz market. A quiet lamentation, particularly from the older Jews, tore from their hearts.

The older ones lifted their heads, seeking the Jewish God and reciting the vide [confession recited before death and on Yom Kippur]. The young ones turned their heads in all directions, looking at beautiful, blooming nature for the last time and parting with it for eternity.

Loud shouts and cynical laughter from the blood-thirsty louts [standing] around the line and satisfying their bestial instinct then and quieting their thirst for Jewish blood accompanied the unfortunate Jews on their way to their slaughter – in Motke Kliap's cellar. They were shut in there and the doors were locked. Many of the voluntary "accompaniers" offered to stay on guard around the cellar so that, God forbid, no one escaped...

5th Chapter

The Jewish women were told to go to their houses after they had taken part in the ordered "demonstration "in honor" of the Soviet government.

The men who were taken to forced labor were brought back to the shtetl on Friday night and forced into a previously prepared barn at the corner of Dolistower Street. The doors of the barn were nailed shut and the police guard and volunteer guards all armed with clubs in their hands stood watch around the barn.

The rear part of Motke Kliap's brick house
From the left, underneath in the foundation, the window of the cellar where the Jews were held until being murdered. Dr. Szer is accompanied by the commandant of the shtetl during his visit to Goniadz [1956].

The lack of space and heat inside was indescribable. Only those who had entered first could lie half-sitting on the dusty, sandy ground and make a "bed" for themselves. The majority had to stand, one family member holding on to another or to a wall. The suffocating heat led to several weak, old Jews fainting and there was no water with which to revive them. Great fear gripped everyone when night came. They heard more and more Poles assembling outside. At times several of them wanted to frighten the Jews by throwing stones at the doors of the barn. Each blow of a stone was accompanied with great laughter...

Their hearts were all full... They were tired, broken spiritually and physically. It was very rare to hear someone speak.

A little later a conversation among the Jews began to develop about their fate. The majority said that today they would surely ignite the barn with the Jews [inside], because nailing the door shut and the influx of many Poles pointed to this. "They will now fulfill their wish," one called out. "What they were incapable of doing during the day in the house of prayer they would do." The despondent conversations extended more and more deeply into the night until snoring by several people was heard. This had a very bad effect on the nerves as an accompaniment to the terrible mood that held sway over everyone.

Suddenly in the stillness of the night three rifle shots were heard in the distance that surprised everyone who was awake. Their hearts began to beat strongly and the fear grew from minute to minute. A voice was heard from a corner: "Who knows which three Jews were just shot?" A second voice called out: "Will we enjoy such an easy death?" The blow of a stone on the door interrupted the conversation and they listened to the noises outside with perked up ears.

The night passed peacefully. Gray rays of light sneaked in through the cracks and revealed that morning was coming. Everyone stood up on their feet and waited for something. What – no one knew; their eyes now turned to the door. They heard the nails in the doors being torn out outside. The guards opened the locks and opened wide the doors.

There was a new feeling among all of them. They began to have conversations among themselves. A happy look appeared on many faces. Women with pots of food nearing the barn and asking the guards to give them to their husbands and children was observed from afar. The guards fulfilled their requests. Little by little women from all corners of the shtetl began to come with baskets of food in their hands for their family members who were languishing in jail.

Several Christians appeared near the barn in the afternoon demanding Jews to work for them. A stampede of Jews began near the Christians. Everyone wanted to work in the open to wrest themselves from the crowded, dark barn. However the Christians only took their old Jewish acquaintances or the men and children whose families had paid for this well in advance. Little by little, more Jews left for work until the remaining remnant was taken for highway construction. The imprisoned Jews again breathed freer air and several of the older ones among them had gebentsht goyml [a prayer recited after escaping from great danger], taking out a small prayer book from a pocket. They worked vigorously. The fear of receiving blows drove the momentum because if a Jew did not appear thankful for his work, one of the Polish foremen immediately hit him across his shoulders with his [the foreman's] club.

Little by little the hour for lunch neared. The women with the baskets of food and with...yellow patches on their chests began to appear. A shudder of horror went through everyone when they saw the yellow patches on Jewish hearts. The yellow patch is so much the frightening sign of shame. "Yes!" said one of the Jews. "The world has regressed back to 600 years ago." A great sigh and regretful look from hundreds of Jews welcomed their wives and daughters who had brought them food.

Everyone turned to the women with the question: "What has happened to those imprisoned in Motke Kliap's cellar?" The answer was: "They are still there. Three of them had been removed the night before and taken away somewhere (This was: Shimeon Jewrajski, Alter Michnowski and Meylakh Feldman). What had happened to them was unknown... Many women had turned to Adam Potocki (Muche), Balonowski, Kempa and to the remaining bandits; they brought them much gold and dollars to free their men and children. We could not approach the priest, who called all of the shots. There were expectations that others would free them. In addition, they [the Jews] had to have treasures; the bandits had received great control... They could only provide food for those in the cellar through the small and only window. Their cries and entreaties – to be saved – were heart- rending. "The fire is great!" [translators note: an indication that this was a very dangerous time for the Jews] another woman called, "They [the Jews] are running around as if crazy; they are carrying possessions to the bandits and they celebrate that there is something to give."

Everyone remained at a loss for words, with pale faces and sighing to themselves. Others, who had children in the cellar, wringed their hands and cried in grief. A louder shout, "Do roboti!!"[to work] interrupted the conversations and all of the men, many already with yellow patches on their chests, took their shovels in their hands and continued their work, but this time without as much energy and desire as earlier.

Night came and the foreman gave a shout: "Fajrant!" [Quitting time] – the well-known announcement that work was ending. They lay down their tools in one place and, tired, broken physically and spiritually, the Jews marched as one under the whips of their torturers into the large stall.

6th Chapter

The barn containing the imprisoned Jews was at the disposal of every Pole, let alone to every German soldier, who would come to the shtetl, seeking people for work. The majority of them were taken away for work on Sunday, too, right in the morning. A smaller number also were employed by German soldiers, mostly with serving them. The mood in the shtetl became one of devastation: when bringing the breakfast to the "men in cellar" they learned that 11 men had been taken out of the cellar on Shabbos. They were placed in pairs with their hands shackled one to another and taken somewhere. The wives of those taken away immediately began to have spasms and cry loudly when they heard the "news." The policemen who guarded the cellar told them to go right home. When other women did not do so immediately they were beaten so badly they barely could reach home. Many women ran straight to Polish acquaintances in their houses to ask what had happened to the 11 Jews in the cellar. The answer was – "They all had been sent to work; they are all alive." A number of the women were calmed by the answer, but many of them did not want to believe it!

The stampede by the women to the Polish activists, to Balonowski and Kempa, became larger and larger. The wealthier women brought them all of the possessions as the price of freeing their family member from the cellar.

Several Jews were freed from the cellar and brought to the barn on Sunday. They were welcomed there with warm kisses and greetings, just as if they had come from the other world.

Meanwhile, there was a new tumult in the shtetl. The Poles provided the following rumor: armed Jews were hiding among the stalks in the wheat fields around Goniadz and today had shot a Polish girl as she worked in the fields. There was a hunt for the "Jewish murderers." The Jewish women were afraid to appear even in the back-streets. The men were suddenly taken away from their work and brought back to the barn. The policemen went from house to house and gathered small children of 14 years of age who had been free until this day. Everyone was dragged into the barn. The Jews understood that this was linked to great suffering.

Kempa appeared at the barn at night. He announced the following to the Jews: "Today the Jews shot at a Polish girl who was working in the fields. She was wounded in the hand. So far we have not been able to find the murderers. If you yourselves do not give up the murderers, the barn will be burned along with all of you...

He left the barn after giving this order and everyone around began quickly to nail the door shut. A shudder went through all of the Jews. They remained as if frozen. No one could say a word. Many fell down with bitter tears. Others kissed their family members and one said: "They searched for and found a nice blood libel against us; tonight we will burn." The rabbi began to recite Psalms and the Jews followed him. The desperation was great and very few closed their eyes in the nightmare-filled night.

7th Chapter

The night passed quietly. Early in the morning the women brought the following news when they brought breakfast: five young men – Hershl and Yehezkiel Kliap, Yisroel Lewin, Betsalel Zimnach and Zalman Niewodowski – had returned home on foot from Bialystok. Nearing the shtetl, they met a gentile boy with whom they were well acquainted, Alfons Dolinski. The young men asked him if it was quiet in the shtetl and if they could enter it. He answered them: "I will ride to the shtetl on my bicycle and look over the situation and return immediately to let you know. But until I return I would advise you to lie in the cornstalks so that a bad person will not notice you." The young men obeyed their "good friend." Not an hour passed when six policemen and the same young gentile appeared before them in the cornstalks. They dragged the young men out and told them to go with them to the shtetl. The policemen led them to the premises of the German command. Three policemen signed their names to "something." Then they were accompanied by two German soldiers, took the five Jews to the cemetery. There they were told to dig their own graves and then they were shot.

The news made a frightful impression on those listening. Many could not eat their breakfast. Others cried terribly.

The breakfast hour ended. Little by little everyone with his group and its guard began to go to work. On Monday a considerable number of the Jews ransomed from the cellar joined those in the barn.

Monday night the bandits again wanted to hunt for the Zydkes [Jews]. A band of Poles burst in; the greater number of [the band] in the barn were policemen and they began choosing again. They looked for fresh candidates for the cellar because the number there had decreased. Heart-rending scenes took place when children were torn from fathers, brothers from each other. The entreaties and crying did not help. One motion with his hand by a bandit to a young Jewish man decided whether he would live or die. A group of young people was brought together that immediately was taken to the cellar.

This photograph was taken when the Germans led a group of Jews who were praying
Sent by Dr. Szar during his visit to Goniadz in 1956.)

From right to left

First row, standing: 1. Leyzer the blacksmith (Todorowicz), 2._?, 3. the cantor Centure, 4. Yosl Wercilinski, 5. Hilke Biali, 6. Yosef Sztrikdrajer (son of the rope-maker), 7. Yehoshua Cwiklicz and wife.

Second row, sitting: 1. Motele Leibczuk's [son], (Malozowski), 2. Shmul Ber Malozowski, 3. Itshe Biali, 4. Yosl Szajmele's [son] (Tikocki), 5._?, 6. Moshe-Mendl Blum, 7. Alter Garber.

Third row sitting on ground: 1.___?, Yerakhmial Guzowski, 3.___?, 4. Sztrikdrajer (the mother), 5. Moshe-Mendl's daughter, 6. Chaya Biali (Itshe Biali's wife).

On Monday and Tuesday there again was success in ransoming Jews from the cellar, until 17 men remained there. During Tuesday night (15 July 1941) they disappeared without a trace in the same manner as the previous 11 men.

The Jews were held in a barn for another week until Balonowski came and announced the following: "All Jews are now freed from the barn. Everyone can go to his residence, but everyone is obligated to go to work every day, wherever they are sent by the German representatives. He immediately designated three of the formerly rich merchants as Jewish representatives to the Polish city council. These were: Hirsh Finkewicz, Asher Kobrinski and Shmuel Lipsztajn.

Those listening accepted the news with great joy and surprise and everyone quickly went home.

8th Chapter

The question of creating a ghetto became timely immediately after the liberation from the barn. All of the commissions accompanied by the city council members strolled around through all of the streets, alleys and courtyards of the shtetl looking for a suitable place for a ghetto. It was decided to create the ghetto at the old marketplace after long quarrels at the city council among the various commissions. The decision was accepted. The plan for driving the Jews into a ghetto was worked out by the German members of the Gestapo who were supposed to come down from Bialystok for this purpose. The official announcement to the Jews was supposed to be given suddenly and the move was not to last more than a half hour so that the Jews would not be able to take their possessions from their houses and would take along only small packs in their hands under the whips of the Gestapo and the Polish hooligans. The news unofficially reached the Jewish representatives who had formed the so-called Judenrat [Jewish council] (through Polish acquaintances). These [the Judenrat members] did not want to cause an uproar and panic among the population that could disrupt the negotiations with the city leaders about abrogating the decision, it should be understood with the payment of money. Therefore, the Judenrat members entrusted the secret only to their close friends. They told the population
– "They are preparing to create a ghetto and enclose all of the Jews in the ghetto. We need giant sums of money in order to pay a bribe." The Judenrat also sent wagons across the shtetl for the women (it was not "healthy" for the men to hang around) to gather money and gold. Hearing the announcement, very few refused to give. The wealthier ones gave gold coins and gold watches. The poor – jewelry, rings, chains – that they had received as an inheritance from grandfathers and great grandfathers. Poor women gave their wedding rings – everyone gave whatever was possible. They collected 750 grams of gold. As the Judenrat members said, a certain sum was immediately given away. To whom and how much – this was a secret because the city leaders had strongly warned against this. Naturally it was thus that the mayor, Balonowski, his representative, Kempa and the police commandant Muca Potocki received the largest portion.

On the 20th of July, pairs of women again went to the wealthier Jews for more money. "A fire again is burning," they said, and this already was enough to get what they wanted. The foreign currency that the "swindlers" with the gang would take was American dollars. They also ripped [money] from the dead and from the living. Whoever did not have any dollars but did have other valuable things was forced to give them to someone else as a pledge [collateral] for a few dollars for the assessment. The fire was so great – the fund needed to be collected in a few hours...

Later, a rumor appeared at the noon hour that the military headquarters was leaving the shtetl and the population again remained without a government. Everyone was filled with fear at hearing the news. A Pole would again be the leader and judge! Anger and fear of the arbitrary regime that would again begin to rule the shtetl spilled from everyone's face.

Other Jews did not believe the spreading news at first, but when the residents at the market saw through half closed windows how the headquarters was being packed onto military trucks, there was no longer any doubt that it was true...

Night arrived. The gloom among the Jews became greater with the arrival of the commandant. On the other hand, the Poles became lively. Crowds full of young Poles and families with children strolled through the sidewalks of the market with happy faces. Their laughter penetrated into the Jewish houses and was like bullets in the hearts of the Jews who sat there in fear and dread. At times a stone or a stick banged against the closed Jewish doors and shutters. In several Christian houses they became intoxicated with the two barrels of whiskey that had been found buried in Rudski's cellar. The screams and singing of the drunk resounded throughout the market in the shtetl. Evening arrived. The tumult lessened from time to time and it became completely quiet later in the night. The Jews then became a little calmer and they went to sleep.

Suddenly a shout from of a woman's voice was heard around one o'clock at night: "Fire!!!... It's burning!!!... Save [me]!!!" We woke up in our house and everyone ran to take a look in the direction of the market through the closed shutters. My mother said: "There is nothing to see; only a tumult can be heard in the distance." My father and I ran up to the attic to look at the street through an opening in the roof. And thus I saw before my eyes a light summer night. Bands of young, gentile men armed with clubs in their hands walking around through the market of the shtetl. A significant number of them were concentrated near Sonia Luria, the midwife, and the rest left for the old market.

A wagon stood near Chaya-Ruchl Luria's brick building on which sat several Jews. From time to time more Jews were brought and they were thrown into the wagon. Afterwards several Poles were carrying badly wounded or dead bodies that they slid onto the wagons – just like slaughtered cattle. From time to time we heard quiet moaning from dying Jews. When about approximately eight people were on the wagon (in addition to the dead that lay at their feet), the wagon began to move from its spot. It was accompanied by about 10 hooligans and traveled in the direction of Tifle Street. Heart-rending screams of men and women were heard at that moment. But they suddenly became quiet. The hooligans beat them murderously over their heads with the clubs, probably as punishment for the screams. We also saw that the hooligans, about 10 men behind the wagon, were leading several Jewish souls and beating them with their clubs from time to time.

The wagon entered Tifle Street and disappeared from sight. Bands of Poles with clubs in their hands filled the market of the shtetl even more. A number of them went to the old market. Suddenly a shout was heard: "Zlapiacie!!!... Trzymajcie go!!!..." [Catch him! Hold him!] and we immediately saw a man run from the old market lightning fast and several hooligans ran after him at a distance of 15 meters. Several of the strolling bandits at a second corner of the market shouted loudly and ran to catch the Jew. Seeing his situation, the unfortunate one ran to Hershl Khine's brick building with his last strength and knocked on the door of the Pole Woronecki, pleading with him for mercy, that he should open the door and let him in his residence. However, the door did not open. Meanwhile, the bandits caught him. It appeared from afar that they were tying him up and he remained lying on the ground. He was beaten murderously without end. I only wondered at his silence during such a long period of torture. Mostly one murderer, who was the last to remain near him really "excelled," after all of those remaining left him alone. Finally he also left him and went further into the old market to his earlier "work."

The tortured bodies lay drawn out near Woronecki's small bridge and died out like a light.

The traffic did not lessen. Hordes of young and old Poles carried packs with looted Jewish property on their shoulders and in their hands. Finally they were seen carrying kitchen utensils and pails. Suddenly two bandits stopped near Nisen the butcher's house (our neighbor to the right) and knocked with strength on the door, shouting in Polish: "Open it quickly!" A woman's voice was heard: "Immediately! We are coming!" However, the knocking did not stop, but strengthened. The door opened and both bandits entered the residence. Five minutes did not pass and the bandits left. They walked in the direction of the old market where they disappeared. They were there for a short time and returned, accompanied by about 20 bandits with clubs in their hands. They marched from the old market straight to Nisen the butcher's residence.

Around 10 men remained standing, hidden behind the front wall and the rest went inside. Through the opening of the gable that was located five meters from the tragic place, we saw the bandits light matches, candles and go around with the homeowners, looking in every corner and crevice. They asked the owners to open the oven door; it was thoroughly searched, too. In the end, everyone was told to go out. Whoever did not move fast enough received a sharp blow from a club so that he ran in pain on all fours. Finally the entire family left: Nisen the old butcher with both of his daughters, their husbands and small children who numbered in total 10 people. They were all placed in the alley. One of the bandits immediately began to beat Nisen's son-in-law. A second bandit, a "better" one, told him: "Do not hit him so hard! Leave him alone!" When all 10 were outside they told them to walk... Quiet crying was heard. Nisen's daughter held the small hand of her three-year old daughter in one hand and she carried her two-year old little girl with her other hand. The family left the alley and walked along the market.

The bandits who were hidden outside the front wall watched and immediately entered the residence where they robbed everything from the bedding, the furniture to the kitchen dishes. Suddenly a terrible, heart-rending shout from the distant, unfortunate Jewish family.

Mostly, the despairing shouts of the women were heard, but their voices suddenly were silent.

Looking at the market of the shtetl that stood in the grayness of the morning I saw several bandits who were still moving around hurriedly with the clubs. Among them I recognized the well-known bandit, Kuc Branek, both Czajkowskis (brothers) and the Kaminski brothers. The bandits entered Tifle Street where they also had taken Nisen the butcher's family. It already was very light in the street, but we saw no living souls. It appeared that all those taking part had gone with the Jews who had been taken outside the city to finish the "work" that they had begun at night.

The sun rose normally as every day and sent its golden rays to the Goniadz market. The birds flew opposite it with song... At the same time, the bandits did their sinister "work"...

9th Chapter

Early on Monday, the 21st of July 1941, the following information about the terrible Sunday night was provided by an eyewitness.

Twenty victims fell: Sonia Luria, the midwife, Wolf Rajgrodski's entire family – five people, Yosef Kobrinski, and Nisen the butcher's entire family – 10 people. The first "visit" by the bandits was to the midwife. The bandit Olszewski murderously beat her over her head with an iron bar until she fell dead. Her husband tried to escape through the window. Noyza, her daughter, was beaten murderously by Olszewski. She fell on the ground in a faint and gave the impression that she was dead. Therefore, the bandits went to their further "work." Meanwhile, Noyza came to and escaped through the back window into the courtyard to a hiding place. The bandits, returning in a much greater number to take the dead bodies, found only one instead of two. All of their searches brought no results. Therefore, the bandits, alas, had to be satisfied with only one murder victim. The dead body was carried outside and thrown on the previously prepared wagon that stood not far from the residence. Further outrage happened to the

Biali family. A large band of murderers led by Bronek Kuc and the Czajkowskis went there. They knocked on the door that it should be opened.

When Mrs. Biali heard the knocks she immediately told her husband (Hilel [the diminutive is Hilke]) and her oldest son to hide in a hidden room, sure that they would not do anything to women and children. Her husband and son did so and Mrs. Biali and her 10-year old son, Yosef, remained lying in bed. However, when the knocking became stronger, Yosef Kobrinski, who lived in the garret, awoke from his sleep and boldly went to open the door. As soon as he opened the door, he received a club over his head. Despite this he oriented himself, ran through the band and escaped. Four bandits started after him and after a long chase through the courtyards and alleys, Kobrinski ran to his good Christian acquaintance, Waronecki, and asked him for mercy and to let him in. However, the Christian did not open the door for him and he met his terrible death there. As described by the Christian, they bound his hands behind him with telephone wire. They stuffed rags into his mouth and murdered him with clubs.

Meanwhile, the majority of the band entered Biali's house and dragged the woman, Miriam Biali out of her bed in her nightshirt and heavily beat her and led her out on the balcony of her garret. There they bound her throat in barbed wire and hanged her on the balcony until she was dead. The son was murdered with an iron rod. They also murdered Hilke Biali's brother, Motl. The dead bodies were then thrown on the wagon.

The Rajgrodski family, it appears, were placed alive on the wagon. Avraham'l, the oldest son, successfully jumped off the wagon and disappeared. However, not a half hour passed and the Christian woman, Lubecki, came to tell the bandits that Avraham'l Rajgrodski was lying hidden in the bushes in her garden. He also was immediately caught.still alive.

Jewish residents of Tifle Street said that when Nisen the butcher's family was led through their street one of his sons-in-law lay in the wagon in a pool of blood and the bandit Witek Roszinski went after it with a rag in his hand and wiped the blood off the cobblestones so "that there would be no trace!" They were all taken to the Majewo Hill [The Majewo Hill is located beyond the Polish cemetery on the road to the village of Hornostaje] and they were murdered there in a terrible manner and buried. A few days later a Polish peasant acquaintance from that area said that Nisen the butcher had been buried alive. During the early morning hours he succeeded with hard work in crawling out of the grave. However, when a small shepherd noticed this, he immediately ran to the shtetl and reported it to the city hall. Suddenly two policemen with iron bars in their hands rode there on their bicycles and completed the "work." As was corroborated later, at the beginning Nisen the butcher's family strongly resisted the two bandits who came to take them from their residence. However, the bandits returned and brought help.

A Part of the Old Market

First building from the right (two stories) – Hilke Biali's brick building. Miriam Biali (Hilke's wife) was hanged on the balcony. Second building – Chaim Poliak's (Kobrinski's) brick building

10th Chapter

On Monday the 21st of July there was not yet a military regime in the shtetl. Therefore, fear among the Jewish population increased as the witnessed the new methods of annihilation implemented by the bandits. There was no one to complain to about this because there was no military regime in the surrounding area. Their only hope was placed on the Jewish girls who would go on foot every day to the Osowiec Fortress to work for the German officers. They were told not to be afraid and to tell everything that had occurred during the previous night.

With great tension everyone waited for the 15 girls to return from Osowiec, wanting to hear the report from there. It was later revealed that the fortress commandant immediately intervened with the uniformed military police by phone. The answer from the uniformed military police was that they would come to Goniadz on Tuesday (the next day) and make order. The fortress commandant also asked the Jewish girls to write the names of the bandits. The report calmed the Jewish population in the shtetl to a certain degree. However, another night of powerlessness and neglect was approaching and it was possible that the bandits would continue their "work" of the previous night. A plan was created by a group of young men to organize and stage a resistance against the murderers. However, it was unworkable because they did not have any weapons. They also established small groups in many residences, arming themselves with axes and large hammers. It was decided that the first bandit who appeared in the window would have his head chopped off. Then they would wrestle with the remaining bandits with their last strength.

The residences where the older Jews lived remained empty because their owners had left to spend the night in various hiding places and bunkers.

The night passed in complete quiet. The next morning, Tuesday at noon, four uniformed military police appeared in the shtetl on motorcycles, armed with automatic weapons. They immediately went to the residences of the murderers who had been pointed out to them by the Jewish girls. They only found seven of the murderers. The military police carried out thorough searches [of their residences] that provided better results than imagined. In addition to the looted Jewish possessions, they also found looted Soviet military clothing and canned food from the military storehouses. According to the law, death was the punishment for this. The uniformed military police shackled the hands of all seven bandits in chains and took them away to Osowiec. After such a long wave of pogroms, a ray of light and joy appeared for the first time in the dark, frozen, Jewish hearts. The Jews began to breathe more freely. On the other hand, the Poles became fearful. Their commerce in the shtetl decreased greatly and many bandits hid, fearing the uniformed military police. Several days passed and the seven bandits were still being held in Osowiec. The investigation of [the bandits] was continuing. The city council members could not rest and the mayor, Balonowski, and his representative, Kempa, every day would ask the local military regime on their [the seven bandits] behalf for their freedom.

They cited the law, that it was permitted to murder Jews and, therefore, their imprisonment was unlawful. The fortress commandant answered them with these words: "We will annihilate the Jews ourselves without you. With regard to the arrest of the seven Poles, it was not for murdering Jews, but for stealing their possessions. According to the law, the penalty for that is death." The city leaders, "alas," had to return to the shtetl with empty hands. Hearing this report the sorrow of the Polish population increased. However, they did not rest and made every effort until it finally succeeded in freeing one bandit, Paszkowski. Immediately in the morning after his liberation the uniformed military police shot all of the remaining six bandits. From that time on, safety in the shtetl increased from day to day, particularly when a fresh German command arrived in the city three days later.

11th Chapter

The situation in the shtetl "stabilized." Groups of young people would go every day to various work in the shtetl and outside it. The Judenrat, which added three more members and became the official representation of the Goniadz Jewish population, would designate the people for work. It received permission for a premises and arranged it as it wished. Finkewicz was designated as the chairman of the council and Brzaczinski as secretary. Every night, an errand boy would carry the names of the Jews capable of working the next morning who were promised for the needed work. The members of the Judenrat were not freed from wearing the yellow patch, except for the chairman who wore a blue band on his left arm with the lettering Judenrat.

Even though the shtetl had become quiet, the danger again grew during the time when the remaining main bandits strolled freely through the streets and the German uniformed military police did nothing to them. Their self-assurance increased and little by little they again lifted their clubs in their hands and lay stretched out in the dozens at the Jewish Frantowe bridge waiting for the sun and teasing the Jews.

The city council members sat at meetings day and night without interruption. The agenda was always the same and well known – the Jews. The ghetto question again surfaced. The city council members went to the shtetl market, down in the valley, after it was decided to create a ghetto, and reached the decision that this area was suitable and able to receive the 980 Jewish souls in the shtetl. The living conditions needed to be: six men in a small room.

When the Judenrat was informed about this information through the city council, it immediately went through the shtetl for contributions for the city leaders to suppress the plan.

For many in the population their last few dollars had gone for the earlier money collections. Many already had pawned their last holiday suit of clothes. A certain sum of dollars was collected successfully with great difficulty that was divided among the city leaders. It was impossible to talk to the priest himself because he had extracted [bribes] quietly while publicly he made the pretense of being good. Balonowski received the largest sum of dollars as well as a gold pocket watch with a long golden chain. The "remedy" immediately worked on them and the work of burying posts for the ghetto fences was stopped the next morning.

Several quiet days passed until the city leaders were again "hungry." Then they remembered that it had been too long since Jewish victims had fallen. They also made a list of 50 men and told the policemen to bring them to the city hall. When the policemen delivered the requested Jews, another four policemen were told to take them to the fortress commandant as communists. The order was carried out immediately and they began to lead the Jews... A significant number in the group consisted of older Jews. There were women among them and the remainder...the young ones. One [member] of the group succeeded in escaping while still in the shtetl, at the old market. The police all shot at him, but without any success. He jumped over a fence in a fruit garden and disappeared from the shtetl. The majority of the group had no idea why they had been chosen, while there had been certain criticisms of others. For example, the old Moshe Grin had expressed [the opinion] to a Pole during the time of the Soviet regime that the brick cross monument that stood at the market of the shtetl would be taken down. A woman at that time said to a Polish woman when she attacked her: "Do not act like that! Your anti-Semitic regime is finished! The Christians remembered this and when the city council announced in the shtetl and in the villages – "Whoever has a complaint against a Jew should report it at city hall." – This was enough for the city council and they immediately crowned them [the Jews] with the name "communists," so that they would be shot by the Germans.

When they arrived in Osowiec with the group of "communists," the fortress commandant fortuitously was not present. The police stood with the Jews and waited for a considerable time near the headquarters' building. The waiting old Jews with beards and the women aroused astonishment with every German officer driving through and attracted their attention. They stopped and asked the policemen what kind of criminals they were. They were surprised when they heard that they were supposed to be communists, stared, shrugged their shoulders and went further on their way.

Finally the policemen waited for the "fortunate" hour when a Mercedes automobile arrived from which emerged a gray old, bent oberst (colonel). He summoned a policeman. The policeman ran quickly to him with a smile on his face, convinced that finally he would achieve his purpose. The oberst asked him: "Who are these people?" "These are communists, Herr Oberst!," the policeman answered with pride. Hearing such talk, the oberst scowled at him and said: "Whom have you come to confuse? Such old men and women are communists?" He shouted at him: "Let them go home immediately and do not bring them here again!" The oberst went back into his Mercedes automobile and left right away.

Sulczinski, the policeman, remained standing, ashamed, with his head downcast to the ground and did not know how he should give such a "sad" answer to the Jews. He was unable to tolerate that they would be happy, but, "alas," he must. Little by little, bloodthirstily he moved towards the group of Jews, because he could not wait any longer and he said to them: "Listen, you know what I will say to you, come! We will go home." The Jews already understood what was happening because they had heard every word of the oberst that rang through the square. Smiles appeared on their faces, many began to kiss each other in great joy. One woman had spasms and, after half an hour of resting in the nearby pine forest, the policemen returned to Goniadz shamelessly with the Jews. It is impossible to describe the joy among the Jewish population. Wives, husbands, children and grandchildren ran out to their dearest ones, kissed and hugged each other with tears in their eyes. On the other hand, there was great gloom and sadness among the Polish population in general and the state leaders in particular. They were ashamed to show their faces to the Jews. However, the Jews did not celebrate for long and the Poles did not grieve for long. The city council held more meetings and baked a fresh "plan" that it began to carry out three days later.

12th Chapter

Just as every afternoon, on Sunday, too, the labor director of the city council announced the number of required workers for the next day to the chairman of the Judenrat. The only difference was that this time the chairman Finkewicz received a supplementary, detailed list with names of 18 men in addition to the general daily number of workers. These had to appear early in the morning on the synagogue hill to dismantle the only remaining wall of the synagogue that had been burned by the Germans in 1939. The pretext was that the destroyed wall could lead to catastrophe. . The representatives immediately gave the news to the Jews of the shtetl and informed them about the 18 people on the list. A number of the requested people had been among those taken to Osowiec a few says before. It should be understood that it was clear to everyone that something was happening.

The more well-to-do Jews on the supplementary list immediately ran to certain Polish leaders with money to ask to be freed from the next day's work. However, there were weak results from all of the efforts. No more than two young men were freed from work. A number of the 18 wanted to hide somewhere for the day. However, this, too, was not so easy because Christian acquaintances were afraid to let Jews [into their house]. Yet, five Jews succeeded in hiding somewhere. When during the work at the synagogue hill, the policeman learned that five Jews on the list were missing, in addition to the two who were freed, they left immediately to carry out searches in their houses, but no one was found there. The 11 Jews worked hard that day and at night, after the work, the policemen took them to Cerela's new, concrete cellar [Cerela's two-story brick building at the beginning of Dolistower Street, which was built in 1933]. They were held shut in there for about two weeks. It was impossible to ransom any of them. No one knew what they planned to do with them. After the 11 Jews in the cellar had been under arrest for two weeks, two Mercedes automobiles of German gendarmes appeared at the market of the shtetl. A great panic occurred in the shtetl. Other men tried to escape somewhere outside the city. Women ran through the side alleys to learn something about this. Meanwhile, the group of gendarmes entered the residence of the city leader, Balonowski, where they lingered for about half an hour. Then they left accompanied by Balonowski, Kempa and several Polish policemen to visit the city council, militia and so on, until the door of the cellar was opened for them and they saw before their eyes 11 imprisoned, miserable Jews. When the gendarme commandant asked who these people were, Balonowski answered: these are Jewish communists. Then one of the young men (Shmul Hirszfeld [Shmul the son of Ruchl-Leah's son Sholem]) went to the oldest gendarme and said, pointing to Balonowski and Kempa: "The bandits previously took our gold and dollars and then imprisoned us for an unknown reason. Meanwhile, they will not bother those who are rich and still have money, but they want to take our souls from us, the poor Jews. The bandits have already murdered over 60 innocent Jews by their own hands while the shtetl was without a commandant. Not being satisfied with this, they are using the opportunity of there not being a German civil regime in the shtetl and little by little they will murder all of the Jews in the shtetl. Save us, Herr Gendarme Commandant!... Have pity on us and free us from their murderous hands!"... The young man cried, joined by all of the remaining Jews. Balonowski and Kempa stood with bowed heads and pale faces, not saying one word. All of the gendarmes turned to both city leaders and looked at them from head to feet. Suddenly the gendarme commandant shouted out to Balonowski and Kempa: "Do not torture the Jews anymore! Free them immediately!" Both city leaders stood at attention and answered: "Jawhohl [Of course]." The commandant said to the Jews: "Go home! You are free!" The Jews, astonished by the sudden fortunate change, lifted their hats in the air, in honor of the gendarmes, thanking them sincerely for their liberation. The gendarmes, in answer, nodded their heads to the Jews and the imprisoned Jews ran lightning fast to their homes. The gendarmes went back to Balonowski's residence where they carried out a thorough search looking for Jewish gold and dollars. However, it appears that Balonowski had taken care of this and there would be no treasure found in his residence. Thus the search had no positive results. The gendarmes returned to their Mercedes automobiles and left the shtetl.

13ᵗʰ Chapter

After the last two defeats, the ambition of the two city leaders increased. They did not rest long until it occurred to Kempa to send an official report to the central office of the Gestapo in Bialystok about the 11 freed "Jewish communists" and he requested that the Gestapo come to Goniadz and take them. The official report was signed by Balonowski and Kempa and was sent in secret to Bialystok. Meanwhile, five gendarmes arrived, who settled in the shtetl and formed a municipal gendarmerie guard. The commandant of the gendarmes immediately called the chairman of the Judenrat and gave him a list of household articles that the Judenrat had to provide. The list began with furniture, bedding and ended with kitchen utensils. The Judenrat collected everything on the list in the course of 24 hours. Contact was made between the gendarmes and the representatives of the Judenrat and in an intimate conversation, the gendarmerie told them: "If the Jews are good to us we will also be good to them."

The Jews, on their part, did everything to the satisfaction of the gendarmes and "found favor" with the commandant of the gendarmerie, who was the actual boss of the shtetl, although Balonowski still appeared as the mayor. As it turned out, the Polish city leaders lost their power over the shtetl with the arrival of the gendarmes.

The Jews already began to feel freer in the shtetl. Some would go to the villages to work with a peasant and there earn their piece of bread. The peasants from the surrounding villages would come to the shtetl to the Jewish artisans. In a word, contact between the Jews in the shtetl and the village peasants, from whom they drew their livelihood, began to revive.

They again went to the designated places for forced labor every day. Understand that there was no talk about taking off the yellow patch or going for a stroll. Work also began again at the shtetl sawmill. A German military engineering division from Osowiec sent its staff sergeant as its foreman and manager. The sergeant named Franz would employ approximately 30 Jewish workers every day, who would be provided for him by the Judenrat. A small number of Poles, tradesmen who would be employed for the more skilled work of driving the cars, working as blacksmiths and wood sorters and the like worked there in addition to the Jews.

Every three days another group of Jews would go to work, which was extraordinarily difficult, literally forced labor. Franz was a terrifying enemy of the Jews and a sadist. He was a little emotionally abnormal. He would beat [the Jews] murderously while they worked. They would work beyond their strength because not more than three men were permitted to carry a large log on their shoulders. When he would summon a "Jude" to lift a heavy log and the young Jewish man could not move it from the spot, Franz would "stroll" his club over the shoulders, back, feet and nape of the neck, so that the momentum would lift the log – not one's strength. Franz would stand the entire day, in heavy downpours, under the open sky, with a rubber cape over his head and club in his hand, behind the backs of the working Jews and again beat them so that they would run up the hill rolling the giant log to the saw of the sawmill. He also would often say in great irritation: "Because of you Jews my comrades are rotting in the fields." Mainly, he carried a terrible hate for the rich Jews. When one of the workers looked better or wore an entire pair of pants, he would summon him, take him to his small room and brutally torture him there.

It was enough that Franz noticed that one of the Jews had a piece of bread with butter during lunchtime. He would bellow to the Jew "Ah! You are eating butter?!" The Jew was then not one of whom to be envious. Franz also introduced a "custom." Every night at around nine o'clock at the change of the 14-hour workday, he shouted: "Listen all of you Jews!" When all of the Jews immediately stood in two lines opposite him, he would give an order, saying aloud three times: "God punish England and the damned Juden!" When the "prayer" was said loudly there was a second order: run home. The tired Jewish workers would run up-hill to the shtetl with their last strength. However there were always one or two, mainly among the older ones, who had no strength to run up the hill. Franz, standing at the courtyard of the sawmill with his Nagant automatic pistol in his hand, pointing at the running Jews, immediately opened his mouth with resounding shouts to the last Jew in the group ordering him to return immediately. When he obeyed, he was terribly tortured by Franz hearing the same words from him again: "Can you not run, accursed Jew?!" The Jews ran up the hill on all fours until he barely dragged himself to the shtetl. The name Franz threw fear into the Jewish population. Therefore, it is no wonder that other Jews wished death for themselves rather than going to work.

14th Chapter

Several weeks passed during which the gendarmes ruled the shtetl and the Jews appeared to breathe a little easier. Suddenly a report arrived that a district commissioner was coming to Goniadz. The Judenrat had already received an order to prepare a residence, furniture and entire wardrobe for him. Two days had not passed before the district commissioner arrived. He was given Chaim Kopelman's brick house as a residence. The Jews began to fear the new boss. He also immediately summoned the chairman of the Judenrat and asked him to provide a list of valuable articles. Everything was gathered from under the earth to satisfy him. Meanwhile, a fresh misfortune occurred. Three weeks after the freeing of the last 11 Jews from the cellar, an answer arrived from the Bialystok Gestapo for the city council and gendarmerie in Goniadz about the sending of the official report about the 11 "communists," that they should be prepared for jail on the 12th of September 1941. On the date mentioned, the Gestapo would come to take them.

The city council members kept the "happy" news a secret.

On the night of the 11th-12th September 1941, the Polish policemen accompanied by the gendarmes took the 11 people from their beds and imprisoned them in the same cellar as before. In the morning, at exactly eight o'clock, a German truck with Gestapo members appeared in the shtetl and went directly to the house of the gendarmes. They ordered the Polish policemen and two gendarmes to bring the 11 arrested "communists."

One of the Jews [Avraham-Meir Todorowicz] succeeded in escaping from police hands and disappearing while they were being driven through a small alley. Several policemen chased after him, but they did not succeed in catching him. They immediately reported this to the Gestapo commandant who was waiting with the truck at the old market. The Gestapo commander immediately ordered that five other Jews be caught instead of the one who had disappeared. The answer to the policeman's question of which Jews was: "Take those first, best Jews that you meet." The policeman went to the houses at the market in order and took whomever he found in each residence. No one even knew what had happened because the policeman said that he was only taking them to work. Therefore, no one refused to go with him. Arriving at the old market, the Jews saw what was happening, but it was then too late to do anything. The Gestapo member ordered them to climb into the covered trucks at once, where the Knyszyn police commandant Wonszikewicz [former Polish policeman in Goniadz for many years] stood guard. The vehicle with the captured Jews left. The five captured Jews were: Noakh Barski and his 15-year old son, Avraham'le, Asher Kobrinski (member of the Judenrat), Brzizsznski (secretary of the Judenrat) and Feltinowicz.

The wives of the men taken away, learning what had happened, ran into the street. There they saw no one... They cried aloud in great sorrow and had spasms until they returned home barely alive.

Learning that the Gestapo members had taken the Jews to Knyszyn and imprisoned them there, the wives of the five captured Jews immediately left for Knyszyn the next morning. The Judenrat tried with a large amount of money to obtain permission from the district commissioner for the wives to travel there and confirm that their husbands were not communists and had no connection to the arrestees in the cellar. Having received this [permission], the wives were certain that they would free their husbands immediately. However, it turned out differently. The Gestapo demanded a specific amount of gold, two Persian lamb women's coats and other valuables for the freedom of the five people. The demanded items had to be provided within two days. They began collecting from everyone. Early the next morning, not waiting for the [two days to pass] the members of the Gestapo placed all of the arrestees on a truck and took them away to Bialystok. They only freed Barski's 15-year old son Avraham'le in Knyszyn because of his young age. From then on, the 14 Jews were lost and vanished without a trace.

Life again began to flow as usual in Goniadz. The "damage" by the Polish city leaders returned with interest: they [the Polish city leaders] no longer had any worries.

The regime of the district commissioner and the gendarmes strengthened from day to day while the power of the city council was weakened from moment to moment since the arrival [of the district commissioner and gendarmes] in the shtetl.

Finally, after two weeks of rule by the district commissioner, he abolished the Polish civilian city council completely and took over complete control of the shtetl in his own hands.

The district commissioner hung the red Hitlerist flag with the black swastika over his office and the routine Hitlerist civilian rule began to reign in Goniadz just as in all of the surrounding cities and shtetlekh. The number in the work force from the Jewish population rose with the growth and scope of the work. The district commissioner would often summon the chairman of the Judenrat, mainly when he needed something, or about labor questions. As the Judenrat members would describe it, the district commissioner was not bad by nature, except for one defect: "He quickly forgets what we give him." Therefore, the chairman of Judenrat often was forced to travel to other shtetlekh to gather the articles for him that were impossible to obtain in Goniadz.

For this, the district commissioner would provide a travel certificate because it was strongly forbidden to travel somewhere without a certificate.

It was clear that the Judenrat drew its monetary means from the shtetl and, particularly, from the wealthier Jews. In addition to the district commissioner, the Judenrat had to provide new clothing to the five gendarmes and their families living in Germany. In a word: They ceaselessly drew the blood from the Jewish population in Goniadz!

The Jewish population consisted of three classes: The wealthier class – these were the pre-war merchants, mainly the manufacturing branch, leather branch, footwear and the like. They did not need to look for work for their income during the uneasy times because beginning at the end of 1939 the majority of them had hidden goods in various bunkers or with well-acquainted peasants in the villages. From time to time they would slice off a bit of goods that were then terribly expensive and exchange them with a peasant for life's necessities. This secret business could provide good nourishment through the years.

The second class was the artisans. It also was not bad for them. Their ten fingers were enough to earn food for their families. At that time, the peasants paid them well for their work because there were not many artisans; there was a particular lack of tailors. The peasants had more than enough cloth that they had looted from Russian warehouses during the sudden withdrawal of the Red Army. Thus, the majority of the artisans also had enough to eat. It should be emphasized that the artisans were freed from forced labor because they would pay a certain monthly tax to the Judenrat. Understand that this did not free their work-capable children.

Much worse was the poor class. These were: pre-war poor people, employees, and former small businessmen, particularly food sellers. The latter had eaten up their goods a long time ago. A larger total of their goods could not be kept for long; they sold it during the first months of the war. Therefore, they were forced along with all of the oppressed Jews to barter their good Shabbos clothing, household furniture received as a dowry, various work tools, linen, and finally, their bedding with the peasants for life's necessities. The monetary system did not actually exist among the peasants. The reason for this was because there were no open shops. Thus the peasants could not buy anything with their money and therefore requested that they be paid for their goods with other goods. All of the transactions would take place in secret because there was the threat of great punishment for this. Right after the occupation by the German regime, the majority of the poor class had enough for their nourishment because every family found something to sell and they could prepare flour and potatoes for the winter. Even the wagon driver received potatoes for the entire winter for his family for two wheels from his wagon. The situation worsened for the poor class with the arrival of spring. Many of them were forced to go to the villages to help the peasants cultivate the ground for which they received food for themselves and their families. The Jews who were not capable of such work such as: older people, shoykhetim [ritual slaughters], the rabbi and the like would receive support and food from the wealthier class who willingly helped them. Thus no one suffered from hunger. The difference was only in the quality of the food.

And a fresh source of work opened at the Osowiec fortress with the arrival of summer 1942. One hundred and forty Jewish workers, men and women, aged 16 to 50 were employed there daily. Many of them would bring new Russian gas mask sacks from Osowiec every day that were willingly bought by the peasants. They would make various clothing from them, mainly pants. Some of the workers worked sorting left-over Russian ammunition: artillery shells of various calibers, various kinds of grenades and the like. There were no weapons there. The second and larger number worked at the train station loading and unloading tents that arrived from German factories from the train wagons. Osowiec was transformed into a base for various wood and pup tents that would be transferred from there to the front for the German soldiers.

Part 15:

After long efforts and entreaties to the district commissioner, the Judenrat was successful in receiving permission to bring the 20 Jews murdered during the Sunday pogrom night of nine months earlier to the Jewish cemetery for burial. It was learned that the bandits had buried them at the Majewo Hill. The image was terrible and frightening when they were dug up. The murder victims lay on the ground and the family members lay near each dead body and wailed terribly. The frightening crying gripped every Jew standing there. There simply are no words to describe the tragic scene.

It still was possible to recognize the faces of some of the murder victims, others could be identified by their clothing, which was recognized by their family members. Mrs. Biali lay only in her nightshirt in which she was dressed when they had dragged out her out of her bed. The barbed wire with which she had been hanged was still bound around her throat. Her right foot was broken. Yosl Kobrinski lay with his hands tied behind him; his mouth was stuffed with rags and wire. There was an opening in his head and his left foot was broken. All of those remaining had open wounds in their bodies, particularly in their heads. Wolfke Rajgodski's skull was split. The young men standing around tried to lay the murder victims on stretchers to take them away to the cemetery. However, the close relatives of the annihilated ones would not permit it. It was simply impossible for them to take away the murder victims from them. They began to carry them to the Jewish cemetery an hour later. The cries that had been decreasing in the last 10 minutes again increased and they really split the heavens. One word was heard from every mouth: "Revenge!!! – Jews. Whoever among who you survives the war should take revenge for the innocent blood that was spilled!" One called out: "Jews! We all implore you, by the open mass graves, that you take revenge on the bandits!!!..."

They brought the 20 murder victims to the Jewish cemetery. Many Jews immediately went to search for the graves of the Jews in the cellar who had been annihilated, the five found in the wheat field and so on.

After long attempts at digging, they uncovered a mass grave of 17 of those from the cellar (the last group). The tragedy increased more: wives recognized husbands, parents – children and vice-versa. The lamentations, screaming and shaking increased even more at the Jewish cemetery. The 17 murder victims also were murdered in a terrible manner. Several were found with nails hammered into their heads and into their hearts. Others had their heads split completely as by an axe. One had his tongue torn out. Many had broken feet and hands. Eight men had their hands tied behind their backs with barbed wire. Others had deep holes in their heads and necks.

The grave of the five who were shot because of a blood libel, which the Poles had accused them of when they lay hidden in the wheat field, was uncovered after a long search. The documents had not been taken out of their pockets. A pocket watch was found still in the pocket of one of them. The first three shot in the cellar were found lying in separate graves. They were shot in the head.

Goniadz Cemetery – Drawing by Shimeon Halpern, of blessed memory

Because of the limited time for which permission was given, no fresh graves could be dug for the found murder victims. Therefore, all were placed in the same mass grave. The grave of the 11 men from the cellar [the second group in Motke Kliap's cellar, who were removed on the night of Shabbas on the 4th of July] was not found. As was later learned, the bandits buried them somewhere at the Majewo Hill.

The entire multitude of Jews returned in groups to the shtetl leading the unfortunate family members of the uncovered murder victims, lamenting and crying, with their heads on their shoulders, to their homes at six o'clock at night.

16th Chapter

Life in the shtetl in time became calm. Some went to work in Osowiec daily, some went to the villages to seek income, others in their workshops and others lamented and cried, day and night, at the misfortune that had happened to them. The relationship between the district commissioner, the gendarmes and the Judenrat grew better from time to time so that one could "almost" feel that the Hitler regime did not rule the shtetl. At times, after a new Polish denunciation, the district commissioner would become angry with the Judenrat and attack its chairman. Suspicion would fall on the district commissioner's chauffeur, Alszewski, the well-know bandit involved in the Sunday night pogrom. They would also suspect Waliniewicz [the district commissioner's secretary] because of his brother-in-law, the well-known bandit Kaminski. However, the Judenrat would immediately calm the district commissioner with a nice present and he would cool off immediately, as if nothing had happened. Mass employment of the Jewish labor force at Osowiec made the Jewish population important to the district commissioner and to the military commandant in Osowiec. At times it simply brought the assurance of the district administration in Osowiec with the words: If the Gestapo does something to the Jewish population in the surrounding cities and shtetlekh, it absolutely will not touch the Goniadz Jews.

The work at Osowiec was never exhausted. No matter how much work was done, more new work would arrive because with the approach of autumn and winter the provisions of tents for the fighters at the front increased even more and, therefore, the work took on a faster tempo. Train traffic at the Osowiec station was greater. It boiled like a kettle. Trains always were seen traveling through, full of the military, from the front and to the front. Many of the soldiers traveling through would shout out from the wagons – "Accursed Jews!" – when they noticed the working Jews. Others would [indicate the beating of heads] with their canes and so on. It should be understood that such depictions did not give the working Jews any hope for a better tomorrow. They would often console themselves with false rumors that would be spread – "the Russians have marched into Kiev, Minsk, Vilna" and the like. But the truth was revealed quickly when they secretly received a German newspaper in which the map of Kavkaz [Caucasus] was published just that day with the following news: "The German divisions marched into Kavkaz and are stubbornly continuing their great victories." The Jewish reader actually would shudder with great surprise and disappointment. Often they would be drawn to a secret conversation at work with Russian prisoners of war at Osowiec. Alas, they also could not learn anything from them. The unceasing news about victories spread by the German information and propaganda ministry were, it should be understood, not believed very much by the Jews. Often they simply did not want to believe because they knew very well what would happen... In a word, it was as if they were enclosed in a sack.

The Jewish workers were well acquainted with the Russian prisoners as companions in bad misfortune. Every day the majority of the Jewish workers took [the same amount of] bread sacks of food for the prisoners as for themselves. Arriving in Osowiec two young men gathered the food in several large rucksacks for the Russian prisoners of war and placed them in a designated bush, every day in another hiding place so their enemies would not find any trace of them. One of the prisoners would secretly remove the food from the designated spot. The danger was double, both from the Germans and from the Polish workers who searched for material for denunciations. However, everyone would feel fortunate that it went peacefully.

17th Chapter

The good bit of time came to an end several months later.

On a beautiful morning the district commissioner announced that he had received an order to create a ghetto for the Jews, just as in all of the surrounding shtetlekh. The Jewish population in Goniadz had foreseen the great danger to its existence. Therefore, it did everything it could to succeed in having the edict rescinded. The chairman of the Judenrat immediately traveled to Bialystok and bought a leather coat for the district commissioner and a Persian lamb coat for his wife. In addition, he took everything he could from the population and carried it to the district commissioner. No one could understand why he [the commissioner] had suddenly changed.

And so on one Shabbos morning, the district commissioner ordered all the Jews of Dolistower Street to leave their residences over the course of three hours. There was a tumult and chaos in the shtetl. Every Jew from the above-mentioned street ran to a peasant acquaintance for a wagon to carry his things. People from other streets ran to their acquaintances and helped them move into their residences. Wagons fully loaded with bags and baggage left Dolistower Street for other streets and alleys in the shtetl, to occupied Jewish residences. Three days later the district commissioner announced to the Judenrat that the Jews should leave Tifle Street. However, at great cost, there was success in canceling this. Several days passed without any changes. Little by little the Jews began to believe in an improvement of the situation; still greater was the belief when the district commissioner decided to distribute potatoes for the winter to the Goniadz Jews at a lower price than the government price. He ordered the peasants in the villages to provide the designated portions of potatoes for the Goniadz storehouses. When the storehouses were full, every Jew had the right to take his portion from them. It did not take long until this joy also was disturbed. The district commissioner suddenly summoned the chairman of the Judenrat and ordered him to provide 200 furs. He immediately gave the chairman the use of a wagon with a Polish wagon driver for this purpose. The chairman of the Judenrat promised him that he would do this.

At around three o'clock in the afternoon the loaded wagon already stood in front of the district commissioner's house. The member of the Judenrat who gathered [the furs] went in to announce this to the district commissioner. The district commissioner came out of his office accompanied by the Judenrat member and went to the wagon to look over the goods that were brought. Then the Polish wagon driver, Czajkowski, who had brought the furs spoke up saying: "Herr District Commissioner! The Jews hid the good furs and they gave away the worst rags." The district commissioner, hearing such talk, immediately gave the Judenrat member two slaps across his face and said: "If we are not provided with two hundred good furs within three hours, you should send all of the Jewish men into the street." There was turmoil in the shtetl. Jews ran to the nearby villages where they had hidden their possessions and brought the best furs that they had. In a word, they raised the demanded number [of furs] from under the earth and provided them in time. The storm was calmed.

On Shabbos, the 20th of October 1942, during the weekly meeting of the soltisn [village representatives] from all of the villages around Goniadz, the district commissioner announced that on the coming Monday, the 2nd of November, all of the villages should provide him with 200 wagons with high ladders at seven o'clock in the morning. The wagons should be placed in rows that would extend from his office along Dolistower Street. The announcement evoked surprise among the soltisn. When one of them asked him why they needed so many wagons, the district commissioner answered: to bring young tree plants from the Grajewo area. After the meeting, when the news spread among the Jewish population, it surprised a certain number them. However, it did not awaken any bad thoughts among the majority in connection with this. The Judenrat sent its chairman to the district commissioner to learn something about this. Returning from the district commissioner, the chairman said that the district commissioner assured him that the 200 wagons had no connection with the Jews. The Judenrat calmed down...

18th Chapter

Just as every day, on Monday the 2nd of November 1942, all of the workers employed in Osowiec awoke at five o'clock in the morning and everyone left for Osowiec in the darkness with their sack of bread.

Leaving the highway near Guzy where the workers were sent from various corners of the city, met and marched together, not one word of mockery was heard about those who had been afraid of today. Walking a kilometer along the highway, they met German military trucks that were going in the direction of Goniadz. Armed soldiers sat on them. This fact evoked unease among the workers and they began to talk about various hypotheses. Walking two more kilometers, they could see a group of people standing on the highway in the morning grayness. Coming closer to them revealed that two Polish policemen and a German gendarme armed with rifles stood there for a long time and stopped all Jewish workers. They announced to the workers that they must remain standing in this place and not move from the spot. The influx of workers grew larger from time to time until it stopped. It was already light at seven o'clock. Several of the workers asked the policeman Olcik what had happened. With a smile on his face, the policeman answered: - "I do not know," and then sang a tango melody under his breath and danced to its tempo. At seven thirty all of the workers were given the order to return [to Goniadz] in close order and whoever dared to escape would be shot.

The matter was now clear to everyone. Many of the girls immediately began to cry. Both policemen accompanied the line on each side and the gendarmes with the machine guns from behind. Arriving at the village of Guzy they saw many Jews escaping on the Trestine Road. Two Polish policemen were chasing them on bicycles, opening fire at them until they were caught and returned to the shtetl. The sound of continuous shooting reached them from Goniadz. Armed Gestapo posts ringed the shtetl with machine guns, manning all of its exits. When the closed line of workers left the highway for the shtetl they already saw the members of the Gestapo stopping a group of Jews who had tried to escape from the shtetl. When the group of workers went by a member of the Gestapo, he incorporated them into the line of workers and told the gendarme to lead them into the shtetl. They were agitated and could not speak because of their fear. One answer was heard to all of the workers' questions about what had happened in the shtetl: "It is not good!" The workers group was enveloped by terror. A father held his child, a brother held a brother or a sister. They held each other's hands. Everyone wished to be with those closest to them at their last minute before their death and to die with them. The Poles stood arranged along the streets and watched with joy as the Jews were led to the slaughter. Arriving in front of the old market, they saw masses of Jews, young and old, running with one breath, wanting to flee from the shtetl. The members of the Gestapo were running around in the fields of young, sprouting, green blades of rye, shooting [at the Jews] ceaselessly. Those escaping returned to the shtetl. Arriving at the old market, it was not easy to see Jews on the street. Going closer to the Jewish houses, a Jewish woman ran out of a residence and ran rapidly into the line to take out her son from there. However, a German gendarme immediately ordered her to go back into the residence, sticking out his revolver against her breast. The woman turned back with great sobbing. The working masses, women, men, children, were seized by echoing, frightening crying – all crying and lamenting aloud.

The packed group neared the market of the shtetl. On the porch of the former city hall stood: Balonowski, Kempa and their close friends and stung the passing Jews with their cynical laughter. Now their dream would be accomplished.

The 200 ordered wagons, whose purpose was now clear to everyone, were already there when they arrived at the market of the shtetl. Several Gestapo automobiles and Mercedes also stood in the center of the market.

A Gestapo officer, with a pale face, black, long sideburns and murderous eyes, appeared before the masses. Several women, seeing him from a distance immediately began to shake. The entire group was told to stand in a row, in twos. When this was carried out, several uniformed and secret members of the Gestapo neared the rows and one of them, holding a paper in his hand, said the following:

"You are all being taken to work. Each of you is going home now for a half an hour and take: a suit of work clothes, a pair of work shoes, two pairs of underwear, two blankets and small pillowcases, a spoon, a fork and a knife. Everyone must return to the street having the above-mentioned with them."

Hearing such words, the distressed workers breathed more freely. Everyone ran to their houses with renewed hope, to carry out the Gestapo's order. My brother, Zalman and sister Kayla and I found our residence locked. We tore off the lock and went inside. After a short deliberation we decided not to go back out to the street, but to try to conceal ourselves in a hiding place that our father had prepared in the attic until the situation became clearer. We carried up food, water, bedding and other needed things. We closed the disguised door of the room and remained lying there. Little by little we gouged out a small opening in the roof, from which we saw everything that happened in the street.

Jews were gathering more and more. They stood in a long line beginning at Dolistower Street, near the waiting wagons. Their small packs lay on the ground near each family separately. Police and members of the Gestapo walked around the street and shouted out loud to each Jew coming out: "Louse! Louse! Faster, accursed Jew!" When the majority of the Goniadz Jewish population was standing in the street, a series of searches began in all of the Jewish houses and courtyards. When they encountered a Jew who was late, the members of the Gestapo severely beat him and chased him in the street. The Polish population helped the members of the Gestapo search for hidden Jews very energetically. When several Polish young people successfully found a Jewish boy in a cellar on Dolistower Street, they brought him straight to the Polish policeman, Gogol, who immediately shot him on the spot. From time to time more Jews, who had been pulled out of hiding places, were dragged to the crowd standing in the street.

The shooting in the shtetl continued. At 12 o'clock noon, when it became completely calm and no further Jews had been found, the Gestapo ordered [the Jews] to get on the Christian wagons by rows. That lasted approximately half an hour until everyone was sitting on a wagon. The members of the Gestapo were scattered through all of the rows of wagons in order to guard the transport. The Sturmführer [assault leader] gave an order: "Abführen [Lead away]!" the transport of heavily loaded wagons began to move...

It was a horrible picture of how in one moment they had erased a kehile [organized religious community] of about a thousand Jews from its birthplace, which had been inhabited by their grandfathers and great grandfathers over hundreds of years. Many of the Jews driven out cast their last looks at their homes, riding past them and said goodbye to them with bloody tears... Old and young women lay stretched out on the wagons [having] fainted and leaned their heads against their family members who stroked and kissed them. Other old Jews raised their hands to heaven looking for salvation there, but no miracles happened...

Poles stood lined up opposite the moving wagons with happy faces and deriving pleasure [from the scene]. Little by little the last wagon, with which the entire community disappeared and was erased from its old home for an eternity, neared Tifle Street.

19ᵗʰ Chapter

After the transports of the Jewish community, there immediately were new police searches in the shtetl in which the Polish population excelled with its armed policemen at the head. One truck and a Gestapo Mercedes automobile still remained in the shtetl. The Poles apparently advised them to wait several hours while they would "cover the expenses." They [the Poles] would certainly succeed in capturing hidden Jews. A half an hour had not passed and a Polish policeman accompanied by a band of Poles led two Jewish boys from Beis-Medrash Street. They were taken to the members of the Gestapo who were standing at the market of the shtetl near their automobiles. A member of the Gestapo asked the Poles to leave both Jews near the truck and proceed to their "work"...

Whole crowds of Poles, from six year-old gentile boys to 50 year-old men and women with clubs in their hands went with full courage like wild beasts to loot. They searched, rummaged through every street and alley, every courtyard and pathway, every house and stable, every attic and cellar – they actually searched for Jews with a candle. In our residence, too, and in the attic we heard the noise of the "guest." It seemed to us that they had discovered us. We remained lying without breath and did not move any limb. Each of us was as if paralyzed from fear, thinking that we were in the last moments of our lives. However, everything passed peacefully. Not finding anyone, they looted our possessions and left on a further hunt. Little by little we became a little freer and we became ourselves. One of us again crawled on our stomach to the "observation point." We saw how captured Jews were being taken to the Gestapo trucks. It was possible to recognize some Jews from afar; [to recognize] others, mostly women, was more difficult because they often wore shawls over their heads that completely hid their faces. The Poles succeeded in gathering 11 Jews over two hours. Among them was my grandfather, Shimkha Khtiba. The Gestapo officer ordered them to go up onto the truck quickly and they were taken away in the same direction that they had sent all of the Jews several hours earlier. The Gestapo Mercedes automobile also went along. No members of the Gestapo remained in the shtetl, only the local regime. The hunt for Jews continued; it appeared that the youngest gentile boys did not tire of the work. A sort of competition to catch Zydes [Jews] went on among them and the parents experienced pleasure from their brats.

Night approached little by little. It grew calm at the market of the shtetl and there were fewer Poles. Firlus, the policeman who was leading two newly found Jews, reappeared. A gang of young, gentile boys, who were celebrating their success, also accompanied them. They were taken to the district commissioner. Not five minutes had passed and the same door to the district commission opened again and the policemen were leading [the Jews] out and walking in the direction of Tifle Street until they disappeared from our sight. From below, near the wall of our house, a conversation among a group of Poles who were gathered there reached us. It was impossible to see them from the opening in the roof because they were standing right against the wall. One of them called out with great joy: "Janek Staczinski is a skillful person. He was successful in getting a hold of both Fuls brothers, who were hiding in the bathhouse." A second called out: "What do you need more than the blind Szenka, who with one eye found Shmuel Penski and his son in a dark, narrow side street and Firlus, the policeman, just took them to be shot at the Jewish cemetery." A third called out with regrets: "What is the use in catching individuals when so many succeed in escaping?" "Do not worry," another one answered the first voice. "We will get a hold of each one to the last." They began to enumerate the names of the Jews who they had not seen on the wagons. The number reached 30. The pessimistic voice said again, "We know of 30. How many do we not know?" There was no answer to this. However, they quickly consoled themselves that many Jews had been wounded during their escapes. They said that the chairman of the Judenrat, Finkewicz, had been shot through his hand and cheek. They lay him bloodied on the wagon. Several unknown women were also severely wounded while escaping. (They did not mention their names.) The conversation ended little by little and the group dissolved.

It already was twilight. A dead stillness reigned over the shtetl. All of the Jewish houses at the market stood sad and lamenting for their residents who had been torn away from them today. Somewhere from a Jewish stall the chattering of a goose who wanted something to eat or drink was heard. From time to time the lonesome meowing of a cat also was heard. It seemed that everything was lamenting and crying at the great misfortune, at the destruction of Goniadz...

The Polish policemen went from one Jewish house to another and sealed the doors and windows ostensibly so that Jewish possessions would not be stolen. Around six o'clock, when it became very dark, Poles with clubs in their hands were divided into groups as night watchmen, near each Jewish house. Our plan to go out from our hiding place at night and escape came to nothing. We remained lying in fear and dread, desperate and waiting for a suitable moment. The first night after the destruction was frightful. From time to time we heard discovered Jews being taken, who could be recognized by their crying and shouting. Sometimes the moving cries of a woman also was heard that shocked the soul. The frequent shooting during the first half of the night rang in the dark, quiet and shook us, knowing that each shot cost a Jew his life. Our faces began to burn; our hearts beat fast, our bodies trembled and we could not take a deep breath. The hooligan-watchmen, who stood below and sniffed around like bloodhounds, might hear us.

20th Chapter

None of us closed our eyes during the entire night. Morning arrived. A golden beam sneaked in through a small opening in the roof onto us. One of us moved to the "observation point" on his stomach. It was empty and free of people. The entire Polish population was still sleeping. It was very tired from its heavy "day of work" the day before. At around nine o'clock, movement began at the shtetl market. Polish policemen appeared, armed with rifles and, little by little, the civilian population crept out of their houses. They again continued with the work arranged by the Gestapo the previous night. Not half an hour passed and a shout was suddenly heard: "Help!!! Save me!!!"... There was a horrible scene in the street. Gogol, the Polish policeman, led Menasha Krawiec (the blacksmith) and beat him murderously over the head, back and feet – wherever he could – with the butt of his rifle. He took him to the district commissioner and then to the cellar where the arrestees were always kept. Five minutes had not passed and another policeman, Firlus, led the five-year old Sholem'ke Rozental under a gun. He led him into the same cellar. Returning from there, a group of small Polish children ran with him [Firlus] and asked him to go with them to "Maysim Gesl" [the Alley of the Dead]. After 10 minutes, Firlus, the policeman led three new Jews, among them two women. Firlus led them to the guard post of the gendarmes and returned in a quarter of an hour, only with the women who he led to the same cellar in which the previous Jews had been imprisoned. The Poles' "productive" work gave the Germans approximately 30 Jews during the first three days after the destruction.

On the fourth day, Friday, the police led the Jews out of the cellar. They were placed in a line near the district commission. There the "guests" waited, three wagons and the gendarmes' carriage. Then, when the Jews had been standing for a considerable time, the district commissioner went over to them. He slapped several in the face and told them all to go up into the wagons.

Accompanied by two gendarmes and three policemen they were taken away in the same direction as all of the Goniadz Jews.

After the gathered remaining Jews were taken away, the Poles succeeded in catching another Jew. Others would surrender themselves at the gendarmerie, there being no other choice when none of their peasant acquaintances would allow then over their threshold. The district commissioner did not play with them and ordered the police to take them to the Jewish cemetery at night and to shoot them. Many Jews were murdered in such a manner during the first few weeks after the destruction. Now the Polish population could calmly begin to rob the Jewish possessions. Understand that the "work" would be done at night when they themselves were the watchmen of the Jewish possessions. This robbery was officially strongly forbidden according to a law that threatened the death penalty for doing so.

The joy of the Poles was mostly obvious on the first Sunday after the destruction of the Jews. All of the Poles dressed up in holiday clothes, a large number in newly stolen Jewish [clothing], and strolled through the market of the shtetl. The happy conversations and laughter could be heard from afar. They gathered in groups and had joint feasts, sharing among themselves the great joy that had suddenly and unexpectedly arrived. One such revelry occurred at the home of our nearest, next door neighbor, the former policeman and famous bandit, Kaminski. He invited many guests and they got drunk together. The voice and every wish from each one reverberated at the open doors. The call, "Let us drink in honor of the fact they we have lived to see a Jewish-free Goniadz," could be heard often from afar. The voices and the singing of the drunk people, which increased from time to time, had a terrible effect on us and really tore our troubled nerves. The rampage lasted until late at night.

21st Chapter

Lying for a long time confined in hunger, thirst and cold in the narrow, low hiding place, we looked for a suitable moment to get out of there and escape from hell. After two weeks we succeeded in grabbing the moment when the night watchmen had left our residence a half hour earlier than usual. It was six thirty. The gray day began to dawn, but the gentiles, sated with Jewish blood and goods, still slept soundly. At that moment we stood at the edge of a knife and dared quietly to come down from the attic to the residence. We opened the back window that led to the courtyard and one by one we went out through it. We ran through the empty courtyard and alleys until we found ourselves outside of the shtetl and from there we ran to wherever our feet took us... When it was already very light, we were on the other side of the highway. The first snow that had fallen two days earlier had not yet covered all of the fields; it moistened them even more and therefore the way through the wet area was very difficult. Our feet would sink so deep that we had to work hard to pull them back out. The wet wind and the snow slapped us in the face, as if nature was trying to make us equal with all of the Jews. Finally after walking for four kilometers without stop with our last strength, we succeeded in reaching a colony, to a peasant acquaintance. From the beginning, he did not want to let us over his threshold, saying that he would face the threat of a bullet in the head for doing so. After we assured him that we had good clothing in our rucksacks and we would reward him well for [letting us in], he let us come into his residence. We immediately gave him a new man's shirt and two silver spoons and asked him to permit us to stay for the day and as soon as it got dark we would leave from here. The peasant agreed to let us. We learned the following from him: all of the Goniadz Jews were taken to the Bogusze camp, which was located near the eastern Prussian border (three kilometers from Grajewo). Dozens of Jewish communities in the Bialystok and Grodno areas were taken away on the same day at the same hour. Only the Jasionówka community, the Bialystok ghetto and the Grodno ghetto remained in place. The Jews from eight shtetlekh around Grajewo were taken away to Bogusze, including Goniadz and Trestine. The Jews from the shtetlekh around Bialystok were concentrated in the former military camps in Bialystok itself: from the Grodno area – in Kiełbasin [now Kolbasino] (near Grodno). He advised us to turn ourselves in to the German gendarmerie because no on would allow us over their threshold because of the order given out by the district commissioner: "Every Pole who hides a Jews will be shot along with his entire family and his buildings will be burned." We answered him that we would try to struggle as much as we could. We left at night to continue our journey after sitting for the day at the peasant's [house] in a closed, small room in fear and terror...

The door was closed to us wherever we went. None of our peasant acquaintances would allow us to cross their threshold. They just set their dogs against us to chase us more quickly from their courtyards. We also were forced to leave on the most hazardous journey and went through fields and forests to Jasionówka. There we found our father and 26 other Goniadz refugees. Our father told us that on the day of the "aktsia" he succeeded in escaping from Goniadz during the morning hours, forcing himself through the armed Gestapo guard on the highway near Rowy. Our mother, who was following after him was turned back by a member of the Gestapo. She was forlorn, probably the only family member taken to Bogusze.

Around 500 refugees from all of the surrounding shtetlekh had come together in Jasionówka. They sat there for another three months until the Gestapo created another "aktsia" like the one in Goniadz on a beautiful winter morning on the 25th of January 1943.

A small number of Jews successfully left the shtetl during the morning hours. A number escaped from the sleds that took us to the Knyszyn train station where a special train to Treblinka waited for us and a greater number succeeded in jumping through the small windows of the freight wagons in which hundreds of Jews were being taken to the slaughter.

On our long road of suffering, fear of death, struggle and a fight for existence, each of us then was accompanied by a powerful, heartbreaking lamenting shout of tortured, half dead Jews pressed together to the point of asphyxiation in the dark wagons. This was the shout of a testament and request in the last hours of their lives – "Jews! Take revenge for our innocent blood!!! Revenge!!! - - - Revenge!!!..."

Everyone in our family was successful in saving themselves from the "aktsia" in a different way. My brother Zalman immediately during the morning hours of the "aktsia" in Jasionówka escaped from an armed Gestapo guard who held him and guarded him non-stop. The member of the Gestapo chased after him shooting and through a miracle [Zalman] succeeded in disappearing and hiding until night in the barn of the Jasionówka priest. I succeeded in escaping from the sleds loaded with Jasionówka Jews during an evening hour when we were going through Knyszyn in the direction of its train station where the train to Treblinka already was waiting.

My father Khaykl Yevreiski jumped out of the small window in the freight wagon while the train was moving. My sister Kayle remaining alone in the dark, crowded, packed wagon, could no longer bear the terrible tortures and decided to kill herself by jumping from the small window of the freight wagon while the train was moving. She fell on a stone, hit her face and lay unconscious in the snow, in the frosty winter night. A young man who had jumped from the wagon after her, carried her to an unknown peasant in the village of Starosielce (outside of Bialystok) and left her there. She woke up and was surprised to find herself there. The wife of the peasant told her the whole story, gave her breakfast to eat… and told her to go. Kayle then wrapped her wounded, swollen face with her winter headscarf and left on her way on the clear day in the direction of Goniadz. Arriving late at night at [the home of] a peasant acquaintance in the village of Rybaki, she found me. After that we found our father and brother Zalman at Christian acquaintances in the village of Kręźce. Then a new hardship began. It was impossible to find a place for us.

Our father wandered around the entire night until he finally found a peasant in the village of Kosoirki who was ready to hide us in exchange for our possessions (we had succeeded in bringing some of them to a Polish acquaintance in time). We were hidden in Kosoirki in the peasant's stable attic for nine months. Our lives often hung by a hair, mainly when the Goniadz gendarmes visited the peasant, entered the stall to look at his cow and we then lay in the attic over their heads. It was a miracle that they did not notice or detect us. After the peasant had received a considerable wardrobe from us for him and his family, he told us to leave… Again death lay in wait for us on all sides. We wandered around the forests, fields, in potato pits and haystacks for a considerable time. The peasants often noticed us in the fields and ran to inform those in the village. However, we disappeared before the residents of the village came to catch us and turn us in to the Goniadz gendarmerie. In such conditions we wandered around day and night, hungry and cold, trudging in winds in the moist forests (alder groves), in marshes where no one usually would be able to reach. Our father would spend the entire night searching for a place for us. The first approach to a gentile was frightening and the most hazardous, not knowing how he would react when he would first see him [our father]. It is not easy to imagine our suspense and anxiety until we lived to see our father returning from his terrible journey. However, nothing stopped him and despite his age (52) he was agile and hearty. He went to all of the perilous places where certain death was a threat. When my brother and I would want to replace him he did not allow us to do so, saying: "You are still young, children. You must still live. If something happens it is better that I be the victim before you."

We were tormented in such conditions for 20 months. At that time our father felt sick and said to us: "Children! Who knows if I have gotten cancer?" (Alas, he was not wrong.) Although life for him was not dear, suffering so many blows, he did not lessen his heroic efforts to save us until he led us to redemption with his last strength.

He died of cancer on the 22nd of Shvat 5705 (the 5th of February 1945) in the Bialystok hospital after an operation.

Honor his memory!

From right to left: **Tuvya, Kayla and Zalman Jevrajski at the grave of their father before leaving Poland in 1945 (three months after his death)**

22nd Chapter

(The camp in Bogusze)

Bogusze is a village that is located on the border of Poland and eastern Prussia, three kilometers from Grajewo. Before the Jews were brought there, Bogusze was a camp for Russian prisoners of war. This was a large field, fenced in with barbed wire. There were barracks erected in the field, actually dug out pits covered from above with roofs. Inside, in such a barrack, were shelves along the walls made of boards (plank beds) that served as beds.

On the 2nd of November 1942, the Goniadz Jews were brought to Bogusze. They found the Jews from Grajewo, Rajgrad, Szczuszyn, Radzilow and other surrounding shtetlekh already there.

One of the internees wrote the following about Bogusze:

"The confined Jews were not given any food during the first three-four days. Everyone ate what they had brought from home. But on the fifth day, the German regime created four kitchens that were to feed more than 7,000 confined Jews.

They cooked potato soup in the kitchens four or five times a day. Everyone received a half-liter of watery soup and 100 grams of bread a day. The people were starving and besieged the kitchen, grabbing the potatoes peels and swallowing them uncooked.

"Terrible hunger and filth truly reigned in the camp. There was terrible mortality. Every night the dead bodies would be laid in a pit and taken to the camp cemetery for Russian prisoners of war in the morning. From time to time a "selection" would take place in the camp – a designated number of Jews who had been told that the next day they would be sent to work, were separated [from the rest]. In the morning the Jews were taken away, but not one of them came back. It is notable that a rumor already had spread among the Jews in Bogusze that Jews were being sent to Treblinka and Majdanek and they were being burned in the crematoria there.

"On the 22nd of December 1942, at five o'clock in the morning, the Gestapo entered the camp as a group and ordered all of the Jews to leave the barracks for the camp square. When about half of the Bogusze Jews had filled it, the Gestapo told those remaining to remain sitting in their places. The Gestapo told the assembled Jews to stand in-fours in a long line and to march in a circle near the fences of the camp square. No person could be recognized because of the deep darkness. The only thing heard were the steps of people marching and continual shooting from automatic weapons. Later, there was a terrifying picture when the Gestapo opened the gate of the camp and took away the Jews to the train station in Prostken [Prostki]. About 70 Jews lay shot in pools of blood, frozen to the ground. Others were still alive and wrestled with death. However, they could not withstand the terrible suffering and therefore asked the members of the Gestapo to shoot them. The members of the Gestapo did them this favor. In the later morning hours, when the remaining members of the Gestapo in the camp sent out a group of the remaining Jews to gather the dead bodies, it was revealed that the Gestapo had not only shot into the lines of the Jews marching at the camp square, but also along the entire road without end, for a distance of a kilometer to the Prostken train station. Over 50 dead bodies lay on the road, frozen to the ground with their blood. On the same day the train took the Jews from Prostken through Knyszyn-Bialystok to Treblinka.

"The number who remained were sent out on the 3rd of January 1943 in a second transport that numbered approximately 3,000 Jews."

My sister Kayle told of the last journey of the Jews to the crematorium at Treblinka in her description, On the Road to Treblinka [next article in this memorial book]. Fate wanted her to survive the terrible "trip" on the death train to Treblinka with 20 other Goniadz Jews during the liquidation of the Jasionówka Jewish community three weeks after the Jews from Bogusze were taken on the same journey by such a train. These documents that tell of the terrible suffering during the last hours of our martyrs completes the tragic history of the destruction of Goniadz.

[Page 675]

Names and Families Mentioned
in T. Ivry's Destruction of Goniondz
Translated by David Goldman

Avrahamke, the Glazier - Raver (?)

Bialy Hilka - Chaya Tsirel's son

Bzhezhinsky - A family from Botka (1935)

Barsky, Noach - Khatskel-Mendel Burkass' son-in-law

Green, Moshe - Moshe, the Rutkovsker [from Rutkovsk]

Hirshfeld, Shmuel - The son of Sholom Rachel-Leah's

Zimnokh, Betsalel - Alter, the dry goods store owner's son, Itshe Berls

Khazan, Henya - Henya Pesha's, the baker

Khativa, Simkha - The estate lessee

Yevreysky, Shimon - Shimon, the army tailor

Levin, Yisrael - Alter Yehudah's, the son of the butcher

Luria, Sonia - The midwife, Rachel Luria's daughter-in-law.

Lifshitz, Shmuel - Son-in-law of Pesha, the Presser

Luria, Khaya Rachel - One of the Marantz family

Tikotsky, Leibel - Leibel Betsalel's (the butcher)

Mikhnovsky, Alter - A baker, Isaac Aviezer's son-in-law

Nievodovsky, Zalman - Son of Eli-Hershel

Feldman, Meilech - His mother, Zissel, was Mosheke Piekarsky's daughter

Finkevitch, Hirsh - Moshe Mendel's son-in-law

Friedman, Nissan - Nissel, the Butcher

Pletinovitch - A family from Yedvobna that moved to Goniondz in 1931

Tsereleh - Gittel Abba's

Kliap, Motke - Motke Gershons

Kliap, Hershel and Yekhezkel - His sons

Kobrinsky, Asher - A son of Bertchuks Poliak

Kobrinsky, Yosef - Son of Chaim Poliak

Koppelman, Chaim - Chaim Dinkes

Kravitz, Menashe - Son of Reizel, the lady blacksmith (!)

Rubin, Yankel - Yankel Eliyahu's (the blacksmith)

Reigrodsky, Wolf - Khaya Tsirel's son-in-law

Rubin brothers - (Puls [?]), their father was Hershel Velvel Zodchak

Rosenthal, Sholom - His father was Khatskel-Itshe Frantsoizel's

[Pages 677-684]

On the Road to Treblinka
by Keila Yevreyski-Kremer
Translated by Martin Jacobs

Forward

Following the great "campaign" of November 2, 1942, which took in dozens of towns and villages, Goniondz included, the Germans left the Jews of Yashinovka where they were, as a trap for the Jews fleeing from the surrounding areas.

And so it was: Yashinovka was filled with Jewish refugees from all around. Among them were a small number of Goniondzers. Here too the bitter end was not long delayed. On January 25, 1943 the black day came upon all Jews who were in Yashinovka. They were assembled in the market place and transported from there on sleds to the railroad station in Knishin.

***

When we came to the Knishin station we noticed three small closed freight cars which were standing on the tracks and waiting for us, fifteen hundred Jews, to lead us to the slaughter. Frozen, tired, and broken, we slowly get down from the sleds and go along, with the rest of the crowd, to the cars. The noise is loud as we get into the train. In the door stands a Nazi with a rubber stick in his hand and beats us without stop on our heads and faces and quickly shoves us into the car. Everyone is pushing now with all his might, because at least in the last moments of life you want to be with the family and die together with your own. But it isn't to be allowed. The truncheons rain over our heads, children are separated from parents, wives from husbands, sisters from brothers – and there is great panic. My father and I hold each other's hands tightly, so that we, the two left from our whole family, don't lose each other now. One car is already packed with Jews and the door slammed shut. Now they push us into the second car. We rush in first, to avoid the terrible blows and settle in a corner. In minutes this car too is filled above capacity with Jews and the door is shut. Little by little the occupants recover and begin to settle down in the dark, narrow, black box (the so-called railway car).

Tired, depressed, broken, we sit down on the floor. But there isn't room enough for everyone to sit. One sits on top of another and the rest stand, pressed together like sardines. I have a place under the little window, but I give it up for an elderly man and stand pressed up against the wall. We are very crowded. It is impossible to move a limb. Hands and feet get mixed up and everyone is moaning that he has no room. The air is suffocating and the heat great. I slowly lift myself up on to tip-toe, to the little narrow window. I open it, to breathe in a little fresh air and look out for the last time at the world which I would soon have to leave forever...

It is a bright starry winter evening. The earth is covered with a thick layer of snow, shining against the light of the moon. In the wide white field stand little trees, set in rows, standing motionless in the stillness of the evening, listening to the sudden commotion. The air is pure, transparent. A great wide world is around us; no one can be seen anywhere. And here in the car – what a contrast! Hundreds of people lie tossed about, without air, and are being led to the slaughter. But then, through the window, I glimpse the figure of a woman lying motionless on the ground. Later I will find out that this is a 19 year old girl. She was severely beaten and during the trip to the station nearly froze to death. She wasn't able to get down from the sled. The driver went to ask the murderers what to do with her. "Dump her in the field and go home", was their answer. And so he did. Now the 19 year old is lying, eyes half open, in the empty field, being extinguished like a light. But I look on almost with indifference at my frozen friend, because I know that the same fate awaits me, that tomorrow I will also lie as motionless as she, not frozen but gassed and burned. No sympathetic glance will accompany me to my rest. Over me will be the sound of cynical laughter from a Nazi, satisfying his murderous instincts by snuffing out our young lives. I again look at my dying friend, I say goodbye to her with a sympathetic look and close the window, since the children in the car are crying because of the cold. It is cold, crowded, and stuffy in the car. The children don't stop crying. They are hungry, frozen, tired, and sleepy. They huddle, crying, against their mothers' hearts, asking them for help. But unfortunately their mothers cannot now help them. They don't even have the heart to quiet them, and let them go on crying. Other mothers have fainted and their children are crying over them. Then a weak, pleading, woman's voice is heard: "Help, have pity, who has a little water, just a little water, my husband isn't well". The woman's voice repeats her plea several times, but in vain. No one has a drop of water to revive him, and the woman's voice grows silent.

For a short time the human mass keeps still, but soon a mighty uproar breaks out. People become like wild animals and begin pushing and shoving each other. The crowding gets even greater. The crying of children is heard anew. Mothers scream and plead: "Have pity, Jews, don't suffocate my child; you'll suffocate my child". The noise gets louder and louder. A quick rap on the door interrupts the noise. The door opens and everyone springs back from fear. Straightaway a shout is heard: "20 marks for a loaf of bread!" The crowd now begins to press forward; everyone wants to grab a bit of bread. Only three loaves are distributed and the door is again slammed shut. A new uproar starts. People scream and beg a little piece of bread. "Give me a bit of bread. Have pity, I have a little child." "My children are crying for food." "All they could distribute were three loaves of bread for everybody", another man screams. I get a little piece of bread from someone nearby. Little by little the people grow quiet. Now a general discussion starts up; first a middle-aged man "takes the floor" and tells this story: He himself is from a distant town, where the campaign of "Jewish cleansing" [Judenrein] was carried out some months ago. At the time he lost his entire family, his wife and three children. They are all now gone up in smoke. He was able to escape, and with long effort and hardship he reached Yashinovka, where the Jewish community was still in existence. When the decree hit this town too it was already impossible to escape. Actually, on the way here he again tried to save himself, but in vain. He was soon noticed and thrown back on the sled. Nevertheless he had not lost courage and called out in a cheerful voice: "Despite all troubles, Jews, let's not lose courage. We'll never be too late for death. Let's go on running; when the train is moving let's jump through the window. I'll jump; who will come with me?"

Several take courage and agree to jump; others say: "Where will we run? No one will let us cross their threshold; later we won't be able to choose when we die any more than now." One girl tells how several people escaped from their sled. From the middle of the group a male voice is heard: "I must give up my life because of my seven year old." From the corner is heard the weeping voice of a young woman with a little child in her arms; she screams at her mother: "It was too lonely for you to die alone; you had to have me with you. I could have saved myself.", and she bursts into bitter tears.

I stand in the corner next to my father and try to persuade him to escape. He doesn't want to. How, he says, can he escape and leave me behind alone? I explain to him that he can't help me now, because I am doomed in any event. Save yourself, Father, while you can, save yourself and help your son Tevye who has already escaped. "No, I can't", he says. I cry, I beg him, I insist he escape. Why must you lose your life because of me? If I weren't with you you would surely make a run for it. Why should I die having on my conscience that I dragged you to your death with me? This has already been our fate: Mother was led to her death separately; I here, also separately; what is the point of my dragging you with me? Run, Father, I beg him, save yourself. Do it for me. I cry, practically tear myself apart begging him, I give him no peace until he promises me he will run away.

Suddenly the car shakes, the train starts to move. What a frightening moment! How dreadful the moment when conscious human beings ride to their deaths with a clear conscience. "Already", the same screamed sigh is heard from everyone, "already they are leading us to the slaughter." Children begin to cry and scream, women faint, men hide their weeping within themselves and moan silently. Now even the car is weeping. It seems as though even this black box leading hundreds of Jews to their eternal rest is also weeping now. Streams of tears are pouring from its walls, mixed with the cold sweat of the dying. Everything weeps and laments the destruction of the Jewish people. "Enough!", a voice is heard interrupting the lamentation and weeping. "Enough, the time has come to run, who will jump first?" "I", says my father, and falls into my arms. No pen has the power to describe our feelings. I only remember how we wept silently and could not tear ourselves from each other. But I immediately remember that time is short and I say: "Enough, Father, enough", and tear myself from his arms, "Now go! Good luck on your way.", I cry out from the depths of my heart "and be a father to your only remaining child, and take revenge, revenge for innocent blood." -- and father disappears from my eyes. Just as it was from my heart, so now from every Jewish heart the same cry is wrenched. Hundreds of voices are now transformed into one strong and powerful voice, which gets stronger and stronger, more and more powerful as time passes. This is the last cry of farewell and, at the same time, the last will and testament of the half dead, which accompanies all escaping Jews on their anguished road to life.

My father jumps out first, and after him other men jump. They encourage each other in their escape from death. The will to live at such a moment cannot be described. I stand at the window and help the escapees lift themselves up and I watch as they jump. I turn my head back and see how each one embraces those near and dear, how they pour out their pain and anger to each other, share their sorrows, cry their aching hearts out, and take leave before death.

I now stand alone in the corner. The only one of my family, the only one from my town. I don't have anyone to pour my heavy heart out to. I remember my unfortunate mother, how difficult it was for her when, also alone and lonely, she was led to the slaughter, without a child by her side, not being able to cry her heart out and share her grief with even one person. All this seethes within me and tightens about my heart. At that moment I hear one girl saying to another, "Let's jump too, I first and then you." and the girls jump to freedom.

Now a thought flashes through my mind: What am I waiting for? What do I have to lose? In the last minutes of my life I don't even have anyone to pour my heart out to. Must I then suffer and die at the impure hands of Nazis? Is it not better to die right here? Hearing someone say, "Who is jumping now?", I shout ":Help me! I'm jumping!" In a moment I'm in the window, holding on to the iron bars on the other side of the car, and then I jump - - - - - - -

And by jumping to my death I chanced to remain alive.

[Pages 685-700]

How I Survived It...
The Storm Breaks Out
by Shabtai Finkelshtein
Translated by Gloria Berkenstat Freund

Shabtai Finkelshtein, of blessed memory, the writer of this article, was from Jasionówka, but his description includes Goniadz. He lived through the tragedy – the destruction of our hometown and the extermination of our most beloved – and survived it. – The Editor

Shabtai Finkelshtein

On the 22nd of July, 1941, the Germans attacked Russia. Thousands of Jews escaped in the direction of Russia. However, the Germans dispersed everyone along the way, and hundreds of corpses with gunshots covered the roads. No one from the area of Bialystok was successful in saving themselves because the Germans surrounded the entire area with lightning speed and surrounded a large Russian army. There was no shortage of Jaszinowker [Jasionówka in Polish] and Goniadzer young people among the bodies.

The Germans along with the Poles set fire to the *shtetl* [town] in Jasionówka. All of the Jews were driven to the wall of the Polish church. The old and sick who could not leave their homes were shot and burned along with the houses. However, many dozen were successful in escaping into the fields.

The Jews of Jasionówka were at the wall of the church for eight hours, surrounded by Poles and guarded by German with machine guns, until by chance a high German military man arrived and asked what was happening. As it was explained to him that these were "communists," he understood that this was not true of the old men and women – and he freed them.

[Page 686]

I Sneak Into Goniadz

I left Jasionówka after eight months and went to the Bialystok ghetto. This was Passover 1942. After being in Bialystok for a month, I had the premonition that an "*aktsia*" [a roundup or deportation] would take place there, and that I, a man from the provinces, would certainly be the first on the fire. Aizik Rozental (a Knyszyner, who had lived in Jasionówka) and I left the ghetto at dawn, with all of the workers – and Aizik led us to Goniadz, where he knew a family: Feygl Slomianski (Shmuel-Ber Malozowski's daughter). We were delayed for a few days in Knyszyn and from there we left for Goniadz. Arriving in Goniadz, we met a Jew who informed us that it was not good there: the commissar was searching for outsiders. But we still entered. I left for Khatskl Rozental, the *tandetnik.* [ed-Itshe Francolyzl's son: dealt with ready made clothing] His son, Avram'l was my friend. Aizik left for the Slomianski's.

[Page 687]

We learned that a few days earlier there was an incident with "outsiders," but now things are quiet. A few days later, I arrived at the quarters of the Slomianski family on the old market, in the house of Feygl's father, Shmuel Ber Malozowski (Feygl's husband, Moshe'ke Slomianski, died in the time of the Soviets.)

The First Blows

The first blow Goniadz received from the war was from the Poles. The Germans did not even stop in Goniadz. And the Poles carried out methodical pogroms under the secret leadership of the priest (*khomer* – Hebrew word for priest).

Nine months later a mass grave was dug up in the cemetery and everyone was found tortured in the most terrible manner. Their hands were bound behind them with wire and there were nails in their heads (I witnessed this with my own eyes). There was sadness in the city. Sheets were brought and everyone was given a Jewish burial.

All of Goniadz Works in the Fortress

Goniadz was organized for work in the Osowiec Fortress. Osowiec was a general assembly point for all weapons and clothing that the Soviet army had left behind and there *everyone* in the *shtetl* capable of working worked; even a small percent of Poles. Later, after the liquidation of Goniadz, all of the Poles had to work.

Work was varied there. If there were "good" Germans – the work was easier. There were cases of Germans only permitting the Jews to ride in the wagons on the return from work, and not the Poles.

[Page 688]

We Live Together with "Good Germans"

The young people would stroll in Kliap's orchard after work. Incidentally, the orchard was a back way for Jews (from Tiple Street to the old market) to avoid the street. Until the Poles learned that the Jews were holding "communistic meetings" in the orchard. With luck that became known to the Jews before the commissar arrived there with a gun...

Feygle Malozowski-Slomianski had three daughters and two sons; each of the children had friends. This was the only house in the *shtetl* where a great number of young people would come together, up to 50 people. It is worth noting that one of Feygle's daughters – Golda – worked at the gendarmerie (in Chaim Kobrinski's house).

The Germans were so accustomed to Jewish workers that we often discussed with them the defeats that awaited them... (At that time, the front was in Stalingrad). Until a decree came "from above" that Jews must not work for Germans. The situation became strained. It began to be felt in the entire province as if we were on the verge of being imprisoned in a ghetto.

After great efforts by the *Judenrat* – with great sums of money and antiques – it was necessary to move out only from Dolistower Street.

This was on a Thursday and Friday. On *Shabbos*, the commissar declared that he was giving the Jewish population potatoes for the winter for a small amount of money.

[Page 689]

Again joy! Early Sunday, everyone, small and large, dragged potatoes. Rivers of sweat poured out doing this and the cellars were filled for winter. Because the war would not be ending so quickly!

What Do We Need the Wagons For ...

On Sunday night, a peasant, a "*soltis* [village chief]" from a village came to a Jew who was close to him and explained that tomorrow all of the Jews would be taken away and that wagons had already been scheduled. The news was quickly spread in the entire *shtetl*. There was a panic. Representatives of the *Judenrat* – Lipsztajn and Pinkewicz – went to the commissar. The commissar assured them that they could stay calm because the wagons that he had scheduled were for bringing trees to plant along the highway. It was again good!... Particularly, because potatoes were already in the cellars for winter.

"Children, Get Dressed!"

My friend, Aizik, who would work the entire week "as a furrier" (finishing skins) in the village and would come to Goniadz for *Shabbos* and Sunday, woke up on Monday at five o'clock in the morning and left for the village. The workers (of the *shtetl*) again left for work in Osowiec. Shmuel Ber – dressed in his *Shabbos kapote* [long coat worn by pious Jewish men] – came in at seven o'clock and woke everyone up: "Children, get dressed!"

We immediately knew what this meant. We put on our best clothes in seconds. Golda ran to the sawmill where she then worked and came back.

Jews are not working today!

We Escape From a Trap

Berl (Feygl's son) and I escaped to the field. The field was full of escaping Jews. Everyone understood the danger.

[Page 690]

We ran to the bridge in Dolko – and opposite us, a German with a gun appeared from under the bridge. The German said nothing and we went back, no longer running... However, we noticed two young girls running across the highway opposite the booth (the house near the highway that stood between Dolko and Guzy). We ran in the same direction – and also across the highway. At that moment a German gave a shout: *Stop!*

I was 20 meters from the German so I stopped and shouted to Berl, "Berl, Stay!" Berl looked behind him – and ran farther. I – after him... And in front of us – the two girls.

The German began to shoot. The road was up hill. I would fall with each shot. I heard each bullet going by with a whistle. A second German shot at me from the side. I then threw down the *kurtke* (a short topcoat); ran farther – and threw away the *marinarke* (jacket) and the hat. I was left in a shirt.

The shooting was in my direction because I was the closest. When I would fall on the ground while the bullets rushed past, I would place my hand on my chest and take a look to see if there still no blood... Thus we ran breathlessly for a few kilometers uphill until we arrived at the far side of the hill. There we sat for several minutes. The girls were Feitshe and Grune Hirszfeld (daughters of Ruchl- Leah's Sholem [Sholem is possibly Ruchl-Leah's son].

We rested a few minutes – and ran farther, to the Downar Forest. Here we lay down on the grass and did not say anything.

[Page 691]

Each of us knew what was happening there, from where the shooting was coming. After resting for a while, we heard wagons go by. I moved closer to the highway. I lay down on the ground and saw that Trestiner [Trzeszczyn] Jews were being taken.

It happened to be a Polish holiday on that day and they went to their cemeteries and prayed for their dead. This was close to the forest. Then a thought came to me: who would cry over our widely scattered graves?...

I could not find my friends (Berl and the two girls) again. I wandered the entire day until night and did not find them. I sat down in a broken mood. When it became dark, I shouted: Berl! I received a response from the other side of the hill. We did not say anything at first. They were frightened – perhaps I had been caught.

Later, it was clear to us why we had been successful in running across the highway (running out of Goniadz). The Germans, who had been guarding the highway, had gone to Guzy because they were then bringing the Jews from Osowiec (all of those who had gone there to work in the morning) – and this gave us an opportunity to run across the road. A German stood every 20 to 30 meters.

We Look for Aizik – And Find Six Jews in the Forest

When it got very dark, Berl had to take us across the train line because he had worked there for the Russians when they built an aerodrome (airport) there. I knew the way from there to Aizik's (who left in the morning to work in a village) and

[Page 692]

I discussed with Berl where to meet him.

When we had gone back a few kilometers, we met a Christian woman near a peasant's house. She did not yet know what had taken place in Goniadz. She let us stay in the "roost [hay loft]" for a pair of golden *koltshikes* (earrings) that Feitshe had given to her. The train was near the stall. Trains passed one after another – and we lay covered (with hay) in the hay loft. It was clear that I had nothing; Berl was without a *kurtke* [short topcoat].

In the morning, the Christian said that it was not safe here. He had small children and Germans came to him. Berl and I left to look for Aizik and the girls gave the gentiles a small, golden cross and remained there.

We searched for an entire night until we found Aizik's Christian. We saw that there were six people with him – four from Jasionówka and two from Goniadz (young girls) were in the woods in a *skhron* (a bunker, a protective lair.) We stayed with the Christian for the night and in the early morning, when comrades (from the woods) came for food, we met them. We met Kahan, the younger son of Centura, at another Christian's. He came to the city at night. We left for the woods together. We climbed on the mountain and found the bunker. We brought kindling wood. We were nine people all together; seven young men and two young girls.

Everyone described how they had escaped.

Khona explained that he had been brought back from Goniadz with all of the workers from Otowiec. They were all assembled near the fortress.

[Page 693]

Escaping had been difficult; this was a more certain death. Everyone in the city had been stood in the market and a member of the Gestapo gave a speech to them – that they were being taken to work; that each of them needed to bring their work clothes, regular clothing and tools. Everyone had to return in half an hour. Those who did not believe the commissar hid in the city. Many were found and shot. Everyone assembled at the market. They were placed in wagons and taken to Bogusze, a concentration camp near Grajewo.

We "Adopt" the Rawe's Young Boy

Two days later. Aizik went out to a Christian at night and met a 10 year old young Jewish boy there – the son of the Rawers [The young boy's surname is spelled in Yiddish here with and without a final "r"] from the watermill. He brought him to us. The bunker (the protection lair) became very small, so we went out to enlarge it and a Christian noticed this. We were afraid that he would talk about it. We returned to the Christian at night to find out. He told us to escape from there, "Because in the morning they would come to us to burn two villages of peasants."

Outside there was snow and a frost; it was dark – where would we go? 10 people – each wanting to live! We separated. Some went to a Christian acquaintance. I suggested going to a second forest and digging a pit. Meanwhile, we learned that Jasionówka and Bialystok still existed [there were still Jews in Jasionówka and Biakystok.] The Jews were driven out of all of the more distant cities. On 2ⁿᵈ November 1942, dozens of cities and *shtetlekh* in our area were liquidated.

Back to Jasionówka

After a few difficult days lying around in farmyards, without the knowledge of the Christians, in pits of potatoes, in forests and woods, we – Berl, Chana and I – arrived in Jasionówka at night. I went to work in the morning with my uncle and made a bunker in a stall. This was difficult because it was cold, 30 degrees, but we managed to create a hiding place closest to the day that the commissar had assured us that Jasionówka would remain as "always."

[Page 694]

In Jasionówka we met other escapees: Leibl Molozowski (Moshe Molozowski's brother – the ed.), Gedalia Guzowski, Hajkl Jewrejski and his children and others. A few hundred Jews gathered in Jasionówka from all of the surrounding *shtetlekh*. The local commissar did not do anything bad. However, in a short time – the 25ᵗʰ of January, 1943 – Jasionówka was surrounded and the *shtetl* had the same fate as every other one.

In the Stall

14 people arrived in the bunker (from Goniadz: Leibl Molozowski [spelled Malozowski elsewhere], Berl Slomianski and Gedalia Guzowski). There was only room for eight. Almost 22 people – with children – arrived at night. The situation in the bunker was terrible; there was no air. We did not dare open the door because there was a constant vapor and we would surely be caught. We could not light a fire because it would not burn because of a lack of air...

One child had whooping cough; when steps were heard overhead, someone threw themselves on the seven year old girl – and she was suffocated...

After another few days of struggle, people began to leave the bunker and search: perhaps they would be successful in finding a place. Leaving were: Leibl Malozowski, Gedalia Guzowski and a number of y in a pail of snow – with mud, and we would eat raw barley. We felt as if we would die of hunger. And we had already sitting there for two weeks, while in the city there were no Jews and there was a terrible frost outside.

[Page 695]

We Are Discovered – But Not Caught

On the 14th day, a Pole looked for gold in the Jewish stall and – found us. He immediately ran to report to the police. The *shtchit* (top most part of the roof) was a double one; all 14 of us went inside it – with two children. In around five minutes, the stall became full of police and Germans. They shot and searched – and did not find us. We heard how they spoke to each other: "There are no footprints in the snow; it is still warm in the bunker – so where are they?" It was cold; the days were short; it became dark – they only left a guard, and in the morning they would again try to search. We heard the policemen say that there was no need to bother, just to shoot immediately. When the policemen became cold, they shot to frighten us and they went to a neighbor to warm themselves.

Then we went out one by one, agreeing to meet in the field. I and my wife, Liba Azrik, were the last to go down, but we found no one when we arrived at the field...

[Page 696]

We Search for Food – In the Night

Forlorn. Sky and snow – and we were in the middle, not knowing where to turn and what to do. It was foggy, so we wandered back into the city. With luck, no one noticed us and we escaped. After a night of roaming, we shoved ourselves into a pile of hay in the field. We remained there for an entire day. At night, we went out and were drawn to a fire opposite us. We came to a village, went into a house and a Christian welcomed us and gave us food.

We wandered farther until we again became lost and we sat in the forest for a day. At night, we went to a Christian, who told us that during the deportations in

Jasionówka, 40 Jews were shot for trying to escape and that their bodies lay around in the street for two weeks.

And as we were sitting with the Christian, a young boy from Jasionówka entered; we learned from him who had escaped. He and a brother and his two sisters were among the escapees. One sister had frozen feet; she could not walk. She could not live and also could not die. She asked that they kill her, so that she would not fall into the hands of the murderers. She could not hang herself alone. Her brothers and the other sister helped her to hang herself...

We Dig Out a Home in the Woods

We knew a Christian and we lived in his field in a pit of potatoes for a month, in cold and hunger. During the month we learned about the area and dug a small pit in a small woods and camouflaged it so that no one would notice it. We stayed there for five months. In the course of time, we experienced many things. There were days when we had too much to eat and days of literal hunger.

[Page 697]

Once we went to the field at night to find a little tree that would look like a "decoration" over the door of our pit. And when we were walking with the little tree, a man was coming in the opposite direction. We could not escape, so we lay down. The man opposite us did the same... Until he gave a shout, "Jews?" – We answered: "Jews!" This was a Jew from Jasionówka, over 60 years old. He had jumped off a speeding train. He had no money; the money remained with his wife, who remained on the train... He was wandering in the dark like hundreds and thousands looking for bread.

In this way, for the second time, we met two Jews. One of them remained with us.

A False Alarm

Once we were sitting – my wife and I – and we sensed that someone was coming, not far from us. There was a heavy rain outside – and the steps came nearer to our pit. We thought that someone certainly had seen how we had earlier planted trees on the pit and around the pit. We felt that someone was digging and sitting on the little tree that was over the door. We were sure that one had gone for the police and the other was sitting over us and not letting us out... I tried to open the door – someone was sitting! I spoke in Polish, lifted up the door with all of my strength – and turned over a person. As I stuck out my head, I saw how a 12-year old Jewish boy lay confused... We immediately took him in our pit...

The story about the young boy was thus: When Jews were still permitted to live and work, - indeed, before the Germans – the young boy was a shepherd for a Christian. Now he came to his "Christian" in the village for bread. The Christian did not let him in; the young boy left for the nearby woods – and a heavy rain was falling! He buried himself in the trees – so that he would not be seen and so he would be a little protected from the rain. He fell asleep in the rain... So, in such a manner, we met a Jewish child... We had many such cases.

[Page 698]

We Are Denounced

A Christian denounced us, "Jews were going around in the area." A second Christian warned us that we should escape. We escaped four at a time in a large storm and rain, across a river and 10 kilometers from our pit. There on that day two Jews had been shot, one from Jasionówka, the second – a Knisziner. As a response to this, several Jews with rifles shot two policemen the next day.

During the summer we would lie in the corn for weeks. In winter, sleeping was worse. Going out of the pit for food once in two or three weeks. It was approximately two months before the liberation, when we took two more Jews with us. We were now six.

The Last Two Weeks in the Pit

The German artillery was literally on us for the last two weeks. This was five kilometers from Jasionówka. The Soviet artillery was two kilometers on the other side of the *shtetl*, where we had been for five months. We lay for two weeks in hunger and in fear. Over our pit, German was being spoken... We had matches ready: if we were caught, we would set ourselves on fire and not fall in their hands...

[Page 699]

We Are Freed and Reach *Eretz-Yisroel*

After those two weeks, we lay in the pit for two more days not knowing that we had been liberated by the Red Army. We had a warm welcome from the Soviets. They gave us food and things (clothing).

In Jasionówka up to 60 Jews assembled. This was one of the largest percentages of survivors from Jewish cities and *shtetlekh*.

We recovered a little in six months – until an attack of the Polish bandits (A.K. [Polish resistance]) occurred. We heroically defended ourselves with return fire and they retreated with losses. In the morning all of the Jews traveled to Bialystok and we began our wandering across European cemeteries to our goal *Eretz-Yisroel* – and we reached it!

[Page 700]

Epilogue

Two months after we were freed, a "*sheygets*" [gentile boy] named Wladek came into a Jewish house in Jasionówka. He learned that Jews lived here so he returned to his persecuted brothers not wanting to be a "Christian" any longer... This was Leibl Rawer's young boy from Goniadz.

The young boy had escaped from the forest near Downar together with all of us, when we had been discovered. He went many kilometers and presented himself to a peasant as a Polish boy who had escaped from a train when the Germans were taking his family to Germany to work. The peasant believed him because he spoke the language and knew the prayers well and the young boy stayed with him.

When the Jasionowker Jews were taken to Treblinka, the peasant sent him with all of the other peasants to take the Jews by sled to the train... (All of the peasants had to take the Jews to the Knisziner train station). The Rawer "*sheygets*" wrapped himself in a hide and no one recognized him.

[Pages 701-705]

Goniondzers in the Bialystok Ghetto
by Zeydl (Note Dvoshke's son) Altshuld
Translated by Martin Jacobs

Avrom-Leyzer Rubin

The book about the Bialystok ghetto uprising by B. Mark (published by the Jewish Historical Institute, Warsaw 1950) is very one-sided. According to the author (a communist) the uprising was organized by the communists, at a time when all Zionist groups had a large part in this sacred work. The author sins against the heroes and martyrs who fell for the honor of the Jewish people.

Three Goniondzers are named in the book: Avrom-Leyzer Rubin (son of Yankl the blacksmith), the dentist Levi Kopelman, and, on the other side, the scoundrel and informer Yankele Tsviklitsh (son of Yehoshua Tsviklitsh, he was executed in the Bialystok ghetto by revenge-taking Jews).

On *p. 277* the book says about Avrom-Leyzer Rubin–may his memory be honored—: "The members of the anti-fascist self-defense, Avrom-Leyzer Rubin and Natek Goldstein, carried out the death sentence against the vile contemptible informer Yudkovsky (who was the terror of the Bialystok Jews both in and outside the ghetto – Z. A.) and took revenge on the criminal."

On *p. 328* it says: "Breaking into the German arsenals and stealing weapons became a frequent occurrence. The fighters Reuben Levine (Sergei), Nathan Goldstein (Natek), Hershl Rosenthal (from Jasinówka) (a heroic young man, I still remember him from Jasinówka – Z. A.), Avrom-Leyzer Rubin (it does not here give his origins) took these dangerous expeditions upon themselves". "This very bold theft took place in the Gestapo's arsenal at 15 Szenkowicz Street. Avrom-Leyzer Rubin, the refugee from Warsaw (why Warsaw ?! – Z. A.), and Nathan Goldstein, the refugee from Lodz, who were employed outside the ghettos, took 44 different types of weapon from there. This deed made an extraordinary impression on the underground and gave strong encouragement to the members of the self-defense organization."

On Page 458. "The Jewish partisans were of diverse backgrounds. Besides the locksmith Mulye Weiner and the mechanic Benjamin Shleifer, there was the smith from Goniondz (finally the correct designation – Z. A.), Leyzer Rubin." Further on we read: "Besides tried and tested fighters and heroic partisans, besides those who jumped from the trains (Kawe, Mietek Jakubowicz), were those who had already been to Treblinka and 'tasted' it (Avrom-Leyzer Rubin)". Here I must point out that the Treblinka camp, which was located not far from Malkin, annihilated hundreds of thousands of Jews. Only a few individuals came out of there, and among them – our Avrom-Leyzer Rubin of Goniondz. This is an indescribable act of heroism, and if there are miracles here, this one is the greatest.

On Pages 466, 467. "These same heroic girls rescued many Jews, those who escaped from the railway cars and even from the death camps. Among those rescued was the Goniondz blacksmith Leyzer Rubin, who took part in the uprising in Treblinka on August 2, 1943 (this uprising is a legend among all Jews, because a dozen heroes fought almost bare handed against a gang of hundreds of criminals, armed with all sorts of weapons. The heroes killed dozens of the Gestapo, and several succeeded in escaping, among them our Avrom-Leyzer. -- Z.A.) He escaped from there to Bialystok, where he hid at first in the Church of St. Roch (Kośció? Świętego Rocha), until a Polish cobbler put him in touch with the girls, who brought the heroic smith into the woods. Leyzer Rubin suffered a hero's death in the month of June, while rescuing a Serbian partisan."

Thus ended the life of our Goniondz hero Avrom-Leyzer Rubin. All of us, and above all the Goniondzers in Israel, should for ever honor his glorious deeds and extraordinary heroism in an appropriate manner.

Now a few excerpts about Dr. Leon Kopelman z"l.

On Page 126. Some of the coworkers of the "*Judenrat*" [Jewish council], whose names come up here and there in its first meetings as opposing the Barash-Subotnik leadership (these were the principal "leaders" of the *Judenrat* in Bialystok – Z.A.), later no longer appear at the Merchants' House (where the Judenrat "staff" was located – Z.A.). "Thus on September 18, 1941 at the meeting of the *Judenrat* Dr. Segal [The Yiddish says "Froy D"r Segal", which can mean a woman doctor (or dentist), but it can also mean the wife of a doctor named Segal] and Dr. Kopelman protested against the leadership's handling of evacuation. At the same meeting Dr. Kopelman asked for more enthusiasm for intellectuals. Their names do not occur again in the minutes of the *Judenrat*. These were just two people who did indeed draw the right conclusions from the Barash-Subotnik policies."

The withdrawal of Dr. Kopelman highlights his moral values and honorable behavior. He did not wish to work with the *Judenrat,* which acted (directly or indirectly) as a spokesperson of the Gestapo, assisting in the annihilation of their own brothers and sisters. A small number of Jews had the courage and the conscience to act in this manner. Honor his memory! (Z.A.)

On Page 104. "There were also democratic elements among the people who devoted themselves to fighting hunger. The hungry intellectual got a free or inexpensive meal in the 'intellectual's kitchen' organized by Drs. Segal and Kopelman."

Dr. Kopelman, our friend and fellow townsman, gave great help to everyone who turned to him for help, especially our townspeople. He was killed, with the other millions of Jews, at the hands of the murderers, in the crematorium. His wife went mad from the frequent upheavals in the ghetto, and she and her daughter were also gassed. (Z.A.)

By the way, heroic figures from the collective Tel-Hai also appear in the book. In the list of the 32 members are mentioned the following names: Reuben Rosenberg from Suchowola, Hershl Rosenthal from Jasinówka (whose heroic deeds are mentioned again and again, as he was one of the leaders of the uprising in the Bialystok ghetto – Z.A.), Menukha Plaskowska from Jasinówka, Jochebed Weinstein, Gedaliah Pitliuk, Peitshka Dorogoy and Yaffa – all from Knyszyn. As we can see, the Knyszyners played an active part, and most of them fought in the woods near Knyszyn. The places around Knyszyn are mentioned numerous times in the book.

[Pages 705-710]

A Visit to the *Shtetl* after the Destruction
by Chaim Krawiec (a grandson of Gedalia Mondres), Tel Aviv
Translated by Gloria Berkenstat Freund

It began right at the outbreak of the Second World War in 1939. The Germans entered Goniadz (the first time) on Rosh Hashanah and they were not there more than 10 days. However, during the 10 days they showed their cruelty towards the Jews.

The first thing they burned was our beautiful synagogue. While they carried this out, the Jews were not permitted to leave their houses. Doors and windows had to be closed; it had to be dark in every house. But everyone took a look through the cracks in the shutters and saw how the Germans labored simply to burn the synagogue. They were not successful with the exterior, because after many attempts, the synagogue did not want to burn...

Everything disappeared in the smoke because we could not save anything, only two walls remained standing – one wall was looted by the Christians in the city, for bricks... There was sadness in the *shtetl*, as after a catastrophe.

Right after this, a new hunt began – seizing young Jews for work. There was a noise, a disturbance; people began running to hide themselves in various places, not knowing what kind of place was suitable – so that the enemy would not find them. This lasted for several days. The Nazis were unsuccessful: no one was then taken and no one was taken away from our *shtetl*.

On the last day of their short reign, various rumors began to be spread about the arrival of the Russian army. This encouraged us a little and a spark of hope again flashed in Jewish hearts. And this is how it was: the Germans began to withdraw from Goniadz in the middle of the day on *Yom-Kippur*. The *shtetl* was empty of Germans before nightfall and the first armored vehicles of the Russian army appeared on the highway to Osowiec.

There was new era in the life of our *shtetl*; our entire way of life changed. Businesses were closed and one general cooperative was created (where besides matches and several grams of salt, there was nothing more to be had). The bakeries went over into the hands of the state. Tradesmen were not permitted to work privately, but general work guilds were created. There was little work and little pay. If only to make it through the day. In September 1940 (a year after the outbreak of the war) I and several other young people from Goniadz were taken to serve in the Red Army.

I only met two soldiers from Goniadz in the Red Army during my entire time in Russia.

I experienced difficult times on the front. I was in various terrible places. Even today, being in Israel, I feel it in my bones. It is difficult to free oneself from this. I tried more than once to run away from them, but I only paid with heavy suffering, hunger and fear.

In 1943 I was transferred from the Red Army to the Polish. I arrived in Warsaw with the Polish army and there I was severely wounded in the right hand. I lay in a hospital for six months and had a rest of several weeks.

This was in February 1945. I decided then to travel for a look at my home city, where I grew up and was educated and for which I yearned and dreamed for five years.

It drew me, although my heart foretold bad things. Yet, I wanted to take a look, perhaps something remained - - - - -

The heart breaks, although it is hardened. The body is engulfed by a cold shiver, a shudder. You become frozen like a piece of ice – you do not move. Your hands shake and your teeth begin to bang against each other. You also feel hot tears on your cheeks – seeing the destruction, the deadness around you.

The heart bursts when you see that the murderers – Poles who murdered our brothers – are living in the remaining Jewish houses. The two common graves are still fresh at the cemetery.

I did not find any Jews in Goniadz itself. The few survivors settled in Bialystok. By fits and starts, one goes there – with fear – to see how the *shtetl* looks.

Seeing the destruction and knowing what happened to our most dear, everything in you begins to waiver: should you remain here? – on Polish soil, where each step is filled and infused with the blood and tears of Jewish fathers, mothers and children, where every stone from the cobblestone pavement is a silent witness for the Jews who were led to the slaughter?

No! Here is not the soil and here the survivors will not find their rest. We must search for a more secure corner. We take various roads and escape from the accursed land. And this – even though we took part in the liberation of "democratic" Poland.

I, myself, was the first to run and after seven months of wandering in various nations of Europe, I succeeded in reaching our holy land – *Eretz-Yisroel.*

A headstone at the "gutn ort" [cemetery] in 1956

[Pages 709-710]

A Holy Community Goniadz…
by Alter Rozen, New York
Translated by Gloria Berkenstat Freund

A holy community Goniadz, may it rest in peace,

You always float before my eyes

As in reality and also in a dream,

Since your pure soul flew away

In high heaven, far.

There are your children driven a long way,

Spread to all corners of the world,

Scattered across Seven Seas.

Each has become a last Goniadzer,

You are lost to them forever.

[Pages 711-712 Yiddish] [Pages 711-712 Hebrew]

A Dream of My *Shtetl*
by Shmuel Farber
Translated by Gloria Berkenstat Freund

…I go through my beloved shtetl [town]
Wander around it lost, as if blind;
The houses are unfamiliar, the streets unknown –
Not recognizing, unrecognized.
I will find the khederim [religious elementary schools],
Where I once studied Khumish, "Swarbe" and Gemara*
Aloud, aloud…
The house of prayer stands orphaned,
Empty and deserted and completely quiet,
Gemarus lie closed – All quiet, all quiet…

Look! The synagogue hill – a cemetery,
Terrifyingly aflame at sunset…
Dear Jews! Where are you?"
All dead, all dead.

*Translator's Note: The *Khumish* is the Five Books of Moses – the Torah. *Swarbe* is an acronym for *esrim-vaarba'a* – the number 24 in Hebrew – the 24 books of the Hebrew Bible: The Torah, the Prophets and the Writings. The *Gemara* contains commentaries on the Torah. The plural of *Gemara* is *Gemarus*

[Pages 713-716]

On the Goniadz Road
by Dovid Treszczanski
Translated by Gloria Berkenstat Freund

"Everyone, everyone is near to me, brothers of my sadness"

Shlomo Shnud

You always follow me as a nightmare, day and night, Goniadz, my dear *shtetele* [little town]!

Home of my childhood years, of my youth. In you I rocked in my straw cradle, studied in kheder [religious elementary school] and – grew into a "person." In you I spent my young years as a victim in the struggle for a better world.

Endless pictures run through my memory!

Friday – a wedding in the shtetl. The groom and bride are accompanied by music to the synagogue hill. The entire shtetl is lively – a wedding in the shtetl, lehavdil[1] – a funeral in the shtetl. Everything draws me to the ghostly alley. Everything is wrapped in sorrow.

Joy and sadness together.

There stands our white synagogue on the hill like a light-tower. Jews would run to the synagogue hill on a warm day to catch a breeze from the river.

The old bathhouse stands beneath. Children running with their fathers to the bath... How lively and familiar – erev [eve of] Pesakh, erev Rosh Hashanah.

Here is the old Beis-Medrash [synagogue or House of Prayer] Mordekhai the shamas [rabbi's assistant] heats the oven and we, friends, bring potatoes to bake.

A group plays cards on a big, long table in the woman's prayer room. Mordekhai the shamas chases them out...

Chana-Dina's son, Yaruhem's gemara [rabbinical commentaries] melody reverberates by the tallow candle on a winter night...

And the bel-tefilah's [person who leads prayer at the lecturn] – the always joyful Reb Eliezar, son of Rywka Ruchl's son Moshe, and Yankl Elia, the blacksmith's son. I see them in front of the synagogue lectern dressed in a kitl[2], in talisim [prayer shawl] asking and crying for a good year.

And the stormy meetings in the Beis-Medrash about all community matters. What was not there in Goniadz? [Political] parties, schools, groups, sport groups, reading circles, libraries and so on.

The dear Y.L. Peretz library! How much love and energy I put in among your walls! Another book! Another book! – And the delight in my heart. I cannot forget the late Leibl Mankowski, the founder and creator of the library who was beloved in all circles of Goniadz society.

I remember the inscription on his headstone: "Here lies a simple member of a Jewish worker family."

A number of young Goniadzers were forced to his grave where they were shot and buried.

I see you all, fathers, mothers, sisters and brothers, how you were forced into the cattle cars to Bogusze[3]... Your last journey.

It is quiet in the shtetl. Death is all around.

It is Friday in the evening. No Shabbos candles. The windows black, dark holes...

... And the Bober swims farther on its way... Dear River Bober! Our mothers would launder our childish shirts in your clear waters. How many dreams did young hearts dream, navigating on your calm waters on summer evenings? How many hearty songs did we sing on boats rented from Mikhal the fisherman?

Jews came to your waters to say Tashlikh[4]. Jewish children will never again swim on your still waters and pious Jews will never come to you again to wash the "sinning" skirts of their garments...

And the frogs at Dolko, Guzy and Rawe [streams] croak as always.

Where are you, dear daughters of Rawe! Your Shabbos pletzlekh [flat rolls] were tasty! A house for everyone who was hungry... Always singing and joyfulness and so much hominess.

For the Goniadz survivors – an eternal, deep wound that will never heal!

However, from the great ruins rises the heroic personality of a young man from Goniadz, Avraham-Leizer Rubin, the son of Yankl the blacksmith. The hero of the uprising in Treblinka and of the partisan movement around Bialystok calls to us and demands that we never forget.

Translator's Footnotes:
1. word usually used to separate the sacred from the profane
2. white robe worn on Rosh Hashanah and Yom Kippur and by the groom at his wedding
3. transit camp near Grajewo
4. the custom of casting bread crumbs into a flowing body of water on Rosh Hashanah to cast away one's sins. It is derived from Micah 7:19 - "You will cast all their sins into the depths of the sea."
5. flat rolls

The Zdroj [Spring]

[Pages 717-720]

Night of Horror
by M. Sh. Ben–Meir
Translated by Selwyn Rose

The night was rainy and after midnight
Blind autumn's fingers o'er the window pane groped,
Tapping her fingers on the tears.
Nestled in the bosom of an armchair
An orphan curled, during a night of cold,
Nestling close to its foster-mother.

Behind me stands the lantern,
Its head droops on the wall before me,
Shedding its light on a picture.
In the picture – the image of a Jew
(A known work of Chagall)
Wrapped in a Talit, crowned with Tephilin.

A crumpled paper I spread before me,
A letter retrieved from the Shoah,
A witness to abomination –
A reminder of the destruction of my town.
From hand to hand, from camp to camp
It coursed its way to arrive in my hand.
The details of a nightmare.
Sanctified names of Men Women and Babes-in-arms.
And at the end one sentence:
The old Rabbi Israel hid in the Yeshiva
Martyred, next the Holy Ark;
Wrapped in his torn and bloodied Talit
His gouged-out eyes on his Tephilin gaze…

My vision is clouded,
My throat chokes up as with a vise.
I heard a heart beating,

I know not whose –
Is it mine or that same old man?
I raised my eyes to the picture.
Gazing for long at the face of the Jew
And a trembling seized me.
My lips contorted and tight in a grimace –
They will open speaking in rage:

Woe to you, O aged Jew enwrapped and adorned!
Art thou not that same Rabbi Israel
From my home town,
Whose blood congealed upon his shawl?
Why hastened thee to conceal thyself here?
Why did you hide? -
Behold your sunken fear-filled eyes
With their frozen look of death.
The look of a dying man,
Gazing on another distant world.
Your cracked and seamed face like a package split open,
Stiffened in death, it thunders a secret.
And your mouth agape as if uttering its final word.
Your hands imprisoned in the leather straps
Are hanging as if paralyzed
Lacking salvation.
And the Totafot between your gloomy, angry eyes
Have slipped and cover your furrowed brow.
In vain: In vain I hid in the House of Prayer!
That which demands blood passed you o'er----
- -
You surely remembered the explicit verse:
"When a man tortures his son"[1]
The killing of sons, strangling of babes –
Is that a fatherly moral?
Is that a fatherly moral?
My head sank onto my arms.
Half asleep, silent in my desolation
With the spheres of my half-closed eyes

The words swallowed up in the sleep of diverse spirits.[2]
And behold – within his frame he stirred and moved,
The Jew in the picture;
He turned his face to me and extended a hand,
And a Divine Voice bellowed a song of praise
Comes forth from the distance:
Who is it here that obscures wisdom,
Burning with sacrificial fires
Burning wisdom, scattering words of chaos,
Measuring with an Earthly scale in a path of human thought
Weighing the life of the world on the scales of earth and ashes?
The concealed secrets of your experience –
The fate of souls thou shalt judge!?
Hidden from you is their meaning
Because the scheming mind
Rest upon faulty perception
And trample on reasoned thought.
The imagination of Man is erred,
His heart a victim, untrustworthy.
I am an old Israel.
I did not seek refuge on the day of death
And from my persecutors I did not hide.
My soul I commended in this Holy place
The end of my flesh is before me,
And receives with grace the Will from above,
May His Name be blessed with love.

Translators Footnotes:
1. A reference to Psalm 43
2. A reference to Isaiah IXX; 14

[Pages 721-722]

The Burning of the Synagogue
by Avraham Yaffe, Tel Aviv
Translated by Amy Samin

In our town, an ancient synagogue stood on a steep hill. The date of its founding is unknown, but the elders of the town would recount that long ago, when the area was ruled by the Prussians, a large prison stood on the spot. And how many benefits there were in that synagogue mount. Aside from the sanctity of the synagogue, and the extensive field around it that isolated it from the town – also of note was the wonderful and spectacular view of the surrounding area. At its feet flowed the Buber River, which wound its course through fields, meadows, and green pastures into the distance, and on the horizon – continuous dense forests which surrounded the area with a blue-green wreath. Not for nothing did the townspeople take pride in the synagogue mount.

On the winter Sabbaths, a *minyan* [ten men, the minimum number required for prayers] of worshipers and synagogue faithful would gather, plodding through the mud or in snow up to the knees. Though as Passover approached and the spring sun began to warm the face of the earth, the residents of the town would throng to the synagogue mount, to see whether the river had awakened from its winter slumber under a thick blanket of ice wrapped in a thin sheet of white snow. On one of the Sabbaths, as the worshippers left the synagogue, chilled to the bone, to warm up a bit in the shining sunlight and to observe the river, suddenly a declaration was heard: the ice is moving! ...In the air could be heard the echoes of the faint sound of the ice cracking, and from the river and beneath it came the trumpeting sound and an amazing noise, which grew louder and louder. That Sabbath day became the festival of Spring, and the synagogue mount would celebrate its victory. During the *Mincha* [afternoon] prayers of the Sabbath, the number of worshippers would greatly increase, and people would stand and watch the flowing ice with joy and trembling...They had just finished studying Psalm 104, and here suddenly they could see with their own eyes "how manifold are thy works", the river killing the ice as it rose up on its banks, its breadth and length in a glorious song of freedom, the song of Spring, a celebration of light and liberty. From Passover to Sukkot and even Simchat Torah, the synagogue was the center of prayer in the town, and the synagogue mount became a destination for day trips, conversations and gatherings for the townspeople.

Lightning struck the roof of the synagogue more than once, and under the roof was kept the lightening-struck timber, in memory of the saving of the synagogue from destruction by fire.

[Page 722]

Many conflagrations befell the town, and during the First World War part of the town was destroyed and burned by the shelling of the Germans and the Russians. The synagogue on its high hill, and with its stone walls, remained unchanged, like an unmovable stone in a stormy sea, "like Mount Zion which cannot be removed," until the blasphemous Nazis invaded the town, those two legged predators, may their names and memories be erased, in the Second World War, at the end of 1938. And so came to an end the fortress of the community of Goniadz.

Rosh Hashanah, 1939. The people demanded in secret: make weak the haters of Israel. But the opposite happened...the bitter enemy of the Jews grew stronger, and with its victory over Poland, the town fell under the government of the filthy, evil Nazis. With the Days of Awe came the real days of horror.

A great fear befell the Jews on the eve of Yom Kippur. Someone spread the word that the Nazis had a terrible plot against the Jews: they were going to blow up the synagogue during the Kol Nidre prayer. The rabbi and the beadles made an announcement not to come to pray at the synagogue on the eve of Yom Kippur. They were barely able to scrape together a *minyan* at the rabbi's house, and there they secretly said the Kol Nidre prayer.

The belief of the townspeople was weakened when they heard that they were to avoid praying in the synagogue on Yom Kippur, because many used to come to pray in the synagogue on that sacred day of fasting, because the pure air there would ease their fast...

The next day, on Yom Kippur, suddenly the sounds of a loud, threatening explosion were heard. Fire and billows of smoke - chunks of the synagogue walls went flying upwards, the roof and ceiling collapsed, and the entire synagogue mount became like a volcano. The Nazis had put their plot into action and blown up the synagogue on Yom Kippur. The Jews of the town prayed brokenheartedly in grief and sorrow: "No prophet and no visionary, like the blind we will cast about and leave. Every day it is said what will be our end, our lives are hanging in the balance..."

During the prayers, weeping and burning tears flowed from their eyes over this new destruction – the destruction of the ancient synagogue that had once been the majesty of the town.

[Pages 723-726 - Yiddish] [Pages 727-730 - Hebrew]

The Synagogue (poem)
by Idl Treszczanski (M. Sh. Ben–Meir) of blessed memory
Translated by Gloria Berkenstat Freund

On the green hill, separated from the shtetl [town]
Chosen on the first day of creation,
Everyone admired your magnificence
And everyone told of the glory of your importance:

"An old castle from Jan Sobieski's time –
In Kingdom Poland, before the Prussians and Russians –
Sanctified him, before God and man,
The great, great grandfather with his accumulation of merit in
heaven"...

From childhood on there has appeared in my dreams
A small temple white and clean,
Where the spirit of peace always floats around,
Like repose with the Divinity itself.
When the swirl of time torments my mood,
When melancholy's wings heavily wave, –
Sorcerer's dreams bring me to the beloved hill,
My eyes and ears – I see and hear...

I see the mantel lamps blazing in holiness, –
The candles sparkle on two arches...

I hear the prayers pour together
With the twitter of birds, – there they fly! –

[Page 725-726]

I see – talisim [prayer shawls] swaying, without end,
Rabbi Gdalye stretches out his hands for the priestly blessing – – –
The voice of Kopl the melamed's [religious school teacher] shofar
[ram's horn] – – –
And Meir Budner's melody split the walls...

A Rosh Hashanah sigh – – a holiday "Amen" – –
A knock of a rattle – – – a sip of Kiddush [prayer over the] wine – – –
And on Simkhas Torah[1] one is called by name.
And the dead pray by moon shine – – –

See – yahrzeit lich [memorial candles] which die at Neilah[2],
The last cry breaks out in the women's synagogue – – –
And after the tumult of the quiet Kadeyshim[3]
Miller approaches with his fire [wagon][4]

My synagogue is a ruin – my most beautiful dream!
The villain destroyed my childhood world!
The Shkhine [Divine Presence] cries – – – and the angels of peace –
They have hidden their face

And we cry with them...
          But I – I cannot cry, –
As there are devastated worlds everywhere!
Oh, synagogue mine, with your thousands of charms,
I will quietly hide you in my heart.

Translator's Notes:
1. *Simkhas Torah* is the autumn holiday commemorating the giving of the Torah by God to the Jewish   people.
2. Closing prayer on Yom Kippur.
3. Prayers of mourning.
4. It was a common occurrence for fires to occur in synagogues on Yom Kippur because of the many memorial candles burning there.

The Synagogue and Officials

[Pages 731-732]

[blank]

[Pages 733-734]

Lamentations
Translated by Gloria Berkenstat Freund

Eikhah [Lamentations] How destroyed and empty has become the deep-rooted traditional, old *kehile* [organized Jewish community] in Goniadz! Her sons and daughters, sacred and pure, righteous and honest people in deed and work, were tortured for the *Yidishkeit* [a Jewish way of life] and met a violent death through the blood thirsty murderers, may their names and their memory be erased, and their bones were seeded and spread across the blood soaked Polish ground and they were not given a burial.

Let us stand sadly and quietly in our great sorrow for the taking of our holy. Let us engrave their dear memory in the depth of our hearts and may their dear images always float before our eyes!

Let their desperate cry of pain not leave our ears and our sadness not cease until the shame and the curse of exile is erased and our people will build and be reestablished in its land, Israel!

[Pages 735-736]

[blank]

[Page 737]

Let us remember them in all prayers,
We will lament them in all prayers for the dead.
Let us recognize them in all *Yisgadals*[1],
May they exist in all our *Hatikvah*[2]

Yakov Glatstein

[Page 738]

***Shema Yisroel*[3]**

Translator's Notes:
1. *Yisgadal* is the opening word of the *Kaddish* recited by mourners.
2. *Hatikvah – The Hope –* an anthem adopted by the Zionist movement and now the national anthem of the State of Israel.
3. *Shema Yizroel –* "Hear, O Israel" – the central prayer of Jewish worship.

[Pages 739-740]

[blank]

[Page 741-754]

List of the Families Who Perished
Translated by Gloria Berkenstat Freund

א **Alef:**

Family   Atlas Hershl
Atlas Nekhemia
Atlas Dworya
Atlas Zelda
Izraelowicz Moshe
Izraelowicz Ezrial
Izraelski Avraham'l
Alszancki Khackl

ב **Beis:**

Family   Bialostocki Leibl
Blum Moshe–Mendl
Biali Hilel (Hilke)
Biali Motl
Brumer Yehosha
Brumer Chaim Hershl
Baidan Zalman
Bajnsztain Sura
Brustyn Yosef (Avraham–Moshe the author's son–in–law)
Braski Noakh
Boyarski Yudl
Barelkowski Bajlach
Barelowski Chaim (Chaim the glazier)
Barelowski Yizroel
Blacharcz Mendl
Bialosukenski Moshe Feywl
Bialosukenski Benim'ka
Bialosukenski Shlomo'ka
Beris Chaim
Berniker Itshe (Chana Dina's son)

ג **Gimel:**

Family   Goldiner Faya
Goldiner Chaim
Goldiner Yenta
Gerzon Notke
Gerzon Yankl
Gerzon Avraham'l
Garbar Alter
Gelbard Avraham (Czudak)
Gelbard Faygl (Czudak)
Gelbard Avraham (Gnendl's)
Gelbard Shayna (Fenikl)
Gelbard Henya
Gelbard Akhr'ka
Gelbard Matisyahu (Mates)
Gelbard Yudl
Gelbard Gershon
Gelbard Henekh (the son of Itshe the water carrier)
Goniadski Avrhaham'l
Goniadski Leibl
Goniadski Hirsh
Gozowski Avraham–Hersh
Gozowski Yerakhmiel
Gozowski Alter
Gopsztajn Shprinca
Gryn Moshe
Gryn Yankl
Grodzinski Moshe–Leyzer
Gornastajski Beylka

ד **Daled:**

Family   Dlugolenski Diodia
Downarski Leibl
Downarski Sheyna–Malka

ה Hey:

Family Hausman Eliezer (Lazer)
Hirszfeld Sholem
Halpern Meri
Halpern Hinda (Szpaira)
Halpern Yehoshaya (Nisl the butcher's son–in–law)
Halpern Yankl
Halpern Leah (?)
Halpern Avrahaml
Halpern Itke
Halpern Yerakhmial

ו Vav:

Family Wigodski (Yankl Rayzl Meir'ke's)
Wercelinski Yosl
Waser Hershl (Chaim Polak's son–in–law)
Welwelewicz – (glass shopkeeper)
Weiner Shmulke (Shmulke Plamczuk's)
Weiner Avraham (Shmulke Plamczuk's)
Weiner Avraham'l (Alter Plamczuk's)
Weiner Zajdke (Alter Plamczuk's)
Weiner Avraham'l
Weiner Sura'ke (Alter Plamczuk's)
Weil Leibl

ז Zayen:

Family Zachariasz Shmuel
Zachariasz Elihu
Zachariasz Ester (Luria)
Zachariasz Moshe
Zimnach Alter
Zarbentszanski Leibl

ח Khet:

Family Khtiba Shimkha
Khazan Henya
Khazan Zeydl

ט **Tet:**

Family	Todorowicz Leyzer
	Todorowicz Moshe Mordekhai
	Todorowicz Yankl (the tailor)
	Todorowicz Ahron Meir
	Todorowicz Pesha Rywka (Shepsl's wife)
	Treszczanski Rywka (Itshe Gela's)
	Treszczanski Rywka
	Treszczanski Yudl
	Treszczanski Yankl (Gela's)
	Treszczanski Leyzer
	Treszczanski Sender
	Treszczanski Feywl
	Treszczanski Henokh (the religious teacher)
	Treszczanski Itshe (Henokh's)
	Treszczanski Leah (Alter Yisroel's daughter)
	Treszczanski Yehoshua (Shia Leib)
	Treszczanski Sender (Jaszwiler)
	Tikocki Yosl (Shaymela's)
	Tikocki Yankl (Shmerka's)
	Tikocki Leibl (Tzlal's)
	Tikocki Ayzyk
	Tikocki Berl
	Tikocki Mendl (Hershl–Leib's)
	Tikocki Berl (Peshkela's son–in–law)
	Trachimowski Chana
	Trachimowski Itshe
	Trachimowski Neshka
	Tyukl Leah

י **Yud:**

Family	Yanowski Etl
	Yanowski Shajnka
	Yanowski Yankl
	Yanowski Moshe'l (Yankl's son)
	Yewrejski Kheikl
	Yewrejski Shimeon
	Yewrejski Ruwin
	Yewrejski Riwa
	Yewrejski Rajkhl (Shaya–Yankl's daughter)

כ Kaf:

Family　Chonowski Etka
　　　　Kohen Yoal–Meir
　　　　Kohen Gedalia (Tuvya–Motl's)
　　　　Kohen (Tuvya–Motl's daughter)
　　　　Katz (Medrash's son–in–law)

ל Lamed:

Family　Linczewski Yudl (son–in–law of Nisl the butcher)
　　　　Lewin Moshe (the rope maker)
　　　　Lewin Ruchl (Noske's)
　　　　Lewin Mailakh
　　　　Lewin Alter (Yehuda's)
　　　　Lewin Avraham'l
　　　　Lewin Yankl (Shmuel the blacksmith's)
　　　　Lewin Henya–Dwora
　　　　Landenberg Shimeon (the rag man)
　　　　Lopczinski Baylka (Kliap)
　　　　Luria Nusan
　　　　Lewar Pesakh (Mariasha's)
　　　　Lewar Yankl (Mariasha's)
　　　　Lewit Avraham–Yakov
　　　　Lifsztajn Shmuel (Pesha the Stozonower's son–in–law)
　　　　Liach Rayzl (Fayga–Ruchl's)

מ Mem:

Family　Malozowski Shmuel–Ber
　　　　Malozowski Motl
　　　　Malozowski Shlomo
　　　　Malozowski Moshe'ke (Itshe Anshel's son)
　　　　Mareina Yisroel
　　　　Michnowski Alter
　　　　Miltszan Zerakh
　　　　Miltszan Fraydka (Wilenski)
　　　　Miltszan Golda
　　　　Menkes Etl (Menkes Etl)
　　　　Mali Leyzer
　　　　Mankowski Rayza
　　　　Mechaver Simke
　　　　Mechaver Yudl

Markus Yirmya
Milwer Alter
Milwer Hershl
Milwer–Kaminski Sheyna

נ Nun:

Family Niewadowski Zelig
Niewadowksi Chaim
Niewadowski Shmuel
Niewadowski Faytshe (Shayna–Malka's daughter)
Niemoi Zerakh
Nozshik (the shoemaker)

ס Samekh:

Family Slomianski Faygl
Stolnicki Mikhal (Fayga–Ruchl's son–in–law)
Sidranski Zeyd (Wichne's)
Sidranski Yankl (Wichne's)
Suraski Chana

פ Peh/Feh:

Family Plaskowski Meir
Fishbein Moshe (Mazur)
Fishbein Mendl
Feldman Hershl
Predmeski Rywka–Dwoyra
Predmeski Moshe'l
Predmeski Leibl
Pinkewicz Hershl (Moshe Mendl's son–in–law)
Pekarski Wolf
Perlowa–Gura Tzadik
Poswietnianska Gershon (Paluch)
Poswietnianski Meir (Paluch)
Poliak Zelig
Piechota Moshe
Fiszer Pesakh
Penski Shifra
Penski Shmuel
Piekarcz Liba (came from Jedwabne)
Peltinowicz –
Farbar Avraham

Farbar Blumka (Yisroel–Yitzhak's widow)
Farbar Chaim
Fridman Leah'ke (Rathaus)
Fridman Pesha (Stoznower)
Fridman Moshe (the tinsmith)
Fridman Yankl (Dolker)
Fridman Nisl
Fridman Manasha
Furman Diodke (the teacher)
Furman Yitzhak (Joske's son)
Furman Chaya

צ Tsadek:

Family   Centura (the cantor)
Cwiklic Yehoshua

ק Kuf:

Family   Kobrinski Yankl
Kobrinski Motl
Kobrinski Yosl
Kobrinski Asher
Kobrinski Basya (Bertshuk's)
Krawiec Rayzl (the blacksmith's wife)
Krawiec Yosl
Krawiec Berl
Krawiec Efroim
Krawiec Gedelia (Rywka's, Mondres)
Krawiec Avraham–Ahron
Krawiec Alter (Czaczuk's)
Krawiec Yitzhak (Czaczuk's)
Krawiec Yisroel (Mordekhai the *Shamas*'
[synagogue sexton] son–in–law)
Kliap Motke
Katinke Moshe
Katinke Chaya–Nekha (Szajnberg)
Kopelman Golka
Kirzczner Chana–Gitl
Kirzczner Yosl
Kirzczner Welwl
Kosoy Avraham'l

ר **Resh:**

Family   Ribak Yankl

Ribak Leah'ke

Ribak Motke

Ribak Ahr'tshik

Ribak Mordekhai (the baker)

Ruski Itke

Rozental Yankl (Berl Rudski's son–in–law)

Rozental Khatskl

Rawer Ayzyk

Rawer Yerakhmiel

Rawer Leibl

Rawer Ber

Rawer Ahr'ke

Rawer Avraham'ke

Rubin Tsipa

Rubin Yankl (Shmuel Yoske's)

Rubin Moshe–Ahron

Rubin Manasha'ka

Rubin Yankl (Libke's)

Rubin Hershl (Pul's)

Rubin Khina

Rubin (Nekhemia's family)

Rubin Hershl (Wrocenier)

Reznicki Baylka

Reznicki Ahron

Reznicki Faywl

Reznicki Itsl

ש **Shin:**

Family   the Rabbi Szlumowicz

Szirotes Asher

Szczuczinksi Moshe (Dinke's)

Sztrikdreyer Yitzhak

Szuster Leibl

Szegftz Moshe

Szachnbaum Tserl

[Unnumbered in the book – pp. 755-756]

לזכר אחינו הקדושים
שנפלו בידי עריצים
בעירי מולדתנו
גאניאנדז וטרעסטינע
בשנת התשׁב
מצבת יגון ואנחה

A headstone in memory of the martyrs, in New York

A headstone in memory of the martyrs, in New York

[Pages 757-758]

To the Eternal Memory
(Necrology)
Obituaries
Translated by Gloria Berkenstat Freund

[Pages 761-762]

**Leybl Brumer and his wife, Ruchl
(Grodzenski)**

Mordekhai Itshe Grodzenski

**Shifra Penski and her daughters,
Meri and Sara**

**Zev (Wolf) Rejgrodski and his wife, Sara,
and their children, Mine and Zalman**

[Pages 763-764]

**Etl Janowski
and her daughter, Sheyndl**

**Leyzer's Yona Shmuel[1] (Janowski) and the daughters[2]
Chaya Simke, the granddaughter, Ester,
and the daughter-in-law, Etl Janowski**

Lusie Gricman (Beylke Raver's daughter)

Sara Bejnsztejn

Translator's Notes:
1. This is a common usage in Yiddish; a person is identified for example as "Yona Shmuel Leyzer's". This most likely means that Yona Shmuel is Leyzer's son.
2. In this instance the plural form of "daughter" is used, but only one daughter's name is given

[Pages 765-766]

Yakov Ruwin, his wife and children

The family of Simcha Hativa with their relative, Szoszka's Leah and her two daughters

[Pages 767-768]

Rywka Zakimowicz   **Eleizer Zakimowicz**

[Pages 769-700]

Toyba Treczszanski   **Gedelia Treczszanski**

[Pages 765-766]

Yakov Ruwin, his wife and children

The family of Simcha Hativa with their relative, Szoszka's Leah and her two daughters

[Pages 767-768]

Rywka Zakimowicz   **Eleizer Zakimowicz**

[Pages 769-700]

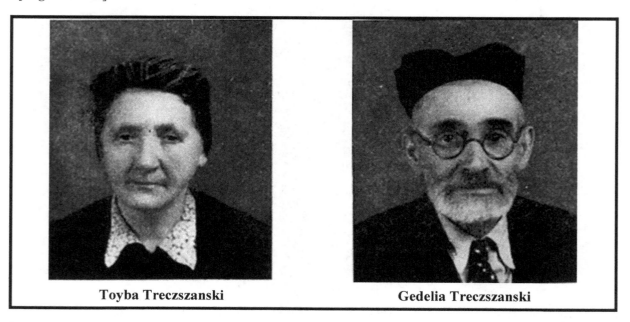

Toyba Treczszanski   **Gedelia Treczszanski**

Ahron Ribak

**Asher Szirotes and his wife, Shifra (Ribak)
and child**

[Pages 771-772]

Yankl Frydman (Dolker) and his family
Standing: Nakhum, Dobke, Moshe; Sitting: Yankl and his wife, Ruchl

[Pages 773-774]

Chaya Plaskowski

Sheyne Plaskowski (Bejlakh)

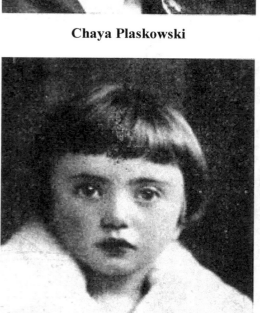

Lusie Gricman (Beylke Raver's daughter)

**Ruchl'ke and Dwoyra Khazan Penina, Beylke
the daughters of Sheyne and Ahron Bejlakh**

[Pages 775-776]

Malka Farber (neé Grican)

Gershon Aryeh (Gershon Leib)

Chaya Grican – Brukh's Chana's daughter

Chana Grican – Brukh's Chana

Pages 778-779]

**Sheyndl (neé Gelbard) and her husband,
Khanan Fenikhl**

Gnendl Gelbard   **Avraham Gelbard**

Yoal Treszczanski (Gele's [possibly Gele's husband]), the son Yitzhak and his wife, Rywka

Ruwin   **Aizik**   **Gitl**   **Yudl**

Children of Yitzhak and Rywka Treszczanski

[Pages 779-780
]

His wife Chaya Malka

Mordekhai Kliap

Their children: Beylke with her husband (Lapczinksi)

Yehezkheil

Hershl

[Pages 781-782]

**To the memory
of our dear husband and father**

Gedelia Sejd
of blessed memory

**His wife Sara
Son Dowid
Daughters, Silve and Perl**

[Pages 783-784]

To the memory of my dear parents

My father, (Eyske Marjanski) and mother

of blessed memory

Their son Yankl (Jack) Marn

Pages 785-786]

To the memory of our dear parents

Our father Mikhal's Moshe [son of Mikhal] Atlas
of blessed memory

**Our mother Shlomo-Moshe's Gitl
[daughter of Shlomo-Moshel]**
of blessed memory

Their daughter Cype

Kate Atlas, Son Michael, Daughters Betty and Lucie, N.Y.

[Pages 787-788]

To the memory of our dear parents

Father Mendl (Max) Szwarc

and mother Yete

Of blessed memory

**Their sons
Irving, Jack**

[Pages 789-790]

To the memory of our
dear husband and father

**Yosef Babdowksi
(Mendele's [Mendel's son])**

Of blessed memory

**his wife
Ester and children**
Norwalk, Conn.

To the memory of our dear parents

Father Hershl Tadarowicz

Mother Sara-Gnendl

Of blessed memory

**Their son Avram'l (Avi) Tadar
and daughter Chaya-Leah Finczuk**
New York

[Pages 791-792]

To the memory of our dear parents
Hershl and Ruchl Rubin
of blessed memory

Meydim Rubin

To the memory of my beloved
deceased parents

Joe and Fanny Goldberg

their son Lewis Goldberg

[Pages 793-794]

To the memory of our dear parents

Motl and Chaya Sara Malazowski

who perished in Goniadz at the hands of the Nazi murderers

Their daughter Teybl, Detroit

To the memory of my dear husband

Philip Szkalnik

who died in Detroiton the 22nd of May 1956

His wife Teybl

To the memory of our dear parents

Hage and Yakov Halpern

and our dear brother

Hershl

Of blessed memory

Berl and Shirley Halpern and children Atlanta

[Pages 795-796]

To the Eternal Memory of our Parents, Sisters, Brother and Relatives*

Rywka Brawerman-Trestine
Mrs. Rebeka Halpern

Trestiner
Mr. & Mrs. Zolty

Senie Berl the miller's [son of Berl the miller]
Mr. & Mrs. Dave Bagel

The cooper's Perl Szake [daughter or wife of the cooper or barrel maker]
Mr. & Mrs. Mayer Francis

Mr. & Mrs. Rochman

Hershl Leib's Motl Mendl [Hershl Leib's son]
Mr. Mrs. Max Tecotzky

Itshe the blond's daughter
Mr. & Mrs. Max Walnock

Chaya Rubin
Mrs. Anna Green

Golde Rubin
Mr. & Mrs. Leonard Herst

Leyzer-Yitzhak Menkis
Mr. & Mrs. Leo Mankes

Hershl Leib's Sholem Mendl [son of Hershl Leib]
Mr. & Mrs. Sam Tecotzky

Khomtshe Tawalinski
Mr. & Mrs. Fouard Monarch

Moshe'ka Dalker
Mr. Maurice Gelbort

Eidl, Avraham Levin's daughter
Mrs. Ida Solomon

Eidl, Salomon's daughter
Mr. & Mrs. Isidor Rappaport
Pearl Corresponding Secretary

Moshe'ka Yankl Szmerkes
Mr. Maurice Tucker

Mashe's Chava
Mr. & Mrs. Samuel Maches

**Mrs. Ida Solomon in memory of her
beloved sister Annie Levin**
Chicago

* Translator's Note: Each name listed is followed on the next line by names in English

[Pages 797-798]

To the Memory of Our Parents, Sisters and Brothers

Mother, Masha, died 29 *Shvat*, February 17, 1912

Father Benyamin-Yosef, died 19 *Kislev*, November 26, 1953

Ruchl, a sister, 14 *Adar* II 5679, March 16, 1919 (died in the typhus epidemic that raged in Goniadz that winter).

Bat-Sheva, a sister, died 26 *Elul* 5705, September 4, 1945

Shmuel, a brother, died October 1947

Benyamin's son-in-law (Sara's husband), **Leibl**, died 5 *Kislev* 5724, November 21, 1953

Leah's husband, Yudl Ribak, died January 1956

The children of Masha and Benyamin-Yosef Baier

To the memory of our dear husband and father

Chaim Hershl Lewin

of blessed memory
(son of Shakar the painter)

Mrs. Beylke Lewin and daughter Hilda

Chaya Leah Markowicz, Keyla Ite's daughter-in-law

To the memory of our dear husband and father

Kalman Ruder Rudski

of blessed memory

from Budne

Mrs. Mini Ruder and daughter Sylwe

[Pages 801-804]

List of Goniondz Natives Who Were Saved
Translated by Shayna Kravetz

ZEIDKE ALTSHULD, Nat'ke the farmer's son, was in Auschwitz. Living in Munich.

BERYL SLOMIONSKY, a grandchild of Shmuel-Ber the tailor. Was in Auschwitz, living in America.

TZADUK SHVECHER, a grandchild of Itshe the blond. Living in America.

LEIZER SHVECHER, Tzaduk's brother, was in Auschwitz. Living in Israel.

YOEL PLUSKOLOVSKI, a grandchild of Itshe2 the water-carrier. Hid himself in a Polish home.

YAAKOV KREPCHIN, Ben-Zion and Chin'ka's son. Was in the Russo-Polish army. Now in America.

DR. EPHRAIM SHOR, formerly doctor in Goniondz. Living in Poland.

KHAYA-ITKE , Shmuel the blacksmith's [daughter?] with her husband and two daughters. Was in Russia. Now living in Israel.

RIVKA, daughter of Zalman-Gershon DOVNARSKI with her daughter Beil'ka . Were in Auschwitz. Living in America.

LIZA RUBIN, Chatzkl Eliyah the blacksmith's daughter. Was in Auschwitz. Now in America.

BEIL'KA4 GRITZMAN, a daughter of Leibl the ditchdigger. Was in Russia. Now in Colombia, South America.

GRUNTSHE SHTSHUTSHINSKI, Moshe Din'ke's daughter. Was in Auschwitz, now in Israel.

TUVIA, ZALMAN, and their sister **KEILA**, the children of Kheikl YEVRAISKI. Hid themselves in Polish houses around Goniondz. Now in Israel.

KHAYIM KRAVIETZ, a son of Avraham-Aharon Gedaliah Mondres. Was in the Russo-Polish army. Now in Israel.

YISASCHAR KRAVIETZ, a son of Gedaliah Mondres. Was in the Russo-Polish army. Now in Canada.

PESAKH TIKOTZKI, a son of Leibl Tzalel . Hid in a Polish home. Now in Israel.

ELIYAHU-HERSHL NIEVODOVSKI, a son of Khayim Leizshke . Was in the Russo-Polish army. Now in Israel.

LEIZER NIEVODOVSKI, a son of Khayim Leizshkei10. Was in Auschwitz. Now in Australia.

ZEIDKE MILTSHAN, a son of Zerakh Shikorer. Was in Russia. Now in Israel.

LEIBL GELBORD and daughter **SONIA**. Leibl's mother was named Khana'tche, n?e Marantz. Leibl was raised by his aunt Khaya-Rokhel Luria. Hid in a forest around Vilna. Now in Israel. Sonia was married here.

MEILECH TRESHTSHANSKI, a son of Zeidke Reuven Drak. Was in Russia. Now in Israel.

GOLDA BURSHTEIN, a daughter of Itshe2-Berl. Was in Auschwitz. Died in Israel.

MUSHKE GENSHOR, a daughter of Itshe2-Berl, was in Auschwitz. Now in Israel.

AVRAHAM'L REZNITZKI, Beil'ke4 Pesha's son. Was in the Russo-Polish army. Now in Israel.

MORDECHAI GRODZENSKI, a son of Moshe-Leizer the watchmaker (GRODZINIAK). Was in the Russo-Polish army. Died in Israel.

KHAYIM ZIMNACH, Alter the dry-goods merchant's son. Itshe2-Berl's grandchild. Was in the Russo-Polish army. Now in Israel.

LEIBL6 GOPSHTEIN, a son of Shprintze , Yehuda the hatter's [wife?]. Was in the Russo-Polish army. Now in Israel.

The **SHLOMOVITSH** brothers and their sister **KHAVA**, children of the last rabbi of Goniondz. Escaped with the Mir yeshiva via Russia, China, and Japan. Now in America.

H. BECKER (PEKARZSH) lived in Goniondz for 9 years. Hid in a Polish home. Now in America.

YOSEF KHAZAN, a son of Henia Pesha. Was a partisan. Now in Russia.

LEIZER-ZELIG TRESHTSHANSKI, a son of Meir the watchmaker. Escaped from Belgium to Portugal. Died in Belgium

KHAVA TRESHTSHANSKI, a sister of Leizer-Zelig. Survived Hitler in Belgium. Now living there.

YOSEF LEV (LEVV), a grandchild of Yoske Rutkovski. Now in Israel.

[Pages 805-806]

Afterword

By Fishl Yitzhaki
Translated by Gloria Berkenstat Freund

Great efforts were invested in this book. The concentration of material, the compilation of documents, the pictures, the ties with our *landsleit* [. people from the same city] throughout the entire world in order to turn to this writing – all of this required a great deal of time and, actually, lasted a long time.

Particular care and attention was dedicated to the content and form of the book. We strove so that a complete, if inadequate, expression of the life of our dear *shtetl* [town] in all of its aspects would be provided as far as possible.

It was clear that not everything received an exhaustive expression, but taking into account the great difficulties with which such a work is bound, we can say that the book gives a sufficiently clear look at our *shtetl* with its population, vivid personalities, works of art, institutions, way of life and destruction.

* *
*

The publication of the book was rendered possible thanks to our *landsleit* in America. Our friend, Meirim Rubin, must particularly be mentioned as the initiator of the idea in America and the main force in collecting the monetary means and for the preparatory work to which he devoted himself with his entire heart.

The editing was done in America and in Israel. The editor in America, the poet, M. Sh. Ben-Meir, of blessed memory, did not spare any effort or exertion – despite his sad family conditions at the time – so that the work would be completed. The remaining members of the editorial group in America, the brothers Moshe and Kalman Bachrach, contributed greatly to the contents of the book with their articles and together with the editorial group member, Moshe Malozowski, skillfully took part in the general editorial work.

Here in Israel, a thank you goes first of all to the editor, Mr. A.L. Fajans, who edited a large part of the book and also reworked all of the material that was edited in America and the Misters Moshe Lewin and Moshe Goelman, who were occupied with the collection and selection of the material.

A special *yasher koyekh* [literally, may your strength be firm – congratulations!] to the Misters Dovid Bachrach, Perec Czerniak and Sora Brkais, who helped with a full effort, each according to their means and abilities, with the realization of this work.

May a deep thank you be expressed here to all who answered our call and took part in the *yizkor bukh* [memorial book] Tovya Evri (Yevraiski), the living witness of the Goniadz destruction, who gave us a strong, shocking description of the destruction, deserves particular thanks.

Let this Goniadz memorial book be a living memorial *matzeyvah* [headstone] to the annihilated-lost splendor of the past – for us and for our children, for eternity.

Translation Coordinator's Note: Pages 807-808 of the Afterword appear to be same (by layout) of pages 805-806 above so they were not translated.

[Pages 817-820]

Index of Images
Translated by Shayna Kravetz
Edited by David Goldman and Marvin Galper

[Note: Pages cited are the page numbers in the original Yizkor Book, not the page numbers of this book translation.]

Translator's Notes:
1. The word "payen" is unknown, but PAY might be an acronym for something like **P**oalei **E**retz **Y**israel
2. An international organization
3. Lit. "To go up to the land"
4. Abbreviation for "zichrono/zichrona li-vrocho" - "of blessed memory" (for a man/woman)
5. Honorific in Yiddish for a rabbi's wife
6. "Elijah the Prophet" - A song traditionally chanted after the Havdalah service marking the ends of the Sabbath and festivals, at which time Elijah is expected to appear to announce the coming of the Messiah
7. **Lit.** "The good place" - the cemetery is considered good, not evil, because that is where a person goes to his eternal reward.

[Pages 821-824]

Participants in the Memorial Book
Translated by Shayna Kravetz

-------, Feigl Bat Binyamin	A daughter of Rabbi Binyamin the scribe[1]
Altshuld, Zeidl	A son of Nat'ke the tenant farmer
Arad (Axelrod), Aryeh	Director of the Hebrew school, before the outbreak of World War II
Avshalom, Prof. L. Mordechai	Motye Leib Fridman, a son of Peshe the Staznover[2]
Bachrach, David, Moshe, & Kalman	Sheina-Beil'ka Rokhel and Moshe's sons
Barqait, Sarah	A daughter of Dvorah and Meir Raigrodski. Meir's father - Avraham-Aharon Dolistover[3]
Ben-Meir, M.S.	Idel Treshtshanski, a son of Meir the watchmaker
Karmin, Dr. Yosef	A son of Yehoshua Charmi (Storozum[4])
Ellen, Isaac	A relative of Khaya-Vichne. Left Goniondz in the [18]90s
Farber, Miriam	Miriam [daughter?] of Gershon-Leib. A sister of Shmuel'ke
Farber, Shmuel	Shmuel [son?] of Gershon-Leib, lived in Bialystok since 1912
Finkelshtein, Shabtai	From Yashinovke
Forman, David	A son of Nisan the tailor
Fridman, Aharon	A brother of Niss'l the butcher
Gelbord, Gershon	A son of Gnend'l and Avraham Gelbord, a grandchild of Gershon Kliap

Gelbord, Morris	Moshe'ke Berl Dolker
Goelman, Moshe	Teacher in the Hebrew school during the [19]20s - Keila Bachrach is his wife.
Graubard, Shalom	A native of Trestine, lived in Goniondz for a short time
Halpern, Yosef	A son of Ephraim Eliyahu Nekhemiah
Halpern, Ephraim	Ephraim the writer, Ephraim Eliyahu Nekhemiah
Hertzig, Yosef	Yos'l Yehudah
Ivri, Keile	Tev'l's sister
Ivri, Tuvia	Tev'l Yevraiski, a son of Kheik'l the hatter
Kamenietzki, ------ (wife)	Wife of Moshe-Meir, a son of R. Gedaliah, the Rov
Kamenietzki, Zeev	Velvel, the rov's [son]. A son of R. Gedaliah, the Rov
Khativah, Aryeh	A son of Simkhah the tenant-farmer
Kravietz, Khayim	A son of Avraham-Aryeh, Gedaliah Mondres
Levin, Moshe	Moshe'ke Klevianker, the Hebrew teacher
Levinshal-Mali, Yonah	Daughter of Moshe Bandkes[5]
Levin, Yerukham	A native of Bialystok, teacher and journalist
Malozovski, Moshe	Moshe'ke, [son?] of Shmuel-Ber
Miltshan, Alexander	Sender, [son?] of Moshe-Yos'l Zerakh
Neiman, Khanah	Khanah-Reizl, a grandchild of R. Gedaliah the Rov
Neiman, Yonatan	A brother of Khanah Neiman
Niyelovitzki, Mordechai	A teacher in the Hebrew school in the [19]20s - His wife

	Beil'ke was a daughter of Sender the writer
Rozen, Alter	A son of Rokhel Leah, daughter of Betzalel (Tikotzki)
Rubin, Meirim	Meirim, [a relative of?] Hersh'l Vrotzenier
Sheinenzon, Elimelech	His mother was called Mot'l, his father - Leib'l, a brother of Khayim and Yehoshua Sheinenzon, who lived in Warsaw
Shtshutshinski, Asher	A son of Itshe and Leah [a daughter of?] Asher
Shvartz, Avraham	Avraham'l, [a son of?] Sender the writer, lived in Trestine since 1912
Treshtshanski, David	A son of Gedaliah Gershon the carpenter
Tsherniak, Yehezkel-Peretz	Chatzk'l-Peretz, [husband?] of Khaya-It'ke
Yafe, Avraham	Avraham the decisor. Left Goniondz in 1907
Yardeni,Y.D.	Yisroel-David Yarushevski, a son of Moshe-Mich'l the dyer
Yitzkhaki (Treshtshanski), Fish'l	Fish'l, [son?] of Itshe the blond

Translator's Notes:
1. No last name is given, Hebrew "Bat Binyamin" - daughter of Binyamin
2. Possibly a geographic nickname, from the town of Staznov
3. Possibly a geographic nickname, from the town of Dolistov
4. Possibly a nickname derived from Yiddish "storozimnik" -wise or knowledgable person.
5. Possibly a professional nickname, from Yiddish "Bander" -cooper

INDEX

APPENDIX – Not Part of the Original Yizkor Book

The Town

The Synagogue on the Hill

[photograph courtesy of Yad Vashem]

The Synagogue on the Hill
[1923; photograph courtesy of Michael Rothschild]

The Synagogue
[photograph courtesy of Yad Vashem]

In the Cheder (school room)
[1923; photograph courtesy of Michael Rothschild]

Inside the Shul
[1923; photograph courtesy of Michael Rothschild]

House of Learning

[1923; photograph courtesy of Michael Rothschild]

Monday Market [1923; photograph courtesy of Michael Rothschild]

Monday Market [1923; photograph courtesy of Michael Rothschild]

Moses - Gershon de Blecher's son at the Goniadz market

[1923; photograph courtesy of Michael Rothschild]

Goniadz Street

[1923; photograph Courtesy of Michael Rothschild]

Street in front of the home of Yoel Treszczanski
[1923; photograph courtesy of Michael Rothschild]

Treszczanski Family Album

Dave Bloom (1893-1987) was born in New York City shortly after his parents - Moses Treszczanski and Dora Bloom (nee Ponemonsky) - emigrated to the United States from Goniadz in 1891. Soon after arriving, Moses changed the family name to Bloom. Dave was one of nine surviving children In 1923, Dave traveled to Goniadz to meet his relatives in the old country for the first time, and took most of the photos in this section.

Photographs Courtesy of Michael Rothschild, Grandson

David Bloom with his Uncle Yoel at dinner in Goniadz

Tobe Tresczcanski

Alter Burak, Itzhak Treszczanski

Chana Burak, ?, Itchie (Isadore) Stabinsk

Yaakov (Jacob) Treszczanski, Arie Treszczanski, Sheina Yafa Ribak

Olszanicki Family

Back row: ?, Khinke Treszczanski, Josef Olszanicki

Front row: Rachel Olszanicki, Jechezkiel Olszanicki, Fishel Olszanicki, Chaja Olszanicki

Marcus and Gedalin Schuster (?)

Beilah's daughter, Beilah Treszczanski Tsevar, Dworka Treszczanski

Michael Atlas (ferry boat owner), Ruben Treszczanski

Itzhak Treszczanski, Yoel Treszczanski

Mareuses, a daughter of Chayeh Rochel Lurie

Goniadz family

Unidentified Goniadz couple in 1923

Treszczanski Family Portrait-
[not by Dave Bloom]

Standing: Ruven, Fischl, Yehuda, Meir, Issik, Gitl
Seated: Itzhak, Yoel Velvil, Rivka Zabludovski (Itzhak's wife)

Khinke Treszczanski

Khinke Tresczanski, Yoel Treszczanski, ?, ?, Gela, ?

Blum Family Album

[photographs courtesy of Suzanne Scheraga

Blum Family Group

Right to left, Elke Blum Pinkevitch with child, brother Nathan Blum and
another sibling, possibly Khaia Basche Blum.

Elke Blum

Back of postcard above

Translation: Dear Sister, I am sending you a picture and asking you to send us one, too. We are all well and healthy. I am sending two pictures. The girls you know already and who they are. There is nothing else to write. Be well and dear God should write us into the book of life. "Ahikima Tovah" and also for you to ask God for a good year from me your sister who hopes to meet with you. Your sister, Elke Blum".

Elke Blum Pinkevich and husband Hershl

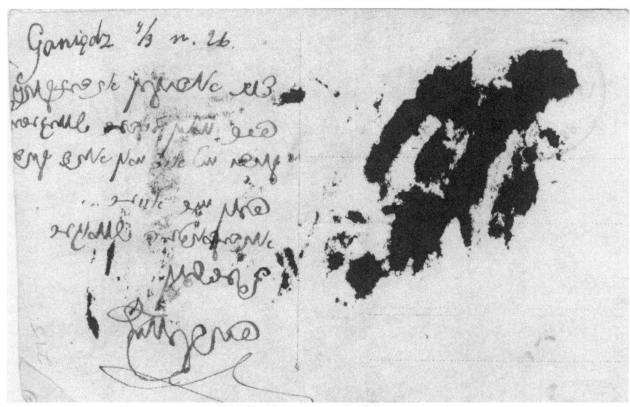

Back of Postcard Above

Translation: "Goniadz on September 4, 1926. As a rememberance to our dear beloved sister-in- law and children and husband, from your unknown brother-in-law, Hershl Pinkevitch."

Unidentified woman, probably Elke Blum Pinkevitch.

Blum sibling, possibly Khaia Basche

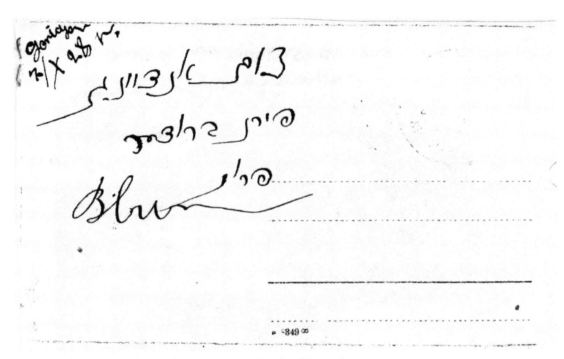

Back of Postcard Above

Translation: 'Goniadz Feb 4, 1928; As a souvenir for my brother; Blum'

More Photos

Chaim Velvel Dovnarsky
[photograph courtesy of Suzanne Scheraga]

Lazar Isaac Vitkowski and wife Chana Treschansky
[photograph courtesy of Carole Rosenfeld]

Goniadz section of Cedar Park cemetery in Paramus, NJ
[photograph courtesy of Michael Rothschild]

CPSIA information can be obtained
at www.ICGtesting.com
Printed in the USA
LVHW061141190723
752798LV00008B/689

9 781939 561404